D0948729

Fritz Reiner, Maestro and Martinet

_____

MUSIC IN AMERICAN LIFE

A list of books in the series
appears at the end of this book.

FRITZ REINER

Maestro and Martinet

Kenneth Morgan

UNIVERSITY OF ILLINOIS PRESS

URBANA AND CHICAGO

Library of Congress Cataloging-in-Publication
Data

Morgan, Kenneth, 1953–
Fritz Reiner, maestro and martinet /
Kenneth Morgan.
p.   cm. — (Music in American life)
Includes bibliographical references (p.)
and index.
Discography: p.
ISBN 0-252-02935-6 (cloth : alk. paper)
1. Reiner, Fritz, 1888–1963.
2. Conductors (Music)—United States—Biography.
I. Title. II. Series.
ML422.R38M6   2004
784.2′092—dc20   2003026968

*To the memory of Alfred Griffin Morgan
and Janet Morgan*

Contents

Illustrations follow page 146

Preface

This book provides a comprehensive scholarly appraisal of the life and musical career of Fritz Reiner, the notable Hungarian conductor whose main musical achievements occurred in the United States between the early 1920s and the early 1960s. In those four decades Reiner made a significant contribution to the teaching of conducting at the Curtis Institute of Music in Philadelphia; he built up the personnel and standing of the Cincinnati, Pittsburgh, and Chicago Symphony Orchestras; and he played a leading role in the opera house, primarily at the Metropolitan Opera in New York. Reiner also made many records of a wide repertoire that have been frequently reissued since his death, recordings that critics esteem more now than when they were first made. His musical impact on American orchestras was filtered through the lens of his formative years in Hungary and Germany. A study of his musical legacy must therefore discuss the musical training he brought with him as an immigrant to the United States at the age of thirty-three and then trace how he adapted to the new cultural situation across the Atlantic.

Reiner's career has been outlined in a number of short articles, but the only book devoted to him is Philip Hart's *Fritz Reiner: A Biography.* Based on wide reading and familiarity with the subject, Hart provides a useful sketch of Reiner's career and is helpful on two issues in particular. He portrays Reiner's marriages in detail, showing especially how his third wife, Carlotta, protected and supported his career. He also discusses Reiner's period as music director of the Chicago Symphony Orchestra from an informed (if one-sided) perspective (Hart was assistant manager of the orchestra at the time). Virtually a third of the biography concentrates on Reiner's connection with Chicago, and these are its best pages. Hart includes appendices listing Reiner's repertoire and the complex legal details pertaining to the custody of his personal papers after his death, a story that leads up to the deposit of most of them at Northwestern University in the 1980s. There is also a helpful discography, updated for the paperback edition published in 1997.

My book differs from Hart's in several respects. I give more attention than Hart to Reiner's musical aesthetic, quoting from the conductor's valuable but scattered pieces on conducting and musical performance. I devote more space to analysis of Reiner's recordings in the context of performance practice; to material gathered from musicians who performed with Reiner; to the European background that laid the foundation for his career; and to the complexity of Reiner's personality. By concentrating on these themes, I aim to convey the controversial personality and to pinpoint the musical legacy of one of the most remarkable musicians to follow a career mainly in the United States. For this reassessment I have brought to bear, for the first time, numerous important items such as newspapers and repertoire details from Reiner's early years in Budapest and Dresden, modern discussions of performance practice, and accounts of opera productions that Reiner conducted by those involved as producers (including books by Herbert Graf and Tyrone Guthrie). I have given full citations to source materials (discussed below in a note on sources and listed in the bibliography) so that those interested in Reiner may now consult them directly.

Chapter 1 of my account of Reiner's career analyzes the conductor's personality in depth, showing how his background and psychological complexity crucially affected his music making. Reiner was always regarded as a "conductor's conductor," someone that fellow practitioners considered superlative. The opening chapter indicates the musical reasons why Reiner earned this accolade by investigating his methods of preparing scores, his baton technique, and his ideas on the presentation of opera and orchestral music. Chapter 2 discusses Reiner's formative musical training and early conducting experiences in Hungary, Slovenia, and Germany before he quit Europe for the United States. It establishes the thorough musical grounding he received at the Franz Liszt Academy of Music in Budapest; traces the influence of Artur Nikisch and Richard Strauss on his conducting; and shows how Reiner gained valuable, sustained experience in the opera house as well as taking his first steps toward conducting well-planned orchestral programs.

Chapters 3 through 8 explore Reiner's contribution to musical life in America, looking at his training of conducting students and orchestras, his cultivation of an eclectic repertoire, his attempts to further the cause of opera, the musical and civic atmosphere of the American cities where he worked, and his dealings with musicians and management. Reiner's encouragement of contemporary music, including works by American composers, is documented. The climax of his career as conductor of the Chicago Symphony Orchestra is analyzed in detail, with attention to the musical triumphs and the disaster of the orchestra's abandoned tour of Europe and the Middle East in 1959. Reiner's demise through ill health, politicking by the orchestra's management, and the influence of Claudia Cassidy's critical commentaries on the Chicago musical scene are woven into the story.

Chapters 9 and 10 conclude the book by investigating Reiner's rich recorded legacy. Particular attention is paid to his interpretative qualities and to the changing context of the record industry through the 78 rpm era to mono LPs, stereophonic sound, and the coming of CDs. Reiner's artistic approach to different repertoire is explored along with his views on recording, the technical aspects of discs he made for American Columbia and RCA Victor, and their reception by critics. My hope is that the book will illuminate the musical legacy of one of the acknowledged master-conductors of the twentieth century and the impact of serious art music and its performance on American life in the half-century after World War I.

Acknowledgments

The extent of research required for this book has obliged me to call on the services of many individuals and institutions. First and foremost, I must thank the British Academy for awarding me a personal research grant to undertake extensive work on this project in the United States and Europe. Additional research funding from Brunel University enabled me to undertake some return trips to the United States in search of elusive information concerning Fritz Reiner. I should like to thank David Wootton, our former Dean of the Faculty of Arts, for his support for this project at a crucial stage of my career. In the early stages of the research, Don L. Roberts, the chief music librarian at Northwestern University, showed me the Reiner Collection in the Deering Music Library and allowed me access to this wonderful resource. I have to thank him and his colleagues, notably Debora Campana, for their prompt help on several research trips to Evanston, Illinois. While there I met Stephen C. Hillyer, the former president of the Fritz Reiner Society, who has kept me up to the mark with a steady stream of offprints, cassette tapes, and conversation on Reiner. Steve has done much to promote Reiner's legacy, notably through his editorship of *The Podium: The Magazine of the Fritz Reiner Society,* and I am grateful for his support during the long gestation period of this project. Roger Dettmer deserves warm thanks for his critical support for my endeavors, granting me the favor of insights from his regular observance of Reiner's conducting in Chicago and serving as a friendly if exacting reviewer of draft chapters. It is also a pleasure to record my thanks to Leonard Slatkin for acting as the other reader for this book and for finding my efforts of merit.

Grateful acknowledgments are made to the following individuals and institutions in the United States for their help with my research requests: John Shepard and the staff of the New York Public Library's Performing Arts Library at Lincoln Center; the staff of the Music Division, the Recorded Sound Division, and the Newspaper and Periodical Division of the Library of Congress;

Ronald Grele and the staff of Columbia University's Oral History Collection; the staff of Columbia University's Special Collections; Barbara Haws and Richard Wandel at the New York Philharmonic-Symphony Orchestra's Archives; Brenda Nelson-Strauss at the Rosenthal Archives of the Chicago Symphony Orchestra; John D. Thompson at the Hillman Library, University of Pittsburgh; John Pennino at the Metropolitan Opera Archives in New York; Carol Jacobs at the Cleveland Orchestra's Archives; Fred Lerdahl at Columbia University; the staff of the Urban Archives Center at Temple University; Elizabeth Walker at the Curtis Institute of Music; Debra Podjed at the publications department of the San Francisco Symphony Orchestra; Koraljka Lockhart at the San Francisco Opera; Orrin Howard at the archives department of the Los Angeles Philharmonic Orchestra; John C. Loomans at the Detroit Symphony Orchestra; Suzanne M. Eggleston at the Sterling Memorial Library, Yale University; and the administrative staff of the Minnesota Orchestral Association, the Boston Symphony Orchestra, and the Rochester Philharmonic Orchestra. Among the North American archives and libraries that facilitated my research were the Mugar Library at Boston University; the Boston Public Library; Case Western Reserve University Library in Cleveland; the Free Library of Philadelphia; the Cincinnati Historical Society; and the San Francisco Performing Arts Library and Museum.

A fruitful research trip to central Europe in the winter of 1994 turned up material that could not be tracked down elsewhere. For their help in locating this material I would like to extend my appreciation to Hedvig Belitska-Scholtz, Katalin Szőnyiné Szerző, and István Horváth at the National Széchényi Library in Budapest and Karl Wilhelm Geck and Ludwig Müller at the Sächsische Landesbibliothek in Dresden. Dr. Geck was instrumental in gaining permission for me to use material from the Sächsische Staatsoper, Dresden, through the auspices of Frau Brigitte Euler. Dr. Müller undertook research on my behalf on Dresden newspapers. Joyce Perry also kindly aided my research. Peter Mackertich gave me professional help with the photographs. In England I received help from the staff of the following libraries: the British Library, Richmond Reference Library, the Royal College of Music's library, the Barbican Music Library, the Westminster Music Library in Victoria, and the National Sound Archives, then on Exhibition Road, South Kensington, and now part of the British Library.

Finding out about Reiner was enlivened by the memories of his daughter, Mrs. Eva Bartenstein, who, helped by her daughter and son-in-law, graciously talked to me in Zürich about her father's personality. A number of distinguished musicians also agreed to let me interview them. Each interview increased my perception of Reiner's achievements, and some of the musicians generously spoke at length. My appreciation goes to Risë Stevens, Lukas Foss, the late Max Rudolf, Walter Hendl, the late Ezra Rachlin, Leonard Sharrow, János Starker,

Irving Sarin, the late Jerry Sirucek, the late Josef Kovacs, the late Robert Mayer, John de Lancie, Samuel Thaviu, George Gaber, Victor Aitay, David Walter, David Diamond, Abraham Marcus, and the late Igor Kipnis. Mr. de Lancie also sent helpful written remarks on Reiner. Among others who wrote me about Reiner were Eugene Weintraub, Mary Ellen Evans, Jean-Do. Mondoloni, Gardner Read, Gina Pia Cooper, and Fred Lerdahl. I thank them all for agreeing to let me draw on their opinions for this book.

Several people gave advice on written drafts. William Ashbrook offered sound editorial advice for an earlier version of chapter 5, which appeared in the *Opera Quarterly* in 1996. Jacques Voois, Hanny Bleeker White, and John Moye all helped with portions of chapters 2 and 4, which appeared in the *Journal of the Conductors' Guild* in 1994 and 1998. Alan Sanders helped with the publication of part of chapter 9 in the *International Classical Record Collector* in 1996. I am grateful for permission to reprint portions of these articles in this book. José Antonio Bowen provided a helpful critique of chapter 10. David Ryden gave sterling support in preparing the typescript on computer diskette. The Archives of Musical America, the Fritz Reiner Society, and the late Igor Kipnis granted me permission to reproduce photographs. I wish to thank Judith McCulloh of the University of Illinois Press for realizing the potential of my project and for her warm support in seeing this book through to publication. My family have offered support throughout the project. Leigh Morgan, in particular, will be pleased to see the book in print. The book is dedicated to my late uncle and late aunt, who played an important role in shaping my musical appreciation.

Fritz Reiner, Maestro and Martinet

1. THE MAN AND
THE MUSICIAN

For forty years musical audiences in America were used to seeing a stocky figure around five feet, five inches in height, with hooded eyes like a falcon, a serious look, and tremendous discipline, conduct operatic and symphonic performances. After a brief handshake with the leader of an orchestra and an almost curt nod of the head to the audience, a hand with a baton almost sixteen inches long gave the upbeat, and the evening's performance started with perfect discipline, rhythmic vitality, and acute attention to the balance and sonorities of an orchestra. From the auditorium, however, it appeared that nothing was happening because of the "singular immobility" of the conductor's features.[1] What the orchestra but not the audience could see was the sheer finesse with which a small man with pudgy hands could wield a baton in a miniscule yet absolutely meaningful way to elicit performances of proportion, style, accuracy, and imagination from his players. If the baton was ever raised as far as the shoulder, the orchestra knew that was the signal to play at full tilt, yet the conducting seemed to be based as much on eye contact, a varied range of bodily gestures, and psychological probing of the musicians as on the tip of the baton. The conductor's control of complicated rhythms was phenomenal. When necessary, in complex modern pieces, his stick would beat three, his elbows four, his hips seven, and his left hand dealt with any other rhythms.[2] Here, indeed, was a virtuoso drillmaster. Yet the building of climaxes, the structural understanding of scores, the balance of different instrumental choirs, the clarification of very complex counterpoint, the transparency of sound, and the imaginative suggestiveness of the performances all proclaimed the re-creative art of a fastidious, subtle master.

The conductor was Fritz Reiner. He had a major career that began in his native Budapest before the First World War and ended in New York in 1963. Reiner's musical appointments until 1922 were in Budapest, Laibach (now Ljubljana), and Dresden, where he conducted operas, operettas, and symphonic concerts. Thereafter he was based in the United States, where he held several significant positions. He was musical director of three symphony orchestras, in Cincinnati, Pittsburgh, and Chicago (in the years 1922–31, 1938–48, and 1953–63, respectively). He was also head of conducting at the Curtis Institute of Music in Philadelphia for ten years after 1931 and a leading conductor at the Metropolitan Opera in New York between 1949 and 1953. In addition, he undertook extensive work as a guest conductor in America and Europe. To all his engagements he brought high professional standards, dynamic energy in galvanizing orchestras to give of their best, technical competence probably unrivaled by any other conductor, a vast repertoire stretching from the baroque period to contemporary music, and a commitment to the promotion of serious music.

Contemporaries always acknowledged Reiner as a complete professional in his conducting. Probably no other conductor has ever gained such a reputation for precise, virtuosic use of the baton. Reiner was very much a "conductor's conductor," the "one conductor whom conductors themselves consider[ed] superlative."[3] This ability was reflected in his complete authority on the podium. According to Yehudi Menuhin, Reiner, along with George Szell, was the only conductor he played for who had to make a show of authority. Menuhin admired Reiner's technical command and orchestral training, whereby musicians played fortissimo when his baton was raised one inch and pianissimo when it was lifted merely a quarter of an inch.[4] As the critic Lawrence Gilman put it, Reiner was "a technician of uncommon adroitness and security. The orchestra is no siren-sealed body of mystery to him . . . it is a vehicle lucidly and realistically understood, and he employs it with clear-cut imperious authority."[5]

These were not encomiums given to a highly efficient *kapellmeister;* they were recognition of Reiner's special qualities. Two factors lifted him above the level of an exceptionally competent craftsman. One was his unerring sense of form and proportion. He could conduct over long time spans—an act, for instance, of a Mozart or Richard Strauss opera—and plan each tempo and transition so that one section dovetailed logically with the next. This was made possible by his concern for structural breadth and depth when conducting. Reiner's second distinctive skill, raising music making to a higher plane, was his ability to forge an "equilibrium between an explosive, almost menacingly elemental temperament and a strong, mature, immensely disciplined intellect which exerts a constant effort to keep that temperament in check."[6] He himself recognized the need to balance these two facets of his character, noting that a conductor "must speak the two languages of intellect and emotion at the same moment. Intellect without emotion is not art. And emotion without intellect is sentimentality."[7]

Fellow conductors recognized Reiner's talents. Serge Koussevitzky and Dimitri Mitropoulos, for instance, made a point of attending his rehearsals in Boston and New York.[8] The composer and critic Virgil Thomson once remarked that he thought Reiner "a sounder musician than Toscanini and a more complete master of his art than [Bruno] Walter."[9] He was well qualified to make this judgement since, in his capacity as music critic for the *New York Herald-Tribune,* he heard all three conductors regularly. The violinist Isaac Stern considered Reiner the equal of Toscanini and Wilhelm Furtwängler in his mastery of conducting and, when on top form, unequaled by anybody.[10] Leonard Bernstein, who had studied conducting with Reiner, stated that the Hungarian maestro was "a supreme master of the baton" and probably the greatest living conductor at the time.[11] The violinist Joseph Szigeti greatly esteemed Reiner's conducting; he always felt at ease performing with him because the Hungarian maestro knew his scores so well.[12] The cellist János Starker agreed. In his experience, Reiner's knowledge of scores "was total and greater than anyone I personally faced in my life."[13]

Despite these plaudits, Reiner's career has been relatively neglected. He is invariably referred to with respect, and many of his recordings have been reissued on compact disc. But neither during his distinguished career nor since his death has he received sufficient attention for his contribution to musical performance. Now that he has been dead for forty years, it is time to take stock of his achievements. Philip Hart's *Fritz Reiner: A Biography* has begun the task of reassessment. My book aims to further that goal through a more comprehensive study of Reiner's personality, musical ideas, career, and recordings. To understand why Reiner has not received the acclaim he deserves, one needs to examine his temperament and private life as well as his approach to music making: the man and the musician were inseparable.

By temperament, Reiner was a loner who did not make many close friends. Coming from a middle-class Hungarian background and with an imperious air about him, like a little Roman emperor, he had a stern, reserved, commanding presence. Formal in dealing with musicians, he liked to be addressed as "Dr. Reiner" (the doctorates he acquired were honorary ones).[14] Proud, stubborn, and disciplined, he expected colleagues to meet his own high standards of thorough preparation and musical knowledge and was scathing about those who fell short of the mark. When faced with ignorance and folly, he was irascible and explosive.[15] "Any day on which he failed to lose his temper," one critic remarked, "was a day on which he was actually too sick to conduct."[16] He could be ill-mannered with subordinates, and his rudeness sometimes made a bad first impression on other musicians. Some disliked his inflated ego and thought he had a Napoleon complex.[17] A New York musician who did not admire Reiner or his music making once remarked, "if Genghis Khan had an orchestra, it would have sounded like Reiner's."[18]

A draconian presence was accompanied by a disapproving, almost severe look, which became more accentuated as Reiner grew older, as crease folds appeared around his mouth and his eyebrows became increasingly hooded. His facial expressions ranged from Mephistophelean to a good imitation of Bela Lugosi. He did not smile often, and when he did it was invariably with a cruel curl of the lip. His sharp tongue added to the intimidating impression. He had a habit of criticizing musicians shortly after he had praised them. Thus Robert Mayer, cor anglais player with the Chicago Symphony, was praised by Reiner for his solo playing in *The Swan of Tuonela* only to be told the following week, when he experienced a problem playing another piece, that it was no good looking at his instrument or the reed and that maybe if he practiced more he would play better.[19]

Reiner was a man of few words yet never at a loss for an appropriate phrase; he always expressed strong opinions succinctly. His tongue had a quick response for every situation. When Morton Gould failed to go to Pittsburgh to hear his Second Symphonette performed, Reiner asked why he was absent. Gould replied that his piece was only nine minutes long and that it scarcely seemed worth making the trip from New York. "It might have been only nine minutes," came the reply, "but *Reiner* did it."[20] Auditioning a horn player who fluffed some notes, Reiner interjected, "No. No. Stop. You play like a baby." As the embarrassed player walked to the side of the stage, Reiner called out, just before he made his exit, "Wait. Not a baby. An embryo."[21] Reiner once replied dryly to a photographer's complaint that all pictures of him were serious: "Young man, I have no other expression."[22] A music critic in New York who reminded Reiner that he had once played in an orchestra under him was greeted with the remark, "So you've heard he's a son-of-a-bitch too."[23]

Yet there was a more human side to Reiner that was not displayed so much in public, a side "kept under strict control when the private person gave way to the maestro."[24] Privately he was a witty, relaxed, cultivated man who read widely. He took a keen interest in politics and current affairs and, in later years, watched the television avidly when items of international political importance were covered.[25] The contrast between his public persona on the podium and his private charm was striking. He preferred to spend much of his time working on scores, preparing concert schedules, rehearsing, and conducting, but he was a good host and participated in cocktail parties with orchestral players. On these occasions he was genial and appreciated a good joke; he enjoyed being a bon vivant in a restrained way. He could be kindly to those in need, playing an important role in sustaining Bartók in his last years in the United States, when he was riddled with serious illness, and helping other musicians, too. But he hated to publicize the fact. Because he was essentially a private person, he disdained attention-grabbing tactics and thus rarely saw his name in the headlines. He could also be vulnerable and thin-skinned. Despite an iron will, he always got butterflies and stage fright before, but not during, a performance. Though one would never guess it from his calmness and composed demeanor when walking out from the wings, he confessed to approaching the podium "as if it were the first concert of my life."[26]

Reiner's personal life was eventful; he married three times and found his career seriously impeded by scandals surrounding the two divorces. His first wife, Angela (Elça) Jelaçin, was a native of Laibach, the capital of Slovenia. The couple married there in 1911 when Reiner was conducting at the local opera house. They had two daughters—Berta (abbreviated to Tuśy, the diminutive of Bertushka), born in Budapest on September 5, 1912, and Eva, born in 1915 after the Reiners had moved to Dresden, where Fritz was a leading conductor at the Semperoper. The marriage was unsuccessful. Angela Reiner poured her energies into bringing up a young family and expected her husband to lavish time and attention on the home. But he, on the threshold of a major career, immersed himself in work and enjoyed the stimulus of artistic circles where she felt uncomfortable. The love did not last. Reiner had a brief affair with Charlotte Benedict, a young singer in Dresden, and their baby daughter was born in February 1916. He then abruptly broke off relations with Benedict, whose family brought up the child (Erika). But it was Reiner's affair with Berta Gerster-Gardini, who was to become his second wife, that proved the breaking point in the marriage. Angela Reiner separated from her husband in July 1916 and left Dresden with her two daughters to return to her parents' home.[27]

Reiner alleged that his wife had set up home in Laibach with a married man. He tried to gain custody of his daughters, without success. After an acrimonious set of divorce proceedings, the marriage between Fritz and Angela Reiner was dissolved by settlement in Budapest in January 1920 and in Dresden in May 1921. Reiner kept in touch with Tuśy and Eva but did not see a great deal of them for the rest of his life. Tuśy attended school in the United States between 1926 and 1929 before returning to Ljubljana. Eva remained in Yugoslavia.[28] Tuśy was grateful for the American education she received but saddened by her father's unwillingness to spend much time with her. She married, had one child (Vovcek), and worked from time to time as a translator. In her later years she had constant money troubles and sought help from her father. Reiner sent food packages, money, and clothing to her but eventually became exasperated with her expectation that other people should feed and clothe her.[29] Eva married a Swiss man, Werner Bartenstein, settled in Zurich, and had three children.[30]

Reiner's second wife, Berta, was the daughter of Etelka Gerster, a famous Hungarian coloratura soprano, and Carlo Gardini, formerly the American consul at Bologna. Berta came from a background of wealth and social connections. Her sister was married to an Italian count, and Berta was a frequent guest at her sister and brother-in-law's home, the Villa di Cipressi, surrounded by large vineyards, at Pontecchio near Bologna. Berta and Fritz were both married when they met, and they began an adulterous affair; she was the wife of a German tenor, Walter Kirchhoff. She divorced him in 1915, the year after she met Reiner in Hamburg. Berta and Fritz's relationship created a scandal in Dresden, especially among stuffier patrons of the opera house. Among those who disapproved of the liaison was Kaiser Wilhelm II, an admirer of Kirchhoff's singing.[31]

Berta and Fritz married in Berlin on November 19, 1921, and repeated the ceremony in Rome on May 29, 1922. The first occasion seems to have been a civil wedding; the second may have been arranged to please Berta's Italian family. There were no children of the marriage.[32] Pictures from the 1920s reveal that Berta was a large-framed woman, with a full, round face and a cheerful smile; she was two years older than Fritz. She always wanted to be a famous singer but never had her mother's ability.[33] Frustrated in her professional singing career, she turned to teaching. She had run a vocal school in Berlin before she met Reiner. After the couple emigrated to the United States in 1922, she became head of a special class of singers at the Cincinnati Conservatory of Music and presented her best pupils at recitals in New York.[34]

Berta and Fritz had strong personalities. Jealous of her husband's attention to his daughter when Tuśy lived briefly in the United States, Berta tried to dominate Fritz, and he resisted.[35] Towards the end of the 1920s the couple fell out once and for all over Fritz's affair with an American actress, Carlotta Irwin. Reiner and Berta divorced in 1930 in bitter circumstances. Berta, corroborated by two witnesses, stated in court that she and her husband separated on April 14, 1929, after he struck and abused her. Berta was granted a divorce on the grounds of cruelty and neglect.[36]

The divorce created a scandal that partly led to Reiner leaving the Cincinnati Symphony Orchestra. While still married he openly courted Carlotta Irwin in too blatant a manner for the orchestra's board of directors and their wives. They disliked Reiner's treatment of Berta, who was admired and respected locally.[37] Throughout the early thirties the taint of disgrace counted against him at a time when jobs were scarce: various organizations, including the Hollywood Bowl summer concerts, refused to hire him. After the divorce Berta continued her work as a vocal coach at the Gerster-Gardini School of Singing in Manhattan. In 1945, during a bout of illness, she sought extra financial assistance from her ex-husband, but Reiner refused, saying he had paid a large divorce settlement in full and lacked the means to provide any more money.[38] His divorce from Berta, who died in 1951, was still talked about by older members of the Cincinnati Symphony Orchestra in the late 1950s.[39]

Carlotta (originally Charlotte) Irwin became Reiner's third and last wife. She was the daughter of an American father of Irish extraction and a younger German mother. Her father, Thomas W. Irwin, was a wealthy designer and manufacturer of steel cornice roofing in Pittsburgh. Carlotta was the only child of his second marriage. Born in the Steel City, she aspired to be an actress from the age of four and prepared for the stage at the Sargeant School in New York, beginning her theatrical career before 1920.[40] Having appeared on Broadway, she met Reiner when she visited Cincinnati with the Stuart Walker Repertory Company in 1928. The conductor visited the show at the time when his second marriage was on the rocks and was bowled over by Carlotta. After his divorce from Berta, Fritz married Carlotta on April 23, 1930. She decided at once to quit the stage, thinking it impossible to sustain two independent careers in the performing arts in a marriage. She did not regret this decision for long, though she kept many thespian friends. She enjoyed music, without having any real knowledge of it, and there were no musical clashes with her husband. She was an avid reader and an outgoing person with lively opinions on people, politics, and the arts. When she wanted to act like a lady she played the part well, but her language could also be forthright.[41]

Carlotta was her husband's companion, valet, and secretary. She was a fine cook in her younger years, using a lot of Hungarian recipes, which she prepared herself or supervised in the kitchen. She arranged her husband's change of linen for concerts, attended nearly all his rehearsals and performances, and typed and maintained his correspondence.[42] Carlotta was devoted to her husband, and they remained together for thirty-three years until his death; they had no children. She expressed no bitterness about his previous wives. Enormously proud of her husband's achievements, she claimed that Mrs. Reiner was the greatest part she ever played.[43] During the American presidential election campaign of 1936, when her husband was conducting in Los Angeles, Carlotta found a newspaper with the front-page headline, "F. R. Leads in California," promptly bought two hundred copies, and sent them to puzzled friends and colleagues all over the world.[44]

After her husband's death Carlotta lived for another twenty years, leading a lonely existence enlivened by occasional weekend guests and admirers of her late husband. In old age her lively tongue became irascible, and alcohol eased the physical pain from stomach and digestive problems. A sufferer from epilepsy (which she kept secret) and from emphysema (though she refused to stop smoking), she also had a painful deviated septum as a result of drinking too much vodka. She died in 1983 after an epileptic seizure followed by two and a half weeks in a coma.[45]

By the time he married Carlotta, Reiner had fully adjusted to American life. Though he retained his thickly accented English and exuded a measured style more common in the Old World than in the New, he embraced the American way of life rapidly. In an interview published in the *Cincinnati Times-Star* on April 21, 1925, Reiner stated that he "was born Americanized. It is true. Always I felt that surge, that need for active work, that impelling impulse to do things which is American." In his eyes, to be American was to be able to do what he wanted without political or social constraints. Reiner regarded moving to America as a positive step towards a better future; he did not dwell upon past achievements or draw attention to them. By September 1926 he was "sick of Europe" and hoped soon to become an American citizen. He and his second wife were granted American citizenship on May 28, 1928.[46]

Reiner threw himself wholeheartedly into American life. This could be attributed superficially to his linguistic ability. He spoke Magyar, Italian, German, Slovenian, and English, and this made him adaptable to the melting pot of musicians, many of them fellow European emigrés, who surrounded him in the orchestra pit and the opera house. His acceptance of the American way of life was helped by lack of nostalgia for the days in Budapest and Dresden, which he rarely talked about.[47] More mundane ways in which Reiner adapted to American life were to take a midwesterner as his third spouse and to acquire a house in Connecticut with every new gadget installed, plus a swimming pool and a station wagon.[48]

In the early 1930s the Reiners lived mainly in a spacious Manhattan apartment on Park Avenue, with seventeenth-century Venetian furnishings brought from Italy. Their home from 1938 onwards was a forty-three-acre property, based around a two-story French villa called "Rambleside," near Westport, Connecticut. The white stucco house was designed according to the Reiners' specifications. In the house Reiner kept a large library, his scores, and a darkroom for photography. In the studio he had a large carved mahogany desk for study, and around the room were various musical pictures, including a rare portrait of Brahms; an etching of Richard Strauss, inscribed to Reiner in 1916 after a performance of *Salome* in Dresden; a picture of Stravinsky playing the organ in Paris when Reiner first knew him; and a color portrait of Reiner himself. There was also a photograph of Reiner standing beside a touring car with Toscanini in a flyer's cap and goggles, taken when they were touring the Italian lakes together.[49]

Surrounding the house at Rambleside were extensive lawns, a formal garden, a swimming pool, and acres of woods. Reiner kept Rhode Island red chickens at a farmhouse and had an Irish red setter called Rambler. His outdoor swimming pool became the setting for informal meetings of fellow musicians and members of Connecticut's intelligentsia during the summer.[50] On these occasions the Reiners liked to relax and act the part of equable, gracious hosts. Wherever Fritz was conducting in the last twenty-five years of his life, he and his wife lived in temporary accommodations, usually a hotel apartment, and returned to Rambleside as frequently as the concert schedule permitted.

In his studio at Rambleside, Reiner prepared scores and concert programs in a secluded, private atmosphere protected by a doting wife. In earlier years he had mastered scores either by silent contemplation, by studying them at sight, or by playing them on the piano. Later, however, he sometimes used recordings to help with preparation.[51] At Rambleside his study scores lined the studio walls, and many of these were heavily marked in various colored pencils. They include a score of Beethoven's *Choral* Symphony, with red markings in German and Italian, and another of Bartók's Concerto for Orchestra, which was a photocopy of a handwritten score corrected by the composer. Reiner's library included marked scores he studied but never conducted in public. Among these were Debussy's early cantata *La Damoiselle élue*, Mahler's Symphony no. 8, Walton's Violin Concerto, Delius's *North Country Sketches* (heavily annotated), and Milhaud's opera *Cristophe Colomb*.[52]

In translating study of scores to performing in public, Reiner placed great store on an effective conducting technique, leadership, and an understanding of human psychology. His own conducting technique was visibly unemotional. "He conducted," John Briggs has written, "as if balancing a toothpick on the tip of his baton."[53] A fastidiously tidy conductor who was restrained in his motions, he never danced around the platform or exhorted players like a half-drunken parson.[54] Reiner's stick technique was immaculate even in the most complex passages. It was so precise and flawless that players knew exactly what to do a split second before playing.[55] There was nothing pyrotechnical about his wielding of the baton, but every move and gesture conveyed perfect control and mastery.[56] Anyone who complained that his beat was too small received the retort, "Yes, it's small but good."[57]

Despite minimal movements, Reiner's beat was very firm and conveyed a great deal of energy in a small physical space.[58] He deliberately compressed the beat if he thought players were lagging behind to force them to concentrate. To keep musicians on their toes in concerts, Reiner sometimes beat loud passages after the manner of beating soft ones or vice versa, cued explicitly or did not cue at all, and occasionally abandoned beating altogether.[59] He believed in the expressive communication of gesture and followed his precepts by indicating precisely ritardando or accelerando markings in a score by a glance of his eyes. These gestures are discernible in a video recording of a televised concert he gave of Beethoven's Seventh Symphony with the Chicago Symphony Orchestra.[60]

Another crucial quality needed in a conductor was leadership. Reiner believed that a conductor must display authority by demonstrating his complete knowledge of the music performed; mistakes led to sacrifice of command. Once, when rehearsing *Lohengrin* in Philadelphia, he uttered an angry outburst at a wrong entry by a quartet of pages in act 2, scene 4. The singers were alarmed because the error was a small one that could have been rectified easily. Reiner later justified his action by saying that a conductor with a fine reputation should stop at an appropriate point in rehearsal and assert his importance and authority.[61] The need for leadership meant that Reiner was opposed to conductor-less orchestras; such ensembles would have to be guided by someone, usually the concertmaster, but a conductor was the best person to do this "if the performance is to seek out and re-create the musical thought of a work, instead of giving forth a mere string of nicely played notes."[62] Reiner was always totally prepared, and everything about a particular piece of music was in place in his mind before he got to the first rehearsal.[63]

An understanding of human psychology was another aspect of musical leadership, for one had to handle experienced musicians, sometimes older and as knowledgeable as oneself. Actions, emotions, a dynamic personality, and re-creative imagination could not be achieved by study alone. These attributes existed in embryo in a young conductor but took years of experience, study, and practical music making to perfect. "The great conductor," Reiner once remarked, differed from an ordinary leader "because he has a heart, a soul, the fire of genius, learning, suggestive power, memory and the ability to command."[64] To offer a convincing interpretation a conductor needed to "live" a piece heart and soul, until it almost became his own composition: "an orchestra conductor must feel intensely the music that he is conducting or else his music falls coldly on the heart."[65] Similarly, he listened to music in a single-minded, concentrated way. "Music never relaxes me," he once remarked, adding that he could not "take it as a lukewarm bath, as some people do, and soak in it."[66]

Despite attempts to pigeonhole him as primarily an exponent of Austro-German music, Reiner's repertoire was vast, his taste broad, and his approach to different music varied. He conducted music from the baroque period through the classical, romantic, and impressionistic schools and did a fair share of contemporary music, too. He was as interested in Russian, Czech, American, French, Hungarian, Italian, and Spanish music as in the mainstream Austro-German classical and romantic tradition (though not so much in British, Polish, or Scandinavian music). He mainly concentrated on operas and orchestral repertoire, with only occasional forays into oratorios and choral music. His greatest blind spot was Sibelius. He declared in front of his students that Sibelius was an amateur: his First Symphony was a poor imitation of Tchaikovsky, and his Second Symphony had many structural weaknesses plus a lazy, excessive use of tremolandi from beginning to end.[67]

Reiner brought the same attention to bear on lighter pieces as on weighty symphonies; in that respect, he was similar to Beecham. Yet he adamantly opposed the popularization of extracts from longer pieces—the sort of thing that was staple fare for a conductor like André Kostelanetz, who made a highly successful career as a conductor on the radio and as a popularizer of the symphonic repertoire. Performing only the love music from act 2 of *Tristan und Isolde* or the second movement of Rachmaninov's Second Piano Concerto were to Reiner merely "glorifying musical impotence and decking oneself in borrowed plumes."[68]

Through the study of history and civilization, Reiner thought a conductor could learn to distinguish between the different styles of composers so that Stravinsky was not played like Schoenberg, Honegger like Strauss, or Hindemith like Prokofiev. Though he excelled at conducting program music, Reiner told a reporter for the *New York Evening Post* that "music should not be pictorially descriptive. It must be effective in itself. If a guide is needed the music is faulty." He added, with reference to Debussy's *Ibéria* and Stravinsky's *Petrushka*, that "it is the musical values that we should seek. Debussy's perfumes of the night must be fragrant to the ear, and Stravinsky's dancing bear must be heard."[69] When conducting early twentieth-century music, Reiner excelled at clarifying complex rhythms and counterpoint, and he had the ability to achieve precise ensemble, elucidate complex textures, and balance a large orchestra.[70] When guest conducting the NBC Symphony Orchestra in the 1940s, players and critics marveled at the way he conjured up pristine playing in complex modern scores after only a few rehearsals.[71]

Reiner considered it a conductor's duty to know about contemporary music. He was familiar, especially when younger, with the latest tendencies in composition, taking a pile of new scores wherever he conducted and looking out for good, new music, whether American or European.[72] His interest in contemporary music was stimulated by personal friendships with Respighi, Malipiero, Bartók, Kodály, Weiner, Richard Strauss, Casella, Stravinsky, Schoenberg, and other composers; he felt that he knew what they were trying to express. Casella, Stravinsky, Malipiero, Bartók, and Dohnanyi gave Reiner signed photos and drawings as mementoes of their friendship: several of these are now in the possession of the Reiner professorship at Columbia University. Through his interest in music by living composers, Reiner attended the International Festival of Contemporary Music in Prague in 1924 and served on a jury in 1927 for a prize, organized by the Musical Fund of Philadelphia, for a new chamber composition (the prize was shared by Casella and Bartók).[73] He was knowledgeable about new music and in his Pittsburgh days was particularly interested in the work of contemporary Russian composers.[74] His programs reflected this interest. Some 47 percent of the works Reiner performed in Cincinnati were twentieth-century compositions; the figures for his seasons in Pittsburgh and Chicago were 59 and 57 percent, respectively.[75]

Reiner was selective about the new scores he agreed to conduct. He turned down works by Roy Harris and Howard Hanson, among others, and refused to play a concerto by his friend Abram Chasins because he thought it derivative and boring.[76] Sometimes he presented a contemporary score even if he had some misgivings about it. For instance, he conducted Louis Gruenberg's *Jazz Suite* several times, even though he found its dissonance a little problematic; attention to balance was needed to prevent the piece from becoming raucous.[77] But though Reiner was a firm judge, once he had agreed to conduct a work he did so to the highest professional standards, which met the satisfaction of the composers.[78] Moreover, in selecting works to conduct by living composers, Reiner was not unduly concerned with the publicity associated with first performances.

In the 1930s and 1940s, Reiner was one of the first choices of conductor by composers who wanted an accurate, lucid presentation of a new score.[79] Richard Strauss sent cable after cable to Cincinnati requesting Reiner to come to Vienna to direct performances of his latest opera, insisting that the Hungarian maestro had a better grasp of the meaning and technique of his music than any other living conductor.[80] Strauss's composition of his Oboe Concerto in old age was indirectly attributable to Reiner. In 1945 John de Lancie, who had been principal oboe in Pittsburgh under Reiner, visited Strauss at his home in Garmisch, in the Bavarian Alps, and noted in conversation that he had played many fine oboe solos in Strauss's works under Reiner's direction. Strauss recalled memories of the conductor but stated at the time that he had no intention of writing an oboe concerto. Shortly afterwards, however, he composed such a piece, inspired by the memories triggered by de Lancie's visit. This proved to be one of the fruits of Strauss's Indian summer as a composer.[81] American composers were grateful for the care with which Reiner conducted their works. Gershwin requested him to conduct concerts that included his music, noting that his works received better performances with Reiner than any other conductor. Copland wanted Reiner to conduct the premiere of his *Danzon Cubano*. Morton Gould was impressed by Reiner's ability to bring out the lighter, jazzy qualities of some of his works.[82]

Reiner lacked interest in experimental music and had little time for serialism; he thought Schoenberg had developed atonal music as far as it could be taken. Polytonality had a much sounder foundation over the centuries and more scope for future development.[83] Reiner did not understand the music of Pierre Boulez and Karlheinz Stockhausen and only grasped Stravinsky's works up to *Agon*. He thought the twelve-tone system would pass; it was entirely arithmetic rather than music.[84] He preferred to speak of contemporary music rather than modern music because, for him, the latter term was synonymous with eccentricities.[85] Contemporary composers were mistaken, he thought, when they tried to reproduce literally the noise of the streets. "Art is not the literal reproduction of the exterior world," he once remarked, "it is the harmonious arrangement of seemingly unrelated things. . . . Art should go beyond 'life,' and show us the hidden meanings behind the obvious."[86]

Reiner's interest in contemporary music has been recognized posthumously by the establishment in 1984 of the Fritz Reiner Center for Contemporary Music at Columbia University. Established by Carlotta in her will, the center is directed to help pay the salary of the Reiner Professor of Music, to support concert activities and possibly recordings of contemporary works, and to assist in musical education in ways that promote contemporary music. Each year the Fritz Reiner Center mounts ambitious concerts of new music, using the best professional ensembles in New York City. These events receive additional support from the Alice M. Ditson Fund at Columbia. In 1999 Fred Lerdahl, the current Reiner Professor, expanded these concerts by founding the Columbia Sinfonietta, a cohesive new-music ensemble with enough personnel to play works that require up to twenty performers. The Reiner Center also plays a vital role in Columbia University's music department by helping fund colloquia of visiting composers, by financing readings of student compositions, and by supporting public concerts by student composers.[87]

Throughout his career, Reiner was thoroughly at home in the theater and the concert hall; he divided his energies equally between operas and symphonic music and mastered the dual responsibilities of these roles very effectively. In a late interview he confessed, "When I am conducting opera, I'd rather be conducting a concert; and when I conduct a concert, I'd rather be in the opera pit. It's been that way all my life."[88] Conducting symphonic and operatic music offered different challenges; one was met by imprinting his own technical preparation on an orchestra he had trained to a high quality, the other was achieved through a combination of conducting, singing, lighting, scenery, and action.[89]

Reiner believed that opera was essentially a show and should have a broad appeal through presentation in English so that American audiences could understand it. He knew there were advantages in giving opera in its original language, but he wanted to avoid the idea "that opera must always remain something exotic, something that is difficult to understand and enjoy, something apart from our lives and thought."[90] In more pessimistic moments, Reiner felt that contact with so many diverse personalities when conducting opera and the need for constant readjustments meant that performances could scarcely be called the conductor's at all, whereas musical problems with a symphony orchestra could be sorted out in rehearsal.[91] Thus Wagner's music was often better presented at concerts than in the opera house, where so many problems (the appearance of the singers, their lack of dramatic skill, and so on) might disillusion an audience.[92] Nevertheless, the opera house gave conductors a thorough training; Reiner lamented the lack of American opera houses and the limited opportunities for young American conductors to learn their trade other than at the Met.[93]

Reiner frequently had difficulty putting his musical ideals into practice, however, because of tense relations with conductors, managers, trustees, and players. During the years when he established himself in the United States, Toscanini, Koussevitzky, and Leopold Stokowski were all prominent conductors. Though Reiner had closer dealings with Toscanini and Stokowski than with Koussevitzky, he admired the quality of the Boston Symphony Orchestra under the latter's direction. He praised the Russian emigré for helping younger composers and his courage in pursuing his musical ideals despite all obstacles.[94] But Reiner had virtually no social connections in Boston, and this precluded becoming friendly with Koussevitzky or being offered guest engagements with his orchestra. There may also have been a touch of professional jealousy, for when Leonard Bernstein decided to leave Reiner's conducting class at the Curtis Institute for Tanglewood, where Koussevitzky presided, Reiner commented that the two schools did not mix.

Toscanini was the conductor for whom Reiner had unreserved admiration.[95] In the 1920s, while traveling in Italy, Reiner became friendly with Toscanini, and this led the Italian maestro to request that Reiner replace him in concerts in New York when he was indisposed. Reiner appreciated Toscanini's art, as the following statement indicates: "I admire Toscanini most highly and for two reasons: first, for his superb artistic ability; secondly, because he possesses something that all the rest of us conductors haven't got—a huge, a colossal, a concentrated energy. There is nothing like his concentrated energy in all the world, nothing like his great genius for the dramatic. He conducts in a veritable paroxysm of musical excitement. And he maintains this sublimation to the very end of the performance, without becoming distracted or exhausted. He plays with absolute reverence and fidelity to the composer—plays the composer's music, not Toscanini's. Of course, I was delighted that this great conductor was so kind and friendly to me, and that we found we had many similar ideas."[96]

Unfortunately, the congenial friendship between Toscanini and Reiner fell foul of political disagreements. In May 1931 at Bologna, a group of young Fascists beat up Toscanini after he refused to precede a commemorative concert for the composer Giuseppe Martucci with the Fascist hymn. Toscanini's passport was seized, his home placed under round-the-clock surveillance, and his visitors named on a list. Reiner was included among the visitors. Around the same time, Reiner was conducting the Scala orchestra and complied with a request to play *Giovinezza* at his concerts.[97] Toscanini exiled himself from Italy after his clash with the Fascists and never forgave Reiner's decision to conduct there later in the thirties under Mussolini's regime.[98] He never spoke to Reiner again but always had some good things to say about him. He had sufficient respect for Reiner's musical abilities to insist that he should be a periodic guest conductor of the NBC Symphony Orchestra from 1941 onwards.[99] Reiner recognized Toscanini's prominence and fame and sometimes liked to tease those who referred to the great Italian as "Maestro" by asking, "Maestro? Maestro who?" Reiner was a little jealous of Toscanini's fame and of the fact that no one had created an orchestra for him as NBC had done for Toscanini.[100] When Reiner heard of Toscanini's death in 1957, he realized that an era in conducting had come to an end. He smiled sadly and commented, "Ah . . . only Walter and Monteux. Then R-r-reiner might be the Grand Old Man of the world."[101]

Reiner had a long and generally cooperative acquaintance with Stokowski, who invited him to share conducting duties with the Philadelphia Orchestra in the 1920s and enabled him to conduct operas in the Quaker City in the 1930s. Stokowski traveled with Fritz and Carlotta Reiner on their honeymoon as far as Berlin and introduced them to Otto Klemperer and Erich Kleiber.[102] But in private Reiner was sometimes miffed at Stokowski's success. Not only had Stokowski been chief conductor of the Philadelphia Orchestra, the ensemble with the most finesse in the United States in the twenties and thirties, rivaled in sonority and precision only by the Boston Symphony and, to a lesser extent, the New York Philharmonic; he had also become a glamorous Hollywood figure thanks to the success of Walt Disney's *Fantasia*. Reiner's efforts to appear on the silver screen, by contrast, came to nothing (until he played a cameo part in an indifferent movie called *Carnegie Hall* in 1947). Rivalry existed between the two conductors. When Stokowski got wind that Reiner had commissioned an orchestral suite from *Porgy and Bess,* he announced that he was going to make his own transcription; to which Reiner commented in private that he was "more than ever convinced that Stokowski's mother must have barked with joy when he was born."[103]

Reiner's career in America suffered from poor relations with some of his managers. For over a quarter-century after his arrival in the United States, he was affiliated with Arthur Judson, who dominated orchestral management in America. Judson was manager of the New York Philharmonic-Symphony Orchestra (1922–56), manager of the Philadelphia Orchestra (1915–35), in charge of the Lewisohn Stadium concerts (1920–43), founder of the Robin Hood Dell concerts in Philadelphia, advisory manager of the Cincinnati Symphony Orchestra for five years during the 1920s, and a chief organizer of the Columbia

Broadcasting System in 1927 and of Columbia Concerts, Inc., later known as Columbia Artists Management. From 1930 until about 1950, Columbia was known as "the Judson empire." Dressed like a solid businessman, Judson was highly influential with boards of directors, thought all conductorial positions lay within his gift, and hated to see appointments made outside of his control.[104] While under Judson's management, Reiner progressed at first, but after leaving Cincinnati he never gained the positions he deserved given his ability and experience. And relations with Judson gradually deteriorated. Judson apparently considered Reiner difficult, and it is true that he tended to quarrel with all of his managers. Judson promoted less experienced conductors on his books; witness the elevation of Ormandy to music director of the Philadelphia Orchestra in 1938, or Mitropoulos to leadership of the New York Philharmonic-Symphony Orchestra in 1950.[105] When Reiner heard of the last appointment, he was somber and disappointed.[106]

By 1946–47 Reiner and Judson parted company, and Andrew Schulhof became Reiner's new manager.[107] In 1948 Reiner switched his allegiance to the Russian impresario Sol Hurok, who managed an illustrious group of emigrés, including Heifetz, Horowitz, and Piatigorsky.[108] Marks Levine, president of the National Concerts and Artists Corporation, assisted Hurok in handling Reiner's career by providing bookings arranged via his own organization.[109] But none of Reiner's managers could secure him the two positions he coveted, as head of the New York Philharmonic-Symphony and Boston Symphony Orchestras, when they fell vacant.[110] He came to realize that New York in particular was a graveyard for conductors, a place where entrepreneurs and management interfered too much in musical matters.[111] It was fortunate for Reiner that, when he became head of the Chicago Symphony in 1953, he found himself beyond the control of Judson, who had never wielded influence in the Second City.

Reiner could be very difficult in rehearsing an orchestra. Musicians frequently referred to him as "the great leveller."[112] A perfectionist who demanded plenty of rehearsals and the highest professional standards, he had both an intellectual and nervous intolerance of poor musicianship.[113] He did not want unreliable players in his orchestras because they would jeopardize concerts, so he challenged sections or individuals in rehearsal to find out who was unsure. He expected musicians to overcome stage fright and adopt *his* conception of a piece of music.[114] Usually there was nothing personal in his musical demands; he just expected perfect discipline and completely assured playing.[115] To him, making music was a serious business; sometimes he smiled feintly in rehearsals if he responded to humor in an individual or situation, but he never laughed out loud.[116]

When in a genial mood, Reiner might have appeared momentarily to relax, but his iron will always gave priority to musical demands. Philip Farkas, the former principal horn in the Chicago Symphony Orchestra, recalled how Reiner, in a sociable mood at a cocktail party, extolled the virtues of the horn players in the Vienna Philharmonic, whom he had recently conducted. On hearing Reiner's verdict that these musicians were wonderful, Farkas plucked up the nerve to point out that the Viennese horn players frequently missed notes. Reiner continued the conversation, saying that the Vienna horn players explained that they were not commercial but took chances when they made music; he then declared: "This will be our new attitude. We may take chances but we will make music." At the next rehearsal of the Chicago Symphony, the horns cracked a note. Reiner stopped the orchestra and snapped in the silent hall: "No cracked notes. I don't accept that standard of playing in this orchestra."[117] The honeymoon was over.

One tactic Reiner used occasionally was to stop an orchestra during rehearsal, tell an individual musician he was playing wrong without any explanation, and then continue to do this until the player (who was not making an error) had demonstrated he would not become nervous.[118] Reiner expected musicians to play in time, with correct phrasing and intonation, and conducting pupils had to know scores thoroughly before they began to work with him. Anyone who could not meet his exacting standards was treated with sarcasm and withering contempt. He was impatient with mediocrity and merciless in his criticisms. "Fritz Reiner treats his orchestra," it was once said, "to a sustained and unrelenting course of icy verbal browbeating."[119] On one occasion the New York Philharmonic, incensed by his cutting remarks about their quality, tried to spoil a performance by responding slowly to his directions. Reiner realized what was happening and reduced his beat to the absolute minimum so that they were forced to follow him to maintain a professional standard. Musicians reckoned that if they could fulfill Reiner's musical demands within two years, they could play to an acceptable level in any orchestra in the world.[120]

Reiner's inability to control his anger when errors occurred was one of his greatest failings.[121] While conducting the Pittsburgh Symphony Orchestra, he was accused of intentional bad treatment of musicians during rehearsals, humiliating them in front of the whole orchestra. He was accused of lowering his voice so that it could hardly be heard, beating so faintly that his baton movement could barely be seen, and then raising the roof with players who missed his beat.[122] He failed to understand the complaints and was reprimanded by the musicians' union for his behavior.[123] At the Met he was asked to apologize to the orchestra for his rudeness on one occasion.[124]

Reiner could also be prickly with managers, as his relations with Gaetano Merola in San Francisco, Edward Specter in Pittsburgh, and Rudolf Bing at the Met illustrate. Fellow Hungarians also received no special sympathy from Reiner if he felt they could not meet his musical demands; sentimentality was not part of his nature. In Chicago he became irritated with some Hungarians in the orchestra who tried to gain favor with him by speaking Magyar. His reaction was curt: "You are in America now. Speak English."[125] When, at a Chicago Symphony rehearsal, a Hungarian cellist muffed a passage in Prokofiev's Second Violin Concerto, Reiner showed no sympathy for his compatriot; instead he exclaimed in a fluster, "Oh, we have a very romantic Hungarian here."[126]

Reiner's feisty nature was combined with pride, so he found it difficult to admit temperamental errors. He expected people to come to him and defer to his authority; he rarely reached out with humility to others. Behind this behavior probably lay a great disdain for servility and the extramusical social chores necessary to promote a career—good public relations with managers, boards of trustees, and patrons; small talk with subscribers in the green room; compromises on living arrangements in cities where he was music director; and so on. Reiner frequently turned down requests for interviews and, in fact, only ever made two broadcast interviews.[127] He was not, by nature, much of a social human being and did not alter his behavior to gain positions by acting in a friendly, approachable way. He deliberately avoided social engagements, especially in middle age, because he considered music a demanding art that left little time for social activity. Unfortunately, his intransigence worked against him; a more ingratiating nature would no doubt have helped to open doors that remained closed.[128]

This reserve and dislike of compromise permeated his musical life, too. As János Starker, one of his greatest admirers, has admitted, Reiner was not truly a great performing artist. He did not wish to see his name in the headlines with fanfares accorded to him; he was uninterested in giving performances only to appear successful; he was unwilling to travel extensively in later years to spread his reputation; he had no interest in planning "career moves." He never became a household name, whereas lesser conductors, now forgotten, gained much better publicity at the time. Unloved by the public at large, he never achieved the popularity his artistry justified.[129] There was a total separation between the public's perception of Reiner and the musician's knowledge of his skills, and this can be attributed to his lack of showmanship.[130] He was an idealist dedicated to the art of music; to securing readings of scores infused with authority, color, and discipline; and to training orchestras and singers, spending as many hours as necessary to ensure perfection.

When Reiner had achieved his goal in conducting a certain piece of music, he was not interested in repeating it at the same level to another audience because he felt that the highest standards of music making had already been achieved.[131] He knew that it was not possible to maintain freshness every day while conducting.[132] He sometimes gave the impression he could conduct in his sleep, and boredom and routine marred some of his performances; on the contrary, a conductor like Koussevitzky always conducted everything—even the most familiar Tchaikovsky symphonies—with the freshness of first discovery.[133] Reiner also had a curious habit in performance. If a player entered in a wrong place or committed some other musical error, he switched off, almost entering a world of his own, while still maintaining a highly professional routine standard of performance; it was as if all his years of preparation and knowledge of scores had been desecrated, and he lost that last ounce of interest necessary to give of his best.[134] At such times his beat became so small that it was difficult to follow, but then the mood passed, and the pulse revived. This could be quite alarming for musicians.[135]

Sometimes Reiner could be remarkably insensitive to those musicians he considered his peers and with whom he was generally on good terms. One wounded victim of his sarcasm was the famous Russian bass singer Alexander Kipnis, who sang with Reiner in his Pittsburgh days and whose family home was near the Reiners' in Connecticut. One day while browsing in a book store in Westport, Reiner spotted Kipnis and called out loudly, "And how is your Russian now?" an embarrassing question for the singer whose first tongue was neither Russian nor English but Yiddish and who had escaped privation in Russia at a young age. Kipnis thought that the words hurled at him by Reiner were intended to wound.[136]

Though Reiner was often sarcastic and forthright in personal affairs, he was more circumspect with regard to politics. He emigrated to the United States in part because he was democratically minded. While in Dresden, he became disenchanted with the the protocol of working in a royal court and, subsequently, with the more extreme political groups that flourished in Germany immediately after the end of the First World War. These were both reasons why he relinquished his life position in the capital of Saxony.[137] When he was clear about the political issues, Reiner allowed his name to be used to support democracy and to oppose fascism and communism. On April 1, 1933, along with ten other conductors, including Toscanini and Koussevitzky, he cabled a telegram to Hitler to request a stop to the persecution of colleagues in Germany for religious or political reasons. A reply from the National Socialist commissarial head of the radio department noted that the records and compositions of certain Jewish and Marxist musicians would no longer be performed in Germany.[138] Long after Hitler had gone, Reiner stated, music would still be heard; it would not be goose-stepped out of existence. Once the martial music glorified by Hitler had passed, music would no longer be "regimented according to the ideas of a man who knows nothing about music but wants to pretend that he does."[139] Five years earlier, Reiner began the orchestral season in Pittsburgh with prevailingly Russian music at a time "when everyone's sympathies are sensitive to their titanic struggle."[140] Later, at the time of the Hungarian Revolution of 1956, he replaced Shostakovich's Fifth Symphony on a Chicago Symphony program with Bartók's Concerto for Orchestra as a protest against the Russian invasion of his native land.

Reiner never played an active role in politics. Rather than devote his leisure time to public affairs, he followed private interests and hobbies. Throughout his life he was an avid reader, not only of books on music but also of biographies and fiction. One of his favorite works was Schiller's *Wallenstein* trilogy, which he found stirring and dramatic. His library shelves included the works of Nietzsche and Shakespeare. He liked to keep up his languages and in the 1940s read a daily Hungarian newspaper published in Cleveland.[141] In his early years in America he occasionally relaxed by gardening, especially cultivating roses. In Cincinnati he walked two white Italian shepherd dogs, swam, and played tennis at the Eden Park Tennis Club during summer vacations.[142] Another hobby was driving. Before leaving Europe Reiner had passed an examination proving a general knowledge of mechanics in order to drive. He could identify many problems with car engines. This love of cars continued into the 1930s; when he taught at Curtis, he frequently turned up in a sixteen-cylinder black Cadillac convertible.[143] He was also a member of a musical society called the Bohemians.[144]

Reiner's most serious hobby, however, was photography, which had been his main recreation since childhood.[145] When he arrived in Cincinnati in 1922, he brought his camera from Europe and showed pictures of his children in Italy on a motion-picture projecting machine. He was interested in all aspects of photography, from the snapshot to artistic portraits and motion pictures. He was familiar with all types of cameras and was always on the lookout for one slightly better than the model he already had. While guest conducting at the Hollywood Bowl in the summer of 1925 Reiner visited the motion picture studios, where he was most interested not in the famous stars but in the movie cameramen, several of whom he interviewed to pick up tips. He was competent enough to develop his own film. When he and his wife designed Rambleside, they gave as much thought to the darkroom as to the music room.[146] Reiner was a member of a camera club called the Circle of Confusion and had many photographs reproduced in magazines.[147] He photographed every possible subject, including all the places he had visited—Italy, Austria, Cape Cod, and the Yosemite Valley among them. He produced landscapes, stills, portraits, country scenes, mountain views, and many other subjects.[148]

Reiner's interest in photography extended to a curiosity about all modern gadgets and inventions. He experimented with television as an aid to opera performances in Cincinnati in 1928 and used loudspeakers to create a stereophonic effect for a performance of Richard Strauss's *Elektra* in Philadelphia in 1931. He participated, along with Stokowski, in Bell Laboratories' experimental stereo recordings in the Academy of Music with the Philadelphia Orchestra in 1931–32 and was keen to appear in movies with a musical theme.[149] Reiner was particularly interested in radio as a means of increasing the audience for classical music. In the late twenties he called for a radio foundation, financed by private endowment, so that the finest music could be broadcast regularly.[150] Reiner thought the establishment of an artistic laboratory at Radio City, New York, would be beneficial; conductors, musicians, and engineers could collaborate there on the best way of picking up and amplifying sounds by large orchestral groups. In due course this would be carried out by automatic apparatus linked to the microphone amplifier, rather than by a manual operator, "to preserve the strict balance of tonal quality striven for by the orchestra director."[151]

On radio, Reiner noted, one could adjust orchestral balance by placing instruments in different places, but often a live performance was being broadcast, so it was difficult to guarantee high quality. In conducting orchestras for films, sufficient rehearsal time was available to record and re-record until a satisfactory rendition was achieved. Instruments could be placed by conductors and technicians without concentrating on their visual layout. But television was the most difficult medium for presenting orchestral performances, because music making occurred without the advantages of time and budgets found in films. Reiner gave hundreds of radio broadcasts during his career and participated in many live telecasts with the Chicago Symphony Orchestra. The overriding purpose of these forms of media, as Reiner saw it, was to create a much larger audience for classical music. Appearances on radio, television, and in films helped to identify musical personalities with the public and spread music to the thousands.[152]

The Reiners enjoyed travel in the years before they moved to Chicago. They frequently visited Europe for Fritz's guest engagements in Rome, Milan, Vienna, London, and other musical centers. In the twenties Reiner spent several summer vacations in Italy, at his then-sister-in-law's villa, and cited it as his home.[153] On one trip in 1929 he visited Venice, which he explored with his composer friend Malipiero, followed by a holiday off the Dalmatian coast. When asked where he would like to settle, he always named Italy. In particular he recalled with affection a vacation in Sicily in 1931, when he and Carlotta visited the remains of Greek temples and amphitheaters.[154] Later in his career, as age took its toll, he became more slothful, hailing a cab to travel three or four blocks on Michigan Avenue in Chicago rather than walk. He grew to dislike the discomfort of travel, with a particular antipathy for airplanes.[155] There was the added difficulty of not being able to transport his music library and scores with him when on vacation outside the United States.[156]

Reiner's leisure interests and his geniality in private company were unknown except to a select few in the musical world—a striking reflection of his essential privacy. His reputation today is still very much that of the martinet, and, in some quarters, his ability and achievements have been recognized grudgingly perhaps because of his own lack of interest in promoting himself as a famous maestro. An understanding of his personality reveals him as a most demanding conductor and teacher, subject to whims and difficult moods, but also as someone who attempted to instill in other musicians all the ingredients of technique and personality necessary to meet exacting standards of musical performance. Once one has peeled back all the protective layers he displayed in public to maintain authority and yet preserve his sensitivity, he still seems an enigma. As Virgil Thomson put it so well, Reiner was "as calculable as the stars and about as distant."[157] Today's orchestral scene exhibits many features that Reiner would have abhorred—the homogeneous sound and style of many orchestras, the effects of the corporate world on symphonic organizations, the prolonged absences of conductors away from the orchestras they direct, the ever creeping importance of public relations.[158] All the more reason, then, to analyze Reiner's achievements in building orchestras, teaching conducting, presenting a wide repertoire, and leaving a distinguished recorded legacy.

2. EARLY YEARS IN EUROPE

Fritz Reiner—Reiner Frigyes in Magyar—was born in Budapest on December 19, 1888, the son of upper-middle-class Hungarian Jews who took a cultivated interest in the arts. Ignácx, his father, was a prosperous textile merchant with a wide social circle. Though he was no performer, he had a keen interest in music and could sing most of Schumann's songs from memory. His mother, Vilma (née Pollak), was an accomplished amateur pianist. With this background the young Fritz Reiner was, not surprisingly, exposed to music at an early age. Chopin's piano music was played regularly in the home along with Schubert's songs and excerpts from operas by Rossini and Meyerbeer arranged for piano. At family gatherings Fritz's uncle Hermann, an amateur violinist, played the concertos of the Belgian virtuoso Charles Auguste Bériot and other pieces. There were other early musical influences while Fritz was still a child. On daily excursions with his brother and a nurse into Budapest, he became keenly interested in the military bands that played in the city's beer gardens. Peering through the railings at the musicians, he was gripped by the motions of the conductor, with his bright uniform, and by the cymbal player, with his loud clashes. When he arrived home, he tried to imitate the players by using the bath tub as a drum and by rattling and banging pots and kettles in the kitchen. At home Reiner also became fascinated by his grandfather's musical clock, which played excerpts from *Lucia di Lamermoor,* especially the sextet and the aria of the last act. In all these ways Reiner was stimulated by music in his household and surroundings before he reached the age of six.[1]

Fritz's fascination with his grandfather's musical clock and the military bands persuaded his parents to arrange piano lessons for him. He was not a model pupil. Several teachers were hired, but none succeeded in making him practice. He was required to write out a hundred times, as a punishment, "If I am questioned, I must answer."[2] But soon the difficulties were overcome. By the age of eight he was playing piano studies by Duvernois and Czerny and, with greater interest, the piano scores of Haydn and Beethoven symphonies and of operas such as *Cavalleria Rusticana*. A family friend also introduced him to piano versions of Wagnerian operas. He practiced these and other scores by playing piano duets with his mother but soon became more interested in the orchestra than the piano.

Reiner's parents whetted their son's musical appetite further by taking him to see operas, including *Lucia* (which he later conducted in Budapest). During performances at the opera, the six-year-old Reiner was more fascinated by the orchestra than by the characters on stage. He watched intently as the musicians moved their bows and the conductor waved his baton. Ignácx Reiner, encouraged by his son's interest, bought seats for the family at the Budapest Royal Opera House along with musical scores. By the age of ten, Fritz regularly waited in the crowd for the cheap gallery seats at the opera. He recalled standing in the queue a long time to get a ticket and then dashing wildly to the gallery to be the first person there.[3] Inside the building he sat with a score and pencil, listening carefully, and marking the parts played by various instruments.

Though Reiner revealed a strong interest in the opera orchestra and displayed some talent for piano playing, he learned no other musical instrument, and there were no early signs that he would follow a musical career. But a turning point came in 1899 during a vacation at Budakesz, a village about an hour from Budapest and a favorite summer resort of the Reiner family. While there he became absorbed in the piano score of the *Tannhäuser* Overture, which he had memorized. One day a young man passed the farm house where the Reiners were staying, heard strains of music from the open window, and knocked on the door to introduce himself. The visitor was Leó Weiner.[4] Two years older than Reiner and already a composition student at the Budapest Academy of Music, Weiner wanted a partner to play piano duets. He asked Reiner to join him; the offer was immediately accepted. After their chance meeting, the two young men regularly played piano duets—arrangements of Schumann's symphonies and Piano Quartet and music by Mozart and Grieg but no Beethoven because Weiner, for whatever reason, did not approve of him at the time.

This sharing of musical interests was important for both young men. Weiner became not only one of Reiner's leading musical patrons in Budapest but his greatest supporter. Reiner later paid homage to his friend as the man who taught him more about music than any other person, and by performing his works and arrangements at concerts. From Leó Weiner, Reiner learned the necessity of hearing the total score rather than just linear musical progression. In other words, he absorbed structural musical knowledge rather than mere acquaintance with the melody or bass line.[5] Reiner later acknowledged that Weiner's influence persuaded him, when he was only eleven years old, to seek a musical career rather than playing music simply for his own enjoyment.[6]

Leó persuaded Fritz to apply for scholarships in piano and composition at the Budapest Academy of Music (renamed the Franz Liszt Academy in 1925). This was (and is) the chief center of musical education in Hungary.[7] Reiner composed a Schumannesque piano piece for his entrance examination, won two scholarships, and entered the academy at the age of ten. He was exempt from paying tuition fees because of his scholarships. While attending the academy Reiner continued to study at secondary school (or gymnasium), specializing in piano, composition, and English. He was always first in his class in Latin, and he also learned Greek. He read the biographies and letters of famous men, especially Horace and Tacitus, but did not care much for adventure stories, romantic fiction, or poetry. He played rugby for diversion, even though Hungarian schools of the time gave little priority to sport.[8]

Reiner concentrated most of all on his piano studies and soon developed a prodigious musical memory. At the age of ten he could play the piano version of the first act of *Die Walküre* without a score. His first public appearance as a pianist followed—a performance of Mozart's Piano Concerto no. 26 in D Major (the *Coronation*) when he was thirteen. While only fourteen, he played piano accompaniment for visiting artists from the Hungarian provinces, Germany, and France. During his teenage years he developed a facility for sight-reading scores and also absorbed much orchestral and operatic literature. Besides piano playing, Reiner became fascinated by the timpani and various percussion instruments. Since all pupils were expected to be members of the orchestra, he played the kettledrums while studying at the academy. This must have left a deep impression on him, for his knowledge of percussion instruments, according to later testimony, was second to no other conductor.[9]

Reiner was a hard-working, gifted student who took the highest honors in his classes. He graduated summa cum laude from both his school and the Budapest Academy of Music in 1904, soon after his sixteenth birthday. Reiner's father supported his son's musical interests but was concerned, like many parents before and since, that a musical career was too precarious an occupation for a gentleman. He therefore persuaded his son to pursue legal studies at the University of Budapest. In deference to his father's wishes, Fritz spent a year studying law at the university; but he did so with reluctance.

After his father's death in 1905, Reiner abandoned the law to follow a professional musical career. He began his studies at the academy by concentrating on the piano but later broadened his musical education to incorporate composition and other skills. Between 1903 and 1905 he studied the piano with István Thomán. From 1905 to 1908 he was a member of the composition class of Hans Koessler. From 1907 until 1909 he studied piano pedagogy with Kálmán Chován.[10] Thomán, a pupil of Liszt, was a greatly esteemed Hungarian teacher and pianist who taught many generations of Hungarian pianists. The German composer, organist, and teacher Koessler was in charge of the composition department at the academy, where he was a member of the faculty for over twenty-five years.[11] His illustrious list of pupils included Béla Bartók, Zoltán Kodály, Leó Weiner, Ernö Dohnanyi, and Emmerich Kálmán. Under Koessler, Reiner followed a rigorous program of academic study, including courses on musical aesthetics, Hungarian musical history, instrumentation, score reading, conducting, study of liturgical music, and piano studies. He received a thorough and demanding training. In the 1906–7 academic year he was required to study pieces by Czerny, Clementi, Haydn, Mozart, and Beethoven. He was awarded the highest grade in all these branches of study apart from score reading and piano studies, in which he achieved a second grade.[12]

In his last two years at the academy, Reiner was also taught piano by Bartók, then a concert pianist with an international career and only beginning with Kodály to collect and study authentic Hungarian folk music as part of a growing nationalist interest in Magyar culture.[13] Among the works Reiner studied with Bartók were Beethoven's Piano Sonata no. 32 in C Minor, Op. 111, and Liszt's B Minor Piano Sonata. Even to attempt to play these pieces suggests that Reiner must have had a very good keyboard technique. In 1906–7 Reiner was one of a handful of pupils in the third class of piano students taught by Bartók. In 1907–8 he was promoted to the fourth class (the fifth being the highest). His studies with Bartók included work on chamber music as well as on the piano.[14] Bartók was a temporary teacher at the academy in 1906–7, but in the following year his appointment was made permanent after the retirement of his teacher, Thomán. An austere, reserved man who was nonetheless an esteemed teacher, Bartók aimed to instill imaginative musicianship into his pupils rather than just technical perfection.[15] He never taught composition but was a pianist par excellence from whom Reiner learned much. Reiner was to become a great champion of Bartók's works in the United States from the 1920s onwards.

During his studies at the academy, Reiner occasionally played in public in the Old Music Academy (now the Liszt Museum). Among the works he performed in recitals at student concerts were Weiner's "Tarantella" for two pianos and the first movement of one of Beethoven's F minor piano sonatas. He was also the accompanist in a performance of Karl Goldmark's Suite for Violin and Piano.[16] As interested in musical interpretation as in performing in public, he forthrightly told his professors that their rendition of certain classic pieces was wrong and that they should be played in another way. To the amazement of his teachers, these suggestions nearly always led to more convincing interpretations. Though startled by his boldness, they held him in high esteem for his musical knowledge and understanding.[17]

After he graduated from the Budapest Academy, Reiner continued to play the piano and kept up his theoretical and practical studies in music. He taught music privately, especially the piano. One of his students at the time recalled that he was a demanding teacher who expected pupils to equal his musicianship; he sometimes ended lessons by telling students not to return next week because he did not care to listen to bad musicians. The same student was nevertheless grateful that Reiner took the trouble to play and teach her all the Beethoven and Brahms symphonies in four-handed piano versions.[18] Thus, even at a young age, Reiner's personality and musical demands were severe, but he had a genuine pedagogical mission.

In addition to teaching the piano, Reiner toured throughout Hungary, accompanying singers and instrumentalists in recitals. In 1910 he was the piano accompanist for a recital in Budapest by his compatriot, the violinist Joseph Szigeti, and for the German soprano Frieda Hempel.[19] He also accompanied the violinist Joan Manén, the cellist David Popper, and the mezzo-soprano Elena Gerhardt.[20] These activities were vital for gaining experience and for earning a living for himself and his mother, whom he supported after his father's death.

Reiner moved away from his Jewish heritage, in what seems a self-conscious act to suppress a potential source of prejudice towards him. By 1900 Jews comprised nearly a quarter of Budapest's population; they dominated artistic and literary patronage in that city.[21] Both Reiner and his mother relinquished their Jewish faith in 1908 and converted to Roman Catholicism.[22] The reasons for this dual conversion are not entirely clear. Reiner's daughter Eva was convinced that her father and grandmother acted with foresight by reacting to the extensive anti-Semitism then common in Budapest. Becoming a Catholic meant greater assimilation into central European society. Reiner and his mother realized that Catholicism would be a more acceptable faith than the Jewish religion for someone wishing to pursue a musical career in central Europe.[23] Despite this conversion, deep religious convictions never played a major part in Reiner's subsequent career.

Reiner was fortunate to spend his formative years in a rapidly growing city with a flourishing musical tradition. Founded in 1873 by the unification of three towns—Buda, Obuda, and Pest—Budapest doubled in size in the last twenty years of the nineteenth century. New districts grew up on both sides of the River Danube, which flowed southward through the city. This major metropolis of the old Austro-Hungarian Empire was perhaps the most bourgeois city in eastern Europe at that time. Political and cultural affairs were discussed in the six hundred coffee houses scattered throughout a city that had a knowledgeable and enthusiastic public for opera and the other arts. Around 1900 the official musical language in Hungary was German; so were the professors at the Budapest Academy of Music. The director of the academy, Edmund von Mihálovich, though a Hungarian composer, was a great champion of German music. But with the emergence of Kodály and Bartók, Hungarian musical nationalism was burgeoning. For Reiner, this fusion of a new Hungarian school of composition with long-established German cultural traditions must have been bracing.[24]

Moreover, Hungary was a focal point for musical creativity at this time. It was the home of great instrumentalists who influenced modern string playing, men such as Joseph Joachim, Leopold Auer, and Carl Flesch. Budapest had a National Opera and Philharmonic Society, plenty of operetta, many concerts by native and foreign artists, visits from Viennese orchestral societies, and recitals by fine instrumentalists such as Bronislaw Huberman, Artur Schnabel, Pablo Casals, Georges Enesco, Artur Rubinstein, Ossip Gabrilowitsch, Josef Lhévinne, and Leopold Godowsky.[25] These talented performers created the perfect setting for awakening the musical interests of Reiner and other young Hungarians.

Throughout his student years, Reiner became increasingly fascinated by the art of conducting. He realized that his capacity for musical expression lay more in directing orchestras than in writing music even though he composed some youthful string quartets and songs.[26] His first efforts on the podium came at the age of twelve, when he conducted his school orchestra in Beethoven's First Symphony. He continued to conduct at annual school concerts. His composition teacher, Koessler, encouraged him to pursue conducting as a career, but in those days conducting was not taught at musical academies, and there were no competitions or prizes or any other formal training available. One simply had to wait for suitable opportunities to conduct for one's talents to be recognized.

After graduation from the Budapest Academy Reiner received personal instruction in conducting by Jenö Hubay, a noted Hungarian violinist and composer. But it is doubtful whether he learned much from him. One day at a rehearsal at the academy, Reiner, who was playing percussion, interrupted Hubay, who was conducting, to ask whether a difficult entry could be indicated with a clear cue from the baton. Hubay looked perplexed and then leafed through the score only to inform Reiner that, at that point, he could not give a cue because he was too busy conducting.[27]

Reiner absorbed much more from watching his idol, István Kerner, who conducted the Budapest Philharmonic Orchestra and at the city's opera houses.

Kerner was heir to a Hungarian school of conducting that included Sándor Erkel, Artur Nikisch, and Hans Richter; Reiner was deeply impressed with him. "It was not any kind of choreography," he later wrote, "but a conducting style of fine, small movements." Kerner was a "fantastically precise man with a fantastic ear and memory. Broad, big movements were utterly alien to him."[28] It was from Kerner that Reiner first absorbed his conviction that the main aim of a conductor is to achieve the maximum result on the podium with the minimum effort.[29] Reiner also learned from Kerner that "art begins where technique leaves off."[30] Reiner was fortunate in having these exemplars and the tradition of conducting in Budapest during his apprentice years.

Leó Weiner encouraged Reiner in his choice of profession, but conducting positions were hard to come by. Reiner's first professional opportunities arose through the kindness of his piano duet partner. Weiner had taken a position as coach at the Budapest Opéra-Comique (the Komisch Oper or Népszínhaz-Vígopera). A bachelor and somewhat of a loner, totally absorbed in music, Weiner was an excellent musician who became a revered teacher and a great influence on Hungarian musicians who began their careers in the first half of the twentieth century. Among his pupils were other notable Hungarian conductors such as Antal Dorati, István Kertesz, and Ferenc Fricsay.[31] Unfortunately, Weiner had an Achilles Heel: he could not conduct. Yet he had the self-knowledge to realize quickly this limitation to his musical ability. He soon resigned as coach and chorus director at the Vígopera and nominated Reiner in his place. Reiner got this chance partly through his friendship with Weiner and partly through his quick sight-reading and good piano playing. He accepted the post without hesitation. The year was 1908; he was only nineteen. This was his chance to pursue his vocation, and he took it. Reiner later mentioned that he owed more gratitude to Weiner, for recognizing that he should be a conductor, than to anyone else.[32]

While at this post, Reiner avidly familiarized himself with all the major features of an opera house—the pit, proscenium, back stage, acoustics, staging, lighting, direction of soloists, chorus, orchestra, and so forth. Initially he had few conducting opportunities, though he did conduct some unspecified music to accompany a performance on June 24, 1908, of Imre Madach's nineteenth-century Hungarian play *The Tragedy of Man*.[33] After only six months in the position, a new opportunity arose. This time it was a stroke of luck. Reiner was called upon to conduct a performance of *Carmen* without rehearsal when the regular conductor fell ill. "It was sink or swim," Reiner later confessed. "I swam."[34] Nothing had ever been so difficult for him. Fortunately, despite his nerves, he revered Bizet, had studied his music extensively, and had discussed *Carmen* with Weiner (who was often known as the "Hungarian Bizet" because of the delicate craftsmanship of his compositions).[35] It was just the good fortune he needed at the start of a conducting career. Reiner later emphasized to his own pupils the necessity of taking such an opportunity in an emergency to get a foot through the door.[36]

The success, however, was short-lived because the Vígopera fell into financial trouble, went bankrupt, and closed its doors forever in 1909. At the end of his one season there, Reiner received the equivalent of 150 dollars. Conducting opportunities had dried up. Thinking that he might need to choose an alternative career, he tried to triple his earnings by gambling. This proved unsuccessful: the money was frittered away, and he turned against gambling for good.[37] He desperately wanted to continue the career he had started, but a member of the Budapest Royal Opera House advised him to leave Hungary and learn his profession elsewhere.[38] Possibly this was because Gustav Mahler was the only Jew who had ever conducted at that opera house; but the recommendation also suggested that Reiner would find greater opportunities if he expanded his horizons beyond his native country. For the time being, however, Reiner stayed in Budapest. All was not gloom. In 1909 Reiner was awarded his diploma from the Academy of Music, with Bartók's signature at the head of the document. This was a moment for proud reflection on his musical achievements so far. The collapse of the Vígopera meant, however, that Reiner once again needed to earn a living through piano teaching and coaching.

If this seemed a step backwards, it was only a temporary one: another conducting position soon came his way. One day in 1910 Reiner accompanied a soprano being auditioned for the opera company in Laibach (now Ljubljana), a town of a hundred thousand that was the capital of Slovenia and part of the Austro-Hungarian Dual Monarchy. The singer was rejected, but Reiner, still only twenty-one years old, was offered a contract as head of the Laibach Opera House, one of the oldest establishments of its kind in Europe. This was an Austrian-style opera house in which a large repertory was performed in either German or Slovenian. It was the home of the Slovene Provincial Theater (Slovensko Dezelno Gledalisče), and was built in 1892 with a seating capacity of seven hundred. It succeeded the German Landestheater, burned down in 1887, where Mahler had served as an apprentice conductor in 1881.[39] Reiner, listed as Friderik Reiner, worked in an opera house where the other main conductor was the Czech maestro Václav Talich, later to become a renowned conductor of the Czech Philharmonic Orchestra.[40]

In Laibach Reiner quickly learned the Slovenian tongue and in a six-month season (October 2, 1910, through March 30, 1911) conducted a varied repertoire that ran the spectrum from light opera and operetta to tragedy. Altogether he conducted fifty-seven performances of ten works by nine composers. His first production was Smetana's heroic opera *Dalibor*, which he never conducted again. He followed this with Puccini's *La bohème*, Weber's *Der Freis-*

chütz, Gounod's *Faust,* Lehar's *Das Fürstenkind* and *Der Graf von Luxem-
burg,* Hervé's *Mam'zelle Nitouche,* Wagner's *Tannhäuser,* Leo Fall's *Die Dol-
larprinzessin,* and Kálmán's *Ein Herbstmanöver (The Gay Hussar).* He also
directed the music for two plays by Slovenian writers—Ivo Vojnovic's *Ekvi-
nokcij* and Johann Nepomuk Nestroy's *Hudobui Duh Lumpacij Vagabund ali
Zanikrna Trojica.*[41]

These productions were well received, but conditions must have been trying for a man who was later a master of opulent orchestral sound, for Reiner's
pit orchestra only consisted of twenty-five players. *Tannhäuser* was performed
with an orchestra of thirty, including only one cello, and Beethoven's *Eroica*
Symphony was performed with less than thirty-five players.[42] While in Laibach
Reiner also directed the city's Grand Symphony concerts with an orchestra of
similar size. The manager of the newly opened Budapest Volksoper (or Népopera) attended one of his Beethoven programs at these concerts and promptly
offered him a three-year contract to return to his native city.

So after only one year in Laibach, Reiner returned home to Budapest with
his wife, whom he had married in October 1911. Their first child, Tuśy, was
born soon afterwards. From 1911 until May 1914 Reiner remained at the Budapest Népopera (known since 1953 as the Erkel Színház and not to be confused with the Royal Hungarian Opera House in the city). The Népopera, on
the Pest side of the Danube, had a capacity of three thousand and offered low
prices and a varied repertoire to a popular audience. Reiner extended his repertoire considerably from the works he had performed in Laibach. At the Népopera he conducted 191 performances of twenty-three operas and operettas
by thirteen composers between December 22, 1911, and April 29, 1914.[43] Leó
Weiner was then head coach at this theater. He and Reiner resumed their
friendship and worked together on all productions. They scheduled lighter
fare, including Robert Planquette's operetta *Les cloches de Courneville.* They
also put on two Hungarian operas: Weiner's *Kozjatek* (one performance) and
Clement Karoly's *Radda* (two performances).[44]

Reiner gave much more attention, however, to Italian opera. He conducted
Rossini's *Il barbiere di Siviglia,* Donizetti's *Lucia di Lammermoor* and *La fille
du régiment,* Wolf-Ferrari's *I gioielli della Madonna,* and several Verdi operas
(*La traviata, Il trovatore, Rigoletto,* and *Un ballo in maschera*). Puccini was represented by *La bohème* and *Tosca.* Critical commentary in the periodical *A Zene*
was complimentary. The notice for a performance of *La traviata* in July 1912 is
typical: "Reiner Frigyes ügyesen véset az eloadást, amelynek egyeten fogy-
atékosága a lehetlen magyar szöveg volt" (Fritz Reiner skillfully directed that
chiseled performance, the only deficiency of which was the former Hungarian
ending).[45] Reiner also covered French opera, conducting Ambroise Thomas's
Hamlet and *Mignon,* Meyerbeer's *Les Huguenots,* Gounod's *Faust,* Bizet's *Car-*

men, and Offenbach's *Les contes d'Hoffmann. Carmen,* one of his favorite operas, was warmly received: "Reiner karmester fényesen oldotta meg a zenei feladatokat, oszinte gyönyörüségünk telt a preciz eroteljes produdukciókban" (Reiner conducted a lustrous, relaxed performance but one that was precise and magnificent).[46]

Reiner's remaining repertoire consisted of the Wagnerian music dramas that had absorbed his attention in his teens. At the Népopera he conducted *Tannhäuser, Die Meistersinger von Nurnberg, Lohengrin,* and *Parsifal.* His greatest coup was to conduct a completely uncut *Parsifal* at the Népopera at one minute past midnight on December 31, 1913. This was the first time that the sacred music drama was officially allowed to be played in public outside Bayreuth after Wagner's death (a rule favored by the composer's sponsor, King Ludwig XI of Bavaria, and by Cosima Wagner, and one that lasted for thirty years). Reiner's production finished at 5 A.M., just ahead of similar productions of *Parsifal* outside Bayreuth by Eduard Mörike in Berlin and André Messager in Paris.[47] The daily Budapest paper *Magyar Estilap* included a one-and-a-half-page report of the production. "Frigyes Reiner, the brilliant young musician," it noted, "accomplished an excellent piece of work by rehearsing this very difficult opera and one must write of him with the highest praise."[48]

Most productions at the Népopera included Hungarian singers, but the leading roles were taken by international artists, several of whom subsequently had leading careers in opera houses throughout the world. One of the leading singers was the Latvian lyric tenor Hermann Jadlowker, who sang Don José in *Carmen,* the title roles in *Faust* and *Lohengrin,* and Cavaradossi in *Tosca,* all under Reiner's direction.[49] He was a favorite singer at the Népopera, and his name always appeared in bold capitals on the performance playbills. Reiner also directed the English tenor Alfred Piccaver as the Duke of Mantua in *Rigoletto,* the powerful Italian baritone Titta Ruffo as Figaro in *Il barbiere di Siviglia,* the Czech soprano Maria Jeritza as Elsa in *Lohengrin,* and the Russian soprano Lydia Lipkowska as Gilda in *Rigoletto,* as Rosina in *Il barbiere di Siviglia,* and as Micaëla in *Carmen.*

Reiner's reputation soon spread, and he planned to extend the scope of his musical activities in Europe as the First World War broke out.[50] The opportunity to expand his musical horizons occurred after three stars of the Dresden Opera sang under his baton at the Budapest premiere of *I gioielli della Madonna* in 1914. The singers recommended him to the director of the Semperoper. The success of the production was such that he was invited to Dresden for an interview. Ten days later Reiner was offered a five-year contract to conduct the Dresden Royal Opera in succession to Ernst von Schuch, who had just died. Schuch had been associated with the Semperoper for forty-two years and was its music director for over thirty years. In Dresden Schuch conducted fifty-one world premieres and added another 117 operas to the repertory.[51] He was renowned, in particular, as a champion of Richard Strauss's operas. Reiner could not match this record of achievement. He was still only twenty-five and had to compete with several older capable competitors for the post, including Karl Muck and Felix Weingartner. But Reiner prevailed largely through the support of the opera house's powerful director, Count Nikolaus von Seebach, who obstinately rejected Muck's candidacy.[52] This was undoubtedly a major breakthrough in Reiner's career and quite a coup for someone born outside Germany.

For most of his time in Dresden, Reiner shared conducting duties at the opera with the experienced Hermann Kutzschbach, who had been associated with the orchestra from his youth, and with Kurt Striegler. In 1918 and 1919 a fourth conductor, Karl Pembaur, was also employed for some performances. Reiner settled down to live in Dresden but moved house frequently. He had residences in Hübnerstrasse, Lilienstrasse, the Hotel Bellevue (opposite the opera house), and Hospitalstrasse.[53] An extended stay in a leading center of opera and symphonic music was just what Reiner needed to consolidate his musical experience. He approached his position with relish even though performing opera in Dresden during wartime was subject to many limitations and privations.[54]

The Dresden Royal Opera was, along with the Berlin, Munich, and Vienna State Operas, one of the most coveted operatic establishments in Europe. Dresden had become the seat of a royal court with the establishment of the Kingdom of Saxony at the Vienna Congress in 1815. Its Royal Saxon Opera House opened in 1841. For six years after 1843 its opera and orchestra were conducted by Wagner, whose operas *Rienzi, Der fliegende Holländer,* and *Tannhäuser* were premiered there. Reiner noted, on arrival in Dresden, that he never imagined that he would one day conduct at a great center of Wagnerian opera.[55] The Dresden Opera had a long and distinguished tradition of performing Wagner and the mainstream Germanic opera repertoire. The city itself, situated on the Elbe, was adorned with many splendid medieval and baroque buildings and the dignity of a royal court. Clustered around the city center were the Royal Palace, with the Zwinger's renowned collection of old master paintings; the Semperoper, built between 1871 and 1878; and the Catholic Hofkirche. Dresden had a lot of high-quality music making, including regular quartet societies and a robust choral tradition associated with the choir of the Kreuzschule, founded in the thirteenth century. The Saxon State Orchestra (the Dresden Staatskapelle of today) played at the opera and at symphonic concerts. There was another orchestra in the city, the Dresden Philharmonic, and a conservatory of music. Dresden gloried in a distinguished tradition of music making harking back over four hundred years to the time of Martin Luther and Heinrich Schütz.[56]

Reiner was fortunate in having a patron to promote him in Dresden. He was the protégé of Seebach, who, on September 23, 1915, over a year after his debut in the Saxon capital, appointed him Royal Court Conductor (Königlicher Hofkapellmeister). This position was as important as it sounds, and it included a lifetime contract. The prospect of tenure until he chose to retire reflected Dresden's confidence in Reiner's abilities and gave him the security to pursue his chosen vocation. In June 1916 he was appointed to the permanent conducting staff of the royal house of von Metzsch, and he also conducted the Saxon State Orchestra in Dresden. Reiner's initial salary in Dresden, on checks signed by the King of Saxony, was nine thousand marks.[57] In February 1915 he negotiated a two-thousand-mark advance to cover moving expenses and his family needs. These were not princely sums despite the prestige of the position. They were, for instance, a good deal less than a conductor could command for work with an American orchestra on the eve of the First World War.[58] Reiner's salary improved substantially after several years, however. At the time he left Dresden, he was reputedly earning six million marks per season—a salary magnified falsely by the rampant inflation then common throughout Germany.[59]

The Dresden Opera had a splendid auditorium and all sorts of theatrical equipment and technical devices.[60] Artistic standards were high. Reiner's experience in the opera house progressed rapidly as a result of working with a highly accomplished orchestra and the best-known singers of the day. His technical proficiency with the baton was aided by the sheer amount of work undertaken, for operas were performed on virtually every day of the week during a season lasting from September to June. During eight years in the city, Reiner conducted some 536 performances of fifty different operas by thirty composers. He directed fourteen new productions, four world premieres, and five first performances in Dresden.[61] All performances were sung in German; French, Italian, and German operas predominated. The Italian selection included only one Rossini opera, *Il barbiere di Siviglia*. Verdi was better represented by *Aida*, *Rigoletto*, *Un ballo in maschera*, *La traviata*, and *Il trovatore*. The other Italian operas conducted by Reiner were Donizetti's *La fille du régiment*, Wolf-Ferrari's *I gioielli della Madonna*, and Puccini's *La bohème* and *Tosca*. From the French repertoire, Reiner conducted Offenbach's *Les contes d'Hoffmann* and *Faust*, Auber's *Fra Diavolo*, Meyerbeer's *L'Africaine*, and Flotow's *Martha*. But pride of place in this repertoire went to *Carmen*. Reiner conducted it thirty-four times, more than any other single opera during his Dresden years.[62]

The German operatic repertoire dominated Reiner's conducting at the Semperoper. This was partly a necessity, because the political regime in Saxony insisted that the performance of German operas should be given prominence during the First World War.[63] Reiner conducted Haydn's *Lo Speziale*,

Mozart's *Die Zauberflöte* and *Le nozze di Figaro,* and Beethoven's *Fidelio* (including one performance, on December 16, 1920, to celebrate the 150th anniversary of Beethoven's birth). The early German romantic repertoire was also represented. Reiner conducted Weber's *Der Freischütz,* including the seven hundredth Dresden performance of the opera,[64] and Marschner's *Hans Heiling,* a German opera written between the time of Weber and that of Wagner. Among lighter works he conducted Franz von Suppé's *Die schöne Galathea* and Dohnányi's music to Schnitzler's pantomime *Der Schleier der Pierrette.*

From the musical legacy of the city Reiner absorbed at first hand the traditions of the Wagnerian Gesamtkunstwerk (or all-embracing work of art). When he first came to Dresden he felt that he did not conduct the orchestra so much as the orchestra conducted him in Wagnerian matters.[65] He learned by experience, and more than a quarter of his opera performances in Dresden consisted of music by Wagner. One of his earliest successes in this repertoire was a complete *Ring* cycle in the 1915–16 season. This was another emergency, in which he substituted for another conductor, but he passed the ordeal. He stayed up nights to prepare the scores, worked with the singers during the day, but had few orchestral rehearsals. His absorption of Wagner in his teenage years was such that he could write out in his piano score the orchestration for *Tristan und Isolde* from memory.[66] His Wagnerian performances in Dresden included eight complete performances of the *Ring,* the only time in his long career that he conducted such cycles (apart from a substantially cut concert version of the tetralogy given at Lewisohn Stadium in New York in summer 1937).[67] He also directed *Lohengrin, Parsifal, Die Meistersinger von Nurnberg, Tannhäuser, Tristan, Der fliegende Holländer,* and *Rienzi.* In 1919 he conducted a festival performance of the *Ring* in Halle, partly with singers from the Dresden Opera.[68]

Richard Strauss's works featured prominently in Reiner's orchestral and operatic programs, and it was during his stay in Dresden that Reiner became one of Strauss's favorite conductors of his own music. Dresden was, of course, one of Strauss's cherished musical venues—as one can tell from the rich lament he poured out for the destruction of the city by Allied bombers near the end of World War II in his *Metamorphosen* for twenty-three solo strings. Before coming to the Saxon capital, Reiner had never directed any of Strauss's operas. But it was unthinkable that he should remain there and not absorb these works in a city that had already witnessed the premieres of *Der Rosenkavalier, Salome,* and *Elektra* only a few years before his arrival.[69]

When Reiner came to Dresden, Strauss was insufficiently assured that he would prove a worthy successor to von Schuch in conducting his operas. The composer therefore arranged for the premiere of *Ariadne auf Naxos,* completed in 1916, to be given in Vienna rather than Dresden.[70] But Strauss soon heard that Reiner had maintained the high standards of his predecessor, and Reiner took the opportunity to familiarize himself with Strauss's works. In Dresden, Reiner conducted the German premiere and five additional performances of one of Strauss's most difficult works for the stage, *Die Frau ohne Schatten.* He also conducted *Salome* (which had been premiered in the city in 1905). These performances were not all undivided successes. In the case of *Die Frau,* first produced in Dresden on October 22, 1919, only twelve days after the Vienna premiere, unsatisfactory casting and designs coupled with political intrigue made the German premiere a trying occasion for Reiner and one that almost ended the long association between Strauss and Dresden. Strauss was displeased at the modest scale of the sets (a necessity, however, due to postwar financial stringency). He postponed the first performance for several days after the leading soprano, Eva von der Osten, had, according to the composer, ruined her voice by taking on too many dramatic roles.[71] Ernst Krause considered that Reiner threw away the opportunity to present a great artistic demonstration of a new democratically founded opera house, soon to become the State Opera of Saxony, by not taking charge of a dull and ill-designed stage set.[72] But it is clear that many decisions about the production were not in Reiner's hands, and he cannot be blamed for its lack of success.[73]

Fortunately, the debacle of the production of *Die Frau ohne Schatten* did not mar the friendship between Reiner and Strauss. In Dresden the two men became friends and regularly played card games until a few minutes before Strauss was due to conduct at the Semperoper.[74] Many years later, when Reiner became head of the German wing of New York's Metropolitan Opera, Strauss wrote to him in warm terms ("mit dankbarkeit gedwidmeter") about memories of a marvelous Dresden production of *Salome* on January 12, 1916. The letter was accompanied by a beautiful pencil drawing of Strauss (now in the possession of the Reiner professorship at Columbia University).[75] While in Dresden, Reiner heard Strauss conduct *Der Rosenkavalier, Die Frau,* and several of his tone poems, including *Don Quixote* and *Tod und Verklärung.* Reiner later admitted that his whole career was affected by watching and hearing Strauss conduct at this time.[76] No doubt he was impressed by Strauss's economical conducting, something that became a hallmark of his own style. In later years he became very much a Strauss specialist and regularly performed and made records of Strauss's operatic and orchestral works.

Reiner's varied operatic repertoire in Dresden included Tchaikovsky's *Eugene Onegin,* Johann Strauss's *Die Fledermaus,* Goldmark's *Die Königin von Saba,* and Ede Poldini's comic opera *Vagabund und Prinzessen.* He led contemporary German operas, including *Der Bärenhäuter* (a premiere) and *Sonnenflammen,* both by Siegfried Wagner, the son of Richard; Clemens von Franckenstein's *Rahab;* Hans Pfitzner's *Das Christelflein;* Eugène d'Albert's

Die toten Augen (premiere); Paul Graener's *Theophano* and *Schirin und Gertraude;* and Hugo Kaun's *Der Fremde.* He also conducted the Austrian composer Franz Schreker's *Der ferne Klang* (premiere) and the Czech composer Joseph Mraczek's *Ikdar.*[77] This list of contemporary operas reveals the progressive policies of the Dresden Opera in the years during and after the First World War. It shows that Reiner was willing to take on many new scores. He never again conducted any of these contemporary operas after he left Dresden, however: many opera houses in which he subsequently appeared were more conservative in their choice of repertoire.

The prestige of the Dresden Opera was sufficient to attract many leading singers. Among those who appeared regularly with Reiner in Dresden were the tenors Tino Pattiera and Richard Tauber, who sang his first *Zauberflöte* under Reiner's direction. Elisabeth Rethberg, the soprano, also began her career with Reiner's advocacy. He heard her sing at her maiden recital in Dresden, when she was unknown, and was so impressed with her voice that he took her at once to Count Seebach, who gave her a hearing and then offered her a five-year contract. This was extended, and she stayed with the Dresden company for seven years between 1915 and 1922.[78] She sang eight different roles under Reiner's direction.

The press notices of Eugen Schmitz, a leading Dresden music critic, point to the versatility of Reiner's conducting in a wide repertoire and to the appreciation of his abilities by (frequently) sold-out houses that sometimes included the King of Saxony himself. At the lighter end of the scale, Reiner's conducting of a new production of *Fra Diavolo* achieved an airiness and grace. This was an ideal interpretation, in Schmitz's opinion, and Reiner combined with the producer, Rüdiger, to maintain a racy, comic tone throughout the opera.[79] At the darker end, Reiner led a new production of *Fidelio* that emphasized that the work was not merely an opera but a tragedy of great suffering rising from the utter darkness. He plumbed the depths of Beethoven's music to highlight every detail of instrumental tone color and to make careful tempo modifications. In Schmitz's view, this was carried out in such a distinguished way that mention of the soloists justified taking second place in his review.[80]

Reiner's conducting of *Carmen* was praised for its fire and verve; his reading of *Il barbiere di Siviglia* was admired for securing an Italian lightness of touch; and his direction of *Un ballo in maschera* was applauded for an understanding of the dynamic and animated characteristics of Italian taste, for achieving a brilliant sound from the orchestra, and for first-rate subtlety in the vocal ensembles.[81] Reiner's conducting of *Rigoletto* was especially singled out for the skill with which he practiced his studies of the traditions of Italian opera. Reiner conducted the revenge finale of the third act, which most German conductors usually took in a square 4/4 time, as a fiery alla breve section; he molded even the most ordinary cantilena into a noble sound; and planned everything down to the smallest detail with affection and dedication, from the tone color of the orchestra to the finely differentiated choruses and ensembles.[82]

To please the opera-going public in Dresden, Reiner was expected to be a capable Wagnerian conductor. Schmitz's press notices of his performances suggest that he met this challenge. A new production of *Rienzi* had a very successful performance in August 1919. Temperament and tone color were the foundations on which Reiner and the chorus built this work after a memorable atmosphere had been established at the outset by the rich, vivacious sound of the overture, which was greeted with a storm of applause.[83] Reiner ably oversaw a *Ring* cycle in 1918 that was presented in less than ideal circumstances. On the opening night of *Das Rheingold*, a shortage of personnel, owing to wartime depletion of singers, was noticeable on stage. Worse than that, during the first scene change a rock in the middle of the stage fell over with a great crash, and during the voyage to Nibelheim, in the scene change between the second and third acts, scenic irregularities caused a disturbance in the music. Only Reiner's presence of mind and lively conducting saved the evening.[84] Things improved during the rest of the cycle. Reiner's performance of *Die Walküre* was notable for a rich orchestral sound that was at times too sumptuous. He conducted *Siegfried* with a fresh, light beat to emphasize the character of a sunny, fairy-tale idyll within a tragic framework. He brought the cycle to a close with a *Götterdämmerung* full of imaginative atmosphere, in which all the scenic effects worked smoothly.[85]

Besides his work at the opera, Reiner also conducted concerts by the Saxon State Orchestra. These were presented, as they are today, in the Semperoper. They took place periodically during the long opera season. Two sets of concerts were scheduled each year—an A and a B series. Reiner gave several cycles of different composers, including Mozart, Beethoven, and Schumann. The Dresden public attended these occasions well and felt they were accomplishing something by concentrating on a specific composer. By 1922 the orchestra had 127 musicians—a very large ensemble by any standard. Besides a full body of strings, there were twelve horns and six of each woodwind. Technical excellence in all sections plus finely honed instrumental timbres were the hallmarks of the Dresden Staatskapelle. Its superb cohesion, virtuosity, magnificent tone and an outstanding bowing technique among the strings were fully in evidence toward the end of Reiner's tenure at a time when postwar inflation in Germany was leading to all sorts of problems in the world outside the opera house.[86]

Some concerts by the Dresden Staatskapelle were interrupted by wartime difficulties, notably by conscription. Reiner and Kutzschbach were also under pressure to concentrate, for nationalistic purposes, on the German and Austrian repertoire.[87] Nevertheless, Reiner had the opportunity to conduct a varied repertory at his concerts in Dresden.[88] He scheduled the occasional Haydn or Mozart symphony, but most of his selections from the classical repertoire were works by Beethoven, including all the symphonies save the first and seventh. Perhaps because he had such a large orchestra at his disposal, Reiner scheduled works from the nineteenth- and early twentieth-century repertoire that required augmented forces. These included complete performances of Liszt's *Dante* and *Faust* symphonies, the latter with Tauber as the tenor soloist; Tchaikovsky's *Manfred* Symphony; Bruckner's symphonies nos. 3, 7, 8, and 9, and his *Te Deum;* Richard Strauss's *Macbeth* and his *Alpine* and *Domestic* symphonies; and Mahler's first and fourth symphonies along with *Das Lied von der Erde.* The performance of the *Alpine* symphony, dedicated to the Dresden Orchestra, was given by Reiner the day after its premiere in Berlin.[89]

Reiner's programming of orchestral music in Dresden was pioneering in its scope and coherence. Arriving in Dresden from an increasingly nationalist musical atmosphere in Hungary, Reiner developed programs that prefigure the themed approach to concertizing one finds today. To be sure, he gave concerts based around music by either contemporary Hungarian or German composers, notably those based in or near Dresden, and in so doing became an early exponent of ethnocentric programming. But he also presented works by a variety of living composers and constructed programs devoted to a single theme, composer, or style-based selections. He celebrated leading composers' anniversaries. He championed the music of a handful of living composers, interspersing their works across programs throughout his tenure in Dresden. He also devised eclectic concerts that went beyond what his administrative superiors thought desirable during the First World War. Such practices appear to have been ahead of their time, even though they are common tendencies in the first decade of the twenty-first century.

Reiner devoted a whole program (on October 20, 1916) to works by Max Reger (the *Symphonischer Prolog zu einer Tragödie,* the Chaconne for violin and orchestra, *An die Hoffnung* for alto solo and orchestra, and the *Variations and Fugue on a Theme by J. A. Hiller*). He introduced two works by his teacher and compatriot Bartók to a Dresden audience—the *Two Portraits* Op. 10 and the Suite no. 1 for Orchestra. On January 13, 1915, he scheduled a program of Hungarian works: Goldmark's overture *Im Frühling,* Leó Weiner's orchestral suite *Csongar und Tunde,* Edmund von Mihálovich's Ballade for large orchestra, and Victor von Herzfeld's *Festival March in the Hungarian Style.* And on June 28, 1919, he programmed a concert devoted entirely to works by composers based in Saxony—Georg Gobler's Symphony in D Major, Johannes Schanze's Two Songs with Orchestra, and Karg-Elert's *Sigfrid,* a chamber symphony. Reiner included contemporary works by composers active in Germany, such as Felix Draeseke's *Symphonia Tragica* and his Serenade in D Major; Hugo Kaun's Third Symphony; and Mraczek's *Orientalische Skizzen für Kammerorchester*. The works by Draeseke and Mraczek were performed no doubt because both composers were then resident teachers at the Dresden Conservatory of Music.[90] Altogether, Reiner directed fifty-eight concerts during his seven years in the Saxon capital.[91]

Reiner developed his conducting skills in Dresden not merely by performing the daily duties of a Royal Court Conductor but by taking the opportunity, whenever possible, to see and hear Artur Nikisch, the great Hungarian conductor, in concert. At the peak of his career during the First World War, Nikisch was concurrently the chief conductor of the Berlin Philharmonic and Leipzig Gewandhaus Orchestras. He conducted with a long baton and avoided excessive use of the left hand for expressive purposes. He did not indulge in lengthy verbal explanations at rehearsals but achieved marvelous results from musicians by use of a deliberately restrained technique. Nikisch influenced many conductors. Sir Adrian Boult, for instance, recalled a thrilling performance of the Brahms First Symphony conducted by Nikisch in Leipzig—the finest performance of this work that he ever heard—and realized after the final movement that the maestro had never raised his hand higher than the level of his face.[92]

Reiner was also deeply impressed with Nikisch and benefited from his personal counsel and advice.[93] He later commented that he learned more about conducting from him than from anyone else: "it was he who told me that I should never wave my arms in conducting and that I should use my eyes to give cues."[94] On one occasion Reiner tried to copy Nikisch's conducting of a fortissimo chord just before the allegro in Weber's *Oberon* Overture by drawing two full circles of the baton and then making a firm downbeat. He used exactly the same gestures as Nikisch but was totally unable to produce the same effect.[95] But if direct imitation proved futile, Reiner nevertheless developed some of his characteristic conducting skills from observing Nikisch—economy of motion, use of the eyes for direction, a persistent right-hand beat, and sparing use of the left hand. Reiner's conducting became renowned for an array of meaningful yet pared down gestures that elicited precise yet imaginative responses from orchestral musicians.

Reiner's Dresden years were wonderful, in terms of musical experience, and they gained him a wide reputation.[96] They also brought recognition in the form of decorations. Reiner was awarded the War Cross of Honor from the King of Saxony in 1916, a civilian war cross from Hungary in 1918, and the award of Knight First Class (Ritterkrenz) from the Duke of Saxe-Coburg-Gotha.[97] Reiner's personal life was turbulent at this time. His first wife Elça, whom he had met in Laibach, produced a second daughter in 1915, but the marriage soon ran into trouble partly because the Reiners were growing apart emotionally, and partly because of Fritz's affair with Berta Gerster-Gardini. Fritz and Berta cohabited before they divorced their respective partners, which shocked the more respectable burghers of Dresden.[98]

Serious musical problems also impeded Reiner's progress during the latter part of his stay in Dresden. The First World War made the cultivation of music difficult in Germany. At the end of the conflict, in November 1918, the Saxon monarchy was deposed, and a revolutionary soldiers' and workers' council set up a republican government with the red flag flown above the palace. The Royal Court Opera (or *hoftheater*) became the State Opera (or Sächsisches Staatstheater). In January 1919 the Marxist Spartacist rebellion led to counterrevolutionary measures and the rejection of the Communists. By November 1920 Saxony was given a new constitution with a state parliament and government based in Dresden, but the political regime was subject to interference by the German army. Reiner was seriously disturbed by the rampant nationalism he saw around him. His Jewish heritage enabled him to sense some of the prejudice that became uglier in Europe a decade and more later. Members of the Dresden Staatskapelle had been resisting his leadership during the First World War; anti-Semitism was already evident then.[99] The one story that circulated in Dresden about Reiner for years after he left was that the orchestra played the first act of *La bohème* at a steady mezzo-forte, without any deviation from this dynamic level. When asked why they did so, a spokesman replied that this was how Reiner conducted it; but clearly this was a collective act of noncooperation.[100]

Reiner also believed that without a "von" in front of his name he would never be taken seriously by Dresden's middle classes. Count von Seebach, his patron, was removed from his position as head of the Dresden Opera in 1919, and a committee of successors clashed with Reiner, who felt that decisions in the opera house were increasingly being made for nonartistic reasons, something he always detested. In December 1920 Reiner's feelings were deeply hurt by the committee's decision to ask Fritz Busch to conduct most symphony concerts in the A series at the Semperoper at his expense. Reiner did not know Busch well. But he felt he had been passed over—as had his colleague Kutzschbach—without consultation, and he announced that he would not conduct the first symphony concert in the A series on January 7, 1921. He complained to the administration about the engagement of an outside conductor.[101] Busch was apparently the choice of the orchestra, and it seems that neither Reiner nor Kutzschbach were deemed suitable for the position of music director.[102]

As opposition began to mount against Reiner in Dresden, the managing board of the Semperoper began to invite guest conductors to take his place in the 1921–22 season.[103] There were also restrictions on Reiner's conducting outside Dresden, and this was to prove the sticking point for his continuance in his post there. While in the Saxon capital, Reiner had conducted in Berlin, Hamburg, Lübeck, Düsseldorf, Budapest, Vienna, and Rome.[104] In Budapest, for instance, he led performances of *Rigoletto, La bohème,* and *Tannhäuser* at the Városi Theater in May 1918.[105] He made six appearances with the Berlin Philharmonic that included an all-Wagnerian program, a concert devoted to works by Hugo Kaun, and performances of Dohnányi's Violin Concerto, Bartók's Suite no. 1, Wladigeroff's Violin Concerto in F Minor, and Manén's *Nova Catalonia* (a first performance).[106]

Reiner wanted to continue guest conducting to gain extra experience and to spread his reputation. It was unlikely that he would return to his native country, for Hungary had been devastated by the First World War, by the diminished size of its territory after the Treaty of Versailles, and by the Red Terror and White Terror that had occurred there by 1920. Reiner's links with Hungary seemed severed. Though keen to travel, he found that political conditions were similarly far from ideal elsewhere. In December 1921 he requested permission from his Saxon employers to conduct in Rome, but the request was turned down flatly on government orders.[107] This led to a courageous decision for a young conductor who was by no means wealthy: he was so fed up with restrictions placed on his activities in Dresden and the change of artistic policy there that he relinquished his life contract. He was succeeded by Busch, who also specialized in conducting the operas of Richard Strauss and who remained in Dresden until driven out by the Nazis in 1933.

Dresden was always a city where Reiner hoped to develop his artistic goals; in no sense was it merely a port of call. It was where he honed his conducting technique and performed a broad repertoire, both of which stood him in good stead for the future. He also achieved high artistic standards in Dresden. His operatic and orchestral conducting at the Semperoper consolidated his devotion to performing Wagner's music and began his championing of Richard Strauss and Bartók, specialities that lasted for a lifetime. His thematic programming, promotion of music produced locally, espousal of living composers, and celebration of composer anniversaries were probably not widespread practices at the time, but, looking back, one can see that he anticipated programming practices that are now staple fare. Reiner would undoubtedly have continued these concertizing trends in Dresden, but changed conditions there led him to seek a world elsewhere. His departure from Dresden presaged two later leave-takings from musical organizations amid controversial circumstances. The farewell to Dresden was by no means easy; it was an end to a promising European career and a great personal disappointment to be passed over as musical director of the State Opera of Saxony.

After quitting Dresden, Reiner initially turned to guest conducting. In late

1921 and 1922 he conducted opera and symphonic concerts in Rome, Barcelona, and Palma, Majorca. In Rome he conducted opera at the Teatro Costanzi (now the Teatro dell'Opera), including *Die Meistersinger, Tannhäuser,* and *Boris Godunov;* he also led symphony concerts at the Augusteo.[108] While in Rome he met Puccini and attended a performance of *Tosca* with him.[109] He also promoted his friend Respighi's *Ballata delle gnomidi* at a concert but found, ironically, that the work was less well received in Italy than it had been in Germany, where he had already conducted it several times.[110] Reiner's guest engagement at the Gran Teatre del Liceu in Barcelona in spring 1922 included performances of four Wagnerian operas—*Lohengrin, Die Meistersinger, Die Walküre,* and *Tristan und Isolde.*[111]

Several American agents attempted to secure Reiner for concert performances in the United States. The most fruitful of these overtures was made by César Saerchinger, the European correspondent of the *Musical Courier* and a musical adviser to Anna Sinton Taft, the president of the Cincinnati Symphony Orchestra. This led to an offer for Reiner to become chief conductor of that orchestra.[112] The offer was cabled through to Zurich and passed on to Berta, who was resting at her family's Italian villa near Bologna. She contacted Reiner, but the message was garbled, so her husband told her to use her discretion in replying to it. She signaled acceptance in March 1922, and Reiner was appointed as music director of the Cincinnati Symphony Orchestra on May 26 of that year.[113] Reiner was pleased; only a few months before he had tried unsuccessfully to arrange conducting appointments in the United States. He now benefited from American orchestras looking towards Europe for conductors and musicians who would carry Austro-German cultural traditions to the New World.[114] The Reiners returned to Rome, where Fritz carried out a final conducting engagement, then traveled to Dresden. They sailed from Hamburg on September 16, 1922, on the Cunard steamer *Caronia,* arriving in New York on September 26 and Cincinnati on October 1, where Fritz Reiner began an illustrious yet stormy conducting career in America.[115]

3. CINCINNATI

Reiner was selected as music director of the Cincinnati Symphony Orchestra from a shortlist of four highly respected, European-trained conductors. The other three candidates turned down the position. Serge Koussevitzky lost interest when his salary demand of thirty thousand dollars per season could not be met. Wilhelm Furtwängler and Felix Weingartner decided not to leave their well-established positions in Berlin and Vienna, respectively.[1] The path was therefore clear for Reiner to come to Cincinnati. News of his ability had reached America before his appointment. The father of the orchestra's concertmaster, Emil Heermann, had written to his son from Geneva about the sensation created by Reiner in the musical centers of Europe, where he was looked upon as a second Nikisch and where critics compared his work favorably with that of Weingartner.[2] For his part, Reiner stated, when interviewed before leaving Europe, that from childhood he had always wanted to go to America. He was familiar with the development of the Cincinnati Symphony Orchestra, which was based in a city where he wanted to conduct. When the Reiners arrived in Manhattan in late September 1922, many musicians flocked to meet them. Fritz was persuaded to listen to a jazz band for the first time and felt flattered by the professional attention he received.[3]

Reiner came to a city blessed with a fine natural setting, overlooking the Kentucky foothills from the banks of the Ohio River, a symbol of the dividing line between North and South in the American Midwest. Known since the early nineteenth century as the Queen City—or "Queen of the West," in Longfellow's description—Cincinnati by the 1920s was a large commercial center, a hub of the pork-packing industry, and a city noted for civic pride and cultural philanthropy.[4] Among its wealthier citizens were descendants of German immigrants who loved music. Already by 1873 they had helped to organize the first May Festival in the city to celebrate their choral traditions.⁵ This community cultivated a *gemütlichkeit* atmosphere that sought to replicate the sophistication of European music centers before the First World War.⁶ Cincinnati's strong German orientation probably made Reiner feel more at home after Budapest, Dresden, and the Austro-Hungarian milieu in which he grew up than any other American city would have done.

Succeeding the popular Belgian violinist and conductor Eugene Ysaÿe as music director, Reiner was initially offered a twenty-thousand-dollar contract for one season.⁷ He took over an orchestra that was among the oldest permanent symphonic organizations in the United States. The Cincinnati Symphony, founded in 1894, was the only professional orchestra west of the Appalachians besides the Chicago Symphony to give regular concert seasons at the turn of the twentieth century. Regular subscription seasons took place at Emery Auditorium, erected in 1911 as part of the Ohio Mechanics Institute. This had a rather cramped stage for a large orchestra. Sunday popular concerts were given in the Music Hall, opened in 1876 as part of the Third Cincinnati May Festival. This was the largest concert hall then used by an American orchestra; it could seat 3,600 people. The orchestra's board of trustees was entirely composed of women; men only served on an advisory board. This remained the case until 1929.⁸

The orchestra was well supported by benefactors from the outset, notably by the wealthy, socially prominent Taft family, who were the most generous patrons of the arts in the Queen City. Anna Sinton (Mrs. Charles P.) Taft helped to found the orchestra. She was president and a member of the orchestra's board for thirty-five years until her death in January 1931. Her husband was a member of the orchestra's executive committee and proprietor of the *Cincinnati Times-Star*. On average the Tafts contributed over a hundred thousand dollars per annum to the orchestra during the 1920s. In 1928 they transferred a million dollars in securities and real estate to the Cincinnati Fine Arts Institute, along with their collection of paintings, porcelain, other art works, and property on Pike Street, to set up a permanent endowment fund for the orchestra—a gift conditional on other parties raising an additional $2.5 million before the end of the year. The target was duly achieved and the permanency of the orchestra assured. This generosity was matched by full support for Reiner. The Tafts admired his enthusiasm and plans for the orchestra, supported many of his requests, and gave him free rein to boost the orchestra's prestige by improving it technically and artistically. They were delighted when Reiner was reengaged, with a four-year contract, in 1923. Anna Sinton Taft showed her gratitude to the Reiners by paying for the remodeling of their home at 3818 Winding Way in the fashionable Avondale section of Cincinnati.

When the Cincinnati Institute of Fine Arts assumed control of the orchestra on January 1, 1929, Reiner was allowed to continue as director of the orchestra's artistic development.[9] The donation of large sums of private money by the Tafts gave the orchestra financial security and helped musicians to preserve their vitality and concentrate on maintaining high artistic standards.[10]

Reiner's career in Cincinnati was also supported by his manager, Arthur Judson. The most powerful man pulling strings behind the scenes in American classical music, Judson was an eminence grise if ever there was one. In addition to his managerial posts with the New York Philharmonic-Symphony and Philadelphia Orchestras, he became advisor to the board of directors of the Cincinnati Symphony in 1923. That appointment also gave him control over Reiner as music director of the orchestra.[11] Reiner and Judson had a gentleman's agreement until 1929, when they entered into a contract.[12] Judson wanted to expand the Cincinnati Orchestra's activities and to place it on a sound and permanent financial footing. In 1925 he announced plans to extend the concert season to twenty pairs of concerts in twenty-eight weeks; to establish a regular touring schedule of twenty-four concerts in four weeks; to increase season ticket prices; to appoint a special assistant conductor for popular Sunday concerts; and to set up a permanent endowment fund of $2 million.[13] Judson influenced the personnel manager of the New York Philharmonic, Maurice Van Praag, not to take players that Reiner wanted in Cincinnati and to offer jobs to musicians that Reiner intended to release from his orchestra.[14]

Helped by secure financial backing and managerial support, Reiner intended to make the Cincinnati Symphony the best orchestra in America. He later remarked that his ideals and hopes for Cincinnati were to create "an orchestra of unsurpassed artistic merit."[15] To achieve this goal, he chose challenging orchestral repertoire and put musicians through their paces. Reiner thought local audiences had sufficient musical interest to appreciate interesting programs. Within two weeks of arriving in the Queen City, he had planned a season's concerts.[16] Though generally satisfied with the quality of the orchestra's musicians, he wanted to augment the orchestra for special needs—to engage a second harp, for instance, and to enlarge certain sections, especially the woodwinds.[17] He hoped to import some European musicians for the orchestra, but he only succeeded in a handful of cases. He abandoned the plan when it became clear that immigration laws and the strict rules of the musicians' union would not permit such hiring.[18]

At his first rehearsal in Cincinnati, Reiner drove the eighty-seven orchestral players hard but was nevertheless courteous. He addressed the orchestra on the importance of precision, attack, phrasing, and nuance but said nothing about interpretation. He used a range of gestures to indicate what effects he wanted. To suggest the degree of pianissimo needed, he measured off fractional inches on his baton. He assumed positions of bowing and handling as if he were playing the instruments himself and then rehearsed Beethoven's *Leonore* Overture no. 3 in depth.[19] After an hour and a half of intensive work, he was still only halfway through the piece. This rigor and attention to detail was a sign of things to come and a complete contrast to the easygoing, spontaneous conducting of Ysaÿe.[20]

By 1924 Reiner had already made rehearsals more exacting and frequent. Desiring perfection and absolute control, he increasingly played the role of a martinet after he received his four-year contract. By the 1925–26 season, rehearsals had a tense atmosphere. Reiner commented sarcastically about musicians who made errors of rhythm or intonation. Addressing the orchestra mainly in English but with a smattering of French, Italian, and German, phrases such as "dummkopf," "shoemaker," or "you should get your money back" were hurled at wayward players, along with requests that the offending musician should play a particular passage repeatedly until the results were satisfactory. Some musicians felt that he was a sadist in his unrelenting demands and never forgot the stress of his rehearsals.[21]

Reiner's use of a large baton with a tiny beat forced musicians to watch him very carefully. They took their parts home so that they could meet his unremitting desire for perfection. An example of his demands came during a rehearsal of the *Tannhäuser* Overture on Thanksgiving Day. Unaware that this was a national holiday, Reiner insisted on every violinist playing difficult scale passages over and over until both terror and hunger seized the musicians. Finally, one player explained the significance of Thanksgiving. Reiner was puzzled. He dismissed the rehearsal but did not abandon the tactic.[22] In fact, he did not relent even when rehearsals were proceeding smoothly. He was sparing with praise, and, if he did get the results he wanted, his most favorable comment was, "well, it's not impossible."[23]

Reiner's authoritarian approach is evident in his reaction to sloppy behavior by players during a tour in the 1926–27 season. He sent a memorandum insisting that in the future the musicians should neither shoot craps nor indulge in other forms of gambling while on tour. Certain rules were to be observed on the concert platform. The entrance of the orchestra should follow a set plan whereby the second, third, and fourth wind players came on stage, then the first men of each group, and finally the concertmaster. Tuning on the platform was forbidden, and fines were to be exacted for insubordination. Reiner wanted players on stage for all of the first or second part of a program, even if they were not required for all the pieces. He discouraged walking between the music stands, especially in the percussion section, and frowned on excessive talking by players on stage (a fine for such behavior was recommended after due warning). All members of the orchestra had to wear dress suits rather than tuxedos.[24]

Faced with these demands, one wonders why so many players remained in the Cincinnati Symphony during the 1920s. The answer lies in Reiner's maintenance of high artistic standards. Ineffective, lax players were not rehired. After his initial season in Cincinnati, Reiner replaced virtually one-third of the orchestra. The rate of changeover ranged from 15 to 29 percent during the next five seasons but then decreased substantially for the rest of his stay in the Queen City. Some losses came through retirement and through players not meeting Reiner's standards; others resulted from musicians being lured to New York, where good money could be earned for freelance engagements.[25] Most musicians in the orchestra were either German or of German-Jewish extraction. Though still a young man himself, Reiner preferred experienced orchestral players, especially those born in Europe, because they were more accustomed to the tight discipline he wanted.[26]

Musicians remaining in the orchestra derived great satisfaction from Reiner's exacting musicianship even if they had reservations about him as a person.[27] A distinguished visiting violinist, Joseph Szigeti, who admired Reiner, tried to assess his musical abilities. He noted that "the new spirit of music shows itself in all that Reiner does; in his precision, his conciseness; in that gesture of his, which I have not observed in any other conductor—that beat that stops dead, unequivocal, utterly final. It shows in the vividness, the color, the pulsing nerve of the effects he unerringly accomplishes."[28]

Reiner planned his concerts carefully. "If better programs are built," he once wrote, "Reiner will build them."[29] Aiming to present a varied repertoire to Cincinnati's musical public, he conducted eleven world and twenty-two American premieres plus 183 works performed for the first time in Cincinnati.[30] The world premieres included two modern transcriptions of works by Bach that were dedicated to Reiner: Joseph Mraczek's orchestration of the Chromatic Fantasy and Fugue and Respighi's arrangement of the Prelude and Fugue in D Major. Two organ pieces received their American premieres: Desider d'Antalffy's *Festival Prologue* for organ, strings, and brass and Marcel Dupré's *Cortège et Litanie* for organ and orchestra. Other works that Reiner selected for their first American performances were Daniel Gregory Mason's *Chanticleer* Overture and Second Symphony; Roger Sessions's *Black Maskers Suite;* Henry Hadley's *Streets of Pekin;* Samuel Barlow's symphonic poem *Alba;* and Bloch's *America,* an epic rhapsody in three parts for orchestra and chorus. The latter was simultaneously premiered on December 20, 1928, by the symphony orchestras of Cincinnati, Chicago, Boston, Philadelphia, San Francisco, and New York.

Among the American premieres presented by Reiner in Cincinnati were several pieces by his friends and compatriots, including Leó Weiner's *Carnival,* a humoresque for small orchestra, and three pieces by Bartók—the Dance Suite, the Suite no. 1, and the Piano Concerto no. 1. Reiner gave the American premieres of several concerted works: Milhaud's Viola Concerto; Honegger's Concertino for Piano and Orchestra; Ferruccio Busoni's Concerto for Piano, Orchestra, and Male Chorus; Kurt Weill's Concerto for Violin and Wind Orchestra; and Vittorio Rieti's Concerto for Wind Quintet and Orchestra. The other American premieres conducted by Reiner included a wide range of composers and musical styles: Mraczek's *Orientalische Skizzen für Kammerorchester*, Ravel's *Menuet antique*, Richard Strauss's suite from *Le bourgeois gentilhomme*, Louis Gruenberg's Jazz Suite, Leo Sowerby's *From the Northland*, Glazunov's Symphony no. 3, Filip Lazar's scherzo for orchestra *Tziganes*, Joseph Marx's *Spanische nachtmusik*, Rieti's *Noah's Ark*, Wilhelm Grosz's *Prelude to a Comic Opera*, Maximilian Steinberg's orchestration of the Chaconne from Bach's Violin Partita no. 2, and Arthur Bliss's *Hymn to Apollo*.

Reiner took great care when compiling standard orchestral programs. Even concerts devoted to a single composer were planned astutely. For the opening of the 1928–29 season, he scheduled a concert devoted entirely to Schubert to commemorate the centenary of the composer's death. The *Unfinished* Symphony was included because it showed Schubert "in the height of his power and pathos" and was very popular with the public. The Great C Major Symphony followed after the interval. Reiner thought a casual listener who heard only those two compositions would conclude that Schubert was a melancholy, introspective spirit, so he scheduled the *Rosamunde* Overture to begin the concert, because it displayed "the real boyishness of his fine artistry, his gaiety, abandon, quenchless optimism and flowing love of lyricism." The program thus displayed Schubert's art from several points of view.[31]

Similar thought lay behind an all-Beethoven program scheduled to open the Cincinnati Symphony Orchestra's 1925–26 season. In a concert year that was "an adventure into the seven seas of music," Reiner scheduled works by Beethoven as an embarkation point to illustrate the mainstream orchestral repertoire. He did not select Beethoven's well-known serious works, such as the *Eroica* or Fifth Symphonies. Instead he chose more cheerful compositions such as the *Fidelio* Overture and the Eighth Symphony. The second half of the concert included lesser known works—the *Grosse Fuge*, orchestrated by Weingartner, as an example of the Beethoven of the mysterious last quartets, and the ballet music to *The Creatures of Prometheus* to represent the budding composer at the start of his career. "Thus we have our program," Reiner wrote, "the jovial, the subtle, and the merry—and thus we have the *point d'appui* for our journey of the year."[32]

Reiner played much standard orchestral repertoire during his years in Cincinnati. He performed all of the Beethoven, Brahms, and Schumann symphonies, though there were no cycles. In the 1926–27 season he wanted to play

Beethoven's symphonies in numerical order to commemorate the centenary of the composer's death.[33] He interspersed the first eight symphonies in succession among the season's concerts, but there was no performance of the *Choral* Symphony to cap the cycle. He conducted three Mahler symphonies (nos. 2, 4, and 7), four Bruckner symphonies (nos. 4, 7, 8, and 9), five Mozart symphonies (nos. 29, 38, 39, 40, and 41), and all of the Tchaikovsky symphonies save number three. He conducted plenty of Johann Strauss waltzes. Every year he presented one major work by Richard Strauss in Cincinnati. He scheduled substantial extracts from Wagner's operas, often with guest singers as soloists. These excerpts were performed from the original complete scores secured while Reiner was in Europe during the summer of 1923.[34]

Reiner's programs included several innovations. Marcel Dupré's appearance with the orchestra in 1925 was the first time that an entire concert devoted to organ and orchestra had been presented in the United States.[35] The program consisted of Bach's Toccata, Adagio, and Fugue in C Major, arranged by the organ soloist, followed by Dupré's *Cortège et Litanie* for organ and orchestra and Saint-Saëns' Symphony no. 3 (the *Organ* Symphony). In 1929 Reiner performed Haydn's *Farewell* Symphony with electric candles to illuminate the players in a darkened auditorium.[36] He presented the *1812* Overture with thirty extra brasses at a popular concert.[37] He allowed the orchestra to begin a concert without him conducting, selecting Schubert's *Unfinished* Symphony as the ideal work for this approach. This was not a stunt to gain attention; it was an opportunity for adequately rehearsed musicians to perform with collective responsibility. Reiner was pleased with the experiment and intended to repeat it. Apparently, this was the first time that a symphony had been performed at a concert in America without a conductor for guidance.[38] For performances of John Alden Carpenter's *Skyscrapers* Suite in Cincinnati and Philadelphia in the 1927–28 season, Reiner caused a stir among the audience by using blinking traffic lights.[39] Another Reiner innovation was the use of placards bearing the descriptive titles of various tableaux of Stravinsky's *Petrushka* at the Cincinnati premiere of the ballet.[40] Finally, Reiner arranged for television apparatus to be installed when he conducted Mahler's Second Symphony, so that an offstage group of players could see him on a screen and hear the orchestra playing on stage. This was achieved by wiring the equipment from microphones on the conductor's podium through to a screen behind the stage.[41]

From the start, Reiner was keen to conduct new works. He practiced what he preached: 47 percent of the compositions performed during his era in the Queen City were written after 1900.[42] Barely a third of the twentieth century had passed by the time Reiner left Cincinnati, which is testimony to his commitment to programming music by living composers. Careful in his choice of composers, Reiner wanted the public to appreciate serious contemporary music and hear the best new compositions (which, to his mind, were based on the foundations of classical music).[43] Contemporary music needed careful programming among more traditional fare and was best introduced to audiences in small doses.[44] Reiner played any new score of musical merit on the piano, trying it out for sound, themes, and harmonies. He then eliminated works whose only value was that they were new. "It is not enough that they present a novelty," he commented; "they must also present something worth hearing and worth thinking about."[45] He took account of practical difficulties in performing new music—the availability of scores only on certain dates, the renting or buying of orchestral parts, the securing of permissions and granting of royalties, the difficulty of planning programs that required extra rehearsal time.[46]

Reiner liked to know all the latest tendencies in music and enjoyed introducing promising composers to the public. In 1922 he stated that Stravinsky, Bartók, and Schoenberg were "the present great names" to follow. Younger composers of the German school that interested him included Webern, Wellesz, Hába, Erdmann, Hindemith, Pisk, and Rosenstock. Among the Italians he esteemed highly who deserved greater notice were Pizzetti, Respighi, Casella, Tommasini, and Domenico Alaleona. Scriabin and Medtner were important Russian composers, and he singled out Schmitt, Poulenc, and Honegger among the French school. British composers of note included Bax, Goossens, Bliss, Holst, and Vaughan Williams.[47]

When Reiner conducted in 1924 at the Prague Festival concerts of the International Society for Contemporary Music (ISCM), he heard several modern works that impressed him, including Schoenberg's monodrama *Erwartung* and Honegger's *Pacific 231*. He brought back a stock of new scores from the festival in the hope of performing some in America.[48] One work was Rieti's Concerto for Wind Quintet and Orchestra, for which Reiner secured permission from Universal Edition for its first American performance after he had heard its premiere in Prague. After visiting Italy in the summer of 1927, Reiner returned to the American Midwest with a further batch of new music he intended to perform.[49]

Reiner introduced a handful of new English scores to Cincinnati audiences. One was Holst's suite *The Planets*, which he conducted in 1923 when it was still in manuscript (though it had already been performed in the United States). In 1925 he conducted Bliss's picturesque *Colour Symphony* and wrote to the composer after the concert that the performance "was really very good, and the men of the orchestra liked it more from rehearsal to rehearsal." Bliss was so impressed with the reception of his symphony in the Midwest that he wrote his *Hymn to Apollo* for Reiner and his Cincinnatians.[50]

Some contemporary compositions presented by Reiner aroused the ire of both concertgoers and musical critics in Cincinnati. When he opened a concert in 1929 with a performance of Hindemith's Concerto for Orchestra, the audience failed to applaud at the end.[51] Similarly hostile reactions greeted the performances of Honegger's *Pacific 231* in 1925 and Kurt Weill's Concerto for Violin and Wind Orchestra in 1930. Most of the audience resented the cacophonous *Pacific 231,* and one of the Cincinnati music critics could not "shake off the feeling" that the "traditional dignity of the symphony concert was violated." Weill's dissonant concerto was equally unpopular. This time a local music critic reported that a string on the concertmaster's bow broke during the performance and that, if it had not, "something might have happened to the audience."[52]

These criticisms from local conservative critics did not deter Reiner from performing a highly eclectic repertoire. Among other new works that he introduced to Cincinnati audiences were Busoni's *Turandot* Suite, Pizzetti's suite *La Pisanella,* Kodály's *Dances of Marosszék,* Respighi's *The Birds,* Bloch's *Psalm 22* for low voice and orchestra, Volkmann's Serenade in F Major for String Orchestra, Franz Schreker's *Prelude to a Drama,* and Grosz's *Prelude to a Comic Opera.* Reiner knew Schreker and his work well and presented this piece to show an American audience the trend in contemporary composition in Germany and Austria before and after World War I. Grosz was a student of Schreker, who had recommended his pupil's work to Reiner. Grosz's *Serenade* had already been performed by Reiner in Dresden; he heard the *Prelude to a Comic Opera* in a piano version in Prague in 1924 and asked to present it in Cincinnati.[53] Reiner also programmed Hans Barth's Concerto for Quartertone Piano and Strings (played by the composer). This piece was a novelty that the composer had performed since 1925, when the Baldwin Piano Company, based in Cincinnati, turned out a device that looked like a piano but consisted of two keyboards, each with eighty-eight notes. The upper keyboard was tuned to regular international pitch and had the usual black and white keys; the lower keyboard was pitched a quarter-tone lower and had blue and red keys.[54]

More popular with Cincinnati audiences than any of these pieces was, predictably, Ravel's *Boléro.* When Reiner discussed the interpretation of this work with the composer in France in the summer of 1930, Ravel insisted that it should be played with a slow, measured beat all the way through, never changing in spite of different variations on the theme. He wanted performances to observe the sliding effects on the trombone and saxophone and was caustic about musicians who lacked the temperament to "jazz it up."[55] Reiner's performances of *Boléro* in the 1929–30 season were received enthusiastically, and Cincinnati music critics regarded them as the musical sensation of the season.[56]

Whenever possible Reiner invited composers to play and conduct their music in Cincinnati; this was a common practice at the time. Ernst von Dohnányi and Respighi conducted and played their own compositions in the

Queen City during the Reiner era; they were highly complimentary about the standard of playing in the orchestra.[57] Reiner knew Dohnányi from his days in Budapest before the First World War: both were pupils and friends of Leó Weiner. Reiner was also friendly with Respighi, whom he had met in Italy in the early 1920s. Particularly keen to perform the *Pines of Rome,* Reiner requested the New York office of the music publisher Ricordi to send him the score as soon as they received it; he wanted exclusive rights to conduct it in different American cities during the 1924–25 season. He also hoped to introduce the work to the London and Berlin public. Respighi, in gratitude, dedicated his orchestration of Bach's Prelude and Fugue in D Major to Reiner. This transcription was performed in Cincinnati during the 1929–30 season.[58]

Of all contemporary European composers, Reiner especially promoted the music of Bartók and Stravinsky. The strong bond between Bartók and Reiner was a legacy from their days at the Budapest Academy of Music. "I have an especial interest in a young Hungarian, Béla Bartók," Reiner noted in an interview on his arrival in Cincinnati, adding that "it would be a gratifying thing to know, some time, that some great master had emerged from obscurity—or taken the first step in that direction—through one's own assistance."[59] This was a prescient comment about the musical quality of one of the twentieth century's acknowledged major composers. Reiner introduced several of Bartók's works to Cincinnatians, including the Dance Suite, *Deux Images,* the Suite no. 1 for Orchestra, and two scenes from *The Miraculous Mandarin.*

Bartók appeared with Reiner and his orchestra in New York in February 1928 when he played his First Piano Concerto in a concert of music by living Hungarian composers. Although the concerto was technically difficult, it drew a capacity audience. Critics unanimously praised the performance, and Reiner was applauded by Toscanini for his enterprise.[60] The concert was remarkable partly because Bartók, on his first visit to the United States, expected to play his concerto with the Philharmonic-Symphony Orchestra of New York; but Willem Mengelberg refused to conduct, advising the composer-pianist that the orchestral score was unplayable.[61] It was a coup for Reiner to step into the breach and show that the work could be performed well, and to do so on tour in Carnegie Hall. Reiner realized that the concerto was "an extremely difficult work, especially so for the pianist and conductor," but that it was also "of the highest interest."[62] Bartók and Reiner repeated the concerto in Cincinnati shortly afterwards. After playing his concerto several times in Europe, Bartók wrote Reiner to say that none of the performances "came up to the standard of precision shown in Cincinnati."[63]

Already by 1923 Reiner wanted to include *Le Sacre du printemps* on his programs because he considered it to be "the most important contemporary musical document."[64] But he never performed the work, no doubt because of its technical difficulties. Reiner met Stravinsky in Paris in the summer of 1924, however, and became very interested in his music. He invited Stravinsky to Cincinnati to play his new Piano Concerto during the next season. The visit was arranged, and the concert was a success. Stravinsky recorded his appreciation of Reiner's conducting of his difficult work when the performance was repeated in Philadelphia.[65] During the twenties Reiner conducted several of Stravinsky's works, including the *Song of the Nightingale* and *Petrushka*.[66] In March 1925 Stravinsky conducted the Cincinnati Symphony in a program of his own music. The concert introduced local audiences to music from *Pulcinella* and *Petrushka* and was well received by a Saturday-night audience. The composer was pleased with the discipline of the orchestra and with the players' interest in his music.[67]

Though he never matched the record of Koussevitzky in Boston in commissioning new works, especially by American composers, Reiner still actively promoted American music. In the early 1920s he recognized talent among American composers. John Alden Carpenter and Charles Griffes were gifted, he thought, and Deems Taylor (a New York critic as well as a composer) had composed some delightful music. But there was no commanding figure, no genius.[68] The best-known younger American composer Reiner promoted was George Gershwin. In December 1926 Gershwin agreed to play his Piano Concerto in F Major with the Cincinnati Symphony for a fee of one thousand dollars. He was delighted at this opportunity to perform in the Midwest.[69] In fact, Gershwin appeared in a pair of concerts during the 1926–27 season in which he played *Rhapsody in Blue* as well as his Piano Concerto. Reiner placed these works, both partly inspired by the jazz idiom, in a concert that included Beethoven's Seventh Symphony and Richard Strauss's *Till Eulenspiegel*. Several local music critics pointed out the lack of serious musicianship, as they saw it, in Gershwin's scores and criticized the Gershwin works as musically inferior to the Beethoven and Strauss. The entertainer Al Jolson, then in town, came to the rescue of his friend Gershwin by making a curtain speech at the Saturday matinee repeat of the concert that ridiculed the men who penned the criticisms.[70]

Reiner himself was sceptical about the lasting value of jazz, which he felt was limited in its musical elements. On first coming to the United States, he was taken to hear jazz performed by Paul Whiteman and His Orchestra but felt "lost" and only heard "a lot of noise." He also considered Gershwin a clever rather than a great composer.[71] Yet Reiner recognized the tremendous public interest in Gershwin's music; with proper handling of publicity, it could stimulate curiosity and act as a chief box-office lure for the public.[72] Though an unlikely musical combination, in person Reiner and Gershwin got on well. Gershwin returned to Cincinnati to hear *An American in Paris* performed under Reiner in the spring of 1929. He arrived with the battery of taxi horns specified in his score and later declared that the performance was the best the work had yet received—it was, in fact, only its second public professional performance anywhere.[73]

Reiner conducted other new American compositions during his Cincinnati years. Some were inspired by jazz, such as Louis Gruenberg's *Jazz Suite;* others were more difficult for audiences to grasp. One of the more demanding pieces was Sessions's *Black Maskers* Suite, written at a time when expressionism in American music was still in its infancy.[74] Reiner learned of this composition while guest conducting in Philadelphia and immediately asked Sessions for a copy of the manuscript. Performances of the work were canceled in spring 1929 owing to delays in copying the parts. But on December 5, 1930, it received its premiere under Reiner and the Cincinnati Symphony Orchestra. The performance went well, and Reiner sent an enthusiastic letter to the composer congratulating him on the work.[75] Another new American work that Reiner performed in Cincinnati and also in Philadelphia was the scherzo of Copland's First Symphony. The composer expected that Reiner's reputation would ensure that his scherzo received "a really first-class performance."[76] The Australian composer Percy Grainger, then residing in New York, contacted Reiner about performing some of his scores. He received a favorable response, but it came in Reiner's final season in the Queen City, and the idea was not followed up.[77]

To secure the best performances of this wide repertoire, Reiner had carte blanche to select the finest soloists "on the basis of their necessary co-operation in certain musical works of importance which demand their participation or in view of their reputation and rank from a box-office standpoint."[78] The roll call of illustrious soloists who appeared under his baton in Cincinnati is impressive. Among the pianists were Walter Gieseking, Alfred Cortot, Vladimir Horowitz, Josef Hofmann, Myra Hess, and Wilhelm Backhaus. Solo violinists included Joseph Szigeti, Carl Flesch, Jacques Thibaud, Mischa Elman, Nathan Milstein, and Bronislaw Huberman. The cellist Pablo Casals and the harpsichordist Wanda Landowska played in Cincinnati. And the appearance of Elisabeth Rethberg, Lily Pons, Rosa Ponselle, Florence Austral, Alexander Kipnis, Richard Crooks, and Lauritz Melchior testified to Reiner's insistence on having celebrated singers for his concerts.

Reiner soon improved playing standards in the Cincinnati Symphony Orchestra, though technical perfection took time to achieve. His first concerts in the Queen City were greeted favorably; within a few weeks he had infused life and vitality into performances.[79] His early achievements were given wider circulation by Deems Taylor's report in the *New York World* that Reiner was a conductor of "extraordinary talent" who had imagination, a great sense of rhythm, and a grasp of the technical structure of music and a composer's intentions. Taylor found the orchestra alert and enthusiastic. The first violins were the best section; they had exceptional quality and solidity. But the second violins were "disconcertingly weak" at times, and the wind instruments needed to blend better.[80] By the 1926–27 season the string section had improved; it played collectively with "marvellous tone quality" and, at Reiner's insistence, with absolute uniformity in bowing. The woodwind and brass players now played with accomplishment and an even projection of tone.[81] Conductor-composers such as Dohnányi and Respighi made highly complimentary comments about the orchestra's technical standard.[82]

The technical and musical progress of the orchestra gave Reiner grounds for satisfaction. After five years' work with them, he praised the "exactness of rhythm and dynamics, perfection of attack, absolute cleanliness, purity and transparency of tone—no mud, no sluggishness." These, he felt, were the fundamentals from which he could develop orchestral life, form, and color.[83] He placed great emphasis on good ensemble work, realizing that much orchestral music consisted of chamber-music textures rather than tuttis and that "the clarity and brilliance of performance is far more likely to rest upon sympathy between small, interacting units than upon any sum total effect of magnificence." Reiner was particularly interested in developing strong dynamic contrasts—from the softest of pianissimos to brilliant, powerful fortes.[84] But he did not wish to be overdidactic; once he had placed before players his essential conception of a piece, he had confidence in their individual musicianship to attain the ensemble performance he desired.[85]

Reiner promoted his career by taking the Cincinnati Symphony Orchestra on tour and by accepting various guest engagements. In 1922, when the yearly deficit of the orchestra was $150,000, he tried to save money by cutting back on tours to small towns in the United States.[86] But for most of his stay in Cincinnati the orchestra undertook short tours in North America, usually in January or February. In the 1923–24 season Reiner directed seventeen concerts outside of Cincinnati, including three each in Pittsburgh and Indianapolis and two each in Louisville and Urbana, Illinois. Other cities visited by Reiner and his orchestra during the 1920s were Toronto; New York; Coatesville, N.Y.; Buffalo; Washington, D.C.; Detroit; Oberlin, Ohio; Cleveland; Wheeling, W.V.; and a series of towns and cities in Pennsylvania—Reading, York, Scranton, and Philadelphia.[87] Reiner only traveled to towns where he felt that his talents and those of his orchestra would be appreciated. In 1927 he canceled plans to perform in Pittsburgh after unfavorable comments had been made there about his orchestra.[88]

Highlights of these tours were visits to Toronto and, especially, to New York City. In concerts in Toronto in 1926, 1927, 1929, and 1930, the orchestra collaborated with the Mendelssohn choir of that city, a body of 240 singers that had appeared in Cincinnati in 1925. The alliance with the Toronto-based choir arose partly because the choral directors of Cincinnati's annual May Festival wanted little to do with Reiner, who had made patronizing remarks about the quality of the local choruses.[89] Reiner set greater store by concerts in Manhattan, where music critics could compare the quality and discipline of his orchestra with more prestigious ensembles in New York and Philadelphia. Reiner conducted the Cincinnatians at Carnegie Hall in three successive years—1926, 1927, and 1928. He selected these appearances carefully, with regard to timing and repertoire, because he wanted the approval of East Coast music critics. He developed his orchestra satisfactorily before running the gauntlet in major musical strongholds.[90] A proposed trip during the 1923–24 season was canceled because the Cincinnati Symphony Orchestra was committed to a recording session with the Columbia Gramophone Company whenever it visited New York, and Reiner would only record if paid personally by Columbia. The record company would not agree to these terms. Reiner defended his actions by stating that no suitable concert venue was available at the time of the proposed visit.[91] During the 1930–31 season, the Cincinnati Symphony did not tour because of financial restrictions.[92]

In Cincinnati, Reiner conducted the vast majority of concerts himself. He had two associate conductors. Ralph Lyford, who held the position from 1925 until 1927, was appointed after Reiner failed to enlist the services of Eugene Ormandy, then playing the violin and conducting a pit band at the Capitol Theater in New York.[93] Then Vladimir Bakaleinikoff was appointed assistant conductor and principal viola after Reiner heard him direct the opera branch of the Moscow Art Theater when it toured America and was favorably impressed. Bakaleinikoff (known as "Bak" or "Baki") was a much-loved, easygoing figure who assumed special responsibility for the Popular and Young People's concerts. He later became Reiner's principal viola and associate conductor with the Pittsburgh Symphony Orchestra.[94]

Few guest conductors were engaged apart from composers conducting their own music. However, Reiner hired the film composer Alfred Newman as a guest conductor after being impressed with his conducting on a visit to Hollywood.[95] The leading guest conductor was the Italian Victor de Sabata, who came to Cincinnati in 1927 on the advice and with the approval of Reiner. He was a pupil and protégé of Toscanini and was known throughout Italy as "the young maestro." He had conducted throughout his native land and at the Monte Carlo Opera for several years.[96] Reiner was never afraid of allowing high-quality guest conductors to substitute for him. He had no doubts about de Sabata's musicianship before the appointment, noting that his orchestra would be in reliable hands in his absence "and that my work of so many years shall not be destroyed by some sort of dilletantic baton hero."[97]

On several occasions Reiner emphasized the menace of too many guest conductors for building up traditions of playing and interpretation in an orchestra.[98] Despite reservations, he himself took advantage of many opportunities to guest conduct in the United States during the twenties. These engagements spread his reputation further. For his debut in Manhattan, he directed the New York Philharmonic-Symphony Orchestra in open-air summer concerts at Lewisohn Stadium in 1924 and 1925, selecting mainly standard repertoire.[99] In a short speech at the end of these concerts, he said that the stadium audiences were the most appreciative he had ever encountered: they comprehended a wide range of musical styles and included many European emigrés with a strong interest in music. Though initially disconcerted at the prospect of daily rehearsals and nightly changes of program, Reiner enjoyed performing before a regular audience of eight to nine thousand at Lewisohn Stadium.[100]

Reiner also conducted open-air summer concerts on the West Coast. Mrs. Artie Mason Carter, the founder of the Hollywood Bowl concerts, heard Reiner conduct in Cincinnati and was impressed enough to invite him to conduct at the bowl, an open-air amphitheater capable of holding twenty thousand. She informed Reiner that his ability in conducting modern music led to the invitation—the sponsors of the concerts wanted more of this played in Los Angeles.[101] The audience, however, was fairly conservative in its musical taste; when Reiner conducted *Petrushka*, the patrons laughed, thinking it was a joke.[102] Californian audiences warmly applauded his work, and local critics singled him out as one of the few internationally conspicuous musical leaders.[103]

Besides summer concerts, Reiner also served as guest conductor in Philadelphia and New York during the regular orchestral season. In 1925 he conducted Stravinsky's Piano Concerto with the composer as soloist and the Philadelphia Orchestra. Stravinsky arrived at the last minute, on the afternoon of the concert, leaving time for only half an hour's rehearsal. "There was a miracle," he later recounted, "for there was not a single hitch. It was as though Reiner had played it time and again with that orchestra. Such an extraordinary phenomenon could not have occurred, notwithstanding the prodigious technique of the conductor and the high quality of the orchestra, if Reiner had not acquired a perfect knowledge of my score, which he had procured some time before. One could aptly apply to him the familiar saying: he has the score in his head but not his head in the score."[104]

Reiner guest conducted the Philadelphia Orchestra in forty-seven concerts during the 1926–27 and 1927–28 seasons, having been hired at the suggestion of Judson, the orchestra's manager.[105] Most of these programs were given in the autumn of 1927 when he was granted a leave of absence from Cincinnati to appear in Philadelphia while Stokowski was on sabbatical in the Orient.[106] For four programs presented in April 1928 he was offered $2,400 plus railroad and reasonable living expenses.[107] Among the contemporary pieces he presented were Rieti's suite *Noah's Ark,* Casella's *Italia* rhapsody, Honegger's *King David,* and Bartók's Rhapsody for Piano and Orchestra (with the composer as soloist). Reiner was popular with audiences during his guest tenure in the Quaker City.[108] He thought Philadelphia had a larger proportion of people who enjoyed good music than any other American city, and audiences there seemed just as interested in contemporary music as in the standard classics.[109] Reiner won the accolade of the orchestra. After concerts with them in the autumn of 1927, he was presented with a beautiful gold and enamel cigarette case by the orchestra's musicians "in commemoration of the many happy and inspiring moments spent together in Philadelphia."[110]

Reiner's first winter appearance in New York City was in late 1925, when he was a guest conductor at Aeolian Hall for the International Composers' Guild on a program of contemporary music that included works by Hindemith and Casella.[111] He also conducted the New York Philharmonic-Symphony Orchestra at their subscription concerts in the mid to late twenties. This arose through the backing of Judson as manager of the orchestra and through the invitation of Toscanini, who was co-conductor of the orchestra with Mengelberg for two seasons (1927–29) before assuming the title of chief conductor. Reiner and Toscanini had met in New York and Italy and had become friends.[112] Reiner guest conducted the Philharmonic in eleven concerts spread over three seasons—1925–26, 1926–27, and 1928–29.[113]

Reiner enhanced his musical reputation during the 1920s by accepting many engagements outside the United States. Most of these appearances were in Europe during the summer, after the end of the concert season in Cincinnati; they were combined with a vacation. In 1923 the Reiners spent a summer vacation with the conductor's two daughters at Berta Reiner's Italian country estate. While there, Reiner relaxed but also conversed with musical friends, including Respighi. At the end of the summer the Reiners returned to Dresden to pack up their remaining possessions for transit to Cincinnati. Reiner was only allowed to take their furniture and other belongings out of Germany after he agreed to pay 40 percent of his previous year's income in tax to the Weimar government.[114]

The Reiners visited Europe again in the summer of 1924. Fritz conducted at a Beethoven festival in Budapest on May 19 and directed performances at the Charlottenburg Opera House in Berlin and at the Royal Hungarian Opera. He made his British debut in London—a concert with the London Symphony Orchestra, in the Queen's Hall, in which Mahler's *Kindertotenlieder* and songs by Richard Strauss, with Elena Gerhardt as soloist, were coupled with Brahms's Fourth Symphony. He then traveled to Prague to represent America at the

ISCM Festival in June.[115] Among the works he directed there were Prokofiev's First Violin Concerto, with Szigeti as soloist, and Bax's First Symphony. In the same summer, as noted above, he also met Stravinsky in Paris.[116]

Reiner turned down guest engagements in Britain and Russia later in 1924 and refused the offer of the post of musical intendant for the Berlin Volksoper. In 1926 he resumed his guest appearances abroad. In May of that year he conducted at the Budapest Opera and later conducted in Turin and Genoa.[117] But the highlight of 1926 was the performance of German operas at the Teatro Colón in Buenos Aires in July and August, the only time that Reiner appeared in South America. Opened in 1908 with a capacity of 2,500 seats, the Colón was one of the most beautiful large opera houses in the world.[118] It presented the only important season of opera in South America. Reiner conducted three renditions of the first German-language production of *Die Walküre* in the Argentinian capital and *Die Meistersinger, Tannhäuser, Tristan und Isolde,* and *Der Freischütz.* He had some major singers in the productions, including Friedrich Schorr and Alexander Kipnis.[119]

Music critics in Buenos Aires praised Reiner's conducting.[120] They noted that he triumphed over adverse conditions, for the orchestra was not really first-rate, had not been given adequate rehearsal time, and was unfamiliar with Wagner's music. In addition, some performances were given in substantially cut versions. For the production of *Der Freischütz,* commemorating the centenary of Weber's death, Reiner had to make do with a highly unsatisfactory set from the previous Italian production of the opera in which a particularly important aria by the hermit had been cut and the role of Max had been assigned to a heroic rather than a lyric tenor. When conducting *Die Walküre,* Reiner shaped the music impulsively with a finely attuned ear for tone quality, bringing out the natural line of the voice in the orchestral parts and giving the dramatic climaxes time to breathe. His conducting of *Freischütz* was musically rounded, maintaining the essential connection between the orchestra and the stage action.[121]

During the summer of 1927, the Reiners stayed in Europe for four months. They traveled over six thousand miles by car, so that they could see people in different countries and observe their way of life. Included in the itinerary were visits to Karlsbad and Bayreuth.[122] In June 1927 Reiner conducted five concerts at La Scala, Milan, at Toscanini's invitation.[123] Proud to be the first conductor of an American orchestra invited to such an illustrious venue, Reiner cut a popular figure in Italy and was recognized as an outstanding exponent of Wagnerian opera.[124] He was invited to return to La Scala in the summer of 1928, but his American commitments forced him to decline an offer by the Italian government to conduct operas in Italian in Cairo and concerts in Turin during the following winter.[125]

Reiner soon revisited Europe. In 1928 he returned to Dresden to attend the premiere of Richard Strauss's opera *Die ägyptische Helena* and renewed his friendship with the composer.[126] In the summer of 1929 he spent part of a vacation on an island in the Adriatic, off the Dalmatian coast, attended a music festival in Berlin, and visited Venice in the company of the composer Malipiero, who had a wide knowledge not only of music but also of painting, sculpture, architecture, and other arts. In 1930 Reiner spent part of the summer in France, where, as noted above, he met Ravel.[127]

After several years conducting in Cincinnati, with regular summer visits to Europe, Reiner decided by the late 1920s to commit himself permanently to a career in the United States. For several reasons he felt that "the future of music and art is here in America."[128] The atmosphere of American life nurtured the need for active work, for initiative, and for doing the things he wanted to achieve. The material wealth of the United States brought opportunities and security to the American people, in his view, and this produced "a sense of responsiveness for the efforts of artists."[129] Moreover, American orchestras had rapidly improved at the expense of their European counterparts. At the turn of the twentieth century only three professional symphony orchestras existed in the United States; by 1923 there were forty-four, and new ones were being organized in Syracuse and Rochester.[130] These orchestras usually had more generous endowments, better rehearsal conditions, and fewer concerts than was common in Europe, rendering music making much more agreeable. Reiner cited as an example his visit to the International Festival for Contemporary Music in Prague in 1924, a three-day event with five conductors. Some pieces were performed without rehearsal because the conductors all wanted rehearsal time with the Czech Philharmonic Orchestra before the final concert.[131]

Reiner felt there were greater opportunities for promoting orchestral music in America and a more progressive spirit than in Europe. He praised the virtuosity of American musicians in playing new pieces and coping with technical pitfalls and appreciated the enthusiasm of New York audiences, especially their acceptance of new music by composers such as Stravinsky. He noted, for instance, that ten thousand would attend concerts at Lewisohn Stadium but doubted whether this would happen even in a city as deeply steeped in music as Vienna.[132] By contrast, he found musical conditions in Europe extremely unsatisfactory. Before 1918 opera and music generally were topics of everyday conversation among many people in Europe, but by 1923 political and economic problems filled their minds instead. Reiner deplored the poverty, unrest, and high taxation evident on his visit to Germany in the summer of 1923.[133]

Reiner attended operas and concerts in Germany during that summer, but "no vestige of the former brilliance and excellence of rendition was apparent."[134] He asked himself whether the voyage to Europe had impaired his hearing when he first listened to an orchestra perform. "Are they playing on cigar boxes," he queried, "or what is it?"[135] In 1927 he found the presentations at Bayreuth second-rate, like a poor regional opera house, and lacking the excellence of prewar productions. Many Germans no longer had money to attend musical performances during the hyperinflation of the 1920s, and generally there had been a dearth of significant new composition in Europe since the First World War. In the United States, on the contrary, music was progressing partly because of the lack of tradition; audiences were willing to listen to new music.[136]

There were, however, two respects in which America lagged behind Europe in musical performance. Opera was one area, partly because the grasp of languages needed to perform the classic German, French, and Italian repertoire often eluded American singers.[137] Secondly, American municipalities needed to develop musical institutions to support conservatoires, opera houses, and symphony orchestras, as in Europe.[138] In time, Reiner thought, America would develop her own great composers. These were all reasons why he stated in a 1926 interview that he would live in America and forsake Europe. He was already thinking of American citizenship, and he and his wife became U.S. citizens in 1928.[139]

Towards the end of the 1920s Reiner's position in Cincinnati deteriorated, for professional and personal reasons. As his four-year contract drew to a close in 1927, he began to look for pastures new. He was asked to conduct part of the season of the New York Symphony Orchestra but kept the negotiations quiet so that his patrons in Cincinnati would not think he wanted to leave the Midwest.[140] It seems that he was already contemplating a move to the East Coast, where he would have a higher musical profile. This surely explains his remark to Judson that an opportunity to conduct the American premiere of Schoenberg's *Gurrelieder* in New York and Philadelphia would help "your and my future plans."[141]

Reiner nevertheless stayed in Cincinnati for the time being. He was offered a one-year contract worth thirty-six thousand dollars for the 1927–28 season, but his professional situation in the Queen City was now uncertain. He was irritated by comments from the orchestral board that he should be grateful for being allowed to conduct in Philadelphia during the autumn of 1927, especially since the same people had approved of his undertaking guest assignments. He was also perturbed by Louis More, chairman of the orchestra's executive committee, stating that only one-year contracts would be offered him in the future and that musicians' wages might be cut.[142]

Reiner had worked hard to build up the orchestra's personnel but was disappointed that, after several years' effort, he was still on a short contract. He stated that no lasting and permanent work could be carried out under these conditions. To ease a difficult financial position, however, he agreed to save twenty-five thousand dollars for the 1929–30 season by reducing the orchestra's size to ninety-four or ninety-five players.[143] The Orchestral Association's reply expressed appreciation for his work in Cincinnati and thanked him for cooperating with the cutback.[144] Yet Reiner thought his talents were not appreciated in Cincinnati, "that the people there do not consider my fellow-citizenship as something to make use of or to be proud of."[145] By spring 1929 he requested that a new orchestral manager be found. He was also still on a one-year contract.[146]

By this time his second marriage had crumbled. All the reasons for this breakdown are difficult to determine, but Reiner's difficult moods and Berta's jealousy and frequent absences in New York, where she had a vocal studio, did not help. During the 1929–30 season there was marital mayhem at the Reiner home. "Big Berta" pushed her husband down the steps outside their home when she decided that the marital cheating had gone too far. He then conducted with his right arm in a sling and his head patched up, while she watched him from a box and was similarly covered with bandages and patches. Newspaper photographs showed the wounded pair without providing an explanation for the injuries.[147]

On February 5, 1930, Berta Reiner, aged forty-four, filed a petition of divorce in the Hamilton County Court of Common Pleas, alleging that her husband had struck her at least once and had taunted her about her age (though she was only three years older than he). She claimed that Reiner had brought an Italian consul to her and insisted that she sign away her Italian property. She produced as a witness a female student lodger who stated that Berta was forced to pay most of the living expenses at the Avondale home and that Reiner once told her to pay for her board. Reiner failed to appear in court and did not contest the suit. In the divorce papers he was found "guilty of gross neglect of duty and of extreme cruelty toward the plaintiff."[148]

The most important reason for the breakdown of the marriage was Reiner's affair with Carlotta Irwin, who met him in the Queen City, where for two seasons she was a leading lady with the Stuart Walker Players. The romance led to marriage between Fritz and Carlotta on April 26, 1930, less than two months after Reiner's second divorce.[149] News of the marriage, however, led to pursed lips and mutterings about its haste among the ladies who were the backbone of the trustees of the Cincinnati Symphony, many of whom socialized with Berta and held her in high esteem. Provincial morality in the Queen City was shocked at Reiner's divorce and hasty third marriage.[150] The announcement of Reiner's third marriage led to heavy cancellations of subscriptions for the next season (although the onset of the Great Depression was also to blame). The trustees and the board, after extended discussion, agreed unanimously that Reiner's services would not be required after the end of the

1930–31 season and that a new chief conductor should be appointed.[151] Reiner was equally uneasy about staying in Cincinnati, but his negotiations for a post conducting opera in Berlin did not bear fruit.[152]

Reiner's personal problems, along with the takeover of control of the Cincinnati Symphony by the city's Institute of Fine Arts, represented the writing on the wall for him as music director in the Queen City. Moreover, for some time the board of directors had considered him persona non grata because of several indiscreet remarks attributed to him.[153] They wanted to appoint as his successor an English conductor of Belgian descent, Eugene Goossens, who had been music director of the newly formed Rochester Philharmonic Orchestra since 1923. Goossens, who was managed by Judson, visited Cincinnati in September 1930.[154] News of his good work in Rochester had reached the Queen City. Besides, a rich patroness there was infatuated with him, which did his candidature no harm. The woman in question, Mrs. Christian R. Holmes, was a resident of Cincinnati and one of the wealthiest widows in the United States. Goossens made use of her patronage but later married a younger woman.[155] Eventually, in late December 1930, Goossens's appointment as music director of the Cincinnati Symphony Orchestra was announced, to take effect from the 1931–32 season.

Reiner's resignation letter, published in the local press, stated that he had done everything possible for the musical growth of the orchestra and that a great deal had been achieved musically during the past nine seasons. He mentioned his negotiations with another musical organization (though he did not specify which one). Rumors that he had been offered a post with the St. Louis Symphony Orchestra were not confirmed.[156] Reiner wrote to Judson about the discouraging situation in Cincinnati and realized that, despite public support, nothing could be done to alter the outcome. Worried about money after his second divorce, he became depressed because he could not afford to sit tight and wait for another permanent post to materialize.[157]

Reiner's farewell program in Cincinnati attracted a capacity audience to Emery Auditorium. Local music critics praised his artistic tenure in the city for passing on to his successor a very fine ensemble, one that was much more accomplished than the orchestra he had inherited. Reiner was given a ten-minute applause at the end of his final concert. On taking over from Reiner, Goossens was asked what musical novelties he would present on his programs. He found himself at a loss because Reiner had already scheduled every worthwhile piece during his Cincinnati years with the exception of *Le Sacre du printemps*.[158] Goossens later remarked that he was able to schedule "novelty after novelty with impunity" at his Cincinnati concerts because of Reiner's pioneer work extending the orchestra's repertoire.[159] Goossens found the Cincinnati players responsive but not inspiring. "They produced a torrential sound with great technical accuracy," he noted, "but string phrasing which lacked sweep and spaciousness."[160] Yet by the end of the Reiner era, the Cincinnati Symphony would probably have been ranked fifth of the American orchestras (after the Boston Symphony, Philadelphia, New York Philharmonic-Symphony, and Chicago Symphony Orchestras).[161]

César Saerchinger, director of CBS's European service, thought the best conducting opportunities for Reiner now lay in Italy and Germany.[162] But Reiner remained in the United States. Early in 1931 he announced that he would leave Cincinnati to live in Philadelphia, where he would hold concurrently three positions—principal conductor of the Philadelphia Grand Opera, associate guest conductor of the Philadelphia Orchestra, and head of the orchestra and opera department at the Curtis Institute of Music.[163] With Judson's help, he secured guest conducting appointments with several American orchestras. Judson advised him to stay in America for another year to see whether an important position would open up.[164] In late April and early May 1931, Reiner traveled to Europe to conduct at the Teatro San Carlo in Naples and at La Scala.[165] The future was uncertain, yet the reputation he had established would surely help him secure a music directorship of a major orchestra in the United States. As we shall see, things took a rather more circuitous and less easy route.

4. TEACHING AT CURTIS

In 1931 Reiner was appointed head of the opera and orchestral departments at the Curtis Institute of Music in Philadelphia, a conservatory that catered to young musical talent of a high order. Founded in 1924 by Mary Curtis Bok, the daughter of a successful publisher and serious music lover, this lavishly endowed institution reflected the philanthropic munificence of the Curtis family. The original endowment was five hundred thousand dollars, but Mary Curtis Bok added $12 million in 1927. At the time this was the largest single private fund ever donated for the advancement of music in America. In the same year tuition fees were abolished and scholarships awarded to gifted students to study music. Initially, over 350 students attended the institute at any one time. The original faculty included Carl Flesch, Josef Hofmann, and Leopold Stokowski. By the end of the 1920s, the Curtis Institute already rivaled the Juilliard School of Music in New York as a center of musical excellence. Located in comfortable headquarters on Rittenhouse Square, the Curtis Institute was only a stone's throw from the Academy of Music, the home of the Philadelphia Orchestra. Students at Curtis had a close relationship with the orchestra, which provided instrumental teachers and absorbed many successful students into its ranks. By 1934 nearly half of the players in the Philadelphia Orchestra were Curtis graduates. Among the prominent members of that orchestra who taught at Curtis when Reiner was appointed were William Kincaid, the principal flautist, and Marcel Tabuteau, the principal oboist.[1] The Curtis faculty also included other celebrated musicians, such as the pianist Isabelle Vengerova, the cellist Felix Salmond, the harpist Carlos Salzedo, and the violinists Leah Luboschutz and Leopold Auer.[2]

Reiner agreed to teach at the Curtis Institute for several reasons: he was friendly with Mary Curtis Bok; he had established a reputation as an orchestral builder and trainer of musicians; and, perhaps most importantly, Curtis was seriously interested in expanding its orchestral program.[3] Josef Hofmann, the renowned pianist who became director of the institute in 1927, was also sympathetic to Reiner's lack of a job. Hofmann had been involved in a scandal when he married one of his pupils, and he sympathized with the ostracism Reiner encountered from the puritanically inclined upper class of musical America after his divorce.[4] If Reiner had not left his post in Cincinnati under difficult circumstances, he might never have tried his hand at teaching. He now became one of a small number of significant twentieth-century conductors to direct a training program for young conductors (others included Pierre Monteux, Serge Koussevitzky, Max Rudolf, and Leon Barzin).[5]

The move to Philadelphia provided new opportunities for Reiner. Though not onerous in terms of time, because he only had to take one conducting class a week, his position at Curtis proved invaluable in keeping his name at the forefront of leading conductors on the East Coast of the United States. It also enabled him to develop pedagogic skills and spend time with the illustrious Philadelphia Orchestra. His duties included conducting the Curtis Symphony Orchestra, teaching basic conducting and score reading, and directing the conducting class. His salary for the school year was nine thousand dollars in 1931 and four thousand dollars in 1935; it was later increased to six thousand.[6] These sums presumably reflected the time Reiner devoted to the Curtis Institute in any academic year, but they were not especially generous; he could earn a thousand dollars for directing a one-hour radio broadcast.[7]

Reiner's published and unpublished writings explain how he communicated to students his ideas on conducting and performance while teaching at the Curtis Institute. He did not believe conducting was intuitive; rather, it required learning, skill, and experience.[8] He thought prospective students should know the orchestral repertoire thoroughly before he could talk to them fruitfully about conducting.[9] He formulated specific views about the craft of conducting, one of which was that some prerequisite qualities, personality traits, and talents were vital to an aspiring conductor. Among these *desiderata* were the person's emotions, actions, reactions, and imagination. These characteristics, he believed, could not be acquired through training but needed to be inherent in the conductor's personality. Reiner thought conductors should possess a stimulating and sympathetic personality, expressive eyes, and executive ability. Educationally, they needed a wide knowledge of the sister arts, including painting, sculpture, poetry, and world literature. They should be familiar, in particular, with the literary classics on which much music is based—Shakespeare's plays, Goethe's *Faust,* and Dante's *Inferno*—for no conductor could interpret music based on literary masterpieces without reading and absorbing their texts. A conductor of French music between 1880 and 1920 should be familiar with impressionism and expressionism. Interpreters of Wagner and Richard Strauss should understand the national traditions that underpin the former's music dramas and the legendary figures that formed the programmatic basis for *Till Eulenspiegel* and *Don Juan*. Reiner theorized that a well-read, cultivated individual would have been exposed to universal artistic ideas that could, if applied, significantly enrich the performance of music.[10]

To communicate effectively with his students, Reiner required that each of them have the following musical training and skills: an infallible ear and an in-depth knowledge of harmony, theory, counterpoint, and musical form; studies in or knowledge of compositional techniques (including contemporary perspectives), even though they may never have composed; significant familiarity with the use and nature of musical instruments (including the voice) and a technical understanding of musical acoustics; adequate piano skills that allowed them to work out and transpose scores at the keyboard in order to analyze them melodically, harmonically, and structurally in a critical fashion; and a thorough familiarity with musical literature, especially orchestral compositions but also the opera, chamber, voice, and piano repertoire.[11] Reiner recommended that pupils study orchestration from works and writings by Berlioz and Richard Strauss and pay particular attention to the scores of Hindemith and Stravinsky.[12] He was convinced that a conductor's authority was achieved by demonstrating a complete musical knowledge of and artistic bond with the score being performed; anything less would compromise a conductor's credibility and command.[13] For Reiner, a keen sense of rhythm was the most important conducting skill. He considered meter, pace, and accents to be the propelling force of music and believed that the structural unity of compositions depended upon the interrelationship of the different elements of rhythm.[14] Though he never used a metronome himself, he could accurately gauge the exact mathematical relationship between any two tempi.[15]

Reiner also regarded certain nonmusical abilities as necessary to a successful conductor. Leadership was crucial, and it was vital for conductors to project a sufficient amount of personality while on the podium. Conductors were "the living conscience of the orchestra" who needed to display a sort of "musical generalship, the human power to lead other people in a harmonious way,"[16] so that a composer's music could be presented coherently. Thus not all talented musicians could become successful leaders. Reiner admitted that this projection could not be learned, since it derived essentially from personal character traits.[17] He also concluded, as did Richard Strauss, that the ability to interpret could not be taught or acquired. While all these general attributes must exist in an embryonic state within a young conductor, many years of practical experience were necessary to develop them to the highest level. It is not surprising, then, to learn that Reiner considered it virtually impossible to become a mature, accomplished conductor before the age of fifty.[18]

These personal, musical, and nonmusical attributes formed the foundation upon which Reiner's "teachable science of conducting" could produce a thoroughly trained, skilled, and practical conductor who had the re-creative imagination needed to perform all types of serious music.[19] Like scores of other conducting professionals, Reiner was convinced that the best place to learn conducting skills was in the opera house. "A conductor does not qualify unless he is prepared for everything, and for every instrument—including the human voice," he once remarked.[20] Simply stated, opera conducting required the control of so many different musical and nonmusical elements that orchestral conducting, by comparison, was considered "easy." In central Europe, where Reiner served his conducting apprenticeship, every town of reasonable size had an opera house. Reiner felt that this phenomenon created "a wonderful training ground" in which to acquire a knowledge of the orchestra, singers, and staging as well as learning how to deal with emergencies. He had conducted hundreds of opera performances before emigrating to the United States and decried the lack of such opportunities for young American conductors. Great conductors such as Artur Nikisch, Gustav Mahler, Felix Mottl, Toscanini, and Walter all conducted in the opera pit, and this equipped them with insight and comprehension of dramatic and stage craftsmanship.[21]

In auditions for his conducting class, Reiner established quickly whether a potential student had sufficient prerequisites. Sometimes he set a comparatively easy task, such as placing a score of a Beethoven symphony before the aspirant and accepting him into the class if he identified the music correctly. On other occasions he gave tougher auditions, such as getting a prospective pupil to sight-read extracts from *Salome* and *Elektra* on the piano, fully expecting him to deal with the difficult transpositions.[22] Usually, however, he used a simpler format. Selecting from about twenty standard scores, Reiner would open one at random and ask the student to identify it. If the student could not do so accurately, he was deemed to have insufficient knowledge of the orchestral repertoire and was therefore unsuitable for Reiner's conducting class.[23]

Reiner often used Beethoven's *Leonore* Overtures nos. 2 and 3 for auditions; he expected potential students to know these works and their distinctive trumpet calls. He also tested students' score reading at the piano and asked them some musical questions. When he referred to a movement of a Beethoven symphony, he expected prospective students to know the theme, tempo, key, and instrumental scoring. Reiner rejected candidates whose score reading and transposition were poor and who could not recognize Beethoven symphonies or the *Tannhäuser* Overture: these young people could not hope to become conductors because they lacked essential musical knowledge.[24] Few allowances were made for poor knowledge or execution. In most years a handful of would-be students passed these auditions, but in some years he accepted no one. Age was not a factor. Reiner recruited some pupils as teenagers; they included the fifteen-year-old Lukas Foss, who was still in kneepants. Foss recalls: "Reiner handed me a score and opened it to the slow movement. 'What is this?' he asked. I replied: 'Beethoven's Fourth Symphony.' 'OK. I'll accept you to my class,' Reiner said, and then added: 'You think you are too young to learn how to conduct, but you are almost too old.'" This statement impressed upon Foss that it was never too soon to recognize and practice one's vocation: it was best to start soon and not postpone one's career, because plenty of musical techniques needed to be learned.[25]

Those students accepted by Reiner followed a rigorous two-year course; they studied symphonic music in the first year and operatic repertoire in the second.[26] The conducting class met once a week for two hours and was taught as a workshop, which was quite novel at the time. Reiner began the first meeting of each new class with two statements: He was there to teach students to become conductors, not musicians, and he would soon identify the students who had a talent for conducting; those who did not would be banished from class. Although he was a demanding teacher who maintained high standards of knowledge and preparation, Reiner adjusted his teaching strategies to accommodate the different personalities of his students—the timid, the overconfident, and the tense.[27]

Unlike Toscanini and Ormandy, Reiner believed that physical gestures for conducting could be taught. Thus his primary goal in the conducting class was to develop a student's ability to beat time accurately and with musical sensitivity. He was very strict about the baton's clarity of motion.[28] Through personal experience, he became convinced that an excellent stick technique could overcome many difficulties, which is one reason why he excelled at presenting complex modern scores. Though he always used a baton, he did not insist that students follow suit; they could conduct without one if they found it burdensome. Reiner realized the baton only served as a means of communication; what mattered most were the musical results. Personally, he preferred a baton because of the distance that usually existed between a conductor and those musicians located on the periphery of the ensemble; he considered it integral to a conductor's total musical equipment. The best musical results came not from a stick technique per se but from unbroken concentration by the players, their confidence in the suggestive powers of the conductor's gestures, and a certain amount of freedom given to the individual players in phrasing.[29]

For Reiner the most important beat was the upbeat, and in the conducting classes he spent no less than three months developing it. "The conductor must give his downbeat preceded by its preparation in the form of an upbeat of exactly the same quality" was one of his key maxims.[30] Reiner covered every type of upbeat to every conceivable beginning in a piece of music. Upbeats were practiced for pieces beginning on the last beat of the bar, in the middle of the bar, between beats, and so on. He expected students to convey in the upbeat all the information necessary for the orchestra to enter and play metrically and stylistically correct.[31] The upbeat must be conducted either forcefully or gently, with a legato or staccato movement, to indicate when an orchestra should begin playing and how. Reiner advocated the use of a limited number of beats; he avoided excessive subdividing.[32] He also insisted that all beats were decisive. Precise attack and excellent ensemble were impossible with an unclear downbeat such as that of Furtwängler or Koussevitzky, for whom orchestras began playing when the baton reached the third button of their shirt. The downbeat, according to Reiner, should be crystal clear; a small but exact movement with the wrist achieves this properly.[33]

In Reiner's opinion, baton technique was only useful when it became "unconscious second nature" and achieved excellent musical results without excessive overt movement.[34] He considered unnecessary movements by a conductor as little more than showmanship that did nothing except disturb the musicians' concentration on the music. Since everyone is built differently, he saw no purpose in having students imitate the mechanical gestures of himself or others. Early in his career, he had tried to copy Nikisch's conducting gestures only to find that he failed to produce the same effect.[35] Consequently, Reiner did not expect students to copy him; he counseled them to find the gestures that worked for them, gestures that elicited an appropriate response from the musicians without making them uneasy.

In Reiner's class, a student usually would conduct the other students, who played the scores at the piano. Occasionally, he varied the routine by requiring the students to conduct in silence.[36] He insisted that conducting technique must be learned and practiced before a student mounted the podium, with the teacher taking the place of an attentive, responsive orchestra.[37] He assigned both shorter and longer pieces for students to prepare for class and expected them to arrive with a thorough understanding of the harmony, form, and orchestration of the works.[38] Students were required to learn and assimilate the scores; no one was permitted to mount the podium without having committed the work to memory. Challenges had to be surmounted. A student who only learned part of a work when assigned an entire piece for study would be greeted in class with the news that maybe he would not become a conductor after all.[39] Reiner demonstrated his own vast knowledge of the musical repertoire by playing on the piano excerpts from all sorts of symphonies, solo works, and operas.[40]

During the initial sessions of the conducting class, Reiner assigned the students scores that were concurrently being prepared for performance by the

Curtis Orchestra. He allowed them to prepare the scores as they saw fit.[41] They could learn scores at the piano or by silent contemplation of the music. To imagine the sounds in one's mind was his own preferred approach, but he did not insist that his students memorize in that manner. He recommended conducting in private in front of a mirror, with simple, unforced use of the right hand, but this was not mandatory. The one method to avoid was to learn scores from recordings, since that approach was too passive to master the complexities of melody, harmony, and instrumentation.[42] Reiner always advocated the use of a score while conducting and saw no need to abandon it. Yet he knew every piece he conducted by heart and only consulted the score in rehearsal or performance if it was new.[43] Once, when watching the Greek-born conductor Dimitri Mitropoulos conduct *Salome* at the Met without a score, he was impressed but commented, "he knows the music without a score: I know the music inwardly."[44]

Learning scores was only the beginning of a conductor's work. Reiner explained to his students that they must also possess the three Cs—concept, communication, and command. By "concept," he envisaged that a conductor would work out how he wanted music to sound before mounting the podium. It was important not only to think about tempi and dynamics but also about balancing instrumental choirs. "Communication" conveyed the bidding of the conductor to musicians. Here the conductor must use all the sign language at his disposal—eyes, face, arms, hands, baton—to embellish his technique. By "command," Reiner meant that a conductor should communicate his understanding of music to the players and the audience; his expertise in doing so determined the conviction of a performance. An authoritative conductor should always avoid blurry subdivisions, sloppy cutoffs, and indecisive moments, all of which would undermine his vision of the music.[45] Emotional identification with the music had to be controlled by one's intellect. Thus Reiner considered that a conductor could not afford to let himself go, even in act 2 of *Tristan und Isolde,* or control would be sacrificed.[46] The need for control explains Reiner's remark that his ideal performance would be to conduct *Salome* without perspiring (a metaphorical rather than a literal comment, but a point nevertheless well made).[47]

Reiner did not spend much time talking about interpretation; for him that was a personal matter that evolved from the musical training, experience, knowledge, sensibility, and intelligence of the individual student. To his mind mature interpretation could only be achieved after all the technical groundwork had been laid and experience gained. Reiner spent little time pedantically beating through sections of music, which he saw as a waste of his and the students' time.[48] However, he was convinced that mastery of certain difficult excerpts from orchestral and operatic literature helped students to deal with a variety of complexities that might arise during the course of a career.[49] Students who completed his course could travel anywhere in the world, even to places with unfamiliar languages, and conduct an entire rehearsal without speaking. In his words, they could "stand up before an orchestra they have never seen before and conduct correctly a new piece at first sight without verbal explanation and by means only of manual technique."[50]

During the second year of the course, Reiner devoted much class time to operatic recitatives. This resulted from his view that a conductor should be a good accompanist. Many difficult passages in opera occurred in recitatives that called for coordination with singers, attention to pace, awareness of stage action, and the ability to count silent beats. Coordination of recitatives would provide excellent technical training, as it required students to develop efficient gestures.[51] Reiner had his students memorize recitatives, whether or not they knew the language, and then made them mouth the words and give all the cues.[52] He drilled students in the recitatives of *Carmen, Fidelio,* and *Le nozze di Figaro* as well as the "stop" and "go" sections of Beckmesser's "Serenade" in *Die Meistersinger.*[53] Reiner taught students to be physically spartan in recitatives so that only necessary beats, rather than the whole measure, were conducted. The most common of these procedures was to have the right hand remain motionless in 4/4 time except for the fourth beat.[54] Students had *one* chance to accompany a singer correctly in a recitative before it was performed for Reiner; those who failed were permanently dismissed from the class.[55] Concentration on recitatives served several purposes. Young conductors often began their career as *repetiteurs*, which was essential for learning languages, gaining knowledge of singers, and experiencing stage conditions. Such an apprenticeship taxed their resources but was embedded in them for future use.

During classes Reiner was formal in his manner and generally maintained a personal reserve when interacting with students. He was delighted when talent blossomed but did not tolerate mediocrity, lack of knowledge, or poor musicianship.[56] Anyone ill-prepared or facile was soon caught out, for Reiner had a quick mind and demanded exact answers to questions. Often he would stop a student's conducting at an unexpected point in a score and demand a description of what was happening in the music; the account was expected to include the notes of each instrument at that point from piccolo to double basses. For a work such as the *Leonore* no. 3 Overture, students had to know the score faultlessly so that they could identify the notes played by every instrument at whatever point.[57]

This severe teaching style set great store on musical knowledge and technical accomplishment. Naturally it caused consternation among pupils, but it motivated them to prepare meticulously for his class.[58] Leonard Bernstein has described the technique vividly: "Reiner's way of teaching was tyrannical in the extreme. He demanded total knowledge. You had no right to step up on the podium unless you knew everything about what every member of the orchestra had to do. And if you didn't, God pity you. . . . Reiner would say, 'What is the second clarinet playing at this moment?' He'd stop and you'd think: 'Is there a second clarinet? I really don't know. Do you mean transposed or the way it is in the score?' And you'd freeze up. It was a scary way of teaching."[59]

Reiner deliberately worked students hard, giving difficult assignments that required a dedication to intense, concentrated work. He liked to ask trick questions to keep students on their toes and exposed guesswork and ignorance mercilessly. One of his favorite phrases to describe those found wanting was *total unbegabt* (totally untalented).[60] Once, after observing the work of a less able student during a conducting class, he cast his eyes down, looked grim, then lifted his eyes and said simply and quietly, "Give it up."[61] Nor did he mince words with students whom he considered unsuitable for a career in conducting. Writing to a young woman whom he had removed from the class—a decision the woman was attempting to overturn—Reiner stated that he had no intention of reversing his view regarding her level of scholarship in class. "I feel that you have absolutely no natural aptitude or sufficiently musical background to take up conducting," he wrote, adding that "a burning desire to do something in Art must not be mistaken for talent." He concluded: "I am sorry to have to disappoint you but I hope that this frankness will save you later unhappiness."[62] Most recipients of such forthright criticism soon realized when the time had come to pack their bags and leave. Some could not stand the pressure. After one such dissection, a disturbed student bought a gun and bullets with the intention of shooting Reiner (as well as Leonard Bernstein and Randall Thompson). Fortunately, he was arrested by the police and returned to his home town before matters got out of hand.[63]

Reiner's personality and teaching methods are well illustrated by an anecdote recalled by Boris Goldovsky, one of his students at the Curtis Institute and later an opera producer and music lecturer. On one occasion Reiner assigned his students the last movement of Beethoven's *Choral* Symphony and gave them the Christmas vacation to prepare the score. The students determined to carry out the task as thoroughly as possible, to answer any question they might be asked. When the class reassembled in the new year, Reiner placed a thick score on the piano and asked Goldovsky to describe the instrumentation at a certain point. Goldovsky was puzzled because the music in front of him was not by Beethoven; it was the piano vocal score of an opera, though he did not know which one. He pointed out to Reiner that this was not the score assigned, but his queries were quashed. Other students in the class were then called forward, like lambs to the slaughter, and similarly humiliated. Reiner stood up from his chair, called them a bunch of ignoramuses, and marched out of the room.[64]

Reiner had less than pure motives for this action. The students later found out that he wanted to attend a party that clashed with the class. The incident was his way of cutting the session without losing face, for he was not a man who made excuses. And though it might seem perverse to question students on a piece they had not been asked to prepare, Reiner expected them to know the substitute score. When they became professional conductors, they would need thorough acquaintance with the orchestral and opera repertoire and might be called upon to conduct something unexpected at short notice—which is how he himself gained his first conducting opportunity. The incident was typical of Reiner's teaching and of his personality: the formal distance between teacher and student; the expectations of high standards of musical knowledge; the unexpected questions that found out what pupils really knew; the unsettling temper and spotlight on individual miscreants. Reiner later admitted that he deliberately worked students hard with difficult assignments because this was an infallible way of finding out a student's knowledge and dedication to hard work.[65]

Reiner's students had ample opportunity to study the gestures that characterized his conducting: they were required to play in the Curtis Orchestra (either on an orchestral instrument or, if they were pianists, on percussion).[66] According to Goldovsky, Reiner peered over his half-moon glasses, watching every player closely, listening for imperfections, and giving attention equally to principals and rank-and-file players.[67] He knew that unless the sound was clean and precise, nothing of interpretative significance could be achieved. "The only general rule," he once wrote, "is to infuse all gestures with precision, clarity, and vitality"; he believed that the third attribute followed necessarily from the first two.[68] Reiner's gestures were a choreographic part of his conducting—puffing out his cheeks if he wanted wind instruments to blow strongly and never raising his hands above his shoulders unless he wanted a fortissimo. He used a long baton and conducted in tiny, precise, authoritative movements. There was no flailing of the arms like a windmill and no extraneous use of the left arm, even for expressive purposes; he maintained, logically, that there was no need for the left hand to duplicate the motions of the right hand. He saw no point in moving the left hand in a beseeching way, since it did little or nothing to help the musicians produce the quality of performance required. Reiner wanted the musicians' attention concentrated on the point of his baton and on the coordination between his eyes and his bodily gestures. With these characteristics he was the heir to his hero Nikisch, who believed that a conductor could demand more from musicians through minimal yet expressive gestures than by wild, emotional lurches of the arms.[69]

Reiner normally rehearsed the Curtis Symphony Orchestra for four hours on Monday mornings.[70] He made a formidable impression when he conducted (a task he usually reserved for himself, only allowing students to conduct at weekly chamber music concerts).[71] He did not provide much verbal explanation, on the grounds that words could not be used when conducting in public and were therefore out of place in rehearsals.[72] Goldovsky has described memorably the atmosphere of Reiner's first rehearsal with his student charges: "From the moment Reiner mounted the podium and faced the student orchestra, there was a silence in that hall such as I had never heard before. The man's look was terrifying. He had a gimlet eye that could pierce you like a dagger, even when he was looking at you from the side, and he had a tongue to match. He had a way of rolling his tongue around inside his mouth and behind the bulging cheeks which was particularly unnerving, for it created a kind of anxious suspense as one waited for the climax of this critical rumination to erupt like a whiplash. But on the occasion of his first encounter with the Curtis student orchestra he didn't even have to raise his voice for everyone present to understand that the musical recreation that they had enjoyed under the benign [Emil] Mlynarski was over. The man before them was a taskmaster. He wasn't going to stand for any nonsense or shoddy playing from anybody, and if necessary he would drill them until they were all purple in the face."[73] The composer Gian-Carlo Menotti, who studied at Curtis in the thirties, claimed to have learned more about how music was made in one Reiner rehearsal than in a month of composition lessons.[74]

Sometimes Reiner asked students to play stand by stand to spotlight weaknesses. He dismissed anyone who was not good enough, either temporarily or for good. To commit a technical error for the second time was inexcusable; perpetrators were cast out of the orchestra. No one was absolutely safe from this treatment, for Reiner did not have favorites. Those who failed to meet his standards lived in fear.[75] Occasionally the demands went beyond mere criticism. Reiner thought students should attend orchestral rehearsals whatever the circumstances. Once a student timpanist, who was late because of a family illness, crept into his place soon after the rehearsal began. Reiner noticed him, stopped the orchestra, and requested an explanation from the latecomer; not satisfied with his answer, Reiner ordered him off the platform and banned him from playing there again. Several members of the Curtis faculty tried to intervene, asking for the student to be reinstated on humane grounds, but this had no effect on Reiner.[76]

The Curtis Symphony Orchestra had been directed by two conductors of stature, Stokowski and Artur Rodzinski, during its first four years. But after three years of relatively undistinguished playing under the ineffectual Mlynarski, the time was ripe for Reiner to restore its excellence. He did so immediately, commenting that his student ensemble rivaled the standard of any professional symphony orchestra.[77] Reiner treated his student orchestra no differently from any other orchestra he conducted. On one occasion he was preparing a performance of Beethoven's *Grosse Fuge* with the Curtis string orchestra. He had added a double bass part. At the dress rehearsal Reiner did not like the playing of one passage and asked the last bass player to play it alone. It was unsatisfactory, and Reiner told the player to leave. He continued down the line of bass players and eliminated all of them, so the performance that evening was done without any basses.[78] This is an extreme example of Reiner's insistence on high playing standards, but it shows his determination to weed out mediocrity with no concessions to his youthful charges. The students became used to a hard taskmaster, and many found that playing under such a leader was demanding. Such an approach, however, helped the students in the long term: they had not been lured into complacency by a patient conductor who made allowances for their youth and were thus well prepared for what they would face as professional musicians.[79]

The quality of the orchestra was soon recognized. A music critic in the *Philadelphia Inquirer* praised the Curtis Symphony Orchestra for its precision, finish, and interpretative eloquence under Reiner's baton. Another commentator thought the orchestra had been "brought to its present pitch of ability by Mr. Reiner" and was "a valuable civic asset. If some unforeseen emergency arose that found the Philadelphia Orchestra unable to give a required performance, the Curtis orchestra might quite creditably fill the breach."[80] Reiner's first public engagement with the orchestra was hailed as the finest concert yet given by the students under any leader and an immense improvement on past performances in balance, ensemble, and tone.[81] The high standards achieved are evident on a reissued performance of Brahms's *Academic Festival* Overture, recorded in 1937 at the Old Met as part of Josef Hofmann's Golden Jubilee concert in honor of his fifty years as a concert pianist in the United States. This was one of the most renowned concerts of the twentieth century, and Hofmann's wife hired RCA Custom Recordings (part of the record label) to mark this Golden Jubilee occasion.[82]

The Curtis Symphony Orchestra under Reiner appeared in public concerts and also broadcast regularly on the radio. When Reiner came to Curtis, the orchestra was about to embark on its third annual series of one-hour radio concerts over the CBS network. These programs lasted for twenty weeks and were broadcast over forty-seven radio stations.[83] The quality of the Curtis Symphony under Reiner's direction can be heard on broadcasts of Randall Thompson's Symphony no. 2, Rimsky-Korsakov's *Capriccio Espagnole,* and Tchaikovsky's Piano Concerto no. 1 (with Byron Janis as soloist), all preserved at the Recorded Sound Division of the Library of Congress's Music Section.

Once a year Reiner allowed his better students to conduct at a rehearsal; occasionally he let them conduct at public concerts. However, nearly always he assumed the baton on the grounds that student players and budding conductors learned more from working with an experienced leader than from conducting themselves.[84] Reiner's repertoire for student concerts included frequent performances of Weber overtures and Beethoven and Mozart symphonies, along with pieces by Bach, Mendelssohn, Berlioz, Schumann, Wagner, and Sibelius. In general, he favored German composers. A few contemporary pieces were scheduled, including Alexander Tcherepnin's Five Russian Dances and Walton's *Façade,* but usually the repertoire was conservative. Nevertheless there were some novelties, as in one concert in which the entire first violin section played the solo part in the last movement of Mendelssohn's Violin Concerto. Reiner also scheduled excerpts from opera. For radio broadcasts, he conducted the second act of *Le nozze di Figaro* and Pergolesi's *La serva padrona* (in English).

The Philadelphia Grand Opera, which had close connections with Curtis, collapsed in 1932, but opera training continued at the institute.[85] From time to time, Reiner presented operas with his Curtis forces. This made sense because he was an esteemed opera conductor who directed several memorable stage performances in Philadelphia during the 1930s. He conducted *Il barbiere di Siviglia* in the 1934–35 season with the combined orchestral and opera departments of the Curtis Institute. The libretto was translated into English, and the stage settings were prepared by Dr. Herbert Graf, an Austrian producer and administrator who was a naturalized American and who later had a long career working at the Met. Performances were given for the Philadelphia Forum in the Academy of Music and in the concert hall at Juilliard.[86] According to one witness of the latter, the rendition was "phenomenally polished."[87]

In spring 1937, Reiner persuaded Mary Curtis Bok to finance a presentation of Milhaud's one-act opera *Le pauvre matelot.* She agreed on condition that the program include her protégé Menotti's one-act opera *Amelia al Ballo.* Reiner did not want to conduct this work but relented in order to present the Milhaud opera and to appease Bok. On April 1, 1937, Reiner led performances of both pieces in the Academy of Music; he repeated the program in New York and Baltimore. Presented in an English translation by George Mead as *Amelia Goes to the Ball,* the Menotti opera was staged by the Austrian director Ernst Laert, with whom Reiner had worked at the Teatro Colón, and had settings by Donald Oenslager. The double program proved a good contrast: the Menotti work was an opera buffa and a premiere, while Milhaud's piece was nearer to tragedy. To Reiner's chagrin, the Milhaud opera was a flop, whereas Menotti's piece was highly successful.[88] Reiner wanted to use Curtis forces for the American premiere of Hindemith's three-act comic opera *Neues vom Tage,* which required only a small orchestra, but the idea did not bear fruit.[89] In late 1940 his conducting students traveled to Chicago, with all expenses paid, to observe his performances of *Der Rosenkavalier.*[90]

Many of Reiner's conducting students graduated to become practicing musicians, though relatively few became directors of major symphony orchestras. Among those who became conductors were Saul Caston, Sylvan Levin, Joseph Levine, Louis Vyner, Henry Mazer, Howard Mitchell, Max Goberman, Walter Hendl, Lukas Foss, and Leonard Bernstein. Others who studied conducting with Reiner were the film composer Nino Rota, the violinist-conductor Felix Slatkin, the opera producer Boris Goldovsky, and the composers Vincent Persichetti and Samuel Barber.[91]

The best known of Reiner's pupils to the general musical public were Samuel Barber and Leonard Bernstein. Their dealings with Reiner were very much a study in contrasts. Barber was briefly a member of Reiner's conducting class at the Curtis Institute in 1932. We have no detailed record of the interaction between the two men, but it is clear that things did not go well. Reiner gave Barber the highest possible marks for his "native musical gift" and for his "ear," "rhythm," and "musical intelligence" but detected in him no special talent for conducting. Reiner concluded that Barber's progress in conducting did not warrant retaining him in the class. Barber "would never make a conductor," wrote Reiner. Barber graduated from the Curtis Institute in piano and composition but gave up his conducting studies.[92]

Reiner's dismissal of Barber caused friction, and the composer was irritated at Reiner's unwillingness to conduct his overture *The School for Scandal* soon after it was composed in 1931. But Reiner later took an interest in promoting Barber's symphonic music. He performed the composer's Violin Concerto with the Curtis Symphony Orchestra in 1940 and included several works by Barber on his programs with the Chicago Symphony Orchestra.[93] Barber, a highly self-critical man, later acknowledged that Reiner was right about his conducting ability. In 1950 he recorded several of his works for Decca and conducted occasional concerts but realized that he had neither the projection nor the authority to command an orchestra to give of its best. He also thought composers were generally poor conductors and became bored when rehearsing his own music.[94]

Bernstein, who studied with Reiner from 1939 until 1941, was already a Harvard graduate and one of several college graduates at Curtis. He had never studied conducting before but was encouraged to do so by Mitropoulos, who was convinced, after meeting him, that he must become a conductor. Mitropoulos asked Reiner to audition Bernstein for his class and was supported by Aaron Copland.[95] Reiner took these recommendations seriously. At the audition he opened a score and asked Bernstein to play it on the piano. The music was Brahms's *Academic Festival* Overture. Bernstein did not know the piece and was understandably nervous, but he was a good sight-reader and performed well. Reiner was favorably impressed and agreed to take him into his conducting class. In later years Bernstein always thought of the Brahms overture when

Reiner came to mind, and he chose to play the piece in a broadcast tribute to his teacher.[96] Besides conducting, Bernstein also studied piano, score reading, and composition (the latter with Randall Thompson, the successor to Hofmann as director at Curtis). Reiner assigned Bernstein the Second Symphony by Thompson as his first task and was satisfied with his conducting of the score (which was one of the first modern scores that Bernstein later conducted with the New York Philharmonic).[97]

Bernstein soon experienced the formality of Reiner's teaching—a chummy attempt to call him "Fritz" received an icy stare. Like other students, he found Reiner a harsh taskmaster who could not be hoodwinked. One day when he did not feel like conducting, he turned up to class with his right arm in a sling but was spotted by Reiner immediately. Reiner told him, "Your other arm is still good, I see, so it shouldn't be too bad." Bernstein knew his bluff had been called and gradually, as he conducted with his left arm, let his right arm come out of the sling and began to conduct naturally. Reiner made no further comment, and proceedings continued smoothly.[98] The incident probably jogged Reiner's memory, for he had conducted with his left arm when his right arm was in a sling at the end of his period in Cincinnati. Reiner also wanted to be firm with Bernstein, whom he regarded initially as worse than a show-off because he often disturbed classes by taking everyone's attention while he played the piano.[99]

Bernstein had undertaken detailed analysis of scores while at Harvard from a pianist's or composer's point of view, but only under Reiner's tuition did he begin to look at scores from a conductor's perspective. He admired Reiner's high professional standards and great skill as a baton technician and learned that, unless one knew a score comprehensively and was ready for all musical pitfalls, it was futile to stand on a podium in front of an orchestra.[100] He later recalled that Reiner provided a marvelous antidote to excessive facial and bodily gestures when conducting but that he was also open-minded in allowing Bernstein to abandon the use of a baton when he complained that he did not feel free using it.[101] Bernstein tried to imitate Reiner's technique by using the baton economically, but it did not suit him, and he abandoned it.[102] His conducting had the physical flamboyance and emotional expression characteristic of Koussevitzky or Mitropoulos; it lay at the opposite end of the spectrum from Reiner's precise minimalism. Yet Bernstein later expressed gratitude for the discipline instilled in him by his original mentor, whom he regarded as a "great master and a great teacher" who was underestimated.[103] "I treasure the memory of Reiner," he wrote decades later, "to say nothing of the invaluable teaching and standards he imparted to me. He was a great teacher, stern, demanding, perfectionist, insisting on thorough knowledge and no fakery. He transmitted his own standards of knowledge, preparation, and technical competence in a way that made his students sometimes tremble, but ultimately bless him for it. When one observed the ease, mastery, and economy of Reiner's conducting, one had a model toward which one could strive eternally. I still have that model in mind, and will probably never equal it."[104]

In the summer of 1940 Bernstein applied to study conducting with Koussevitzky, who presided over the Berkshire Summer Music Festival at Tanglewood. This was on the recommendation of Reiner and Mitropoulos, yet Reiner was clearly irritated by this move.[105] Some observers consider that he did not think Bernstein an exceptional student at the time, though he gave Bernstein an A in conducting in 1941 (apparently the only such grade he ever awarded).[106] Whatever he thought of Bernstein's conducting potential, he certainly hated to lose students to rival conductors. Koussevitzky, it should be noted, made no attempt to poach Bernstein; in fact, he was shocked that Bernstein (and Foss) wanted to leave Reiner's tuition and urged them "both very earnestly to return to Philadelphia and resume their work at the Curtis Institute of Music."[107]

When he went to Tanglewood, Bernstein, feeling that he had caused a misunderstanding, wrote to Reiner expressing loyalty to him as a teacher but explaining his need to take the opportunity offered, for he was conducting only one short piece a year in student concerts at Curtis. Financial difficulties also made it preferable for him to live at home in Boston while studying at Tanglewood.[108] After six weeks in western Massachusetts, Bernstein wrote to Reiner, expressing enthusiasm for life at Tanglewood and praising his former teacher for the discipline and knowledge he had imparted.[109] Reiner was gratified that Bernstein gave a good account of himself "and did not disgrace his teacher" and that he would have an opportunity to gain further conducting experience.[110] Relations between the two men cooled, but in 1944 Reiner, hoping to share some of the accolade that Koussevitzky had received as Bernstein's teacher, invited Bernstein to Pittsburgh to conduct his *Jeremiah* Symphony.[111]

Reiner respected the Russian maestro's musicianship but was irritated by Bernstein coming under Koussevitzky's spell. Reiner and Koussevitzky were complete opposites as men and conductors—as different as the North and South Poles.[112] Yet Koussevitzky realized the skills that Reiner could impart. When Bernstein contemplated leaving Curtis for Tanglewood, Koussevitzky advised him to pay attention to all of Reiner's remarks, for he recognized him as a master technician imbued with the best European traditions of musical art.[113] Bernstein was immediately influenced by Koussevitzky's warmth, inspirational teaching, and promotion of American music, and the two men developed almost a father-son relationship.[114] Reiner thought that Bernstein did not deserve the prominence accorded to him during his student years at Tanglewood. By imitating more flamboyant conductors, Bernstein seemed to reject all that he had absorbed from Reiner. In fact, however, the reverse was true: Bernstein learned everything technically about conducting from Reiner rather than from Koussevitzky.[115]

Several of Reiner's other pupils remembered him as a fine teacher who gave interesting lessons and who instilled thorough musicianship. Ezra Rachlin remembered him as having a deeper knowledge of scores than any other musician he ever met.[116] Despite his stern manner, Reiner acted kindly toward musicians who showed promise. Thus he arranged for one student's tuba to be brought by a chauffeur to rehearsals after he discovered that the young player did not have suitable transportation.[117] It is also feasible that his behavior as a martinet was partly an act to disguise a fierce love of music.[118] At any rate, Reiner followed the careers of successful pupils with interest and conducted music by Barber, Bernstein, and Foss in concerts. Though fond of conducting students as a group, Reiner never played the role of a benevolent uncle like Koussevitzky.

Reiner's teaching position at Curtis ended after a change of director and policy. In 1941 Thompson quit the director's job. He had tried to introduce a wider cultural and scholarly content to courses at Curtis in order to broaden the training given to young virtuosi, but this had not been approved by Mary Curtis Bok and some of the resident faculty.[119] His replacement was Efrem Zimbalist, the leader of the violin department at Curtis who married Bok in 1943. Zimbalist was a notorious skinflint who decided to eliminate the orchestra department to save funds (even though much of the institute's fame came from that department). This also marked a return to one of Curtis's foundational principles, which was to provide training for soloists.[120] In early 1941 Mary Curtis Bok wrote Reiner that various alterations were contemplated for the Curtis Institute next year, including changing the orchestral department and eliminating conducting as a major subject. She was not therefore able to offer Reiner a renewed contract.[121] A few days later, after a decade in Philadelphia, Reiner resigned from Curtis, stating that his responsibilities as music director of the Pittsburgh Symphony Orchestra, a post he had taken up in 1938, now prohibited him from spending as much time in Philadelphia as he would have liked.[122] His resignation came only a few hours after Thompson quit his post, prompting some to view Reiner's action as a protest. But Reiner claimed at the time that the two departures were unconnected.[123]

Bok expressed regret at Reiner's resignation but thanked him for the quality of his instruction. She thought his pupils were already demonstrating his principles in the positions they held in various American orchestras.[124] Reiner's years at Curtis had been rewarding. He was able to keep in close touch with major musical events on the East Coast, especially in Philadelphia and New York, and probably felt closer to the hub of the nation's serious musical life than he had while in Cincinnati. He never taught on an extended basis again.

By the mid 1940s it seemed as though Reiner would return to conduct and instruct students on a part-time basis. He outlined plans to conduct the Juilliard student orchestra at the invitation of the school's new president, William Schuman. Reiner wanted to present concerts by the Juilliard orchestra once every three or four weeks and to direct two operas a year. He would train the singers and chorus, with the help of opera coaches and a chorus director, and he would direct rehearsals. He was also willing to take conducting students from the pool of composition graduates at Juilliard, provided that they had a complete background in musical theory.[125] But these plans never materialized. Schuman found out that Reiner would not perform the music of Roy Harris. He decided that any conducting appointment at the Juilliard School should be given to someone more attuned to contemporary American composers that he wished to promote. Reiner and Schuman remained on friendly terms despite this difference of opinion. Two years later, when Juilliard renewed their offer, Reiner lacked the time to take up the appointment and balked at the modest fee.[126] He had become disillusioned with the prospect of further teaching. He informed an inquirer that he no longer accepted conducting students "because the technique of the baton does not interest me. Observing others and learning by experience is the best teacher—provided that you have the natural aptitude for communicating your ideas to a group of people."[127] He later received many applications from prospective conducting students but always turned them down because of his heavy work schedule.[128]

In 1947 Reiner outlined a sketch for a proposed book on conducting at the request of a publisher. He planned chapters covering an historical sketch of the art of conducting, the musical background of the student, elementary training, conducting nonprofessional and professional groups, the art of interpretation, and the personality of the conductor. The project never came to fruition, however, because Reiner did not have three or four free hours a day over three or four months—the time that he estimated would have been necessary to write the book.[129] Only toward the end of his life did he think of teaching again, but hopes that he might instruct students privately rather than in a school were dashed by a series of heart attacks.[130] Bernstein acknowledged Reiner's formative influence on his conducting career in a chapter called "A Tribute to Teachers" in his book *Findings*. This was originally a radio broadcast, taped on November 2, 1963, only a few days before Reiner died.[131] The Hungarian maestro was gratified that his "teaching and ideas about music are remembered by my most brilliant and successful student."[132] Reiner's role as a teacher was also recognized by William Schuman in a funeral eulogy on November 18, 1963—a tribute to Reiner's teaching of students, of orchestras, and of the musical public.[133]

5. A GUEST CONDUCTOR IN THE 1930S

Reiner's teaching position at the Curtis Institute was a useful vantage point for guest appearances conducting operas and symphonic music in the Quaker City and for keeping in touch with musical developments on the East Coast. It also gave him time to pursue other musical activities on a freelance basis. By the 1930s, Philadelphia already had a long tradition of presenting opera. The Academy of Music, when completed in 1857, was the finest opera house in North America. Later the home of the Philadelphia Civic Opera Company (1924–30) and the Philadelphia Grand Opera Company (1926–43), it was also the venue for the annual season presented by New York's Metropolitan Opera in most years between the 1880s and 1968.[1] This abundance of operatic activity did not lead, however, to the foundation of a permanent opera company along the lines of the Met: the offerings, rather, were piecemeal and occupied only part of the winter season of music making.

Reiner wanted to conduct opera in Philadelphia while he worked there. At that time it was unusual for a first-rate conductor in America to be willing to commit time and energy to the preparation and performance of opera, as the obstacles to be surmounted were formidable: casts often changed completely from one performance to the next; rehearsal time was frequently inadequate; and fees for conducting orchestral concerts—to say nothing of appearances on radio—were always higher. The costs of producing opera could be financially prohibitive, and there were few permanent opera companies. These problems deterred major conductors from conducting opera. Arturo Toscanini avoided conducting opera on the American stage after leaving the Met in 1915. Otto Klemperer never conducted opera in the United States after his dazzling spell at the Kroll Opera House in Berlin. Artur Rodzinski and Dimitri Mitropou-

los, both dramatic conductors of opera, largely confined their operatic conducting in America to concerts.[2] But the difficulties of performing opera did
not deter Reiner. Between leaving his post in Cincinnati and becoming music
director of the Pittsburgh Symphony Orchestra, his most significant conducting achievements were in opera, with the Philadelphia Orchestra, the San
Francisco Opera, and at Covent Garden.

During the 1931–32 season Reiner conducted several operas with the Philadelphia Grand Opera Company, which generally presented between twelve and
fifteen productions per season at the Academy of Music.[3] Leopold Stokowski
invited Reiner to conduct seven performances of six operas—Wagner's *Lohengrin* and *Tannhäuser,* Richard Strauss's *Elektra,* Verdi's *Aida,* Mussorgsky's
Boris Godunov, and Bizet's *Carmen.* These were Reiner's first opera performances in the United States. The works were performed in their original languages under the stage direction of Wilhelm von Wymetal Jr.[4] Curtis Institute
singers appeared in the casts along with seasoned operatic soloists, a result of
the affiliation between the institute and the Philadelphia Grand Opera Company that commenced in 1929; orchestral musicians were drawn from the Curtis Institute and the Philadelphia Orchestra.[5] The work of the company was excellent, with a chorus and stage management that compared favorably with
those of the Met.[6]

The cast for *Tannhäuser* included Gotthelf Pistor in the title role, John
Charles Thomas as Wolfram, and Anne Roselle as Elisabeth. Reiner's conducting of the opera was admired; it allowed the singers to be clearly heard
and "aided rather than antagonized the people on stage, without slighting the
orchestral part or dimming the instrumental splendor of the score."[7] Another
highlight of the season was *Boris Godunov,* with Ivan Steschenko in the title
role, Nina Koshetz as Marina, Dimitry Onofrei as the False Dmitry, and Irra
Petina as Fyodor. The performance was praised for an able and individual interpretation of Boris, "the superbly authoritative and intensely vital conducting of Fritz Reiner," and the fine, forceful work of the chorus, which has a
prominent role in the opera.[8]

Elektra contained the most striking individual performance of the season.
Reiner thought that Strauss's blood-curdling opera would not be too modern
for a musical public attuned to the music of Stravinsky and Schoenberg and
that there would not be the sense of shock that was felt at *Elektra*'s Philadelphia premiere (in French) in 1909. Presenting the opera in German for the first
time in the United States, Reiner assembled an enlarged orchestra of ninety-
six musicians for the performance, including players of several Wagner tubas,
which were purchased for the occasion.[9] A novel effect was introduced towards the end of the opera, whereby backstage microphones and amplifiers
projected an impassioned chorus singing behind the stage, and the death cries

of Klytemnästra and Aegisth were electronically amplified; as a result, the Academy of Music was flooded with music.[10]

Reiner excelled in conducting *Elektra*'s complex score, bringing out the "mood of impending horror, dread and gruesome tragedy . . . with vivid comprehension and sensitive art in his energetic, full-blooded conducting."[11] Roselle sang Elektra. Nelson Eddy (later a Hollywood star) took the baritone role of Orestes; Charlotte Boerner was Chrysothemis; Bruno Korell sang Aegisth; and the Hungarian mezzo-soprano Margaret Matzenauer (who later had a distinguished career at the Met) was Klytemnästra. Matzenauer was still in fine voice at the age of fifty. She proved her acting ability as Klytemnästra, looking with her makeup "like a creature that was rotting alive"; her presence drew many opera fans to the performance.[12] Roselle visited Richard Strauss in Garmisch to sing for his approval before this production, and Strauss conveyed his best wishes for Reiner's resumption of opera conducting.[13]

Roselle and Eddy also appeared together in *Lohengrin*, as Elsa and the King's Herald, along with Paolo Marion in the title role. Roselle sang the title role in *Aida*, with Cyrena von Gordon as Amneris and Aroldo Lindi as Radamès. The cast for *Carmen* included Coe Glade (hired from the Chicago Opera) in the title role, Lindi as Don José, Chief Caupolicon (a Native American) as Escamillo, and Natalie Bodonskaya (later Bodanya) as Micaëla.

Unfortunately, the Philadelphia Grand Opera ran into financial problems despite backing from wealthy patrons such as Mary Curtis Bok. In spring 1932 mounting debts forced it to cease operations,[14] but Reiner did not abandon opera conducting. On November 8, 1932, at the Metropolitan Opera, he directed excerpts from *Salome* with the Musicians' Symphony Orchestra, an ensemble of unemployed players, with Nelson Eddy as Jochanaan and the Moravian soprano Maria Jeritza as the heroine.[15] She sang a special concert arrangement of the opera devised by the composer, in which two vocal excerpts (Salome's temptation of Jochanaan and the final scene) were interspersed by a nonchoreographed version of the Dance of the Seven Veils. This was the first time that music from *Salome* had been performed at the Met since 1906, when the score was declared to be depraved and unsuitable for performance in New York. A packed audience applauded both the orchestra, which played well under Reiner's baton, and Jeritza's opulent, sensuous, dramatic rendition of the title role.[16]

Reiner wanted to follow up the performance with more operas but lacked suitable opportunities. When he indicated his willingness to conduct at the Chicago Civic Opera almost a year after appearing with Jeritza, he appears to have been too busy to accept the offer.[17] However, another chance to conduct operas soon arose. In 1934 the Met abandoned its regular Tuesday night performances in Philadelphia owing to financial restrictions necessary during the

Great Depression. Arthur Judson, the manager of the Philadelphia Orchestra, was nevertheless keen to present an opera season at the Academy of Music; by combining operas with the regular orchestral season, subscriptions could be maintained. Stokowski showed little enthusiasm for the venture and, in any case, had requested leave from the Philadelphia Orchestra for the 1934–35 season.[18] But because Judson needed to present something to maintain the interest of Philadelphia's musical public, he devised bold operatic plans for the Quaker City. He wanted a secure financial basis for opera in Philadelphia and, ultimately, throughout the United States but realized that this could not be achieved overnight. An extraordinary season of opera presented at concert prices would create a demand; the following year the prices could be increased until the investment was recouped. He outlined these plans to the committee of the Philadelphia Orchestra, explaining that this was the time to invest and that the opportunity would be lost by false economies. He was helped by an outcry from the Philadelphia musical public, who wanted an opera season to replace that of the Met.[19]

In August 1934 a plan was devised to include ten operas as part of the normal concert season, with a different opera every third week. Stokowski chose the operas but was not interested in conducting them. He had disagreed with the board of the Philadelphia Orchestra over experimental ways of producing operas. He wanted to continue work begun in the early 1930s with scientists and engineers at Bell Laboratories, which entailed amplification of singing parts with actors miming on stage by synchronizing lip movements, so that the sound was projected by speakers from areas hidden from the audience.[20] The board disagreed with him over what it regarded as avant-garde proposals. The task of conducting the operas therefore fell partly on the shoulders of Stokowski's assistant, Alexander Smallens, a Russian-born immigrant who had directed the Philadelphia Civic Opera, and partly on Reiner. This was another chance for Reiner to spread his reputation as an opera conductor, to lead the world-renowned Philadelphia Orchestra, and to demonstrate his capabilities to East Coast music critics—an opportunity he did not intend to waste.[21] For conducting five of the operas to be presented during the season, he was offered ten thousand dollars.[22]

Judson brought in Herbert Graf, a young Viennese producer, as stage director for the operas. Although Graf had never seen any opera productions in America, he felt it incongruous that a nation with such an advanced way of life was still clinging to conservative presentations of grand opera. Accordingly, leading Broadway designers such as Norman Bel Geddes, Donald Oenslager, and Serge Sudeikine were engaged to provide new costumes and scenery. Another of Graf's contributions was a revolving stage, specially built in New York and sent by road to Philadelphia in forty segments. This was the first time that such a stage had been constructed for opera in America; it was used for the performances of *Carmen, Tristan,* and *Der Rosenkavalier.*[23]

Several singers were imported from Europe, but the majority hired were American. All were chosen for the quality of their voices and their ability to act. A young chorus was recruited, and two weeks of piano stage rehearsals and one week of orchestral rehearsals were allowed for each production. Also, for the first time the Philadelphia Orchestra would be seated in the musicians' pit in front of the stage rather than on the stage itself. The operas were presented as part of the Philadelphia Orchestra's regular subscription series, even though the presentation of all ten operas would reduce the duration of its symphonic season from thirty weeks to twenty.[24] Reiner, who had hoped to present at least one American opera during the season, examined "five hundred pounds" of scores that were American in subject, feeling, and treatment but considered none good enough for performance.[25]

Reiner and Smallens divided the conducting responsibilities equally. Reiner took charge of Wagner's *Tristan und Isolde* and *Die Meistersinger,* Mozart's *Le nozze di Figaro,* Richard Strauss's *Der Rosenkavalier,* and Verdi's *Falstaff.* Reiner conducted *Der Rosenkavalier* and *Falstaff* for the first time in his career.[26] The total cost of three performances each of five productions was estimated at thirty thousand dollars.[27] Smallens directed Bizet's *Carmen,* a double bill of Humperdinck's *Hänsel und Gretel* and Stravinsky's *Mavra* (an American premiere), Mussorgsky's *Boris Godunov,* Gluck's *Iphigénie en Aulide,* and Shostakovich's *Lady Macbeth of the Mtsensk District.* Debussy's *Pelléas et Mélisande* was also scheduled but was dropped because it proved impossible to cast properly.[28]

Reiner and Smallens were not on the best of terms. At a cocktail party held during the grand opera season, Smallens had boasted about conductors who did not know how to rehearse and who wasted musicians' time, whereas *he* could prepare the entire *Ring* cycle with a single orchestral rehearsal. Reiner, when asked his reaction to this jibe, at once replied: "With Smallens? But of course it's possible. Why, he wouldn't know what to say at the second rehearsal."[29] The remark, although barbed, was apt. Smallens had the energy and routine skills to present capable performances in the opera house and the concert hall, often at short notice, but Reiner's skills were altogether higher, for he was a conductor's conductor with a complete mastery of baton technique and wide experience in all aspects of opera conducting. He had the ability to clarify very complex counterpoint, achieve perfect transparency of sound, demonstrate the structural unity of scores, galvanize singers and orchestral players to give their best, and bring out the vitality and emotional depth of the music. Fortunately, the differences between the two conductors had little bearing on the success of the season.

Reiner understood the economic plight of opera in the United States and the lack of money for all the arts during the Depression. He lamented the fact that the Met was the nation's only permanent organization where the mainstream operatic repertoire was performed regularly, contrasting European governmental support of opera with the dependence of operatic ventures in America on the bounty of rich patrons. To improve this state of affairs it would be necessary to popularize opera by selling opera performances as well as orchestral concerts to schools, clubs, universities, and labor organizations.[30]

Reiner hoped his operatic plans for Philadelphia would bring about even more sweeping changes. Along with the onstage modernizations under Graf's direction, he further updated casting procedures by abolishing the star system of singers inherited from Italy and presenting works with predominantly American casts in English. Instead of choosing operas to fit the schedules of star singers, he selected artists who fitted particular operas—something else that set the Philadelphia experiment apart from other operatic ventures in America.[31] Another goal was to broaden opera's artistic appeal beyond the socially privileged classes, thereby helping its survival. Anticipating audiences used to the modern theater and cinema, Reiner took steps to have better stage designs for his Philadelphia season. He wanted to avoid the restrictive traditions of grand opera and achieve a more modern type of presentation, one in which music, drama, dance, and the plastic arts united to realize Wagner's dream of the Gesamtkunstwerk.

Reiner faced considerable difficulties in achieving these goals. It was not easy to find American singers with sufficient training and experience for leading roles, but they were given preference wherever possible. It was also difficult to find adequate texts in English for all operas: many of the available translations were banal. But Reiner wanted to find good texts for all the operas presented in English in the belief that "opera cannot approach the intellect and emotions of a people until it speaks to them in their own language."[32] This was not yet a widespread practice because of the snobbish attitude of initiates, the laziness of imported musicians in learning English, and the absence of good translations.[33] In particular, Reiner believed that comic operas such as *Le nozze di Figaro* and *Il barbiere di Siviglia* should be presented in English so that audiences could understand the jokes and the entrances and exits.[34] These aspirations differed from the traditional style of Met productions usually seen in Philadelphia.[35]

Many of these objectives, which Smallens shared, were put into practice in the Philadelphia Orchestra's opera season of 1934–35. During that year Reiner frequently traveled to New York and became familiar with the résumés of more than 250 American singers. He hired the best American voices available for major parts and promising young singers for secondary roles. Among these was

Julius Huehn, a young baritone trained at the Juilliard School, who was chosen to sing Count Almaviva in *Le nozze di Figaro,* Faninal in *Der Rosenkavalier,* Kothner in *Die Meistersinger,* Kurwenal in *Tristan und Isolde,* and the title role in *Falstaff.*[36] Indeed, over 90 percent of the company eventually assembled was American-born, including virtually all the amateur chorus.[37]

The first opera Reiner conducted was *Tristan,* a bold move given its demands on even seasoned opera companies. He decided to perform the five-hour work without cuts and to emphasize scenic splendor. He sketched out some ideas for the stage sets himself. For the opening of the first act he wanted a steeply inclined Viking boat, with Tristan at the rudder, sharply etched against the horizon. For the end of the act he suggested that the landing coast and castle should be visible. For act 2 he insisted that the torch be the center of action in the first scene, placed low enough for Isolde to grasp. The castle and terrace should be submerged in darkness and, at the beginning of the love duet, "a sense of unreality must come over the entire stage through the use of lighting and gauze." In the third act, the sea should be seen beneath the towering ruins of the castle, and a symbolic inclined pathway would lead from Tristan's bed to the doorway of the castle, where Isolde appears at the end of the act. At the end everything would appear to dissolve except for Tristan and Isolde in the middle of the stage.[38]

Unfortunately, problems occurred with the set designs. The sculptor Alexander Archipenko's original stage model for the production consisted of a beautiful longitudinal design of a ship, but the proportions were wrong: the cabin, which was the setting for most of the first act, occupied only a quarter of the stage's width, leaving little room for the singers.[39] This concept was abandoned, and Donald Oenslager, one of America's foremost stage designers, was hired to redeem the situation. This he did, making great use of gauze, lights, and innumerable stairs leading to different stage levels.[40] The most striking visual feature of the production was the ship he designed for the first act, with its prow pointed upstage and into the open sea. A large sail-like drape hid the front of the ship, but when it parted the audience could see Tristan seated high in the prow next to some sailors. When the drape was closed, the audience's attention was directed to the quarters occupied by Isolde and her personal maid, Brangäne. In this way, the shift of focus between the doomed lovers on the ship carrying them from Ireland to Cornwall was managed imaginatively and effectively.[41] Oenslager's sets horrified traditional Wagnerians used to papier-mâché trees and artificial flowers in the second and third acts. Some critics questioned whether these new designs added to the projection of dramatic moods.[42]

Reiner invited the Norwegian soprano Kirsten Flagstad to appear as the heroine, having heard glowing accounts of her singing, but she declined because of prior commitments in Sweden.[43] In keeping with Reiner's artistic policy, the cast assembled was American-born with the exception of Hans Grahl as Tristan, Marga Dannenberg as Isolde, and Emanuel List as King Marke. Grahl was recruited from the Municipal Opera in Hamburg; Dannenberg was a well-known operatic singer in Lübeck and Bayreuth; List was a famous basso at the Met. Philadelphia music critics praised the singing of the entire cast, the artistic lighting effect, and Reiner's authority as an opera conductor, with "the orchestra responding in complete artistic appreciation to every suggestion and demand of his alert and sensitive direction."[44] The full-strength orchestra in the pit almost stole the show, for its "tonal beauty, delicacy and subtlety of shading were revelatory."[45] This was the first time in the United States that an orchestra with the expertise of the Philadelphia had undertaken such an operatic venture.[46] It was also the first full version of *Tristan* ever presented in North America and the only uncut account of the music drama that Reiner conducted in America.[47]

The prior publicity for this venture was so irresistible that First Lady Eleanor Roosevelt came up from Washington to join a capacity audience. She left after the second act. Marcel Tabuteau, the principal oboist, who naturally was obliged to stay till the end, quipped after the performance, "Tell me, mon cher, is Roosevelt still President?"[48] This humorous remark emphasizes that this was probably the longest public performance yet of any musical work in America. Reiner, deciding not to test the patience of the audience again, gave the final two performances of *Tristan* with traditional cuts, omitting about thirty minutes.[49]

Reiner's performance of *Figaro* used an English translation by the musicologist Edward J. Dent. Rehearsals were marked by intensive drilling of the singers and some explosive disagreements with piano accompanists who did not play as Reiner wished.[50] The production included several minor cuts. Reiner was praised as the "dominating figure of the occasion" with a reduced orchestra of forty-five players, for he "gave sparkling pace to the performance" by accompanying recitatives on a piano, modified to suggest a clavichord, in addition to conducting.[51] Working closely with Graf, Reiner imparted zest and life to the stage direction. He conducted in a chamber-music style suitable for the presentation of the opera in the Academy of Music, aided by fine singing from a predominantly youthful cast.[52]

More striking than this production, however, were performances of *Der Rosenkavalier*. Boris Goldovsky, one of the piano accompanists at the rehearsals, noted that Strauss's "complicated scores were a perfect foil" for Reiner's conducting talents and that "of all the Richard Strauss opera conductors I have seen, and I have seen quite a few, Fritz Reiner was undoubtedly the finest."[53] For the production of *Der Rosenkavalier*, Reiner recruited two of the

Vienna Opera's finest stars to play Sophie and the Marschallin—Elisabeth
Schumann and Lotte Lehmann. By doing so he took excellent advantage of the
availability of two of the best exponents of those roles: Schumann was engaged in a concert tour in the United States at the time, and Lehmann had been
singing with the Met since early 1934. From Prague, Reiner brought Eva
Hadrabova to sing Octavian. List portrayed Baron Ochs, a role he had sung
many times in Europe and at the Met.

Reiner's preparation of *Rosenkavalier* was disturbed by List's inability to
follow all the musical cues in rehearsal. Laxity in a professional singer, especially one with an established reputation, would normally enrage Reiner to the
point of firing the individual. However, even though Reiner had difficulty con-
taining his anger at the mistakes, he controlled his feelings as much as possible
because no immediate substitute was available for the role and he did not want
to jeopardize the success of a favorite opera. The upshot was that Goldovsky,
the piano accompanist, took the brunt of the outbursts instead.[54]

The stage scenery and costumes used for this production, set in the rococo
period, were elaborate and colorful. Graf, the stage director, pulled off a considerable theatrical coup by using, with the composer's approval, a revolving
stage in act 3, which turned from Ochs—being chased through an inn and onto
the street by a waltzing chorus of lackeys, musicians, stable boys, and children—to the moonlit garden of the inn, with Vienna as the candlelit backdrop,
in which the famous trio between the Marschallin, Sophie, and Octavian takes
place. This was the perfect setting for the dénouement of the opera. Although
approved by Lehmann and the composer, the revolving stage for *Rosenkavalier* was criticized by the press.[55]

Reiner hoped to present a new piece, Shostakovich's *Lady Macbeth of the
Mtsensk District,* in English. He was persuaded against this, however, because
the opera contained violent and bawdy scenes that, if given in English, might
offend stuffier elements of Philadelphia's musical public. As Reiner had no
wish to begin his grand operatic venture with a fiasco, he set the opera aside
(it was later successfully conducted by Smallens with the "obscene" brass parts
included). Reiner then turned to Verdi's *Falstaff,* a work to which he was
deeply attached and one he was able to present in a new English translation.
His rehearsals for the production were painstaking, especially for the final
episode, in which the ten principal singers mingle their voices in a culminating
fugue. Concerned about the split-second timing of their entries, he gave the
singers a final run-through of the passage during the intermission of all three
performances.[56] For this finale the impressionistic trees and shrubbery of
Windsor Forest were whisked off the stage, leaving the assembled singers
standing on a bare framework against black velvet draperies.[57]

A production of *Die Meistersinger* concluded the operatic season. With such fine soloists as Friedrich Schorr as Hans Sachs, Gustav Schützendorf as Beckmesser, and Charlotte Boerner as Eva, Reiner was inspired to give a majestic reading of the score. He was in his element in coordinating the soloists, chorus, and orchestra in superb ensemble work. The production was so successful that Reiner believed that the Philadelphia public had acquired a lasting taste for opera and would not want to renew their subscriptions unless there was opera in the 1935–36 schedule.[58]

Reiner correctly regarded the first Philadelphia opera season as an artistic and social success. "No effort was spared in tackling the problems of opera productions," Graf recalled. "In addition to the best orchestra any opera could hope for, we had an interesting repertoire, real ensemble, good acting, new scenery and costumes, up-to-date lighting, new artists, and opera sung in English."[59] Graf, Reiner, and Smallens, working hard to encourage good team spirit, all played a full part in the musical and stage direction. Most productions had received three weeks of rehearsal, some as many as five or six weeks. The presentation of opera in English succeeded sufficiently to encourage some observers to think it would become the norm in America. Reiner's skill and vitality in dealing with the manifold elements of operatic performance impressed many observers.[60]

Unfortunately, the season was a financial disaster. To mount ten lavishly staged operas nearly bankrupted the Philadelphia Orchestra; its entire surplus of $250,000, built up carefully over two decades, was consumed by this one season. Why was it so expensive? Costumes and scenery were sumptuous and had to be bought out of one season's funds; stage rehearsals were held on Sundays, the only time when the Academy of Music and the chorus were regularly available, which led to heavy overtime payments; the revolving turntable used for *Der Rosenkavalier* and *Carmen* was very costly; the original lavish scenic design for *Tristan* was abandoned because it was impractical; only three operas presented (*Carmen, Die Meistersinger, Der Rosenkavalier*) were sure box-office draws; and all this when the country was still in the economic mire of the Great Depression. Further seasons of opera in Philadelphia became unviable, and the elaborate scenery and costumes decayed into dust. Decades passed before the Philadelphia Orchestra again presented operas.[61]

The Philadelphia season was beset by other problems. Soon after it began, Judson—no longer friendly with Stokowski and with plenty of other musical interests to pursue—resigned as manager of the Philadelphia Orchestra. At virtually the same time Stokowski announced his resignation after disagreements with the board of directors. These difficulties did not quite mark the end of Reiner's opera conducting in Philadelphia, for he directed several operas with Curtis Institute forces. The Met returned to Philadelphia for guest appearances in the 1935–36 season, but it was not until 1938 that a new opera group emerged in the Quaker City—the Philadelphia Opera Company, under the direction of Sylvan Levin.[62]

Reiner's opera conducting soon focused on two new venues: the San Francisco Opera and Covent Garden. He appeared at the San Francisco Opera in three successive seasons between 1936 and 1938, directing a total of twenty performances of operas from the German repertoire. These took place at the War Memorial Opera House, which had opened in 1932 as the first municipally owned operatic venue in America. This was the home of the San Francisco Opera Company, formed in 1923 under the leadership of the conductor, producer, and impresario Gaetano Merola.[63] He made efforts to secure first-rate conductors for the San Francisco Opera, including Reiner, but the productions he oversaw had uninteresting stage direction, exemplifying what might be called "visual provincialism." In 1935 the San Francisco Opera had presented a full *Ring* cycle under the conductor Artur Bodanzky, hired from the Metropolitan Opera.[64] It had proved popular with the Bay City's musical public, and it was therefore not surprising that Reiner should conduct Wagnerian operas in the next season.

Reiner's involvement in the short San Francisco Opera season of 1936 helped to generate two hundred thousand dollars in advance ticket sales.[65] He conducted three Wagnerian music dramas: two performances of *Die Walküre,* one of *Götterdämmerung,* and two of *Tristan und Isolde.* Reiner put a lot of work into rehearsing the orchestra, drawn from players in the San Francisco Symphony, so that it would be in good form. "I have had gruelling rehearsals here," he noted, adding that the orchestra was good even though it lacked experience playing operas and sufficient rehearsal time.[66] Reiner usually insisted on performing Wagnerian operas with the full score, in the authentic Bayreuth tradition, but on this occasion he sanctioned several cuts.[67] He gave particular attention to hiring *tuben* for the performances of *Die Walküre.* He felt that the instruments (which have four valves instead of three and the same style of mouthpiece as the French horn) were essential for such passages as the scenes of Hunding, the monologue of Siegmund, the end of the first act, and especially the scene between Brunnhilde and Siegmund in the second act, reasoning that if Wagner had wanted to avoid their distinctive sound he would have written the parts for fifth, sixth, seventh, and eighth horns.[68] For the performances, his assistant Karl Riedel taught the local musicians to play the *tuben* (also known as Wagner tubas) he had purchased in Vienna for the Curtis Institute.[69]

The main soloists in the performances of *Tristan* were the two greatest interpreters of the role yet known: the Danish tenor Lauritz Melchior and Flagstad, whom Reiner had directed in performances of the same opera at Covent Garden only a few months earlier. Other members of the cast were Kathryn Meisle and Doris Doe alternating as Brangäne, List as King Marke, and Friedrich Schorr as Kurwenal. Melchior and Flagstad also sang the parts of Siegfried and Brunnhilde in *Götterdämmerung,* joined by Schorr as Gunther, Dorothee Manski as Gutrune, Arnold Gabor as Alberich, List as Hagen, and Meisle as Waltraute. For *Die Walküre,* Flagstad was Brunnhilde, and Melchior was Siegmund. Lehmann appeared as Sieglinde, Schorr as Wotan, List as Hunding, and Meisle as Fricka. Melchior and Flagstad fully appreciated Reiner's gifts. Flagstad greatly admired his conducting and had cordial professional relations with him.[70] Melchior's confidence in Reiner's ability was such that, later in the thirties, he requested Reiner to conduct him in records of Wagnerian opera; RCA Victor did not comply.[71] Reiner treated his two star singers considerately and staggered performances of the Wagnerian music dramas so that they could keep engagements elsewhere.[72]

A local music critic admired the balance achieved between voices and orchestra in the performance of *Götterdämmerung,* and the musicians gave Reiner a tremendous ovation. Despite Reiner's generally slow tempi, a critic writing in the *San Francisco Newsletter* thought the singing and conducting represented "the finest performances of Wagner that can be heard in the world today." The critic for the *San Francisco News* added further praise for the performance of *Tristan:* "Fritz Reiner is unquestionably the finest operatic conductor who has ever directed for the San Francisco Opera Company. For he not only secured a memorably fine (and oft times thrillingly magnificent) orchestral performance in amazingly brief rehearsal time, but he also inspired the singers on the stage to do their finest work."[73]

Reiner's brief time in San Francisco was not without turbulence, for he tried (and failed) to discredit Merola by making direct contact with the president of the Opera Board.[74] He also argued with Armando Agnini, the stage director, over the use of a new steam apparatus in *Götterdämmerung.* The device was intended to aid the realistic depiction of Valhalla being burnt at the end of the opera, but Reiner vetoed it because the steam hissed so loudly that it detracted from the music. Agnini told Reiner that there would be a scandal if the steam was omitted, because the audience expected it; to which Reiner replied that there would indeed be a scandal, since he would leave the pit if the device was used.[75]

Despite these tussles, Reiner was invited to conduct with the company in each of the following two seasons. In 1937 he repeated the success of *Tristan,* presiding over three performances, including one in Los Angeles. Melchior and Flagstad again appeared in the title roles, with Meisle as Brangäne, Huehn as Kurwenal, and Ludwig Hofmann and List alternating as King Marke. An "in-house" recording of act 2 has survived for the performance of November 15, 1937, at the Shrine Auditorium in Los Angeles. The sound is oddly balanced, and there is a fair amount of noise from the deterioration of the original acetate discs. Listening to the performance is thus rather difficult.[76] Nonetheless, the gleaming tones of Flagstad's Isolde can be clearly heard, and Reiner's conducting is more volatile than was the case with his live recording of *Tristan* from Covent Garden in June 1936. The performances of *Tristan* were hailed as the artistic triumph of the season.[77] Reiner conducted three performances of *Lohengrin* and a single performance of *Fidelio*. To prepare the performances of *Fidelio*, Reiner spent three evenings with Graf studying set designs and comparing ideas about the action in order to better put into practice his notion of opera as a vivid theatrical experience.[78]

For his farewell to the San Francisco Opera in October and November 1938, Reiner directed two performances of *Don Giovanni*, three of *Die Meistersinger*, including one in Los Angeles, and four of *Elektra*.[79] Melchior and Flagstad did not take part in these productions, but Reiner still had accomplished singers for the major roles. The cast of *Die Meistersinger* included Schorr, Charles Kullman, Kerstin Thorborg, Irene Jessner, and Arnold Gabor as Hans Sachs, Walther, Magdalene, Eva, and Beckmesser, respectively. Ezio Pinza and Elisabeth Rethberg were the Don and Donna Anna in *Don Giovanni*, in which they were joined by Jessner as Elvira, Dino Borgioli as Ottavio, and Salvatore Baccaloni as Leporello. Rose Pauly and Thorborg sang Elektra and Klytemnästra in *Elektra*, with Huehn as Orestes and Jessner as Chrysosthemis. For these performances of *Elektra*, the San Francisco Opera had the largest orchestra it had ever assembled.[80]

Reiner was dissatisfied with the number of rehearsals available to achieve his artistic goals. He did not have one rehearsal for *Don Giovanni* where all singers were brought together, even though this was an ensemble opera par excellence, and the singers had traveled from many different countries to appear in the Bay City. The improvisatory nature of the performance did not please Reiner—he did not, as he put it, like to specialize in miracles—but the orchestra played well, and the public responded to the performance enthusiastically.[81] It is likely that San Francisco had never before witnessed sustained opera conducting of the class provided by Reiner.

To complement his work in San Francisco, Reiner came to England to conduct in two short seasons at Covent Garden in 1936 and 1937. These were his only performances of opera in London. They came about indirectly. Since 1933 Sir Thomas Beecham, the artistic director at Covent Garden, had attempted to increase the number of performances each season and to broaden the repertory at a time of financial stringency. Beecham wanted to invite guests to conduct Wagner but was unable to secure the services of either Hans Knappertsbusch or Bodansky. Knappertsbusch, a prominent Wagnerian conductor at Bayreuth, could not travel to London because of political tension between Nazi Germany and Britain; he had also lost favor with the Nazi government and could not be guaranteed a return to his post in Munich if he traveled out of Germany. Bodansky, the leading Wagnerian conductor at the Met, was not hired because his requested fee was considered exorbitant.[82] Reiner's wife telegraphed her husband that Beecham wanted him to take their place.[83] Reiner agreed to conduct nine operatic performances for a total fee of six hundred pounds during a short spring season, April 27 through June 12, 1936. He returned to conduct the following year for the Coronation Season, April 19 through June 30, 1937.

Reiner participated in seasons at Covent Garden that also saw Beecham and Wilhelm Furtwängler conduct complete *Ring* cycles and John Barbirolli direct Eva Turner's famous portrayal of *Turandot*.[84] He was determined to make his mark on London's operatic scene, particularly in the light of the high-quality competition provided during a winter 1936 visit from his former company, the renowned Dresden State Opera. Orchestral musicians at Covent Garden found Reiner on his mettle; they became used to "a very professional but rather sour-faced conductor, gifted with a prodigious memory."[85] Reiner himself was impressed with the English public's enthusiasm not only for opera but for a wide range of music, as evidenced by the flourishing choral societies he observed there, the attendance at ballet, and the demand for tickets at opera productions.[86]

In his first season at Covent Garden, Reiner conducted *Parsifal* twice, *Tristan und Isolde* four times, and *Der Rosenkavalier* three times. During his second season, he gave three more performances of *Parsifal*, three of *Der fliegende Holländer*, and three of Gluck's *Orphée*. The Gluck opera, performed in French with the aid of the resident ballet company, was the only one of these works that Reiner did not choose to conduct; he only agreed to the assignment after Beecham withdrew from the engagement. Plagued by last-minute replacements among the singers, it was the least successful of his Covent Garden performances.[87] Richard Capell found the treatment of the score characterless: "It was flat and tired—and not even precise."[88] The *Rosenkavalier* performances of 1936 were more successful. The cast, including Rethberg as the Marschallin, Tiana Lemnitz as Octavian, Stella Andreva as Sophie, and List as Baron Ochs, drew appreciative comments from some but not all London music critics. After praising Rethberg's "lovely" portrayal of the Marschallin and List's "highly effective" singing of Ochs, Ernest Newman referred to Reiner's conducting as very fine in places but superficial in others. Walter Legge complained that the orchestra "played somewhat clumsily and with more volume than vitality," thereby obscuring much of the singing.[89]

The highlight of Reiner's performances at Covent Garden was undoubtedly his conducting of the Wagner operas. In 1936 he led an uncut version of *Parsifal*, in accordance with the composer's wishes but with his own approach to the score.[90] A novel feature of these performances was the use of nonsinging flower maidens miming their parts; the singing chorus was hidden behind various pieces of scenery.[91] Critics commented hardly at all on this novelty; they were more concerned with the overall musical virtues displayed. Newman felt that the sacred music drama was, as the composer had wished, played like spun silk and that Reiner "had a complete understanding of the peculiar texture of the orchestral score."[92] He thought it was the best performance of the work given at Covent Garden and equal to the finest he had seen or heard anywhere—quite an accolade from the doyen of Wagnerian critics. Neville Cardus commented that Reiner offered "a devout and thoroughly German reading" that "skilfully attended to the demands of the text and the music."[93] Capell wrote that Reiner touched the heart of *Parsifal*—"the sense of farewell, the falling leaf, the tolling bell, the sweetness of renunciation, the languor of chromaticism, the repose of its resolution."[94] The singers—Torsten Ralf as Parsifal, Frida Leider as Kundry, Ludwig Weber as Gurnemanz, and Herbert Janssen as Amfortas—were all praised. Reiner too was congratulated on his consideration for the singers. Further performances of *Parsifal* under Reiner in the 1937 season were commended for their passion and sensitivity, and Thorborg, the Swedish mezzo-soprano who replaced Leider as Kundry, was accounted a great success. After witnessing Thorborg's performance, Newman stated that she was the greatest Wagnerian actress of the present day.[95]

Reiner's 1936 performances of *Tristan und Isolde* brought together Flagstad and Melchior, who were *hors concours* in the title roles, along with Janssen as Kurwenal, List as King Marke, and Sabine Kalter as Brangäne. Flagstad was making her debut at Covent Garden at the age of forty-one, only a year after her first appearance at the Met. Melchior was already a centurion in terms of his Tristan performances.[96] Melchior and Flagstad's voices were perfectly blended and imbued with heroic beauty and stamina. All the London critics commented on the great beauty and power of Flagstad's voice. They applauded Melchior's magnificent, sympathetic singing and Reiner's intimate feeling for the music. Flagstad's debut in *Tristan* was greeted with eight curtain calls after act 1, nine at the end of act 2, and fifteen at the conclusion of the opera.[97] Reiner's direction of *Holländer* (with Flagstad, Mary Jarred, Max Lorenz, Janssen, and Ludwig Weber among the cast) never allowed the music to drag, and his grip on the music as a whole was admirable with regard to rhythm and tonal climax.[98] Some of these live performances were recorded and have been issued on CD.[99]

Attempts were made to record Reiner's Wagner performances at Covent Garden for commercial release. These ventures were supervised by Fred Gaisberg of the Gramophone Company, but they unfortunately misfired. Gaisberg approached Reiner soon after the 1936 performances of *Tristan* to say that

HMV wanted to engage him with Melchior and Flagstad to record the entire second act of the opera and excerpts from *Die Walküre* in Vienna. The sessions, with the Vienna Philharmonic Orchestra, were scheduled for September 2–6, 1936. Reiner was offered a flat fee of £250 for the project and informed that the Vienna Philharmonic had been chosen because the London Philharmonic Orchestra, which had performed under him at Covent Garden, was unavailable. However, Gaisberg and the Gramophone Company had already recorded Reiner's Covent Garden performances of *Tristan,* although they had not discussed anything about their release (Reiner knew of the recordings and had traveled to the HMV studios to hear one set).[100] Unfortunately, after Reiner had already left London for Austria, Gaisberg and his team found such good sound on the live performances that they decided to abandon the recording sessions in Vienna.[101] In 1937 the Gramophone Company recorded extracts from performances of *Der fliegende Holländer* that they were keen to release.[102]

Although Reiner was interested in the release of experimental recordings for commercial purposes, he wanted to hear the pressings and insisted that all mistakes be corrected by substituting new sections in the recording studio. From the recorded performance of June 11, 1936, he singled out unsatisfactory playing by the stage horns at the beginning of the second act and some wrong notes in the bass clarinet's solo at the culmination of King Marke's monologue.[103] Reiner and his wife were worried about the release of recordings that included the inevitable slips and audience noise of a live performance.[104] Melchior and Flagstad were infuriated by the near-complete *Tristan* recorded for HMV because each thought that the other received favorable microphone placement. Flagstad was so irritated that she apparently threw her test pressings into a Norwegian fjord.[105] She approved of the fragments from *Holländer,* and so did Reiner, but because of the technical imperfections other participants did not.[106]

The whole episode ended abruptly with Gaisberg deciding that it was impractical to re-record the erroneous parts and rejecting the release of experimental records because too many faults would remain to satisfy all the concerned parties. Moreover, it was impossible to substitute studio versions for unsatisfactory live sections because they would not match up in tone.[107] Reiner did not forget this sequence of events. At a dinner at the Savoy in 1937 to entertain the visiting Berlin Philharmonic Orchestra, Reiner, Beecham, and Furtwängler signed the menu cards of various players invited; the bass clarinet of the London Philharmonic was surprised to receive back his card from Reiner with the words, "You owe me two bars."[108]

Besides appearances at Covent Garden, Reiner visited Europe on numerous occasions during the thirties. He conducted operas and orchestral concerts, but his European trips were less frequent and less extensive than in the 1920s, when he had established a popular reputation as a Wagnerian conductor in Rome and Naples and had become friendly with several Italian composers. At the Venice Festival in 1932 Reiner led the La Scala Orchestra in the premiere of Joseph Achron's orchestral suite *Golem,* in which the last movement is a note-by-note reversal of the first movement, symbolizing the creation and destruction of the monster of Jewish legend.[109] In the same year his work in Italy was recognized by the title Cavaliere Ufficiale (Officer of the Order of the King of Italy) on the personal instruction of the monarch, Victor Emmanuel. At the time, no other foreign conductor had ever received such a decoration.[110]

In April 1933 Reiner sailed to Europe to conduct concerts in Turin and Rome, a Liszt Festival concert in Budapest, a performance of *Tannhäuser* at the Budapest Royal Opera, and a concert with the Budapest Symphony Orchestra at the International Music Festival in Vienna.[111] His direction of *Tannhäuser* combined theatrical effects with the finesse associated with first-rate orchestras in the concert hall. Hailed as the musical highlight of the season in Budapest, Reiner's performance showed his mastery of picturesque sound effects ranging from somber, velvety softness to sparkling brilliance. The Liszt Festival concert was also warmly received; Reiner's conducting displayed dynamic tension and concern for the color and form of pieces such as Liszt's *Les Préludes.*[112]

Reiner returned to Europe in February and March 1934, conducting orchestras in Naples, Rome, Florence, Turin, and Venice.[113] In 1937 he led concerts in Florence, Rome, Vienna, and London and made five guest appearances with the Stockholm Philharmonic Orchestra.[114] The Stockholm concerts included a piece he only conducted once during his career—the Swedish composer Oskar Lindberg's symphonic poem *Florez und Blanzeflor,* written in a late romantic style influenced by Rachmaninov and Sibelius.[115] His London engagements included a broadcast program of Wagner excerpts from the *Ring* with the BBC Symphony Orchestra, for which he received seventy-five guineas.[116] In January 1937 Reiner was warmly greeted at the Teatro Adriano in Rome for a concert of music by Bach, Brahms, Casella, and Stravinsky. Many in the audience remembered his performances of *Die Meistersinger* at the Teatro Costanzi fifteen years earlier and appreciated his efforts to perform contemporary Italian music in foreign centers.[117] These were Reiner's last forays into Europe as a guest conductor before the Second World War. His attempts to conduct opera at the Maggio Musicale in Florence in 1937 and 1939 were abandoned after music making there was restricted by the Fascist regime.[118]

Since he was teaching at the Curtis Institute and conducting opera in Philadelphia, it was natural that Reiner should be a regular guest conductor of the Philadelphia Orchestra during the 1930s. He was recommended by Judson, whose patronage was essential: he was then the only American manager of conductors.[119] Reiner also had the support of local music critics, who lamented his absence from the podium at the Academy of Music, and the backing of the orchestral players.[120] Reiner conducted the orchestra nineteen times in the 1931–32 season, four times in 1934–35, and five times in 1935–36.[121] At these concerts he conducted the American premieres of two works—Toch's little overture to the opera *The Fan* and Richard Strauss's potpourri from *Die schweigsame Frau*. He directed an unpublished sequence of seven short wind concertos by Malipiero dedicated to him and modern choral pieces such as Honegger's *King David* and Kodály's *Psalmus Hungaricus*. He also took part in some experimental recordings of Wagner for Bell Laboratories.

Reiner worked with other American symphony orchestras during the thirties. He conducted eleven concerts in four seasons with the Rochester Philharmonic Orchestra at the Eastman Theater.[122] He repeated an experimental performance of the *Eroica* given in Philadelphia, with the inner movements reversed. His Rochester programs included the world premieres of Leó Weiner's Suite for Orchestra (Hungarian Dances) and his Divertimento for String Orchestra, the first American performances of Casella's symphonic fragments from *La donna serpente*, and Sibelius's tone poem *Night Ride and Sunrise*. Reiner requested extensive rehearsals to conduct *Ein Heldenleben* and *Das Lied von der Erde*. After bargaining, he secured five rehearsals for the former, even though the Rochester Civic Music Association used all the overtime money available to pay players for the rest of the season.[123]

In the 1935–36 season Reiner conducted the Detroit Symphony and St. Louis Symphony Orchestras in addition to his guest appearances in Rochester and Philadelphia.[124] He also led the Detroit Symphony in the following season. He hoped to conduct the prestigious Boston Symphony Orchestra, but this proved impossible to arrange because he had no musical or social connections with Boston.[125] While asking Koussevitzky whether he could substitute as conductor for Stravinsky, who had canceled a tour to America, Reiner noted that it would be "a great honor and one of the most exciting experiences of my life to conduct your beautiful orchestra."[126] But arrangements had already been made for someone to replace Stravinsky, and Reiner's plans were frustrated.[127]

During the thirties Reiner resumed conducting summer concerts. In 1931 he made his debut with the Robin Hood Dell Orchestra—the summer guise of the Philadelphia Orchestra—and again conducted the orchestra in the summer of 1934 at the Robin Hood Dell East in Fairmount Park, Philadelphia.[128] In the summer of 1934 he conducted concerts with the San Francisco Symphony Orchestra at Hillsborough's Woodland Theater and the Civic Auditorium in San Francisco.[129] Another new summer venue for Reiner was Ravinia, where he conducted the Chicago Symphony Orchestra for the first time in August 1937. Large, appreciative audiences attended his one-week engagement. Reiner found the orchestra very well disciplined but not equivalent in quality to the New York Philharmonic.[130] After leaving Ravinia, Reiner went to Los Angeles to conduct two concerts at the Hollywood Bowl for the first time since 1925.[131]

Reiner returned to Lewisohn Stadium to conduct thirty-nine concerts by the New York Philharmonic-Symphony Orchestra in three summer seasons (1931, 1937, and 1939).[132] In 1937 his stadium programs included edited concert versions of the entire *Ring* cycle plus a heavily cut version of *Tristan und Isolde*.[133] These productions enabled him to capitalize on his experience conducting parts of the *Ring* at Covent Garden and San Francisco in the mid thirties. The singers for these productions included Paul Althouse as Loge, Siegmund, Siegfried, and Tristan; Florence Easton as Brunnhilde and Isolde; Meisle as Waltraute and Brangäne; and Huehn as Wotan, Gunther, and Kurwenal.[134] Despite the grind, the performances were enjoyable because "the spirit of cooperation on the part of the men was simply marvellous and they played some beautiful and memorable concerts for me."[135]

Nevertheless, Reiner was dissatisfied with his lack of conducting opportunities in New York. In January 1934 he had conducted a contemporary program consisting of Stravinsky's *L'histoire du soldat* and Hindemith's *Kammermusik* nos. 1 and 2 at a concert sponsored by the League of Composers in New York.[136] Further performances in Manhattan, however, were rare. In 1937 he reminded his manager Judson that they had agreed that he "should have the position of first Wagnerian conductor in New York." But despite his performances of Wagner operas at the stadium that summer and favorable critical comment, only one winter engagement had been arranged for him in New York. Reiner hoped that his concerts might serve as a platform for conducting a cycle of Wagner's music dramas at the World's Fair in 1939.[137] This did not eventuate, yet his occasional stadium appearances were still a success with the public. For instance, on August 8, 1939, he conducted Jascha Heifetz in Beethoven's Violin Concerto on an all-Beethoven program, attracting a capacity audience of twenty-two thousand.[138]

Two new departures for Reiner as a guest conductor in the thirties were his appearances on Ford Sunday Evening Hour concerts and his interest in music for films. The former was a regular set of programs, sponsored by the car firm based in Detroit, that was broadcast at a time when people huddled around the radio to listen to concerts in their leisure time. It was one of a series of one-hour broadcasts of popular orchestral music such as the Firestone Hour and the Cadillac Hour that flourished at the time.[139] The Ford Hour was played by the Detroit Symphony Orchestra, broadcast by CBS, and presumably intended to boost car sales. Catering to people who enjoyed classical music but lacked the

patience to sit through long symphonies, it was deliberately based on the standard classical repertoire. The programs, timed to last for fifty-two minutes, included excerpts from classical music, some choruses (including one as a finale),
and a short interval talk; they took "The Prayer" from Humperdinck's *Hänsel
und Gretel* as their theme music. Reiner conducted forty-one of these concerts
in six consecutive years from 1936 onwards. Although brief extracts and lighter
orchestral fare were the order of the day, first-class soloists were hired for the
concerts. Those who appeared with Reiner on the Ford Hour included the violinists Mischa Elman and Heifetz; the pianists Robert Casadesus and Myra
Hess; and various celebrated singers, including Helen Traubel, Lily Pons, Marian Anderson, Ezio Pinza, Jussi Bjoerling, Richard Crooks, and Rethberg, Melchior, and Flagstad.[140]

Reiner's interest in film stemmed from a proposal that he serve as general
music director for Music Guild Productions, incorporated in 1934 for the purpose of producing musical pictures. Reiner was to conduct excerpts from
Gounod's *Faust* for a color film interspersed with episodes from Marlowe's
Doctor Faustus, in the hope that this initial production would bring good music
to the masses and inspire composers to write especially for the new medium of
talking pictures. But though Reiner's appetite was whetted, and he laid down
terms, the venture came to nothing.[141] His attempts to conduct *Scheherazade*
and a shortened version of *Parsifal* as accompaniments to black-and-white films
(to be screened at Radio City Music Hall, New York) also collapsed.[142]

Reiner's contact with Stokowski no doubt stimulated his interest in music
in films, and perhaps there was an element of jealousy here. At any rate, by
1938 Reiner had seen and enjoyed Walt Disney's *Snow White* and wondered
whether Disney could scoop the entire film industry by promoting the first production of a full-length opera in the movies. Reiner suggested *Hänsel und Gretel,* with himself as conductor, and wanted the idea kept quiet so that no one
could steal it. Humperdinck's opera seemed an ideal vehicle for Disney to bring
fantastic characters to life, and Reiner knew the opera well.[143] Nothing came
of this proposal, and shortly afterwards Stokowski stole the limelight with his
appearance conducting the Philadelphia Orchestra in Disney's *Fantasia.* Reiner wanted to participate in MGM's proposed film on the life of Johann
Strauss and a Warner Brothers projected picture on Tchaikovsky, called *Pathétique,* but once again the plans did not bear fruit.[144]

Though the round of guest conducting proved unsatisfactory, it was necessary for so many years because of Reiner's personal situation. His career suffered in the 1930s because of his second divorce. Berta Gerster-Gardini had
enough friends in musical circles to sabotage conducting opportunities for her
ex-husband. As a result, Reiner was not offered the same number of guest concerts in the United States that he had undertaken a few years earlier. It was not

until the mid 1930s, when he went to Covent Garden, that barriers established by Berta were broken down.[145] Gershwin thought Reiner had made a bigger name for himself through guest conducting than through becoming music director of an orchestra—it enabled him to be seen and heard at many different venues.[146] Yet guest conducting did not really suit Reiner; he preferred to build up orchestras and train musicians, as he had done in Cincinnati in the 1920s.

Carlotta Reiner realized that her husband needed such a position if he were to be satisfied and happy. Early in the 1930s she hoped he would be appointed chief conductor of the St. Louis Symphony Orchestra, but the position went instead to the suave Vladimir Golschmann.[147] A friend of Reiner's suggested that he transfer his conducting career to London but realized this would be difficult for a conductor who had not kept his memory green in a city where concert life was dominated by Beecham, Sir Adrian Boult, and Sir Hamilton Harty like a closed corporation.[148] Reiner's enquiries about a position as director at the Royal Hungarian Opera came to nothing because he was not prepared to agree in advance to accept an invitation.[149]

By 1936 Reiner felt despondent about his situation. Carlotta thought his lack of a major appointment owed much to the intrigues and jealousies of the musical profession. Hoping that the Chicago Symphony Orchestra might offer him some guest appearances in 1937, she noted that Frederick Stock was so well established and esteemed in the Windy City that he could afford to be generous to a colleague. A request led to a brief summer engagement at Ravinia. But Reiner still wanted to conduct an orchestra permanently rather than continue guest conducting ad infinitum, and his wife was solicitous on his behalf, writing often to people in the musical world who she thought could further her husband's career.[150]

Reiner hoped that the success of his summer concerts with the San Francisco Symphony Orchestra in 1933 would help him gain a permanent position in the Bay City, but this did not occur because the Russian conductor Issay Dobrowen still had two years of his contract to run with that orchestra.[151] In 1936 Reiner was frustrated when the board of the Detroit Symphony Orchestra took a long time to decide who should succeed the late Ossip Gabrilowitsch as music director. They eventually ignored Reiner's candidature and appointed Franco Ghione instead.[152] In the same year Judson privately indicated that the board of the New York Philharmonic-Symphony, having tried and failed to appoint Furtwängler as successor to Toscanini on account of Jewish feeling against him, considered that Reiner was "not popular from the public standpoint."[153] Judson nevertheless had great faith in Reiner's conducting ability and pointed out, in Reiner's favor, that he was half Jewish. Reiner's candidacy was not pursued by the board. By the late 1930s he stood little chance of becoming head of a leading symphony orchestra in America. Pierre Monteux and Barbirolli had begun periods in charge of the San Francisco Symphony and New York Philharmonic-Symphony Orchestras, respectively, in 1936; Koussevitzky still reigned supreme in Boston; and Eugene Ormandy had begun his long tenure as music director of the Philadelphia Orchestra. The latter appointment rankled most of all. Reiner hoped to succeed Stokowski and was entitled to think that his efforts with the Philadelphia Orchestra in opera, concerts, and summer programs had given him better credentials than the less-experienced Ormandy. But Judson wanted to promote Ormandy in Philadelphia, having already helped to expand his career from work as a violinist at the Capitol Theater, New York, to guest conducting and the leadership of the Minneapolis Symphony Orchestra.[154] By the midthirties, Stokowski was sufficiently at odds with the orchestra's board that any recommendation from him carried a black spot.[155] The management of the Philadelphia Orchestra also promoted Ormandy; they wanted him rather than Reiner to conduct a recording of the orchestra with Melchior as soloist (though Melchior requested Reiner as the conductor).[156] The opportunity for Reiner to begin his second stint as music director of an American orchestra came, ironically, not from eastern Pennsylvania but from the western part of the state—the beleaguered Pittsburgh Symphony Orchestra.

6. PITTSBURGH

When Reiner became music director of the Pittsburgh Symphony Orchestra, he came to one of the grimiest industrial centers in the United States—a city full of smoke and steel, dominated by river and rail traffic, regular floods, and the smell and pollution of factories. Ash and soot were so prevalent that daylight street lighting was needed, and sewage was regularly dumped in rivers. Reiner also arrived in Pittsburgh at a crucial point in the orchestra's reorganization. An orchestral society in the city dated back to 1873, but the Pittsburgh Orchestra, as it was first called, was not formed until 1895. Over the next forty years it had a checkered history. It flourished briefly at the turn of the century under conductors such as Victor Herbert and Emil Paur but was disbanded in 1910 because of financial problems. Reorganized in 1926 as the Pittsburgh Symphony Orchestra, it struggled to achieve national recognition. In 1937, after seven years' direction by an affable but musically limited local conductor, Antonio Modarelli, the orchestra's board decided to change players and appoint a conductor of international standing who would improve artistic standards. Despite the Great Depression, some auspicious financial news encouraged this plan. In 1936 and 1937 the Pittsburgh Plate Glass Company sponsored the orchestra's nationally broadcast radio concerts. A year later the Buhl Foundation donated fifty thousand dollars to the orchestra's maintenance fund and an equivalent sum to establish a program of school concerts. By 1937, $240,000 had been raised to fund the orchestra and a new chief conductor.[1]

Otto Klemperer, who conducted frequently in the American provinces in the thirties, was asked to reorganize the orchestra. In the 1937–38 season he started to rebuild the ensemble by holding auditions, reshuffling old personnel, and presenting successful performances. Klemperer was offered the permanent job as music director but turned it down, preferring to remain as conductor of the Los Angeles Philharmonic Orchestra; his reasons for staying there are puzzling, because his contract was due to expire and he disliked southern California. Reiner had guest conducted the Pittsburgh Symphony in spring 1938. The players regarded him as a "musician's musician," and he was a popular and critical success.[2] After Klemperer decided to leave, the orchestral board offered Reiner the post of music director, which he accepted. His initial annual salary was twenty-five thousand dollars, but it was scheduled to rise to thirty thousand by the 1940–41 season.[3]

This was an important appointment for Reiner after seven years without a music directorship. He now had the opportunity once again to be an orchestral builder, lead his own players, choose his own repertoire, and hire the best soloists.[4] Ralph Lewando of the *Pittsburgh Press* praised the selection of Reiner, "world famous as a conductor of important symphony orchestras and opera organizations, a musician of unquestioned ability and a man of uncompromising adherence to high ideals."[5] Many hoped that Reiner would restore cultural prestige to the city. His achievements in Pittsburgh, as we shall see, were notable.

The Pittsburgh Symphony Orchestra had several deficiencies when Reiner arrived in the Steel City. It played for twenty weeks during the autumn and winter, which was one of the shortest concert seasons in the United States. Musicians in the Pittsburgh Symphony augmented their work by freelance engagements—for instance, by padding out the orchestra of the Ballet Russes de Monte Carlo on their annual visits.[6] The situation did not change until 1945–46, when the orchestra played for twenty-eight weeks, putting it on an equal footing with six other American cities with concert seasons of similar length.[7] Pittsburgh also lacked an adequate auditorium. Most concerts took place at the Syria Mosque, a garish building erected in 1916 by the Shriners that recently was demolished. This was the home of the orchestra for forty-five years until the splendid Heinz Hall was opened in the downtown area of the city in 1971. The Syria Mosque was located in the Schenley District in Oakland, the cultural heart of the city, near the University of Pittsburgh and the Carnegie Institute of Technology. Despite having seating capacity for 3,370 people, which it rarely filled, it had poor acoustics: its oval-shaped auditorium was at least twice as wide as it was deep, with no proper focus of sound—a particular problem when the orchestra was recorded.[8] Apart from the Mosque, repeat programs were sometimes given in the nearby Carnegie Music Hall. Reiner hoped that this smaller concert venue could be redesigned as a permanent home for the orchestra, but the estimated cost of $950,000 was far too prohibitive.[9]

To help with running the orchestra, Reiner had the assistance of Edward Specter, a lawyer by profession and a trumpet player in the local musical union. Specter had become manager of the orchestra in the mid-1920s and was devoted to its welfare. He had played a leading role in the search for a music director that led to Reiner's appointment.[10] Reiner hired his former Cincinnati colleague Vladimir Bakaleinikoff as assistant conductor and first viola. He was an avuncular, genial man who took charge of popular concerts as well as being on standby when Reiner was indisposed. A marvelous humorist and after-dinner speaker, Bakaleinikoff was much loved by the orchestra. From the 1945–46 season, he relinquished his position as first viola and concentrated entirely on his conducting duties.[11]

Specter and Bakaleinikoff poured a lot of energy into the orchestra, which was invaluable when the Reiners were out of town, a frequent occurrence. Fritz and Carlotta Reiner mainly spent the Pittsburgh concert season in a suite at the Schenley Hotel, though at the beginning and end of their stay in the city they lived in houses (at 1298 Denison Avenue and later at 6953 Edgerton Avenue). They wanted to promote the orchestra as a cultural symbol of the city but preferred to spend as much time as possible—including the entire summer vacation—at Rambleside.[12] Reiner was criticized in Pittsburgh when, during the 1944–45 season, he extended his authorized four-week winter vacation to conduct another orchestra.[13] This action did not endear him to the orchestra's sponsors, for in those days, unlike now, music directors were expected to reside in or near the city where they held full-time appointments. The same problem recurred when Reiner became music director of the Chicago Symphony Orchestra.

Reiner had clear artistic policies for the Pittsburgh Symphony Orchestra. He intended to give Pittsburgh a foremost position on the musical map by creating a great orchestra. The city would then be on the same footing musically as it was industrially. He wanted a longer concert season, a new venue built for staging operas, and a high school devoted to musical education. He criticized the inadequacy of the Syria Mosque as a concert venue and hoped that a new memorial hall could be built at the Point, in the downtown district of the city.[14] Above all, he wanted the best artistic standards for the orchestra. This meant having the wherewithal to hire and fire players as he saw fit.[15] But a fine orchestra could not be created overnight. The utmost work and dedication was needed, with musicians playing together for several years to achieve "that perfect blending which is the essence of artistic endeavor."[16]

Reiner's contract included a clause that gave him the final word on the hiring and repertoire of guest soloists. As far as possible, he treated audiences to the best soloists in the world. Among the figures who appeared with him in Pittsburgh were some of the most celebrated instrumentalists and singers of the twentieth century: violinists such as Yehudi Menuhin, Fritz Kreisler, Jascha Heifetz, and Joseph Szigeti; cellists such as Gregor Piatigorsky and Emanuel

Feuermann; pianists of the caliber of Sergei Rachmaninov, Artur Rubinstein, Vladimir Horowitz, Josef Hofmann, Rudolf Serkin, Artur Schnabel, William Kapell, Rudolf Firkusny, and Earl Wild; and singers such as Lauritz Melchior, Kirsten Flagstad, Elisabeth Schumann, Rose Bampton, Jennie Tourel, Helen Traubel, and Astrid Varnay.[17]

Unfortunately, financial constraints made it difficult to invite many guest conductors to Pittsburgh: in Reiner's first six years there, the only guest leaders were composers conducting their own works (such as Leonard Bernstein and Stravinsky); Edwin McArthur, the disciple of Kirsten Flagstad; and the local protégé Lorin Maazel, who made his conducting debut with the orchestra at the age of twelve (and who later became music director of the orchestra from 1988 until 1996). Inviting composers to conduct their own works continued as a policy. In 1945 and 1946 the orchestra's guest conductors included Lukas Foss, Morton Gould, Zoltan Kodály, Virgil Thomson, and Carlos Chávez. Towards the end of his stay in Pittsburgh, Reiner introduced an apprentice system that gave young American conductors the opportunity to direct the orchestra.[18] During the 1947–48 season, this scheme enabled Walter Hendl, Ezra Rachlin, Henry Mazer, Alvin Etler, and James Guthrie to test their mettle on the podium. Reiner hoped to invite Klemperer as guest leader, but he dropped the idea: Klemperer had been led on and off the stage while appearing at concerts in Mexico City, and his erratic, unstable behavior as a manic depressive might have proven an embarrassment.[19]

Musicians in the Pittsburgh Symphony Orchestra found Reiner always totally prepared for rehearsals and concerts. He absorbed all the notes in a score in advance of performing it and always made up his mind how to conduct passages before meeting the players. He knew how to organize and fit everything together beautifully without too much pressure.[20] With new scores, he was especially concerned that everything be mastered. He had sufficient knowledge of instrumentation to determine whether a composer had made a technical error. When conducting a rehearsal of Lukas Foss's First Symphony, for instance, he was surprised by a piccolo player who articulated a low D-flat written in the score. Reiner stopped the orchestra to ask the player how he had played the note, since he knew that the piccolo's lower register normally extended down only to a low D-natural beneath the treble stave.[21] This knowledge greatly impressed the player and the orchestra. The incident revealed Reiner's understanding of technical problems in new scores while demonstrating that he could not be hoodwinked.

Composers who had new works performed in Pittsburgh during the 1940s appreciated Reiner's ability to master their scores quickly. Foss has remarked that Reiner knew every note of his First Symphony, "made it sound better than the orchestration deserved," and gave "a very, very fine performance" of the piece in concerts on February 9 and 11, 1945.[22] Foss witnessed gratefully the way in which Reiner whipped his symphony into shape from the first rehearsal through to the performance.[23] Randall Thompson came to Pittsburgh to hear his Second Symphony performed, attended rehearsals, and was pleased at Reiner's cooperation over difficulties in the score.[24] Gardner Read was also full of praise for Reiner's conducting. Commissioned to write a *Pennsylvaniana* Suite, based on three folksongs, Read attended the first performances on November 21 and 23, 1947. He was apprehensive about the reception he would receive. "Approaching this first personal encounter with the formidable maestro," he has written, "I was frankly uncomfortable. He had accepted and programmed my demanding sixteen-minute work, but what sort of human being would he be, face to face? Would he be gracious and easy to talk with, or testy and fault-finding? Would he be offended if some crucial matter of tempo or balance needed his co-operative attention? I needn't have worried; Reiner was kindness and affability personified, and his performances were everything I could have hoped. With his characteristic economy of movement, with that miniscule baton, he commanded exactly what the Read work wanted."[25]

Reiner's conducting ability, of course, was not merely limited to technical expertise. Nor were his relations with musicians all sweetness and light. "The crucible of Reiner's art contained elements of a unique discipline," according to Sebastian Caratelli, the principal flautist with the Pittsburgh Symphony at the time, for "here one saw the fusion of intellectual logic and delicate sensuousness, clarity of musical structure and soaring poetic lyricism, while a distinctive economy of gestures unfolded a musical fabric that was bathed in the exquisite light of an endless dynamic gradation. Such were Reiner's gifts. True, one was never in danger of being seared by the intensity of an emotional fire, but the sparkling brilliance of a diamond has a cold beauty that is not devoid of attraction."[26]

The exacting standards that Reiner expected led to a tense atmosphere during rehearsals. He demanded uncompromisingly from his players the same unfailing knowledge, skill, and application he brought to bear on his own conducting. Anyone guilty of sloppy playing—poor phrasing, cracked notes, wrong entries—had to contend with his sharp tongue. Reiner's penchant for brief, acidulous comments put errant musicians in their place: there was none of the genial bonhomie of a Beecham, the warmth of a Koussevitzky, or even the tantrums of a Toscanini. "The score calls for a C-natural," Reiner would say in rehearsal, "but what you have given me is a thud!"[27] This would embarrass the player, and an eerie silence would descend on the orchestra.

Another favorite Reiner remark was to stop the orchestra when something had gone wrong and state: "You either have it or you haven't got it," and then jab his finger toward the miscreant, adding, "and you haven't got it."[28] Pungent criticism was very much a part of Reiner's public persona. To a percussionist who persistently hit a wrong note during a rehearsal of Gershwin's Piano Concerto, Reiner stopped the orchestra and said, "How much will it cost for you to play a D-flat instead of a D-natural?" The percussionist remonstrated, saying that he had no room to perform, since he had to play bells, a xylophone, the cymbals, and a triangle. After this explanation Reiner queried, "Are you through?" "Yes," came the reply. Reiner then wiped his half-moon glasses wearily and capped the dialogue: "Well, how much room do you need for a D-flat?"[29] Sometimes, poor playing had more serious consequences. When rehearsing a difficult trumpet part in Kabalevsky's *Colas Breugnon* Overture, Reiner increased the tempo, but the second and third trumpets could not play the passage correctly. He ordered them out of the orchestra with the words, "I have no need for you."[30] They did not return.

The orchestra under Reiner's direction was no place for the thin-skinned. Some players referred to him as a "musical surgeon" because of his unerring ability to spot weak points in rehearsal or performance. Adopting a dictatorial approach on the podium, where the gulf between himself and his players was recognized and formality maintained, Reiner was sometimes deliberately cruel, staring at players he thought should retire until they nearly blanched or ignoring them altogether when he needed to instill confidence with cues.[31] When a trumpeter missed a crucial note during a rehearsal of Robert Russell Bennett's suite from Gershwin's *Porgy and Bess,* Reiner walked towards the player, pointed his baton at him, and said emphatically, "You cannot miss that note!"[32] If a player did not immediately grasp instructions during a rehearsal, Reiner occasionally dropped a warning about the renewal of contracts for next season.[33] In Reiner's orchestra there was no relaxation; he forbade principal players to delegate work to junior colleagues when they felt exhausted. Reiner's intimidating sarcasm and musical knowledge was enough to quiet musicians, who dared not challenge him unless they wanted a quick response that would cut them down to size.[34]

The Pittsburgh Symphony Orchestra had many changes of personnel during the Reiner era. Shortly after being appointed music director, Reiner auditioned around 150 musicians.[35] Most people hired were young professional musicians enthusiastic to embark on an orchestral career.[36] There were several changes of concertmaster, but Reiner always managed to attract experienced fiddle players. His concertmasters in Pittsburgh included Hugo Kolberg, the former leader of the Berlin Philharmonic; Henri Temianka, who had played with Reiner when he guest conducted in Stockholm; Michael Rosenker, concertmaster at the Met for two years; and Samuel Thaviu, who had led the Baltimore Symphony Orchestra. In the 1943–44 season his assistant concertmaster was Louis Krasner, who had premiered the Berg Violin Concerto (which he recorded) and who was a well-known soloist.[37] Reiner recruited many female players; by 1944 he had more women musicians than in any other major American symphony orchestra.[38] He pruned inadequate and unsuitable musicians, replacing over 90 percent of the players during his first three years in Pittsburgh. It soon became common for almost half of the personnel to change annually. By the end of the 1943–44 season, only two members of the orchestra when he took over had retained their positions. At the start of the 1944–45 season, half of the orchestra consisted of new players, including seven principals.[39] This turnover meant that Reiner had to revive the Pittsburgh Symphony Orchestra not once but several times during his decade in western Pennsylvania.

The turnover was partly the result of losing players to the draft after America entered the Second World War and partly the result of Reiner's desire to create a first-class orchestra.[40] He believed that such a massacre was necessary to weed out incompetent players. Because he appointed and sacked whom he pleased, Reiner built an orchestra based on the judgment of his ears rather than on the decisions of a committee. The changes did not occur without dissent. After Reiner fired forty-one musicians in an orchestra of eighty, a union protest led to an adjudicator from the American Federation of Musicians being appointed to examine the case. The adjudicator was friendly with Reiner and supported him in all except two cases. This action shook up Reiner; thereafter, if he wanted to get rid of incompetent players, he pressurized them to leave the orchestra through fright.[41]

Reiner came around to the view that he could not make the orchestra a permanent success with a turnover rate of a half or a third per season. He was prepared to stay in Pittsburgh and build a permanent first-class orchestra if he could have a season long enough to realize that goal; failing that, he would conduct elsewhere.[42] Reiner tapped gifted young players from his work at the Curtis Institute and had informal connections with musicians graduating from Juilliard.[43] Players joining the orchestra might reasonably have been put off by Reiner's exigencies, for, with a short season and no summer concerts to earn extra money, an average musician could not draw a particularly good salary. But players flocked to Pittsburgh, thinking that if they spent one or two seasons under Reiner's guidance they could pursue a professional career in any orchestra.[44] Reiner's attachment to his players was somewhat different. Never sentimental about musicians, Reiner refused to reappoint four former principal players at the end of World War II, stating that their war service might have made them rusty musicians.[45]

Players who withstood the withering assaults on their musical capabilities realized that there was method in Reiner's behavior. More than anything, he wanted to achieve perfection in his music making. To realize that goal he acted as a drill master and demanded absolute subservience to his authority. This is

not so common among conductors nowadays and would undoubtedly cause
difficulties with the musical unions. But it was the rule rather than the exception in Reiner's heyday, as players who performed for Toscanini, Szell, Stokowski, and Rodzinski could attest. Reiner's perfectionism justified his severity.[46] His disdain was not always wholesome, but such uncompromising artistic
idealism created the atmosphere of an "orchestra being channelled toward an
awareness of what dwelt beyond the printed notes. And while it is true that the
asperity of his strictures had a paralyzing effect on many an orchestra member,
it is equally true that his rigorous discipline accounted for the musical reorien-
tation of many others. For once we were disabused of the notion that our instrumental proficiencies were at the center of the musical universe, the way was
opened for the expansion of our awakened aural faculties."[47]

Reiner liked plenty of rehearsal time, especially for difficult works. He
scheduled Bartók's Concerto for Orchestra and excerpts from *Salome* in the
1945–46 season and insisted on numerous rehearsals, including work with individual sections of the orchestra.[48] Usually, however, his energy was directed
to the entire orchestra; he did not often hold sectional rehearsals, for he expected players to know their parts thoroughly before he mounted the podium.
He rehearsed the strings and the winds alone if a difficult modern score needed
to be mastered, but such occasions were infrequent. Reiner allowed principal
players to take responsibility for their own section. This was particularly the
case with the strings. He himself was not a string player and was happy to
allow the concertmaster and other principal string players to sort out bowing.
Unlike some conductors, he never contradicted principals but still complained
forthrightly if one member of a section played incorrectly. He was also unusual
among conductors in his knowledge of percussion. A player of percussion in
his student days, he thoroughly understood the color, rhythm, and tempo devices characteristic of percussion instruments.[49]

Reiner studied hard and liked nothing better than a musical challenge. All
his resources came to the fore when conducting difficult works—a new score,
a complex set of instrumental parts, a problem in the balance of soloists, chorus, and orchestra.[50] Players joked that Reiner was not happy until he had a
score that looked like fourteen laundry cardboards that produced a draught
when he turned pages and led everyone in the orchestra to catch a cold. For
long stretches of the music Reiner was almost immobile. But then complexities emerged, his eyes lit up, and he conducted some players with his right arm,
others with the left, gave cues with his eyes, and, in all, acted like a little general.[51] His greatest talent was for the clearest possible baton technique, despite
a very small beat. His lucidity with the stick when giving the beat, subdividing it, or indicating cues was unmatched and compelled musicians to concen-

trate on his minimalist gestures on the podium. Excessive words were unnecessary at rehearsal.[52]

In his autobiography, the pianist and wit Oscar Levant, who played several times with the Pittsburgh Symphony in the forties, summarized Reiner's skill memorably. "There are few conductors who impress an orchestra (also composers) at first contact as strongly as does Fritz Reiner, whose knowledge of everything pertaining to the mechanical performance of music is, briefly, unparalleled. He has evolved a personal sign language which leads an orchestra through the most complex scores of Strauss or Stravinsky with the ease and sureness of a tightrope walker who performs a backward somersault blindfolded. Whenever the complexity of the scoring is a sufficient challenge to his skill Reiner will subdivide beats, flash successive cues to remote sections of the orchestra with either hand and meanwhile indicate the pianissimo, in which he takes such great delight, by a bodily movement that totals by a kind of physical mathematics to the exact effect on the printed page." Levant also commented on Reiner's ability to terrorize those of inferior musical ability. "A mere series of facial expressions," he wrote, "can shade his degrees of contempt for a nervous oboist or a fright-palsied violinist as artfully as he fades an orchestra from mezzo piano to pianissimo. His passion for the least audible of possible sounds has created among violinists a new form of occupational ailment known as Reiner-paralysis. When he is sufficiently challenged by an operatic score, such as *Der Rosenkavalier,* or by the collaboration with a fine soloist, to marshal all his virtuosity, he can achieve fabulous results. The reaction he induces from orchestras he has conducted runs the full gamut of all emotions but deep affection."[53]

Musicians often claimed that Reiner's minibeat was too small to decipher. When they mentioned this to Reiner, he usually made the beat even smaller until it nearly disappeared. This drove them to concentrate harder—a deliberate tactic, since Reiner was convinced that forcing players to watch his beat engendered a superior performance.[54] But its singularity attracted attention. In a well-known incident during the 1944–45 season, a young double bass player pulled out a telescope during a rehearsal and focused it on the podium. Such cheekiness was unheard of in any orchestra conducted by Reiner. When asked what he was doing, the player commented that he was looking for the beat. (An apocryphal ending to the incident maintains that Reiner scribbled something on a piece of paper, held it up, and asked the player if he could see it. When he replied that he could not, Reiner read out the words on the paper: "you're fired.")[55] A few months later, while the orchestra was on tour, Reiner and his wife were waiting for a train when, at the end of the station platform, they spotted the same double bass player with his telescope. When Reiner enquired once again what he was doing, the same reply came back: "I'm still looking for the beat."[56] The young player did not last long in the orchestra.

Apparently he had become upset with Reiner for not releasing him from his contract in Pittsburgh after he was offered better-paid work by CBS.[57]

Reiner created a fine orchestra quickly in Pittsburgh. In 1939 the veteran conductor Walter Damrosch, after fulfilling a guest engagement with the orchestra, noted that it was "a remarkable proof" of Reiner's "artistic convictions and technical skill that in so short a time" he had "accomplished this miracle."[58] A local music critic concurred, stating that after only two weeks of rehearsal, the orchestra, with thirty-two new faces, was playing with "uniformity truly amazing." This was a recurrent phenomenon. At the beginning of the 1943–44 season, Reiner within one week "had fused and molded this heterogeneous group into a cohesive, unified orchestral body that followed his beat with almost mid-season certainty and, at certain portions of the evening, gave inspired response."[59] By 1941, after three seasons under Reiner, the Pittsburgh Symphony was considered one of the outstanding orchestras in the United States; and it is no accident that it began to make records regularly for Columbia in that year.[60]

The Pittsburgh Symphony was not on a par with the big four American orchestras—in Boston, Philadelphia, New York, and Chicago—partly because the first-desk musicians were markedly better than rank-and-file players, and thus the ensemble was not always supported by the necessary intensity and volume of sound. Even so, Reiner's ability to galvanize players into a coherent, polished ensemble in so short a time was remarkable. It was made possible by the alertness, precision, and high musical standards that he instilled in them.[61] "His conducting is concise," a music critic wrote in the *Toledo Times,* and there are "no uncertainties of tempi, no inexact phrasing, no loose ends. Yet with all this technical impeccability, he never loses sight of that core of the music which is above and beyond all technical considerations."[62]

Reiner regarded program making as one of his major obligations. He spent much time during summer vacations planning the next season's concerts. His programs in Pittsburgh included a solid core of baroque, classical, and romantic music. He frequently played modern arrangements of pieces by J. S. Bach, including choral preludes, organ fugues, and excerpts from violin partitas and *The Well-Tempered Clavier.* He conducted two of the orchestral suites (nos. 2 and 3, the latter in an arrangement by Max Reger), and the third and fifth Brandenburg Concertos. Reiner played the pianist's part in the latter—the only occasion during his Pittsburgh years that he assumed a soloist's role. He was a skilled keyboard player, but the orchestra nevertheless had to allow for some technical blemishes.[63]

The standard symphonic repertoire was well represented. Reiner performed seven Mozart symphonies in Pittsburgh (nos. 29, 35, 36, and 38–41), two Schubert symphonies (nos. 8 and 9), five Haydn symphonies (nos. 88, 94, 95, 97, 100, 102, and 104), and all four Schumann symphonies (with no. 2

presented in an orchestral revision by Reiner). During his first season in Pittsburgh, Reiner conducted all the Beethoven symphonies; and in his decade in the Steel City he performed all these works at least twice. He also conducted all of Brahms's symphonies at least three times. Not all programs consisted of serious fare, for Reiner often conducted Rossini overtures and was fond of closing concerts with a Johann Strauss waltz.

The size of the Pittsburgh Symphony Orchestra set constraints to the repertoire performed. Reiner only conducted one Bruckner symphony (no. 4). He abandoned attempts to schedule the same composer's Seventh Symphony after management complained about the cost of the extra players needed. And though Reiner played the second movement from Mahler's *Resurrection* Symphony and the "Nachtmusik II" from the Seventh Symphony, the only complete Mahler works he conducted were the Fourth Symphony and *Das Lied von der Erde*. He scheduled virtually all the major tone poems by Richard Strauss. For some years he could not perform *Ein Heldenleben* because the orchestra lacked enough French horns and trumpets, but in 1947 he gave the Pittsburgh premiere of the piece, assembling 102 players, the largest orchestra ever witnessed in the city (the usual size being ninety).[64] Reiner was so keen to make a good impression with this work that he drilled the orchestra for two weeks in rehearsal and worked with the strings, woodwinds, and brass separately.[65] He did not perform Stravinsky's *Le Sacre du printemps*—a work he never conducted—because too large an orchestra was needed.[66]

Sheer cost precluded Reiner from conducting concert versions of operas in Pittsburgh. He thought the city was "opera-minded" and hoped to present Richard Strauss's *Ariadne auf Naxos* to add luster to the regular concert season.[67] This did not happen; presumably the cost of scenery, singers, and a stage director was too great. Nevertheless, aware of the dearth of opera in the Steel City, he presented the second half of a concert on October 25 and 26, 1941, in which soloists sang excerpts from *Der Rosenkavalier*.[68] On February 23 and 25, 1940, the Pittsburgh Symphony presented an entire act from an opera in concert form—act 1 of Wagner's *Die Walküre*.[69] On February 27 and 29, 1948, Reiner conducted, again with soloists, the same act of *Die Walküre* and excerpts from act 3 of *Götterdämmerung*. For these performances he augmented the orchestra with ten extra musicians, making one hundred players altogether, and hired extra instruments (four Wagner tubas and a bass trumpet) from the Curtis Institute.[70] In general, "bleeding chunks" from Wagnerian music dramas, one of Reiner's specialities, were often performed during his decade in Pittsburgh.

Oscar Levant observed that, already by the 1939–40 season, Reiner's programs were the most modern in the country.[71] In 1947, a survey of major American symphony orchestras ranked Pittsburgh first in performing European and

American contemporary music. During Reiner's stay in Pittsburgh, over half the works he conducted were by twentieth-century composers.[72] He actively solicited information on interesting new scores. He had read about Ernest Bloch's opera *Macbeth* in 1938 and wanted to acquire the score to see whether he could schedule a stage performance of the work.[73] This never materialized. He was more successful in arranging to perform a piece by Schoenberg in the 1944–45 season. Reiner wrote the composer to enquire whether he could conduct either a reduced version of his Five Orchestral Pieces, which he considered a landmark in contemporary music, or the *Theme and Variations* Op. 43b for orchestra.[74] Schoenberg, pleased that one of his works was to be given in Pittsburgh, noted that this would be one of the first competent performances he could expect at that time.[75] Reiner decided to perform the *Theme and Variations* and wrote to the composer with critical comments about a broadcast of the piece conducted by Koussevitzky. Reiner thought the latter's performance skimmed the surface and did not reach the core; it lacked rhythmic variety and had insufficient tempo contrasts for individual variations.[76] Schoenberg agreed with these criticisms, noting that Koussevitzky had disregarded metronome markings in the score and had failed to differentiate the character of each variation.[77]

Reiner rejected some modern scores placed before him. Schoenberg tried to persuade him to conduct the orchestral version of his *Kammersymphonie* no. 1, his suite for string orchestra, and his orchestration of the Brahms Piano Quartet in G Minor, but to no avail.[78] Sometimes Reiner informed a composer that he could not perform a score because his allocation of new works was full for a particular season.[79] He also turned down new compositions because he lacked sympathy with the music. He was no respecter of persons, rejecting Howard Hanson's Fourth Symphony after careful examination even though he was friendly with the composer.[80] He found Roy Harris's orchestral music unsympathetic and would not perform it. He turned down a possible performance of George Antheil's Fourth Symphony.[81] He scheduled Prokofiev's *Semyon Kotko* suite but dropped it from the program before the concert because he thought it insufficiently important to receive an American premiere.[82] In his first season in Pittsburgh, Reiner refused to conduct a composition dedicated to him, returning a symphony to Charles Wakefield Cadman, the leading Pittsburgh composer of the day, because he did not think the work merited a performance.[83] Reiner's manager Judson regretted this decision; to ignore a work by a leading local composer was to step on many people's toes.[84] But Reiner did not relent. He was not prejudiced against Cadman's music in general, since he had conducted the composer's *American* suite for strings in Pittsburgh in 1938; the new piece simply seemed less worthy of performance.

Because he wanted to schedule interesting new repertoire, Reiner conducted twenty world premieres in Pittsburgh, all but two of them by American composers; nine American first performances; and no fewer than 137 Pittsburgh premieres. The presentation of new American compositions reflected Reiner's desire to perform works of "high artistic merit" that suited the spirit of the times.[85] Among the world premieres under Reiner's direction were Wallingford Riegger's *New Dance;* Norman Dello Joio's Concert Music for Orchestra and *Three Symphonic Dances* (later renamed *Variations, Chaconne, and Finale*); William Schuman's *Prayer—1943* (later changed to *Prayer in Time of War*) and *Side Show* (later renamed *Circus* Overture); Morton Gould's *Foster Gallery* and First Symphony; Lukas Foss's Symphony; Gardner Read's *Pennsylvaniana* Suite; Paul Creston's *Threnody;* and Milhaud's Concerto for Two Pianos. Reiner very much wanted to conduct the latter, which he considered "a very brilliant piece of writing." He requested a copy of the score from the composer with the orchestral parts checked and corrected.[86] Records of his performance of the piece were sent to Milhaud, who praised the orchestral balance, the soloists, and, most of all, Reiner's direction.[87] Reiner hoped to give the concert premiere of the 1945 version of Stravinsky's *Firebird* Suite, but the composer refused. Nevertheless, Stravinsky agreed that Reiner could conduct the American premiere of his String Concerto in D; this took place in Pittsburgh on January 15 and 16, 1948.[88]

Reiner commissioned a concert version of music from Gershwin's *Porgy and Bess*. The composer's suite from the opera (*Catfish Row*) was unavailable at the time, and Reiner thought Morton Gould would be a good arranger for the music if Robert Russell Bennett was uninterested in the commission.[89] Gould later wrote his own arrangement of the music, but Bennett composed a suite at Reiner's request after a successful revival of *Porgy and Bess* in 1942.[90] Reiner selected the portions of the opera that he wanted to play, set their sequence, and offered ideas about instrumentation. He asked Bennett to make generous use of the banjo and saxophones and to dispense with the piano, Gershwin's favorite instrument. Bennett followed these suggestions and remained faithful to Gershwin's harmonic and orchestral intentions, producing a colorful potpourri.[91] The premiere was scheduled for February 5, 1943, and initially selected for a concert where a soloist did not have the spotlight.[92] This did not exactly work out as planned: it was performed in a concert in which Heifetz played the Tchaikovsky Violin Concerto.

Another work given a first performance in Pittsburgh at this time, though not conducted by Reiner, was Leonard Bernstein's *Jeremiah* Symphony. Koussevitzky was not keen to perform this work by his pupil. Reiner, who had been Bernstein's original conducting teacher, was irritated at the publicity surrounding Bernstein's work with Koussevitzky at Tanglewood. He therefore created some publicity of his own by inviting the composer to conduct the world premiere in Pittsburgh in January 1944.[93] Bernstein thanked Reiner and the Pittsburgh Symphony for their spirit and cooperation, and Reiner was excited by the performance.[94] He liked to assist his better pupils and enjoyed stealing the limelight from Koussevitzky, who was renowned for presenting new American compositions.

A highly eclectic selection of works were given their American premiere under Reiner's baton in Pittsburgh, ranging from Stravinsky's Concerto in D for String Orchestra to Haydn's Elegy for Wind Instruments from his *Seven Last Words of Christ on the Cross*, and from Leó Weiner's *Pastoral, Fantasy, and Fugue* for string orchestra to Casella's *Paganiniana* Suite and Revueltas's *Janitzio*. The latter piece was performed in manuscript not long before the composer's death. Reiner also gave the newly revised version of Schoenberg's *Verklärte Nacht* its first performance.[95]

While in Pittsburgh Reiner renewed his association with Bartók, his friend, former teacher, and compatriot. Bartók came to Pittsburgh in 1941 to play his Second Piano Concerto with Reiner and his orchestra. In rehearsal the two Hungarians were often absorbed in detailed discussions in Magyar, almost oblivious to the orchestra patiently waiting for them to continue.[96] By this time Bartók, who had settled in the United States, was in dire financial straits and in poor health. Reiner wanted to promote his friend's music because of his stature as a composer and was sympathetically concerned with Bartók's welfare. Apart from works already mentioned, Reiner introduced to Pittsburgh audiences a series of pieces by Bartók—the *Divertimento for Strings*, the Suite no. 2, the *Portrait* Op. 5 no. 1, the *Hungarian Sketches, Two Roumanian Dances* (orchestrated by Leó Weiner), excerpts from *The Miraculous Mandarin*, and the Second Violin Concerto (with Menuhin as soloist).

In January 1943 Reiner conducted the New York Philharmonic in a concert at Carnegie Hall in which Bartók and his second wife Ditta performed the American premiere of the Concerto for Two Pianos and Orchestra (a reworked version of the Sonata for Two Pianos and Percussion). Reiner requested the participation of Bartók and his wife, and the Philharmonic complied after finding an extra six hundred dollars.[97] The first performance was nearly a disaster. The composer momentarily lost his way, and Reiner was annoyed at the waste of an opportunity for him to publicize his own music. Though errors were corrected by the time of the repeat performance, Bartók clearly had many distractions on his mind. His research position at Columbia University had come to an end in late 1942, leaving him with hardly any money; he was suffering from polycithemia; and he thought his career as a composer was over. In fact, his performances with Reiner in New York were his last public appearances as a pianist.[98]

Bartók was very proud and intensely disliked the taint of charity. He was sensitive about the fact that Reiner had arranged for him to play at Carnegie

Hall and that this might be criticized as a "family" affair. But this fear was unfounded. Many of Bartók's Hungarian friends rallied in secret to provide him with moral and financial support. Reiner and Szigeti secretly raised money from various organizations to supplement his stipend at Columbia.[99] When that post was due to end, Reiner enquired whether the composer could be found a research position at the Juilliard School or at the Carnegie Institute in Pittsburgh.[100] These requests did not bear fruit. But Reiner continued to help Bartók. Together with Szigeti, he secretly persuaded Koussevitzky to commission the composer to write his Concerto for Orchestra. This work, perhaps Bartók's most accessible masterpiece, was written quickly during two months in the summer of 1943 while the composer convalesced in a sanatorium at Lake Saranac, New York.[101] Koussevitzky conducted its premiere with the Boston Symphony Orchestra, but Reiner made the first commercial recording of the work with his Pittsburgh forces. Bartók was pleased that Reiner planned to perform the Concerto for Orchestra in Pittsburgh in the 1945–46 season, but the composer died before then from leukemia.[102] Szigeti realized how sad all Hungarian expatriates were at Bartók's death. "You have the satisfaction of knowing that you have done nobly by him all along," he wrote to Reiner, "and I must say Bartók always recognized and appreciated the attitude you had towards his works."[103]

Reiner increased his own and his orchestra's reputation by regular broadcast concerts, by recording discs for Columbia Records, and by touring.[104] The Pittsburgh Symphony Orchestra undertook very little touring in the late thirties and early forties apart from regular visits to neighboring states such as Ohio. This reflected the time needed to rebuild the orchestra before exposing it to the wider world, but financial support for touring was also limited. By the mid-1940s, however, the orchestra was sufficiently accomplished to tour and extend its reputation. In February 1944 it gave ten concerts at different venues in New York, Pennsylvania, and Ohio. In November 1945 it played in several southern states, including Alabama, Georgia, and Tennessee, and traveled to Canada.[105] In the following year it gave eleven concerts in the southern states. In the first three months of 1947 it undertook a six-week tour of thirty-seven concerts in twenty-seven cities in the southern United States and Mexico.[106] The Pittsburgh Symphony was the first significant orchestra to play at the Palacio de las Bellas Artes in Mexico City, where it performed six concerts (plus one in Monterrey). On the tour Reiner served as an unofficial ambassador for the arts in the United States. The trip to Mexico embodied the mayor of Pittsburgh's hope that his city would gain recognition as a cultural center.[107]

The problems of touring in the 1940s were considerable. Auditoriums used for concerts were invariably makeshift—a burlesque house in Allentown, Pennsylvania, and an arena in Ottawa that also housed circus acts were used

along with school and college halls. Often the stages were cramped, and violinists risked elbowing each other in the eyes or nose; usually backstage dressing rooms were nonexistent; and in some towns hotel rooms were in short
supply.[108] Partly because of these conditions and partly because he was older,
Reiner was less enthusiastic about touring than he had been in his Cincinnati
days. Upset that none of the orchestra's tours were to established large musical centers, he became fed up with touring and, in an unsent note, considered
leaving Pittsburgh to pursue opera conducting at the Met.[109]

Reiner caused headaches for management with his behavior on tour. Before the Mexican trip, he became tetchy about the itinerary because he had not
been consulted over the transport connections and expenses involved (though
he was right to point out that the tour had a grueling schedule). He argued
with management about staging an outdoor concert in a bullring and was so
worried about drinking water south of the Rio Grande that he ordered many
cases of mineral water for the tour and supervised the loading of the bottles
onto the train.[110] When he was bored conducting in a small provincial town,
he sometimes canceled the concert on the afternoon of the performance, saying he was ill. His assistant, Bakaleinikoff, would take over at short notice.
Reiner insisted on private cars during train journeys but often did not supply
his requirements until the last minute. These peccadilloes created constant
problems for Specter and his assistant, John Edwards, who were responsible
for generating income from tours and who did all they could to assuage Reiner's complaints.[111] The difficulties were overcome eventually, for Reiner used
all his charm to repair the situation. But they pointed to the future in Chicago
during the fifties, when it was well known that Reiner hated touring with its
discomfort and crowded schedules.[112]

Several honors in the 1940s recognized Reiner's services to music. The University of Pennsylvania awarded him an honorary doctorate in 1940 for his
work at the Curtis Institute, for cultural contributions to Philadelphia, for sympathetic understanding and encouragement of young composers, and for raising the standard of opera and orchestral performance in the city. This was followed by an honorary D.Mus. from the University of Pittsburgh in 1941.[113] In
1945 the president of the Bruckner Society of America—an organization devoted to the works of Bruckner and Mahler—presented a Mahler Medal to Reiner in honor of his efforts to promote Mahler's music in America. The award
was made after he conducted Mahler's Fourth Symphony in Pittsburgh.[114]

While based in Pittsburgh, Reiner's guest conducting was more limited
than at any time since he arrived in America. He only conducted two operas
during his years in western Pennsylvania—Douglas Moore's one-act opera *The
Devil and Daniel Webster,* with a libretto by Stephen Vincent Benét, for the
American Lyric Theater in New York in May 1939, and two guest perform-

ances of *Der Rosenkavalier* in Chicago in December 1940.[115] Reiner conducted Moore's work to promote American opera sung in the English language by Americans. The composer Ernest Bloch, who saw the production, referred to the mise-en-scène as perfect and to Reiner as a "superieusement dirigé" who had provided color, precision, and movement in a short time.[116] For the performances of *Der Rosenkavalier,* with the young Risë Stevens in the cast, Reiner arranged for students from his class at Curtis to attend so that they could watch his conducting and principles of direction. Randall Thompson, the director of Curtis, was also present.[117] These renditions of *Der Rosenkavalier* were hailed as the pinnacle of the Chicago opera season.[118]

Reiner resumed guest conducting in Detroit for the Ford Sunday Evening Hour in 1940 and 1941 and gave similar concerts in 1945 and 1946. The main attraction of these engagements was the fee, which was one thousand dollars per broadcast.[119] Reiner could not program ambitious works or neglected compositions; indeed, he found it difficult to schedule works with which the controller of the broadcasts was unfamiliar.[120] He was also barred from playing Johann Strauss's waltz *Wine, Woman, and Song* because the concerts were broadcast on the Sabbath.[121]

Reiner was active as a guest conductor in New York. In 1942–43 he directed a month of concerts during the New York Philharmonic's winter season. In three successive summers, from 1943 to 1945, he conducted special Sunday afternoon broadcasts of the Philharmonic over a coast-to-coast network sponsored by the U.S. Rubber Company. He was allowed one two-and-a-half-hour rehearsal for each concert and allocated a maximum of eighty players; the broadcasts were made in Carnegie Hall. The highlight of these concerts was the premiere, on July 23, 1944, of Shostakovich's orchestration of three monologues from Mussorgsky's *Boris Godunov,* with the distinguished Ukrainian bass Alexander Kipnis (a performance available on compact disc).[122] When Toscanini refused to conduct the NBC Symphony in the 1941–42 season, after finding that the orchestra was not his exclusive preserve, Reiner had an opportunity to conduct the best broadcasting orchestra in the United States. He conducted the NBC Symphony in two concerts in March 1942 and made four Sunday broadcasts with the same orchestra over Christmas and the New Year of 1946–47 (all for a fee of one thousand dollars per broadcast). The concerts were broadcast from the dry acoustic of Studio 8–H in Radio City Music Hall.[123]

Besides these engagements, Reiner conducted four concerts with the Cleveland Orchestra in Severance Hall, their home base, in December 1944 and several concerts with the Boston Symphony Orchestra—the one great American ensemble with which he had never appeared—in the following year.[124] At the first rehearsal of one of his Boston concerts Reiner sensed indifference from the musicians. He deliberately conducted with a vague beat, raised his eyebrows as various principals missed entrances, and then, after the mistakes continued, said sarcastically, "So this is the famous Boston Symphony Orchestra." The orchestra was humiliated, recognized Reiner's authority, tried to reinstate itself, and proceeded to give a very fine concert.[125] The music critic for the *Boston Herald* saluted Reiner as "the finest, most seasoned and well-equipped guest conductor the Boston Symphony has had in at least fifteen years," although not many guest conductors had appeared in Symphony Hall.[126]

After his abortive attempts to appear in films towards the end of the 1930s, Reiner finally made his movie debut in *Carnegie Hall*, which premiered in May 1947. The film is based around a silly story about a charwoman at Carnegie Hall who brings her son to hear the world's greatest classical musicians perform, in the hope that he might be inspired to become a concert pianist. But the film ends with the son conducting Vaughn Monroe's orchestra in jazz, featuring Harry James on the trumpet. The two-and-a-quarter-hour film was notable for being the first feature-length movie with stereophonic sound (and also, incidentally, for being the first film shot in New York City in forty years). Reiner appeared alongside many other musical celebrities, including Lily Pons, Jan Peerce, Risë Stevens, Artur Rubinstein, Gregor Piatigorsky, Ezio Pinza, and Jascha Heifetz. Stokowski promoted the picture, and the New York Philharmonic accompanied these famous artists.[127] In the film Reiner accompanies Heifetz in an abbreviated version of the first movement of Tchaikovsky's Violin Concerto. The music was recorded for the sound track several days before in a specially constructed backstage recording studio at Carnegie Hall. The sound was dubbed: the artists performed with synchronized gestures to sound coming through loudspeakers at the side of the auditorium.[128] Reiner's conducting gestures are noticeably more expansive in the movie than was his wont.

During the 1940s, Reiner only received short-term contracts to remain in Pittsburgh. It was therefore natural for him to look for a permanent position with another major symphony orchestra. When Frederick Stock died in the saddle in 1942, after a very long tenure with the Chicago Symphony, Reiner hoped to succeed him after Rodzinski had decided not to pursue the post. But Chicago's Orchestral Association decided to appoint instead a little-known Belgian, Désiré Defauw. This proved fairly disastrous; it ushered in a decade of turbulence for the orchestra and its music directors.[129]

Reiner wanted further engagements with the New York Philharmonic and was miffed at being overlooked for the orchestra's centennial year, 1941–42. Judson explained that he had constantly put Reiner's name before the Philharmonic Board to no avail.[130] In 1946 Reiner was seriously considered by the board of the Cleveland Orchestra as their new music director, but George Szell was appointed instead.[131] By this time Reiner had pinned his hopes on succeeding Koussevitzky as music director of the Boston Symphony Orchestra. In 1944 he received a confidential letter from a friend noting that Koussevitzky was very interested in who should succeed him in Boston and that it was imperative for Reiner to remain persona grata with the Russian maestro.[132] But Koussevitzky did not retire from his Boston position until 1949; he was succeeded not by Reiner but by the more flamboyant Charles Munch. Reiner was interested in two other musical organizations—the CBS Orchestra, where he wanted the post of music director, and the newly reorganized·National Symphony Orchestra in Washington, D.C. He knew that the Gramophone Company in England intended to issue a recording contract to that orchestra if he became their conductor and was prepared to resign his Pittsburgh position if Washington was to have a major orchestra.[133] None of these proposed plans came to fruition, however.

Reiner had conducted in places where the financial backing for music making was fairly secure (in his later years in Cincinnati and at the Curtis Institute). But he had also experienced lack of money for musical performance, notably the demise of the Philadelphia Orchestra's opera program after the brilliant season of 1934–35. Pittsburgh fell into the latter category. Despite being a city of wealthy industrialists—the Heinz, Carnegie, and Mellon families were all prominent there—the orchestra had financial problems. In 1938 the Pittsburgh Symphony Society only had sufficient money to continue for one more year. It was compelled to begin a campaign for financial support and had no option but to stage a fairly short winter concert season.[134] The situation did not improve. After Reiner's first season as music director, the Symphony Society was $82,000 in the red. In the spring of 1941 it still needed to meet a deficit of $155,000 by private donations, even though it had a gross annual income of around one hundred thousand dollars. These problems were not solved. A couple of months before the start of the 1943–44 season, the orchestra needed $250,000 per annum to survive; it raised one hundred thousand dollars through ticket sales but still fell short of sixty thousand via contributions. Patrons were badly needed, for ticket sales only covered about 40 percent of the orchestra's operating expenses. The solution was to establish an endowment fund to meet the problem, but this did not materialize at the time.[135]

Reiner's search for a new post became more urgent as the forties progressed because of the opposition to his artistic and financial goals in Pittsburgh. He left his post there in 1948 after disagreements with Specter and attempts to cut back the number of players and length of the season. Specter had played a significant part in rebuilding the orchestra during the Reiner era, but by 1948 animosity had long existed between the two men. Specter thought that his contributions as manager were overshadowed by Reiner's status as music director, and Reiner was irritated when Specter advised him on purely musical matters. Both men built factions among members of the orchestral board.[136] Bad feeling reached such a pitch that Reiner took to dealing with Specter indirectly through his assistant, John Edwards. A clumsy attempt by Reiner to topple Specter from his position backfired because the manager was widely respected and supported in the Pittsburgh cultural community.[137]

In 1948 the orchestra reported a deficit of six hundred thousand dollars, and the board of directors voted to reduce the concert season from twenty-eight to twenty-five weeks. There was talk of reducing the number of permanent orchestral players from ninety to eighty-five. For some years Reiner had advocated a longer season to spread the orchestra's reputation and extended contracts to keep good players: these would prove financially beneficial and artistically satisfying, because musicians would be more familiar with the music they played.[138] Less rehearsal time would be needed, and the orchestra would be seen and heard more often, which would increase its chances of being invited to tour and make records. Reiner personally defended the financial demands of players to the management, for he held skilled musicians in high regard.[139]

Plans to reduce the length of the concert season were a blow to Reiner. He thought that his decade of work in Pittsburgh was all in vain and that nothing was left to fight for. It was time to leave. This decision was not made in a fit of pique or for financial reasons; he simply could no longer compromise on artistic policies.[140] Reiner's long-term aims for Pittsburgh were for a new concert hall to seat up to forty-five hundred, a stage equipped with the latest devices for giving concerts and opera, and adequate rehearsal and dressing rooms. He thought Pittsburgh's civic leaders could have established an endowment fund to overcome the financial crisis.[141] He had taken a salary cut in the 1941–42 season to help with the orchestra's running expenses and now agreed to a further reduction in salary if the orchestra board would overturn their decision to cut the length of the concert season or the number of musicians. This proved fruitless; nothing was changed.[142] In private Reiner criticized the "aimless, useless most strenuous touring contrary to my ideas of making the orchestra a success both artistically and financially."[143] There seemed little option but to search for a new position. Besides, he was irked by the orchestra's executive committee banning him from a personal recording contract with Columbia Records, which would enable him to make records with other orchestras.[144]

By 1948 Reiner was in negotiation with the Metropolitan Opera to become its music director, and his appointment there was confirmed shortly after he resigned from Pittsburgh. Some players in the Pittsburgh Symphony Orchestra thought the standard of playing would decline without Reiner's authoritative leadership and decided to move to new pastures.[145] "All musical roads have led to Pittsburgh," wrote Caratelli to Reiner at the time, "and those of us who have made the journey are proud and grateful for the artistic experiences and great precepts you have inculcated in us. This is the testimonial of many a young musician to the imperishable work of a great man and a great artist who has been blessed with an abundance of unique and rare gifts."[146] Over half a century later the double-bass player David Walter, a member of the Pittsburgh Symphony in the early 1940s, recalled the impact of Reiner's musical leadership: "Among professional performers the Reiner legend deals almost wholly with his acerbic, even cruel character in his dealings with his musicians. Overlooked, sadly, are his valuable contributions as performer and teacher—his microscopic understanding of the scores he conducted, most especially Richard Strauss, Wagner and, yes, Beethoven, and his instruction in orchestral techniques which launched the careers of a whole generation of symphonic instrumentalists. Though he used the stick more than the carrot his was a successful leadership and many who played under his small baton remember him with a pleasant nostalgia."[147]

Reiner's farewell speech to the Pittsburgh Symphony Orchestra clarified his artistic policies during his decade in the Steel City. Addressing an audience at the Schenley Hotel at a banquet held in his honor, he explained his desire to create an orchestra proficient enough to perform the best musical compositions and capable of gaining international standing for its musical standards. He was proud of the orchestra's achievements and thought that he had developed a fine ensemble. He noted that he had deliberately offered a mixed pattern of programs. The Austro-German symphonic repertoire had been central, but performance of contemporary music was justified partly because it shed new light on older works when juxtaposed with them. Scheduling performances of American compositions was also important; otherwise, what incentive would Americans have to write music? Reiner liked to conduct five or six new American works each year and was contemptuous of those who regarded such performances as endurance tests. He had wanted to perform large-scale works by Mahler, Richard Strauss, Berlioz, and Stravinsky, but this had not always been feasible because ninety musicians were insufficient for some pieces; about 110 players would have been necessary.

These comments were an implicit criticism of management policy on program building and the size of the orchestra. Reiner also regretted that the board of directors had not done more to promote the cause of young conductors: most leading conductors were now aged over fifty and, to give younger men their chance, a reasonable number of concerts should be set aside so that newcomers could find their feet. This would not harm a well-established orchestra and was preferable to a string of guest conductors concerned mainly with their own egos. If these goals were realized in the future, Reiner thought that the Pittsburgh Symphony Orchestra could "offer long range planning for the future of music all over the country."[148]

Reiner's speech was honest and forthright, but the implied criticism of management shook the socialites present, and the banquet ended without a round of applause. A few days later, the local press announced Reiner's resignation as music director. He came to the next rehearsal after the announcement and said, while introducing excerpts from *Götterdämmerung*, "we shall now rehearse the funeral music." Everyone present knew that this served as an epitaph for his years in Pittsburgh.[149] Reiner stated finally that he cherished his work with the orchestra and gave his "adieux with a feeling of leaving my own baby—and I fervently hope that its future guardians will take good care of it." His years in Pittsburgh had seen the orchestra achieve national standing, reflected in its tours and recordings. He could claim much credit for the success.[150] After Reiner's departure, the Pittsburgh Symphony had Bakaleinikoff as acting music director and several seasons of guest conductors until William Steinberg was hired as permanent conductor in 1952.[151] For Reiner, the farewell to Pittsburgh led to a move eastwards to New York and to his major stint as an opera conductor in the United States.

7. AT THE MET

Reiner made his Met debut with a sensational triumph on February 4, 1949, when he conducted Richard Strauss's *Salome* with Ljuba Welitsch as the acclaimed interpreter of the heroine. This was truly one of the red-letter days in the history of the Metropolitan Opera, for the performance was greeted with a fifteen-minute standing ovation, which was almost unprecedented in the history of the company. Nothing like such applause had been heard at the Met for a generation, and the impact of this production was talked about for years afterwards.[1] The end of Reiner's career at the Met came four years later, on April 11, 1953, with a performance of *Carmen*. His years at the Met were his most sustained period of opera conducting in the United States. While he had conducted opera occasionally in the twenties and thirties, these engagements, despite some illustrious performances, lacked the continuous absorption in opera that had been his staple diet at Budapest and Dresden in the early part of his career. Coming to the Met, Reiner was aware of the famous traditions of North America's foremost opera house. At that time it was based at the "Old Met" on 39th Street, a building modeled after the celebrated Italian opera houses, seating 3,639 people, rather than at today's Lincoln Center.[2] Reiner gave the opera house priority over the concert hall for several years.

Reiner came to the Met at the instigation of Edward Johnson, its general manager. Johnson heard that Reiner intended to leave Pittsburgh and approached him to become the new music director. Contractual arrangements were discussed in the early summer of 1948. Reiner received a series of short contracts for his work at the Met over a period of four and a half years. His fee was either one thousand dollars per performance or twelve hundred dollars per week, with the exception of fifteen hundred dollars per performance for a spring tour in 1952. His contracts usually specified three weeks' unpaid rehearsal time before the opera season began.[3] Although his opera repertoire was subject to discussion, he had the final word in terms of available and desirable talent and insisted on adequate rehearsal time for the orchestra and cast "with mutual understanding of prevailing conditions and artistic requirements."[4]

The announcement of Reiner's move to the Met was greeted with scores of congratulatory messages. Among them were best wishes from Leonard Bernstein, who stated that the Met should have made Reiner their permanent chief conductor years ago, and from the octogenarian Richard Strauss who, after saying "what a blessing for opera," added that "there are plenty of others who can do Brahms and Bruckner. Opera needs men like you."[5] The music critic for *Newsweek* thought it ludicrous that someone with Reiner's fame as an opera conductor had not made his debut at the Met until the age of sixty.[6] But in one sense it was not a surprise, for Reiner had never been asked to conduct there before Johnson approached him.[7]

At the same time, Johnson decided that it was an appropriate time for him to retire from the Met. Rudolf Bing came with good credentials to succeed him as general manager at the end of the 1949–50 season. Bing had been the founding general manager of the Glyndebourne Opera in 1934–35 and a leading figure in the establishment of the Edinburgh Festival in 1947; he was to hold his position at the Met for twenty-two years.[8] Bing's appointment did not meet with Johnson's approval; the coolness was repaid by Bing never seeking advice from Johnson about the Met.[9] The change of general manager led to Reiner's appointment being altered slightly; it now included only conducting duties, to be shared with other regular conductors at the Met, including Fritz Stiedry, Kurt Adler, Max Rudolf, Fausto Cleva, Alberto Erede, and Wilfred Pelletier.[10] In effect, however, Reiner was the leading conductor of this group.

Johnson, the first tenor in the history of the Met to become its general manager, had attracted outstanding singers and notable guest conductors to appear on either side of the famous red and gold curtain. But during his era the repertoire performed was conservative, the stage direction often indifferent, and the costumes and scenery in need of a complete overhaul.[11] Moreover, stage conditions were inadequate. Located in a dingy building dating from the 1880s, the Met was cramped and unsuitable for large productions. It had no side stages, no near stage, and old-fashioned lighting. The area behind the proscenium and the curtain was dirty; there was no soundproofing between access halls and the auditorium; and few promenade areas were available for members of the public not associated with the Metropolitan Opera Guild or the Metropolitan Opera Club. There was inadequate space for storing furniture for even one opera and no room for scenery for forthcoming productions—a major defect in a house that presented a different bill every night. The orchestra pit extended from 39th Street to 40th Street, and it was difficult for players at either side to hear each other. Acoustical defects meant that the sound was only tolerable in the expensive seats.[12]

Many of these problems persisted when Bing was chief impresario at the Met, but he changed what he could. After analyzing the problems during the 1949–50 season, he quickly improved the stage preparation of operas. He made the productions more dramatic by hiring new directors, often from the world of theater, so that operas had a distinctive visual impact as well as distinguished music making.[13] Fervently believing in opera as a theatrical form, he wanted to stage imaginative productions that would bring the audible and visual elements of opera into a harmonious relationship.[14]

Whatever the problems of staging, the Met continued to attract the world's finest singers, and its orchestra was of high quality. After years when it often produced sloppy playing, the Met orchestra became first-class in the late forties and fifties; it had few peers as an operatic ensemble anywhere in the world.[15] This was very much appreciated by Reiner, who found that the Met's orchestral players had a "wonderful spirit" and studied diligently on their own despite a heavy schedule.[16] The Met orchestra was much better than it had been in the days of Mahler and Toscanini and was now versatile enough to play several major operas each week to a very high standard. The Met players were better paid than most orchestral musicians in America at the time, but Reiner considered their pay "blood money" because they worked extremely hard.[17] The grind was partly necessary because he demanded more rehearsals for the orchestra than any conductor since Toscanini.[18]

The fascination of opera, to Reiner's mind, lay in the complex coordination of musical and nonmusical factors. Besides a capable conductor and orchestra, one needed adequate singers in good voice, a properly rehearsed chorus, effective sets, skillful lighting, and a capable stage director. Any one of these elements might compromise quality; thus, in Reiner's view, the mathematical chances of any one performance being outstanding were much greater with a symphony orchestra than with an opera company.[19] Exposure to the varied elements of opera production was sorely needed by young American conductors, but the lack of sufficient opera houses in the United States meant that they could not often learn their "business from the ground up," as had been Reiner's experience in Budapest, Laibach, and Dresden.[20]

Reiner believed, above all, in the theatrical value of opera as drama: teamwork on the stage and in the pit, together with an ensemble spirit, was more important for achieving good performances than appearances by star singers.[21] "Opera is theatre, a show," Reiner commented, "and a good opera conductor looks above all to his showmanship. In opera there can be no devotion to musical problems without devotion to dramatic emphasis. To do this one needs the kind of control that enables one to hold in the palm of one hand the entire action and meaning of the stage, and in the other the entire action and meaning of the music, and with both hands bring about a fusion concealing the separate doings of both in the mutual propulsion of the whole."[22]

When conducting at the Met, Reiner displayed many characteristics familiar from his prior career. Singers were forced to follow his tiny beat as he moved his stick in what Regina Resnik called "little chocolate squares," with no more than an inch up, down, or sideways in movement. This minimal baton gesture was even more difficult to follow from the stage than from the orchestra pit.[23] Reiner, ever the perfectionist, rehearsed the orchestra separately, then the singers at the piano, and finally put singers and orchestra together towards the end of the rehearsal period.[24] As with his other conducting engagements, Reiner demonstrated great knowledge of the orchestra and an ability to get musicians to learn works thoroughly. He talked sparingly but used precise visual and manual gestures to extract the musical effects he wanted from the musicians and had enormous strength of character about the way in which the music should be interpreted.[25] When conducting a rehearsal, he insisted on meticulous attention to nuance, timbre, and intonation. He was widely respected for his professionalism.[26]

Reiner expected singers and orchestral players to be equally well prepared; he did not miss musical errors. Victor Aitay recalls how he came in a bar too early in one of the concertmaster's solos in *Der Rosenkavalier*. Reiner said nothing at the time, but he looked directly at Aitay just before reaching the same point in the score when he conducted the work again a few years later.[27] This was Reiner's signal to the concertmaster about the need to avoid a similar mishap. Mistakes by other players could be dealt with severely. But occasionally the expected scowl disappeared after an orchestral error and Reiner briefly reminded players of his love for the music and of his own humanity. This occurred, for instance, when Gunther Schuller, then a young horn player, fluffed his part in the second act of *Die Meistersinger*. On finding out that Schuller was playing the opera for the first time, Reiner, normally furious at errors, took off his glasses and said gently, "My goodness. What I wouldn't give for the joy of hearing *Meistersinger* for the first time."[28]

Reiner had a reputation for being kinder to singers than to orchestral players, but many singers were scared of him because he could reduce them to size with a few words if they performed indifferently. With singers who missed their notes, Reiner was merciless. Yet if he agreed with a singer's interpretation and thought the person was technically accomplished and could be trusted, he was affable, cooperative, and delightful to work with. He gave a darting glance when singers needed his support over a tempo or dynamic adjustment, and they were always confident of his thorough preparation and musical understanding. Risë

Stevens, who sang under Reiner many times, recalls that his performances were exciting and that she had greater rapport with him than with any other conductor.[29] "His feelings and interpretation of a score," she remembers, with "his uncanny sense for the drama, for the dynamics, resulted most of the time [in] such a high pitch of excitement that after the curtain went down, there was always a complete experience—not only with the audience, but among the singers as well. He had a marvelous sense of humor which often times came out in the music. He was an exciting conductor to sing with, especially on those evenings when he reached incredible heights with the music, then he was magnificent."[30]

Reiner took great care with rehearsals for singers at the Met. He insisted that all of them, however eminent, attend rehearsals because some extra illumination might result. He learned things from rehearsals and logically thought that singers would learn too. Flatly refusing suggestions from principal singers that they knew their parts and should be excused from attendance, he thought that the presence of all the singers at rehearsals was necessary for a true ensemble to shape the spirit of a performance.[31] Occasionally Reiner relented from these ideals, when the alternative was to lose a leading singer from a production. During the preparation of *Don Giovanni* in 1950, Welitsch spared only one day for rehearsal, whereas the rest of the cast had been rehearsing for six weeks with no soprano. Reiner disliked this attitude by his prima donna and was perturbed when Welitsch arrived to sing her part in the first act quartet full-throttle rather than softly, as Reiner had coached the other singers to produce. But he did not criticize Welitsch because he wanted to stage the opera successfully without replacing a leading member of the cast at the eleventh hour.[32]

Reiner was generous in the time he allowed for rehearsing with singers—a reflection, in part, of the central European milieu in which he had served his apprenticeship. Sometimes he coached leading singers privately for major parts; this occurred, for instance, with Eleanor Steber when she was learning the role of the Marschallin in *Der Rosenkavalier*.[33] No one was under any illusions that he or she could avoid hard work. For performances of *Carmen* Reiner was relentless in his coaching, arriving at the Met at 10 A.M. and rehearsing until midnight, with breaks only for lunch and dinner.[34] On the days when *Carmen* was performed, Reiner sometimes rehearsed the act 2 quintet in the singers' rooms backstage so that the ensemble was precise and note perfect.[35] To prepare *Elektra*, he coached the singers at the piano for over a month before beginning full rehearsals with the orchestra. When conducting *Falstaff*, he played the piano score with the singers for two months before the production opened and practiced the closing fugue every morning five times before moving on to the rest of the opera.[36] On the day before performances, Reiner rehearsed ensembles with singers at the piano four, five, or six times before he was satisfied.[37] By rehearsing the singers for hours with piano scores rather than delegating rehearsals to vocal coaches, he ensured that high standards of preparation were observed. By this means, he also imparted to them his vast knowledge of the opera. He was generally impressed with the learning capacity of young American singers at the Met, finding their flexibility and capabilities far above those of comparable European singers.[38]

Reiner conducted 111 performances of twelve operas in New York during his period at the Met. Ninety-four engagements consisted of music by only three composers—Mozart, Wagner, and Richard Strauss. Reiner also conducted operas by Bizet, Verdi, and Stravinsky. On tour Reiner conducted a further forty-four performances, which repeated repertoire given in New York in various North American cities. Twelve performances were presented in Philadelphia and nine in Boston. The rest were given in Birmingham, Ala.; Chicago; Cleveland; Dallas; Houston; Washington, D.C.; Minneapolis; Lafayette, Ind.; Memphis, Tenn.; St. Louis; Montreal; and Toronto.[39]

Reiner's work at the Met won a national reputation through regular touring and television and radio broadcasts. Several of his performances were televised, including *Der Rosenkavalier* on the opening night of the 1949–50 season. Sponsored by Texaco and offered on the ABC network, this was seen in New York, Philadelphia, Baltimore, Washington, Detroit, and Chicago.[40] In December 1952, Reiner's performance of *Carmen* was telecast directly from the Met by Theater Network Television to thirty-one theaters in twenty-seven American cities, the first time that anything of this scope had been attempted. The telecast was in black-and-white, projected by special equipment onto movie-theater screens; close-range shots were more effective than long-distance frames, which sometimes appeared dim and confused.[41] More frequent than these television recordings were transcontinental radio broadcasts, a long-standing Met tradition on Saturday afternoons. Eighteen of Reiner's performances at the Met were broadcast,[42] and many are still preserved on tape in the Metropolitan Opera Archives and the Performing Arts Division of the New York Public Library. The only commercial recording of a complete opera that Reiner made while at the Met—or in his entire career, for that matter—was of *Carmen*, but noncommercial live recordings exist of his performances of *Le nozze di Figaro, Don Giovanni, Der Rosenkavalier, Salome, Elektra, Der fliegende Holländer, Die Meistersinger, Falstaff,* and *The Rake's Progress.*

Before leaving the Met, Reiner named three composers that he especially liked to conduct—"they are Mozart first, Mozart second and Mozart third." He added, "there are others, too."[43] The casts for his performances of *Don Giovanni* included Paul Schoeffler, Paolo Silveri, and George London as the Don; Ljuba Welitsch, Zinka Milanov, and Margaret Harshaw as Donna Anna; Salvatore Baccaloni, Virgilio Lazzari, and Erich Kunz as Leporello; and Jerome Hines, Nicola Moscana, Desző Ernster, and Norman Scott as the Commendatore. Virgil Thomson praised the performance of February 3, 1950, with Schoeffler, Welitsch, Baccaloni, and Hines, as an evening "without flaw." If Reiner's Mozart lacked "a shade in sparkle," Thomson remarked, "it has a dramatic line and a precision of accent that are in every way meaningful . . . his intellectual tone was high, his musical and dramatic communication powerful."[44] In a later broadcast performance of January 6, 1951, Reiner was credited with being "the key element," able to insert energy into the drama and "a classical sense of proportion."[45]

In Reiner's performances of *Le nozze di Figaro,* the title role was taken by Italo Tajo, Cesare Siepi, and Martial Singher, while John Brownlee, Francesco Valentino, and Giuseppe Valdengo sang the Count. Steber and Victoria de los Angeles portrayed the Countess. There were two Cherubinos (Jarmila Novotna and Mildred Miller) and four Susannas (Bidú Sayao, Licia Albanese, Nadine Conner, and Hilde Gueden). Reiner's first performance of *Figaro* on January 4, 1950, with Brownlee, Steber, Sayao, and Tajo, was hailed by Olin Downes in the *New York Times* as "the wittiest and most distinguished reading of the score that has been given in decades in this theatre." Reiner played the secco recitative chords on a small piano in the pit. His treatment of the score was not as heavy as some expected from his penchant for late romantic music, and the performance had plenty of humor and good ensemble work.[46] The performance of March 1, 1952, available on compact disc, is notable for several reasons. It preserves a live rendering of Siepi's accomplished, idiomatic singing of Figaro, a role he sang fifty-six times at the Met;[47] it displays Baccaloni in his element in projecting Bartolo's rapid wordplay; it includes de los Angeles's sole recording in a Mozart opera; and it demonstrates Reiner's incisive conducting and well-paced handling of the ensemble pieces, such as the finale of act 2.[48]

Despite his love of Mozart, Reiner had always been accorded greater acclaim for performances of operas by Wagner and Richard Strauss. He continued this advocacy at the Met, performing *Die Meistersinger, Parsifal, Tristan und Isolde, Der fliegende Holländer, Der Rosenkavalier, Salome,* and *Elektra.* These operas accounted for over half of Reiner's performances at the Met (in New York and on tour). He would probably have liked to conduct more operas by these favorite composers, but performances of the *Ring* cycle in the late forties and fifties were allocated to rival colleagues, notably Stiedry.

Reiner's performances of *Holländer* were all presented in the 1950–51 season. Welitsch, originally scheduled to sing Senta, withdrew and never performed the role. For six performances, Hans Hotter sang the Dutchman and Astrid Varnay was Senta. In the remaining two performances they were replaced by Schoeffler and Harshaw. Set Svanholm sang Erik, save for one performance in which Charles Kullman substituted. Sven Nilsson appeared as Daland. The bass-baritone Hotter's conception of the eponymous hero was praised for being an "impressive and stirring creation," and the first sight of the ship emerging out of the whirling mists over tossing waters was an atmospheric opening for the production.[49] Thomson thought the stage direction by Herbert Graf was clear but not especially imaginative. The production was redeemed musically, however, by an excellent performance "under Fritz Reiner's animated and crystal-clear direction."[50] Reiner's conducting emphasized the legacy of Weber in treating the opera as if part of a folk genre rather than a portentous harbinger of later Wagnerian music drama.[51]

Reiner's performances of *Parsifal* occurred in March and April 1949. Svanholm and Kullman alternated in the title role. Rose Bampton sang Kundry. Herbert Janssen played Amfortas twice, and Osie Hawkins took the role once. Joel Berglund sang Gurnemanz in his farewell performances at the Met. The production elicited contradictory evaluations. To some of the musicians involved the tempi never dragged, but to some critics it was "slow in pace, dull in color, with limited mood or atmosphere" and lacked both sensuousness in the garden scene and the music's humanity in the first half of the last act.[52] Audiences apparently had difficulty in sitting patiently through Reiner's realization of the full score; they were used to abridgements of Wagnerian music dramas.[53]

During the next season, 1949–50, Reiner conducted *Die Meistersinger* with some of the same singers that had appeared in *Parsifal* and *Holländer.* Svanholm sang Walther, Schoeffler appeared as Hans Sachs, Varnay took the role of Eva. The performance on February 8, 1950, marked the final Met appearance of Kerstin Thorborg, a singer long associated with Reiner; she sang Magdalene. Further performances of *Meistersinger* under Reiner's baton took place in the 1951–52 and 1952–53 seasons. Schoeffler continued as Hans Sachs. Walther was performed by Hans Hopf and Svanholm, Beckmesser by Gerhard Pechner and Kunz. Steber, de los Angeles, Walburga Wegner, and Hilde Zadek sang the part of Eva.

According to the critic for the *New York Times,* Reiner's approach to *Die Meistersinger* was "objective," for he did "not whip up the orchestra" but was "content to let the poetic atmosphere emerge slowly and naturally."[54] Reiner was criticized, however, for adopting tempi that were sometimes too fast and sometimes too slow. He was said to have directed a prelude without spaciousness and an introduction to the third act without elevation and spirituality; to have conveyed little tenderness in the scene between Sachs and Eva; and to have understated the summer-night mood of the second act. The production also suffered from cuts, uneven singing by the chorus and some soloists, and a tame riot scene staged by Graf.[55] A live recording of the performance of *Meistersinger* from March 22, 1952, indicates that some of these deficiencies had by then been repaired. On this broadcast Schoeffler, a specialist in Wagnerian roles, sings Sachs with nobility and authority; Walburga

Wegner's attractively warm soprano, with its close vibrato and fine German diction, is ideal for the role of Eva; and the choral contributions and blend of voices in the act 3 quintet add to the vitality of the performance. Reiner conducts the score with affection, and only the unreliable intonation and wobbly vibrato of Hopf's Walther diminishes the occasion.

Reiner's performances of *Tristan* at the Met occurred in the 1950–51 season with varied casts. Tristan was sung by Ramón Vinay, Gunther Treptow, and Svanholm; Isolde by Varnay, Helen Traubel, and Kirsten Flagstad; King Marke by Ernster and Nilsson; and Kurwenal by Schoeffler, Hotter, Janssen, and Ferdinand Frantz. A small cut was made in act 3, a concession that Reiner was forced to adopt to avoid exceeding a budget that did not offer money to pay musicians' overtime after midnight.[56] Perhaps the most notable of these *Tristan* performances was the keenly awaited return of Flagstad, who had not appeared at the Met for almost a decade. At her first performance of *Tristan* on January 22, 1951, she sang, as always, with great amplitude and control and received more curtain calls than any singer since Welitsch's Salome in 1949.[57] She was able to hold back Reiner's tempo in act 2 so that she could place her two high Cs perfectly.[58]

Critics were divided over Reiner's conducting. After one performance he was criticized for being "unconscionably slow" and for directing the first act "as if the music were an oratorio."[59] But on another occasion Thomson declared that Reiner was the star of the evening besides Flagstad. "Transparency in sound, flexibility and firmness in the beat, meaning and incandescence in the whole made the work what it really is, a long symphonic poem with vocal *obbligato*. Mr. Reiner was respectful of that *obbligato* and gave it acoustical elbow room. But his orchestra, where all the real characterization and the continuity take place in this piece, was the source of musical line and substance."[60]

Reiner, a devotee of Richard Strauss, conducted *Salome, Elektra,* and *Der Rosenkavalier* at the Met. These operas were Reiner specialities, and he always conducted them with great fervor, gaining a fiery response and a crystalline transparency from the Met Orchestra. His control of the large forces needed to perform Strauss exceptionally well was unsurpassed.[61] *Der Rosenkavalier* opened the 1949–50 season, with Steber as the Marschallin, Stevens as Octavian, Erna Berger as Sophie, and Emanuel List, with whom Reiner had worked extensively in the thirties, as Baron Ochs. Thomson, usually an admirer of Reiner, thought the orchestra was too powerful on this occasion, because Steber was difficult to hear in act 1.[62] On later hearing a recording of the performance, however, Reiner stated that the orchestra's contribution could not have been better; no doubt he was pleased with the textual clarity and elegance achieved by his players.[63] He secured the perceptive accentuations and inflections that highlighted the Viennese elements in the score. In the second act his waltzes were "pulsatingly alive," and in the last act "he maintained a complete continuity of musical line from first to last, and yet dared to adapt tempos slow enough to let the trio and the duet, for once, achieve complete lyric expressiveness."[64]

Reiner subsequently conducted *Der Rosenkavalier* with many cast changes. Lorenzo Alvary, Endre Koreh, and Fritz Krenn all sang Ochs; Traubel and Varnay appeared as the Marschallin; Conner, Gueden, and Roberta Peters took the role of Sophie; and Miller, Novotna, and Irra Petina all played Octavian. Apparently Graf's staging of the opera was a routine affair; everything went well in conventional terms, but the production lacked fresh ideas.[65] A recording of the performance of December 3, 1949, preserves a distinguished evening's singing. The trio of leading female singers are Stevens as Octavian, Steber as the Marschallin, and Berger as Sophie. They were all experienced in the Straussian idiom. Stevens studied her role in Europe in the thirties with Marie Gutheil-Schoder, who had sung the role at the Viennese premiere of the opera. Steber had made her debut at the Met as Sophie in December 1940. Berger's coloratura had graced the role of Sophie in several leading German opera houses.[66] Their voices blend beautifully in passages such as the presentation of the Silver Rose in act 2 and the trio at the end of the opera. Using Clemens Krauss's 1938 version of the score, Reiner underscores the color and delicacy of much of *Rosenkavalier*'s orchestration, allows the singers time to phrase their long-breathed vocal lines without hurrying, and coaxes a large orchestra to play atmospherically without swamping the voices. A minor bonus is the ideal, ardent voice of Giuseppe di Stefano as the Italian tenor.

Reiner conducted *Elektra* in the 1951–52 season. Varnay sang Elektra; Resnik, then still a soprano, and Walburga Wegner alternated as Chrysothemis; Schoeffler and Hotter shared the role of Orest; Svanholm took the part of Aegisth; and Hoengen was Klytemnästra. The performances made a huge impact. Thomson thought this production of *Elektra* was "the finest musical performance of any opera that I have ever heard . . . the singing shone, and the orchestra glowed. The sound of it all was rich, sombre, complex and at the same time utterly plain and meaningful."[67] Reiner assured Thomson that no other ensemble, not even the Philadelphia Orchestra, with which he performed the work twenty years earlier, had played it so beautifully for him—and he was not an easy man to please.[68] The precision and sound quality produced by the orchestra stemmed partly from Reiner's skill in projecting the stage works of Richard Strauss and partly from Bing allowing him to rehearse the orchestra over a period of three months for this production.[69]

Varnay sang the demanding central role with an uncommon accuracy and freshness, the rest of the cast was outstanding, and Reiner, combining "pinpoint control with dramatic propulsion," paced the music at every juncture to suit the meaning of the words, the dramatic situation, and the practical requirements of the singers. Varnay's acting was first-rate, notably her pent-up rage and dance of exaltation when Orest and his followers slay Klytemnästra and Aegisth. At the end of the performance the audience applauded for fifteen minutes. Varnay has remarked that these five performances of *Elektra* with Reiner in 1952 were the highlight of her Met career.[70] The only serious drawback was Graf's stage direction, which was based on limited rehearsal time with the singers. This made it difficult to mold the individual interpretations of the principals into a satisfactory pictorial unity.[71]

The most illustrious of all Reiner's Strauss performances at the Met, however, was undoubtedly his and Welitsch's joint debut in *Salome,* with stage production by Graf. Six orchestral rehearsals were allowed—a generous recognition of the two important debuts being made.[72] Berglund and Janssen sang Jochanaan, Max Lorenz and Jagel were Herod, and Harshaw and Thorborg alternated as Herodias. The production was preceded by a great deal of excitement among the musical public, with touts selling tickets for around one hundred dollars (equivalent to around seven hundred dollars today). Moreover, as soon as it was announced that Reiner would begin his tenure at the Met with *Salome,* the orchestral parts vanished from the company's library: the players took them home to study and practice, something that touched Reiner greatly.[73]

Welitsch had already sung the part under the composer's direction in Vienna in 1943 and had made acclaimed recordings of the opera's final scene.[74] To her performances at the Met she brought a steely brilliance and vocal power that soared over the enlarged orchestra to great effect. Her pure delivery, suggesting a virginal princess, had the warmth, beauty of timbre, command of German, and sheer stamina to rise above the potentially heavy orchestral textures. Welitsch's Met debut on February 4, 1949, was justly celebrated. "The occasion was instrumentally perfect," wrote Thomson, "vocally well nigh-so, and dramatically sensational. Never before in the hearing of this listener has the work been led so suavely, so powerfully or with so luxurious a sound. Rarely has it been sung so well. And only in the memory of those older opera goers who remember [Olive] Fremstad, [Mary] Garden or [Geneviève] Vix, has it ever been acted so thoroughly." Thomson pronounced it "one of the great musico-dramatic performances of our century" and referred to Reiner's conducting as "the greatest . . . that we have heard here in several decades."[75] Others acclaimed it as a sensational success in which an electrically charged atmosphere pervaded the theater.[76] Richard Strauss wrote to Reiner, thanking him for the performance. "I can well imagine the pleasure you and the splendid Miss Welitsch had in cutting off the head of that locust-eater," Strauss commented. "What a pity we did not have this excellent girl in Dresden, but your orchestral performance was magnificent in those days."[77]

Reiner, the costar of the performance, conducted with perfect control and mounting excitement and conjured from the orchestra an alluring sheen and shimmer that perfectly matched Welitsch's performance on stage. Revelling in the luxuriance and suavity of the score, his "merciless eye and whiplash baton" ensured that the orchestra played an equal role with the singers; this was a "penetrating conductorial discipline of which the Met could use more."[78] Graf's stage direction was worthy of a red-letter occasion, for the details of the production seemingly dovetailed effortlessly. Everything was better prepared and more closely knit than the usual offerings at the Met.[79]

Salome was performed with Puccini's *Gianni Schicchi* as a curtain raiser, which makes the standing ovation that Welitsch received at the end of the opera all the more remarkable. Welitsch, with her flame-colored hair, purple skirt, dazzling green wrap, and amply rounded features, hardly looked like a teenage princess, but she commanded the stage and created "the illusion of everything the psycho-neurotic little fiend is supposed to be."[80] As one critic put it, "one felt this must have been exactly the effect Strauss had in mind—a performer with the voice of a young girl and the sensuous body of a voluptuary."[81] Her nervous, enraged pacing around the cistern, into which Jochanaan has been returned after denouncing and cursing Salome in the third scene, was extraordinarily vivid.[82]

Welitsch later recalled that Reiner was a little fast in places but that "there was give and take with us."[83] She wrote to Reiner to thank him for their performances together and reappeared at the Met in the same role, with Reiner conducting, in January 1952, when she was praised for being "impressive for musicianship, outrageous in her erotic pantomine and a good part of the time plain absurd in movement."[84] Her voice had diminished and lightened since 1949, and, though she sang memorably, there was less intensity in her portrayal. The revival included Svanholm and Kullman singing the part of Herod, Hoengen and Harshaw appearing as Herodias, and Hotter and Schoeffler in the role of Jochanaan. These performances were notable for the atmosphere created by Donald Oenslager's lighting; he provided sulphur-yellow clouds that swept across a green moon to impart an eerie atmosphere appropriate to the events occurring on stage.[85] Reiner also conducted *Salome* at the Met in 1950 with Varnay and Welitsch in the title role, Lorenz and Svanholm singing Herod, Harshaw and Thorborg taking the part of Herodias, and Schoeffler and Hugh Thompson alternating in the role of Jochanaan. But these performances did not garner the acclaim accorded to Welitsch and Reiner in 1949.

Richard Strauss thanked Reiner for his success with *Salome* and gently reminded him that he had written thirteen other operas, besides *Salome* and *Der Rosenkavalier,* that the Met might like to perform. Unfortunately, few of his operas were popular in the United States at that time, so Reiner was unable to schedule them (with the exception of *Elektra*). When Strauss's death was announced in September 1949, Reiner noted that "it was his music and his infallible knowledge of other great composers which gave me for many years inspiration and insight to musical interpretation and the meaning of the theatre." The death of Strauss, Reiner thought, was the "end of an epoch and the end of a friendship and artistic association of over 34 years."[86]

The rest of Reiner's repertoire at the Met consisted of three operas—*Carmen, Falstaff,* and *The Rake's Progress.* His performances of *Carmen,* one of his favorite works, were given in his final two seasons at the Met (1951–52 and 1952–53). Stevens portrayed Carmen in all performances save one, in which Fedora Barbieri was the heroine. Richard Tucker, Mario del Monaco, and Vinay sang Don José; Conner, Gueden, and de los Angeles took the part of Micaëla; and Robert Merrill, Frank Guarrera, London, and Silveri played Escamillo. The production was a great success. With some cast changes and a different orchestra, it was recorded commercially by Reiner and is still available on CD in good mono sound.

Reiner conducted the opera in its full version without many of the cuts often made.[87] *Carmen* "was always a challenge," Reiner commented, "because it is a textbook of orchestration. To squeeze every inch out of it is such a pleasure."[88] Since this was a new production, with costumes and settings by Rolf Gérard, Reiner spent a lot of time preparing the performances and discussing details with the producer, Tyrone Guthrie.[89] This famous theater director, on leave from London's Old Vic, attempted to make the opera more realistic and dramatic than usual in order to bring out the Spanish passion and tragedy of the plot. He set the opera in a Spanish village built around an enormous staircase, with the cast strolling and brawling all over it.[90] Guthrie omitted the boys' chorus in the first act because he thought it dramatically wrong; cut the traditional ballet in the fourth act because it impeded the action; achieved greater realism by eliminating the elegant prima donna's costume often worn by Carmen, so that she appeared more appropriately in peasant garb; and dressed Escamillo not as a toreador but as a man who had shown up in the mountains. Greater dramatic impact was created by setting the fourth act indoors and by making the singers act out the drama in a believable way.[91] The death scene was not, as usual, in the bullring but in Escamillo's seedy hotel room.

Reiner worked well with Guthrie and agreed with most of his suggested changes. But they clashed over one point.[92] Reiner insisted that singers watch his beat for every single second throughout the opera in order to avoid technical errors, while Guthrie thought that sometimes it made little dramatic sense for singers to face the conductor rigidly and not look each other in the eye. Guthrie eventually conceded this point to Reiner, who had greater experience with opera performance. Nevertheless, Guthrie still thought his point was correct.[93]

Stevens reveled in portraying the most famous mezzo-soprano part in the opera repertoire. She learned the castanets and all the dance steps and studied the score and Mérimée's text intensively. The public warmly appreciated Stevens's acting and vocal ability in the title role and applauded the sense of tragedy that permeated the production.[94] "She smoldered with nonchalant sexuality," Robert T. Jones has written, "burst into terrifying rages, fought for her life in a furniture-hurling fury and died hanging on to an immense red drape that ripped apart and fell over her, drenching her in a bloody shroud as the curtain fell."[95] Guthrie's emphasis on acting out the story was always evident, introducing a freshness into many conventionalities associated with the opera; but it did not convince all critics that he had created a single aesthetic viewpoint rather than a series of clever effects.[96] Reiner's conducting achieved the necessary lyricism, balance, natural flow, and "hair-breadth perception of tempos," even if his conception was essentially symphonic.[97] Conducting with his usual incisiveness, he was assisted by the "well balanced, vocally rich singing of the chorus."[98] His vitality and assured control of the music spread from the pit to the audience; together with committed singing and acting, this made the performance almost a Broadway hit. Reiner brought many interesting nuances and portamenti to his conducting of *Carmen,* and RCA Victor decided to record such a highly successful production.[99]

Reiner's only performances of a Verdi opera at the Met were those of *Falstaff* during the 1948–49 season. He conducted the opera three times with the same cast: Leonard Warren in the role of Falstaff, Valdengo as Ford, Resnik as Mistress Ford, Martha Lipton as Mistress Page, Cloe Elmo as Dame Quickly, Albanese as Nannetta, and Giuseppe di Stefano as Fenton. *Falstaff* was Reiner's favorite opera. He always found its music fresh and wonderful and completely unlike anything the aged composer had written before; he thought that *Falstaff* truly illuminated Robert Browning's idea of "the last of life for which the first was made."[100]

Reiner used the Italian text for the opera, rather than the English one Beecham substituted at the Met in 1944. This was validated artistically by an excellent cast fluent in Italian.[101] Olin Downes in the *New York Times* praised the performances of *Falstaff* as ones "that we have not seen equalled on this side of the Atlantic" and considered Reiner to be "the directing mind and authority" behind the production. Paul Jackson, who has listened to more than two hundred broadcast performances preserved from the Johnson era at the Met, considers that this production of *Falstaff* was a great triumph primarily because of Reiner's absolute control: all the great ensembles were exceptionally clear though never dry.[102] Reiner achieved great clarity and precision in conducting a difficult score and "maintained a prescient control of its shifting pace that made everything easy for the players and singers and correct for the musical and dramatic nuances."[103]

The one contemporary opera that Reiner conducted at the Met was Stravinsky's *The Rake's Progress,* which had received its world premiere in Venice in 1951. Stravinsky selected Reiner to conduct the first American performances and attended all the rehearsals. At the dress rehearsal, given before about twelve hundred people, he sat at a lectern near Reiner, following the score, and leaned over several times to offer suggestions to the conductor.[104] This irritated Reiner and disturbed the singers. It followed a piano rehearsal at which, according to Robert Craft, "a truculent dictatorial" Reiner insulted everyone and virtually told Stravinsky to shut up.[105] Stravinsky's hamfisted conducting drove Reiner to distraction. The public performances of the opera, however, papered over the cracks. Reiner's experience with dozens of modern scores made him the ideal clarifier of the music, though forty hours' rehearsal was needed to achieve perfection in the orchestral accompaniments.[106]

The American premiere of *The Rake's Progress* was held on February 14, 1953, at a Saturday matinee. The cast included Norman Scott as Trulove, Gueden as Anne, Mack Harrell as Nick Shadow, Eugene Conley as Tom Rakewell, Lipton as Mother Goose, and Blanche Thebom as Baba the Turk. Some critics thought the opera suffered from bad prosody, as if Stravinsky had distorted the natural cadences and syllabic stresses of the English text by W. H. Auden and Chester Kallman. Yet the careful preparation, Reiner's "zealous and inspired" direction, and George Balanchine's vivid choreography were praised.[107] At the box office the opera was a flop; only six performances were given in two seasons, with the house only half full at best.[108] Nevertheless, the opera was recorded by Columbia after the performances, with the composer as conductor. Reiner had used a piano in his live performances because he felt the sound of a harpsichord would not carry in a large auditorium, but Stravinsky used a harpsichord, as prescribed in the score, for the recording.[109] Reiner attended the recording sessions because he wanted to ensure that the score received a thoroughly professional performance. He conducted with a pencil during parts that Stravinsky himself could not negotiate technically, and some consider that he knew the score better than the composer.[110]

During his final three seasons at the Met, Reiner had to liaise with Rudolf Bing as general manager. From the start, Bing tried to keep Reiner as happy as possible.[111] Though both men agreed in principle on the theatrical values needed in opera productions, their relationship was volatile. Difficulties arose, particularly over a new production of *Die Fledermaus.* The litany of problems that occurred in the preparation of this production cast a harsh light on Reiner's penchant for treating management and producers high-handedly. Disagreements over *Fledermaus* existed from the start. Bing, in his first year at the Met, commissioned a fresh version with a new English libretto by Howard Dietz, the Broadway lyricist. He saw the production as one way in which New

York's operatic and Broadway traditions could mesh. He wanted Danny Kaye to play the spoken part of Frosch, the drunken jailer, and was keen for Welitsch to sing Rosalinde.[112] But Reiner was fussy about who should appear in the cast. After hearing Kaye on the radio, he did not think he was the right man to play Frosch. Instead he preferred Bobby Clark, whom he had heard as Jourdain in Molière's *Le bourgeois gentilhomme*. Reiner thought Kullman preferable to Svanholm for the part of Eisenstein, Dorothy Kirsten a better choice than "the Bulgarian bombshell" Welitsch for Rosalinde, and Lawrence Tibbett the best choice for Frank.[113]

Reiner had more serious differences with the well-known Broadway stage director Garson Kanin, who had taken on this venture as an interesting sideline and who wrote fresh English dialogue for Dietz's new English libretto. Reiner raised a series of musical objections to stage effects that Kanin wanted in his production. Reiner refused Kanin's request to conduct the overture facing the audience; he would not repeat "dui dui" because he did not wish to tamper with the score; he would not insert the *Acceleration* waltz and suggested *Roses from the South* instead because he liked it better. Reiner vetoed the use of a gypsy band for the "Czárdás," believing that skilled orchestral arrangements would be necessary because musicians on the stage would be playing from memory (which he did not trust). He regarded Kanin's production changes as unnecessary tampering with the operetta that would only increase the cost of the production.[114] Bing thought this was a charmless, unhelpful response by Reiner to Kanin even though he agreed with its substance.[115] Kanin, for his part, conceded Reiner's right to conduct the overture as he wished but defended his other ideas.[116]

Kanin and Reiner clashed in particular over a scene in the second act in which the director wanted the principal singers to lie on pillows in a bedroom and sing while in a reclined position. Reiner raised exactly the same objection he had made to Guthrie over *Carmen:* the singers could only sing properly standing up; they should watch him; and he had far more experience in opera than Kanin. While some of Kanin's suggestions were naive, others were well within the province of a stage director, yet Reiner refused to acquiesce.[117] Reiner expected the director to comply with his wishes; he wanted ultimate control. Kanin resisted this stubbornness but deferred to Reiner's musical judgment so that rehearsals could continue.[118] Underlying the dispute may have been jealousy stirred up by Carlotta Reiner, whose claim to fame was that she once, while still an actress, replaced Ruth Gordon, Kanin's wife, in a touring company; Carlotta had always resented an actress whose star shone brighter than her own.[119]

As if disputes over the production of *Die Fledermaus* were not complicated enough, a projected recording posed further problems. While Reiner had already recorded highlights of *Die Fledermaus* for RCA Victor, the Met had a contract to record original casts for Columbia Records. Since the latter was advancing lucrative, five-figure sums to the Met, Columbia Records and Bing were upset when they found that Reiner could not take charge of the recording and that they stood to lose thousands of dollars. The announcement of Reiner's new, exclusive, long-term RCA Red Seal contract, with excerpts from *Die Fledermaus* in English as the first release, added salt to the wounds.[120] At the eleventh hour Reiner asked to be relieved from conducting *Fledermaus*, saying that he was bored with the piece and had just recorded it. Bing agreed but thought Reiner was very uncooperative. He also feared future disputes between the conductor and stage director.[121] Reiner wanted Bing to support him in disputes with Kanin, clearly feeling the need to establish his authority. But he miscalculated. Kanin did not have to continue the job, since he could earn far more as a film director.[122] And Bing wanted to keep Kanin.

Bing cleverly resolved the dispute by recruiting Eugene Ormandy, who had never conducted or even seen *Die Fledermaus*, to lead the new production and record excerpts for Columbia. At the same time, Bing assuaged Reiner by offering him the opportunity to conduct Flagstad in *Tristan und Isolde*.[123] Behind the scenes Reiner and Ormandy had been rivals ever since the younger Hungarian became music director of the Philadelphia Orchestra, a position Reiner coveted. Now they were scarcely on speaking terms.[124] Reiner demanded rudely whether Ormandy was familiar with the score of *Fledermaus*. Ormandy only knew the overture but learned the rest within a week. He promptly assured the musicians that they should follow the stage director's ideas and that he would accompany whatever was required—quite the reverse of Reiner's attitude.[125] *Die Fledermaus* turned out to be Bing's first New York success; it brought the Met to the attention of the general public and was as popular as any Broadway show in town. In fact, it had more performances in one season than any work in the history of the Met.[126]

Reiner continued to conduct orchestral concerts during his period at the Met, but a long winter of engagements at the opera house precluded extended guest conducting. While waiting to come to New York from Pittsburgh, he had led several programs with the Minneapolis Symphony Orchestra "with an iron authority that spelled sound yet sometimes dogmatic readings."[127] His guest conducting during this period consisted mainly of summer concerts, radio broadcasts, and attractive, prestigious foreign bookings. He made sixteen appearances with the New York Philharmonic in summer concerts at Lewisohn Stadium in 1948 and 1949, when he mainly conducted nineteenth- and early twentieth-century orchestral works.[128] He conducted eight one-hour radio concerts by the NBC Symphony Orchestra in New York between 1949 and 1952.[129] The highlight of these broadcasts came on November 6, 1950, when he conducted the premiere of Copland's Clarinet Concerto with Benny Goodman as soloist. Goodman thought that he and the composer were lucky to acquire Reiner's services.[130] In summer 1951 Reiner was busy recording *Carmen* in New York and conducting three orchestral programs with the Philadelphia Orchestra at the Robin Hood Dell.[131]

After leading opera for most of the year, Reiner preferred to conduct concerts only in the summer. He was prepared to change his schedule if something prestigious was offered—at, say, the Salzburg, Lucerne, or Bayreuth Festivals.[132] But no invitations came from these sources during his period at the Met. Other proposed appearances in Europe at this time were largely aborted. Reiner wanted to appear at the new Edinburgh Festival, but his proposal to conduct Richard Strauss's *Ariadne auf Naxos* in 1949 was turned down by the festival committee.[133] He did conduct four performances of *Carmen* at a new open-air theater in San Carlo, Naples, in August 1953, with Giulietta Simionato as Carmen and Franco Corelli as Don José. He found the chorus and chorusmaster very capable and the singers acceptable, but he had to work harder than expected with the orchestra.[134] He conducted two concerts in Mexico City in October 1951 but turned down offers to tour in places farther afield (including Israel and Australia) because he disliked flying.[135]

While conducting at the Met, Reiner said that he could not possibly hold a concurrent position with an orchestra. There were rumors that he would become chief conductor of the San Francisco Symphony Orchestra when Pierre Monteux retired in 1952. At that time, however, Reiner had no intention of leaving the Met.[136] But he was certainly interested in changes of musical chairs in New York and Chicago. In 1951 his manager, Sol Hurok, heard that the New York Philharmonic was looking for a major new conductor and put forward Reiner's name.[137] The answer he received from Judson, as chairman of the board, was blunt: "the rumor about the Philharmonic-Symphony looking for a conductor is false. The Board made up its mind a week ago and there is no opportunity for Reiner."[138] In the same year Reiner heard that Rafael Kubelik might be leaving Chicago and asked to be kept abreast of the situation; he indicated that he wanted the position.[139] Eventually, in 1953, Reiner received the call to become music director of the Chicago Symphony Orchestra, which offered him three times his Met salary.[140]

By the time he left New York for the Midwest, Reiner had become tired of the Met. His moodiness was not suited to performing opera in repertoire at this stage of his career, and sometimes he appeared bored.[141] He could be lackadaisical after the first performance of a production, especially if he was unhappy with compromises made because of rehearsal time or stage direction.[142] He disliked changing casts and was sometimes upset at the quality of substitute singers.[143] "It is probably the most unpredictable theater in the world," he once commented about the Met, "and I am never surprised by any last minute catastrophe."[144] Dissatisfaction can be sensed in a quip he made to Resnik in a New York restaurant one evening. "Good evening, Maestro," she said. "How was the opera?" Reiner glowered sardonically and muttered: "Well, I conducted *Meistersinger*. I don't know what they did on stage."[145] He also became irritated when favorite operas, especially by Verdi and Wagner, were offered by management to second- and third-rate house conductors.[146] The number of opportunities given to Stiedry, a friend of Bing, particularly distressed him. Reiner knew that Stiedry, for all his love of music, was a poor conductor who frequently became lost in rehearsals (and sometimes in performances).[147] Reiner's relationship with Bing had been fairly strained ever since the *Fledermaus* problems. Bing knew that many of the regular conductors were hacks and that Reiner was easily the leading figure at the Met; but he thought Reiner had always regarded his position there as a stopgap while waiting for a major post with an American symphony orchestra.[148] When Reiner left New York, however, Bing sent a telegram saying that "Chicago's gain is our loss," a sentiment echoed by William Schuman.[149]

Reiner was sincerely sad to leave the Met. He considered it a great honor to have been a part of that opera house and regarded his time there as happy despite problems and emergencies that occasionally arose.[150] He left Manhattan with fond memories of Welitsch singing Salome, Warren as Falstaff, and Flagstad's return as Isolde.[151] His chief regret was that he had only conducted one Verdi opera, *Falstaff,* in his years at the Met. He would have liked to perform other Verdi operas, notably *Il trovatore.* He did not intend to give up opera conducting, noting that he would feel cheated if there were no opportunities to conduct his favorite operas for the rest of his life. In the event, Reiner only occasionally conducted performances of opera after 1953.[152]

In spring 1953 Reiner sent his best wishes to Bing for the future of the Met and hoped that he was taking an "au revoir rather than a goodbye."[153] The Met missed his abilities; it had not always had conductors of his quality on a daily basis and soon began to miss his skill at fine tuning an orchestra to give of its best. Some of the luster soon disappeared from the orchestral playing.[154] The opera conductor Robert Lawrence's verdict was that Reiner's days at the Met "contributed much to the richness and precision of operatic performance, as well as to the presence of a generally stirring ensemble on stage."[155] Radio broadcasts of Met performances spread Reiner's fame, and in 1949, 1950, and 1952 he came at the top of a poll conducted by *Musical America* to find the best opera conductor in the United States.[156] But the Met's loss was indeed Chicago's gain, and Reiner's move to the shore of Lake Michigan in autumn 1953 marked the apogee of his career as a conductor and his most fruitful period for making records. It was almost as if his whole career, with all the twists and turns, needed one further period as an orchestral builder to achieve maximum impact.

Portrait of Reiner. Courtesy of the Fritz Reiner Society.

Reiner and his daughter
Eva, ca. 1918. Source:
Eva Reiner Bartenstein.
Courtesy of the Fritz
Reiner Society.

Reiner in his study at Rambleside. Courtesy of the Fritz Reiner Society.

Reiner and his camera, Hollywood, 1924. Source: Fritz Reiner Collection, Deering Music Library, Northwestern University. Courtesy of the Fritz Reiner Society.

DOHNÁNYI

zenekari hangversenye a Népoperában

Vasárnap, 1914. február hó 8-án, délelőtt 11 órakor.

MŰSOR:

1. WAGNER RICHARD:
A MESTERDALNOKOK előjátéka.
Előadja a Népopera zenekara.

2. BEETHOVEN: G-dur zongorahangverseny.
Előadja a zenekar kíséretével DOHNÁNYI ERNŐ.

3. WEINER LEÓ: „KÖZJÁTÉK".
Előadja a Népopera zenekara.

A zenekari számokat REINER FRIGYES karmester vezényli.

4. BRAHMS:
   a) Intermezzo (F-moll)
   b) Capriccio (H-moll)
   c) Rhapsodia (Es-dur)
   Előadja: DOHNÁNYI ERNŐ.

A BÖSENDORFER zongorát CHMEL J. ÉS FIA udvari zongora-
gyárosok szállították.

ÁRA 20 FILLÉR.

Ernö Dohnányi and Reiner, Budapest, February 1914. Source: Budapest
Népopera program. Kenneth Morgan Collection.

Reiner, age four, Budapest, 1892. Source: Fritz Reiner Collection, Deering Music Library, Northwestern University. Courtesy of the Fritz Reiner Society.

Reiner and his mother, Vilma Pollak, ca. 1900. Source: Fritz Reiner Collection, Deering Music Library, Northwestern University. Courtesy of the Fritz Reiner Society.

NÉPOPERA.

A JASA HEIFETZ
HANGVERSENY MŰSORA

VASÁRNAP, 1914 MÁRCIUS 1-ÉN, A NÉPOPERÁBAN.

1. WAGNER: Lohengrin-előjáték.
   Előadja a Népopera zenekara.

2. VITALI (1650?) — LEOPOLD CHARLIER: CHACONNE.
   Hegedün előadja JASA HEIFETZ.

3. BRUCH: G-moll hegedüverseny.
   a) Allegro moderato.
   b) Adagio.
   c) Finale-Allegro energico.
   Hegedün előadja JASA HEIFETZ.
   Kiséri a Népopera zenekara.

4. LISZT: Magyar ábránd. zongorahangverseny zenekarral.
   Zongorán előadja FARAGÓ IBOLYKA.
   Kiséri a Népopera zenekara.

5. BEETHOVEN: Romance G-dur.
   MOZART-BURMESTER: Menuette, D-dur.
   POPPER-AUER: Fonó-dal, Nr. 1.
   Hegedün előadja JASA HEIFETZ.

6. SARASATE: Cigány-nóták.
   Előadja JASA HEIFETZ.

   A zenekart REINER FRIGYES karnagy vezényli.

   A zongorakiséretet WALDEMAR LIACHOWSKY látja el.

A BÖSENDORFER-zongorát CHMEL J. ÉS FIA, udvari zongora-gyárosok
szállitották.

ÁRA 20 FILLÉR.

Reiner and Heifetz at the Budapest Népopera, March 1914. Source: Budapest
Népopera program. Kenneth Morgan Collection.

Reiner conducts *Die Fledermaus*, Dresden, June 1917. Source: Dresden Opera Museum. Courtesy of the Fritz Reiner Society.

Fritz Reiner, *hofkapellmeister*, Dresden. Source: Dresden Opera Museum. Courtesy of the Fritz Reiner Society.

Reiner conducting in Rome, ca. 1921. Kenneth Morgan Collection.

Freitag, am 4. November 1921, Anfang 7 Uhr

1. Sinfonie-Konzert

Reihe B

Leitung: Fritz Reiner

I.

HAYDN, J.: *Sinfonie Es-dur (mit dem Paukenwirbel)*
(Nr. 1 der Breitkopf & Härtelschen Ausgabe)

Adagio — Allegro con spirito — Andante — Menuetto —
Finale — Allegro con spirito

---

15 Minuten Pause

II.

Zum Gedächtnis des 25. Todestages

BRUCKNER, A.: *Siebente Sinfonie (E-dur)*

I. Allegro moderato — II. Adagio (Sehr friedlich und langsam)
III. Scherzo (Sehr schnell) — IV. Finale (Bewegt, doch nicht schnell)

Sämtliche Plätze müssen vor Beginn des Konzerts eingenommen werden

Ende gegen 9 Uhr

Reiner conducts the Dresden Staatskapelle, November 1921. Source: Dresden Opera Museum. Courtesy of the Fritz Reiner Society.

Reiner and his second wife, Berta, arriving in the United States, ca. 1926. Source: Fritz Reiner Collection, Deering Music Library, Northwestern University. Courtesy of the Fritz Reiner Society.

Reiner and Victor de Sabata outside La Scala, Milan, June 1927. Kenneth Morgan Collection.

Reiner studying a score in the music room, 3818 Winding Way, Cincinnati, ca. 1925. Source: Fritz Reiner Collection, Deering Music Library, Northwestern University. Courtesy of the Fritz Reiner Society.

FRITZ
REINER

Mr. FRITZ REINER was for many years Conductor of the Dresden
Opera and at present is Conductor of the Cincinnati Orchestra

WITH

LONDON SYMPHONY
ORCHESTRA

PROGRAMME WILL INCLUDE:
Mahler's Song Cycle "Kinder-Totenlieder"
Songs by Strauss with Orchestral Accompaniment
~~Bela Bartok's First Suite for Orchestra~~
Brahms Fourth Symphony in E minor
TICKETS (including Tax) :
Reserved : 12s., 8s. 6d. and 5s. 9d. Balcony, unreserved, 3s. 6d. Area, unreserved, 3s.
May be obtained at the Box Office, Queen's Hall, Libraries, usual Agents and of
DANIEL MAYER CO., LTD.   Grafton House, Golden Square, Piccadilly, W.1
A stamped addressed envelope must accompany all orders for tickets by post.   Telephones : REGENT 2977, 2978, 2979

Reiner conducts the London Symphony Orchestra, May 1924. Source: London
Symphony Orchestra program. Kenneth Morgan Collection.

Reiner and Samuel Barber
onboard ship, 1936.
Source: The Curtis Institute
of Music, Philadelphia.
Courtesy of the Curtis
Institute.

Reiner with Kirsten Flagstad and Lauritz Melchior, San Francisco, November 1936. Source: The Curtis Institute of Music, Philadelphia. Courtesy of the Curtis Institute.

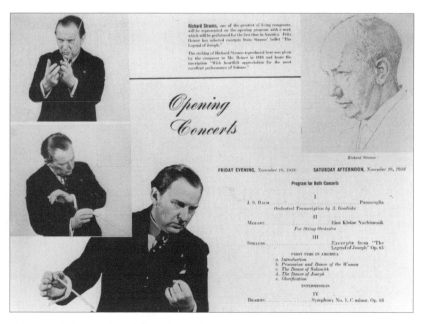

Reiner and the Pittsburgh Symphony Orchestra, 1938–39 season. Source: Pittsburgh Symphony Orchestra program. Kenneth Morgan Collection.

Reiner and Vladimir Horowitz, Pittsburgh, 1943. George Gaber Collection.
Courtesy of George Gaber.

Reiner and Jascha Heifetz, Pittsburgh, February 1943. George Gaber
Collection. Courtesy of George Gaber.

Reiner and Artur Rubinstein, Lewisohn Stadium, New York, 1943. Source:
World Wide Photos. Courtesy of the Fritz Reiner Society.

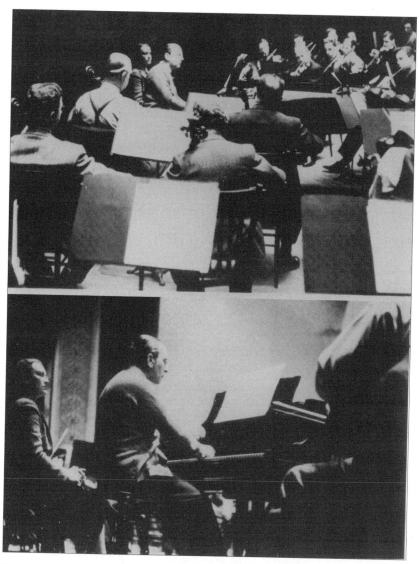

Reiner playing the piano in Bach's Brandenburg Concerto no. 5, Pittsburgh,
February 1941. George Gaber Collection. Courtesy of George Gaber.

Reiner and Béla Bartók, Weston, Connecticut, spring 1942. Taken by the conductor. Source: Fritz Reiner Collection, Deering Music Library, Northwestern University. Courtesy of the Fritz Reiner Society.

Reiner and Alexander Kipnis, ca. 1944. Igor Kipnis Collection. Courtesy of the late Igor Kipnis.

Reiner conducting in Cleveland, 1944–45. Kenneth Morgan Collection.

Reiner with Max Rudolf, Igor Stravinsky, and George Balanchine before rehearsals of *The Rake's Progress*, New York, 1953. Source: Metropolitan Opera Association, New York. Courtesy of the Metropolitan Opera Archives.

Reiner and the Chicago Symphony Orchestra. Source: Chicago Symphony Orchestra. Courtesy of the Fritz Reiner Society.

Reiner and Victor Aitay, ca. 1954. Source: Chicago Symphony Orchestra.
Courtesy of Victor Aitay.

Reiner rehearsing *Götterdämmerung* at the Met, November 1963, a few days before his death. Source: Metropolitan Opera Association. Courtesy of the Fritz Reiner Society.

Reiner and the cast of the RCA Victor recording of *Carmen*, Manhattan Center, New York, May or June 1951. Courtesy of the Fritz Reiner Society.

Reiner records for RCA Victor. Courtesy of the Fritz Reiner Society.

Reiner and Van Cliburn in the music room at Rambleside. Source: Chicago
Symphony Orchestra. Courtesy of the Fritz Reiner Society.

8. CHICAGO

Reiner came to Chicago after a turbulent decade for the orchestra that followed half a century of stability. From its foundation in 1891 until 1942 the Chicago Symphony played under only two chief conductors, Theodore Thomas and Frederick Stock. Both were German-born, and both gained a reputation as orchestral builders and contributors to the civic life of Chicago. After the death of Stock several music directors came and went in quick succession. Désiré Defauw lasted four years (1943–47). Artur Rodzinski stayed for only a single season (1947–48). They were followed by two years of guest conductors. At this time Wilhelm Furtwängler was a leading contender for the post of music director. He withdrew his candidacy, however, when the cultural community of Chicago registered its disapproval: he had made himself persona non grata by continuing to conduct in Nazi Germany throughout the period of the Third Reich. Reiner issued a statement condemning Furtwängler as an opportunist who was morally guilty and supported criticisms of him by American colleagues.[1] In 1950 Rafael Kubelik became the third permanent music director of the Chicago Symphony in seven years, but he occupied the post for only three seasons.

Several reasons account for this quick turnover. Defauw, a Belgian violinist and conductor, scheduled interesting programs. Unfortunately, he was criticized relentlessly by Chicago's most powerful music critic, Claudia Cassidy. Ticket sales dropped, and he made an early departure. Rodzinski's position with the orchestra was canceled after a few months. He argued with management, which accused him of mounting overambitious programs. He was also charged with incurring severe financial problems by performing expensive operas in the concert hall and the Civic Opera House. Kubelik was attacked by

Cassidy for his lack of authority, for conducting the same repertoire over and over, for lack of showmanship, for uneven performances, and for disagreements with the orchestra. He was also accused, somewhat unfairly, of putting too much contemporary music into his programs.[2] Despite these comings and goings, a twelve-CD collection of recordings by the Chicago Symphony Orchestra reveals that Defauw, Rodzinski, and Kubelik all drew impressive playing from the orchestra.[3] Nevertheless, these rapid changes of music director had demoralized the orchestra by 1953.

In that year Reiner became the sixth permanent conductor of the Chicago Symphony Orchestra and its fourth music director in nine years. His appointment arose after discussions with Dr. Eric Oldberg, a prominent Chicago surgeon who was president of the governing Orchestral Association. Oldberg wanted his friend George Szell, then in charge of the Cleveland Orchestra, to lead the Chicago Symphony, but this proved impossible because Cassidy unequivocally opposed Szell. And so the idea was dropped.[4] Cassidy was crucial in deciding who gained preferment with the orchestra. With little formal background in the performing arts, she began to influence Chicago's musical and theatrical life in the twenties. From 1942 until 1965 she was senior music critic for the *Chicago Tribune,* the largest nontabloid newspaper in America, with a daily circulation of more than one million readers. One might question the depth of her musical knowledge, but she had a keen critical instinct, a capacity to wound and destroy with a few barbed words, and a strong impact on the local musical scene. She was critical of the Chicago Symphony's trustees— especially their treatment of Rodzinski—but still wielded influence over them. Though she attacked Defauw and Kubelik, she admired Reiner's work.[5] Oldberg also knew of Reiner's qualities as an orchestral builder and world-famous musician and turned to him as the man to restore lost pride and prestige. He had little difficulty in persuading George A. Kuyper, the orchestra's manager, and the rest of the board likewise.[6]

Reiner had met Cassidy in 1948, when he was about to take up his duties at the Met, and she became friendly with him and his wife.[7] Reiner sounded out Cassidy privately about the Chicago appointment to ensure her support. She had praised his guest appearances in Chicago in 1950, commenting on his ability to secure "pinpoint accuracy and shining tone" in his interpretations and noting that it might be "a long, long time before the orchestra plays again with such magical finesse."[8] At that time, however, Reiner was passed over; his temperament and strong will made the Orchestral Association shy away from him as if he were another Rodzinski.[9] After Kubelik's departure it was a different story; not only did Reiner have the management's support, he also had Cassidy's backing. "I know he will put the Chicago Symphony Orchestra in spectacular shape," she wrote in her column in August 1953, "and that he will restore our sadly dwindled repertory." In private she advised Reiner only to come to Chicago if he had an iron-clad contract.[10] On top of this support, luck also played a part. Arthur Judson, the kingmaker of conductors in the United States, had no influence over Chicago's trustees—a fortunate situation for Reiner, who had fallen out with Judson some years earlier.[11]

With Cassidy's support and Judson at arm's length, Reiner accepted the position, stating that he was "very happy" with the appointment and considered the Chicago Symphony "one of the best orchestras not only in the United States but in the whole world."[12] He had heard the Chicago Symphony play under Stock, and it reminded him of the Berlin Philharmonic.[13] And he was well aware of the Germanic tradition in playing and repertoire built by Thomas and Stock, which he felt he could preserve and extend.[14] Reiner's previous experience of music making in Chicago was intermittent. He had appeared with the orchestra for summer engagements at Ravinia in 1937, 1948, and 1949; had directed a performance of *Der Rosenkavalier* for the Chicago Grand Opera Company in 1940; had led three weeks of subscription concerts in 1950; and had conducted *Die Meistersinger* in Chicago while on tour with the Met in the same year.[15] But coming to Chicago in 1953 was a challenge of a different order; it was the position he needed to cap a distinguished career. After thirty years in the United States, Reiner at last had the opportunity to rebuild an orchestra that was already potentially of high quality. He knew the orchestra was good before he took over but thought it needed a permanent leader to put his personal stamp on the quality of music making.[16] The orchestra and music critics in the Windy City awaited his arrival with great expectations.

The Chicago Symphony was well endowed and able to pay its musicians better salaries than most other American orchestras. In 1953 the orchestra's endowment was some $4 million.[17] By 1959 it was at least $8.2 million, and most players received an annual salary between eight and eleven thousand dollars—not a princely sum, but above average at the time.[18] Reiner was well paid for his services. For most of his time in Chicago, he held short-term contracts as music director that paid between forty-five and fifty-five thousand dollars per season, significantly better than the thirty-five thousand dollars per season Kubelik had received. To boost his income, he received 50 percent of the net royalties of recordings made by the Chicago Symphony Orchestra under his direction.[19]

When Reiner came to Chicago, the city was the second largest in the United States. Winding along the western shore of Lake Michigan, Chicago had a reputation for business, raciness, and culture. It was a major financial, banking, and manufacturing center with a diverse ethnic population, including many blue-collar workers—the "city of big shoulders," in the poet Carl Sandburg's phrase. It had a legacy of underworld violence from Al Capone's activities in the Prohibition era and was known for municipal corruption. But Chicago also had a rich and varied cultural life. It was renowned for architectural novelty, from the birth of the skyscraper under Louis Sullivan to the buildings of Frank Lloyd Wright and Mies van der Rohe; it had many fine museums and educational institutions; and it had a musical public with a taste for everything from jazz and blues to grand opera and orchestral concerts. Two of the greatest symbols of Chicago's claims to artistic eminence faced each other on South Michigan Avenue: Orchestra Hall and the Art Institute of Chicago. Opened in 1904 and seating 2,580 people, Orchestra Hall became the focal point of Reiner's work with the Chicago Symphony.[20]

Reiner enunciated two principles when he assumed the directorship of the orchestra: to transmit to the players the clear meaning of a piece of music as he understood it, and to act as an authority and guide on musical matters for the local community. These dual principles governed his approach to maintaining high orchestral standards and were based on his years of constant study and experience in music making.[21] His first rehearsal as music director in Orchestra Hall was a sign of things to come. He mounted the podium, greeted the musicians briefly, lifted his head to the ceiling, and said, "I call upon God and upon the ghost of Frederick Stock to make this once again a great orchestra."[22] He then rehearsed the orchestra intensively. The principal work was *Ein Heldenleben*. At the beginning of the rehearsal, the players showed signs of low morale, poor discipline, and lack of cohesion. Some musicians feared Reiner, whose reputation as a martinet was well known; but this was accompanied by tremendous respect for his musical knowledge.[23] After three hours of ironing out technical difficulties and polishing the ensemble, Reiner galvanized the orchestra to play to its potential. The experience was grueling and, in fact, one player was fired by Reiner for producing unacceptable playing. As Reiner left the stage at the end of the rehearsal the principal second violinist, Royal Johnson, commented, "Well, not much of a conductor but an awfully nice fellow," a remark that has stayed with the orchestra ever since.[24]

Reiner's rehearsals were closed to outsiders; only the orchestra knew how demanding he could be.[25] Players soon became used to Reiner's unsettling sense of humor. The orchestra's second oboist, Jerry Sirucek, once greeted the maestro with a pleasant "good morning, Dr. Reiner," only to receive the reply, "You're flat" (the last time the conductor had heard the player was in a concert).[26] The violist Robert Glazer, at his first rehearsal upon joining the orchestra, received similar treatment. "Glay-zer isn't it?" "Yes, Dr. Reiner. It's a pleasure to meet you." To which Reiner replied: "You'll see."[27] When rehearsing the slow introduction to Beethoven's Fourth Symphony, Reiner was displeased with some of the strings' bowing. As they played, he commented, "I'm sorry that there will be some new faces in the orchestra next year." As some of the bows began to quaver, Reiner added, "There will be many new faces in the orchestra next year and, as for the few that remain, you will have to make new friends." By this time the players had reached the end of the introduction and launched into the *Allegro* without sufficient drive. Reiner was annoyed and admonished them, "Be happy, be cheerful," because he felt that the music needed this approach.[28] The strings were bewildered at his sudden change of mood; all that mattered to Reiner, however, was a faithful rendition of the music's character.

Reiner constantly tested players in the orchestra. He was especially severe with musicians during the first year that he conducted them. No one, however senior or accomplished, was exempt from this treatment. Sometimes Reiner demanded that individual musicians play alone in order to test their capabilities.[29] Adolph Herseth, the principal trumpeter of the orchestra, always referred to this procedure as Reiner giving players their "week in the barrel."[30] Reiner himself described the technique as needing to know what the players could do in the trenches.[31] Concentrating on troublesome parts of a score, Reiner felt that only those who could stand the pressure would, so far as humanly possible, avoid cracked notes, imprecise rhythm, or other sins against music in performance. He wanted musicians who kept their nerve and did not spoil concerts. Occasionally this extended to the practice of not giving a player a clear cue when one was required to test whether the musician would still play in the right place.[32] If musicians emerged unscathed from this grilling, Reiner generally left them alone. If they performed particularly well, he would occasionally give a salute from his forehead with the palm of his hand to the musician concerned. But a player found wanting after a second opportunity had to leave the orchestra: Reiner believed that good players did not need a third chance.[33] This toughness was familiar to musicians. "To Reiner, the orchestra is like a piano," one player commented; "if a key sticks, he kicks it."[34] Such harshness led several musicians to fear that Reiner kept a long list of those whom he wanted to fire. Some older musicians were worried about losing their positions.[35] Statistics do not bear this out. In his first two seasons Reiner replaced sixteen musicians out of a hundred. By 1960 he still had two-thirds of the personnel inherited from Kubelik: the notion of wholesale replacements is largely a myth. Yet Reiner was unceremonious when musicians were released; there was no need, as he saw it, for commiseration.[36]

Reiner could be savage about mediocrity and was unable to control his anger when faced with shoddy musicianship.[37] The reason for this severity lay in his concern for rehearsing to the highest professional standards and securing playing that did justice to any work being performed. He aimed to produce precision, transparency, and vitality in his music making, believing that the third attribute followed necessarily from the first two.[38] He asked players to make the sound "clean" and once remarked that "nothing was more repulsive" to him "than a muddy sound."[39] To achieve this ideal, technical mistakes had to be eradicated. For someone to commit such an error was, to Reiner, a crime against music. Such instances were not forgotten quickly. Herseth recalls how once he split a note when playing a solo trumpet passage in *Don Juan*. Reiner reached for his chest as if he had been stabbed and stared at the momentarily errant trumpeter as if to say "how dare you."[40] In this respect, his temperament was completely at odds with Toscanini's. Whereas Toscanini was a volatile musician whose mood varied from day to day, who threw tantrums and later forgot them, Reiner was a much more controlled person who did not forget errors: if something went wrong on a Monday, he would remember it each time the piece was rehearsed.[41]

Reiner prepared thoroughly for rehearsals, taking nothing for granted. He plotted rehearsal schedules meticulously and was irritated when his plans were upset. Everything was set in his mind beforehand, as a result of study and experience, except for making acoustic adjustments for different venues.[42] After painstaking work on a score, Reiner often left it alone for six months, yet he expected musicians to remember the pitfalls exactly when it was played again.[43] Players may not always have liked this approach, but they respected him for his musical knowledge and ability to inspire a good orchestra to play consistently well. They also found his rehearsals stimulating, with no time wasted.[44]

Reiner was fortunate in having some top-notch musicians in his orchestra. Among the principal players were the cellist János Starker, the bassoonist Leonard Sharrow, the flautist Donald Peck, the oboist Ray Still, the trumpeter Adolph Herseth, the principal horn Philip Farkas, the harpist Edward Druzinsky, and the percussionist Gordon Peters. For Reiner's first six seasons in Chicago John Weicher was concertmaster, but he agreed to become leader of the second violins after Reiner revealed his intention to invite Sidney Harth to lead the orchestra.[45] Reiner relied on the expertise of these players. He expected some variety from his musicians; he would not casually interfere with solos or cadenzas and delegated responsibility to section principals.[46] Frequently consulting them about the overall sound produced by their sections, he gave them considerable leeway to correct errors by rank-and-file players.[47] He took the advice of string players on bowing, of woodwind players on tonguing and producing trills, and of percussion players on achieving the right timbre from their instruments. He did not like to stop the orchestra in rehearsal to work on technical details—his chief concern was making music—but errors were all logged in his mind and corrected when necessary.[48]

Reiner had a high rehearsal chair from which he constantly controlled the orchestra with his fabulous baton technique by commanding attention with his eyes and by a range of coordinated gestures that soon became familiar to musicians. Good players had no problem with his small beat because it was so clearly defined. Reiner used his beat subtly in rehearsal, often making it smaller and smaller if something needed attention, to compel the musicians to give him their full attention.[49] By deliberately underconducting and reducing the beat, Reiner induced players to listen more carefully to each other. This technique was so well honed that several players suggested to Reiner at a social gathering that perhaps the best way to practice conducting was to trace the outline of a postage stamp on a distant wall.[50]

Reiner's small gestures were quite different from those of many of his illustrious contemporaries. "In contrast to the elaborate gesturing of Stokowski, Ormandy, Bernstein or Mitropoulos, Reiner's movements were spare, dry and sharp," Irving Sablosky wrote. "Not a motion is made that does not result in a sound; if the proper sound will come without a motion, no motion will be made. Sometimes when the music is at its most furious, Reiner's movements will be at a minimum; the music can go on its own momentum, and it may go more freely and vitally if the orchestra can pour it out without interference from the conductor. When the next important movement of the baton occurs its effect will be doubly strong—and it will be exactly as much or as little as is needed to take the orchestra around the next turn."[51] Reiner thought that a large beat was undignified and produced a sense of superficial show and that waving the left hand in a beseeching way did not really help musicians to produce the quality of sound required.[52]

Apart from his use of the baton, Reiner's facial gestures became familiar to players—puffing his cheeks exactly at the point where the wind instruments should play, raising his eyebrows if he wanted a louder crescendo, kicking out his foot to bring in the violas while looking at the first violins, wagging his tongue for a tremolo. Much of the conviction in his conducting came from those watchful, alert eyes, which seemed to probe every player directly.[53] Whichever gestures were used, Chicago Symphony players have testified that they really learned the repertoire under Reiner's tutelage and that his high standards were instilled in them for years to come. He left an indelible impression.[54]

Reiner adjusted the seating of the Chicago Orchestra for concerts because of the characteristic features of its auditorium. Orchestra Hall, in Roger Dettmer's words, was shaped like Nefertiti's eye; it had a wide, shallow stage with the narrowest depth of any major concert venue in America.[55] Though reverberant when empty, the hall had dry acoustics when all seats were occupied, and musicians complained that they could not hear other sections of the orchestra adequately.[56] Reiner experimented with various seating arrangements, because he knew that the hall tended to swallow up string sound. During his first season, he divided the violins.[57] He placed the first violins on his outside left and the seconds on his outside right (with the violas beside the sec-

ond violins and the cellos next to the first violins). This followed Stock's seating of 1923 with the orchestra, and it was naturally effective for antiphonal
passages between the two sets of violins. But it was not so good for playing in
unison or for projecting the sound. Subsequently, Reiner placed the violas on
the outside right and put all the violins together on his left. He later replaced
the violas in that position by the cellos, who generally still play there today.
Reiner rearranged the brass and woodwind seating patterns, but he could not
hear the winds adequately when they were placed to his right, so he reverted
to their normal position centrally behind the main body of strings.[58] In the
1957–58 season he found that removing the velvet half-curtains at the back of
the orchestra—a practice first advocated by Stokowski—improved the textural
clarity and frequency response of the hall's acoustics.[59]

Reiner was assisted in Chicago by an associate conductor. For his first three
years in the post, this was George Schick, who had been appointed to the position under Kubelik. Schick was an accomplished musician who knew the repertoire well; he was also a first-rate pianist, with great facility in sight-reading. Yet
he was a poor conductor who failed to impress either critics or concertgoers.[60]
Some critics campaigned for a long time to oust him; they wanted management
to appoint a more authoritative associate. Virulent press attacks were led by
Cassidy, who referred to the combination of Reiner and Schick on the podium
as "half virtuoso and half hack."[61] It was difficult to replace Schick because of
his close relationship with certain members of the orchestra and the board, but
he eventually resigned his position in the spring of 1956.[62] Reiner offered the job
to his former pupil Lukas Foss, who declined because he wanted to conduct his
own orchestra. Reiner could not understand Foss's refusal to accept a position
bestowed on him by his teacher, and a curtain descended between the two men.[63]
Samuel Antek, then conductor of the New Jersey Symphony Orchestra, was offered the appointment, but he died prematurely before taking up the post.[64]
There was no replacement until early 1958, when Walter Hendl accepted his former teacher's offer to become the associate conductor in Chicago. Hendl was
fired as music director of the Dallas Symphony Orchestra after a tenure of nine
years and came to Chicago as second-in-command because of Reiner. Hendl had
experienced personal as well as professional problems in his last years at Dallas,
and Reiner's offer enabled him to continue his career at a difficult time. Reiner
felt that he could trust Hendl to keep his orchestra in fine fettle but did not interfere with the repertoire that Hendl wished to perform with the orchestra unless it clashed with pieces Reiner had already claimed for himself.[65]

Besides an associate conductor, there was a long list of guest conductors.
Reiner was able to engage many more guests than during his years in Cincinnati and Pittsburgh. He was unafraid of inviting capable conductors—unafraid, that is, about their talents being compared favorably with his own. He

wanted the Chicago Symphony to play under notable guest leaders, something the orchestra very much appreciated.[66] Among the celebrated guest conductors he brought were Sir Thomas Beecham, Sir John Barbirolli, Charles Munch, Eugene Ormandy, Paul Paray, Bruno Walter, Ernest Ansermet, George Szell, Paul Kletzki, and Josef Krips. Reiner's period in Chicago also witnessed the local debuts of Igor Markevitch and Leopold Stokowski and the American debuts of Karl Böhm, Hans Rosbaud, and Carlo Maria Giulini.[67]

Before he came to Chicago, Reiner stated that he wanted to establish a professional chorus to appear with the orchestra in large-scale choral works. He thought the public deserved to hear a good professional chorus and was always leery of amateurs: one might find an excellent college chorus, but personnel changes each year would make it difficult to establish long-term continuity.[68] On his arrival in Chicago, Reiner was quickly displeased by the Northwestern University Choir, which had served as the orchestra's official choral ensemble for several years. In the 1954–55 season, the choir was under strength for a rehearsal because of the Christmas holidays, so Reiner decided it was time to look elsewhere.[69] He turned up in New York in February 1955 with such a mission in mind. On this trip he heard Margaret Hillis's New York Concert Choir, auditioned them briefly in excerpts from Bach's B Minor Mass, and appointed them as the Chicago Symphony Orchestra's official chorus. The arrangement lasted for two seasons (1955–56 and 1956–57).[70]

By 1957 it became apparent that the expense of bringing a full chorus from New York to Chicago was exorbitant; several projected works for concerts had been canceled because of this problem.[71] Reiner therefore decided to establish a Chicago Symphony Chorus with Hillis as its conductor. This was an unusual step at the time, for in America only the Cleveland Orchestra had a permanent chorus attached to it. The Chicago Symphony chorus made its debut in the 1957–58 season at a concert conducted by Bruno Walter. Reiner selected repertoire but discussed his ideas with Hillis and sometimes also relied on her advice about possible soloists. He also held piano rehearsals with the chorus, while Hillis followed his beat.[72] Under Reiner's baton the chorus performed two oratorios by Handel (*Judas Maccabeus* and *Israel in Egypt*), Beethoven's Choral Symphony, Berlioz's dramatic symphony *Roméo et Juliette*, Brahms's *German Requiem*, Prokofiev's cantata *Alexander Nevsky,* and Stravinsky's one-act opera *Mavra.* They also performed Verdi's *Requiem,* one of Reiner's favorite works.[73]

In a speech given on his arrival in Chicago, Reiner outlined his plans for the orchestra's repertoire. He stated that the bulk of his programs would be drawn from the classics, with plenty of Bach, Beethoven, and Brahms, as well as Mozart, Wagner, and Richard Strauss. But there would also be "a liberal sprinkling of the best in contemporary music—carefully selected and painlessly administered." Reiner characterized his programs "as *progressive*, but not too adventurous or in any sense experimental."[74] They would be "a happy mixture to reconcile two opposite parties—those who are lenient towards contemporary music and those who are congenitally opposed to it."[75] Reiner wanted to perform contemporary music, as he had done earlier in his career, with only a few reservations. One was that he had to be convinced that a composition was worthy of performance; he had no interest in performing American music simply because it was written by an American. Secondly, he never considered unsolicited new scores, sending them back unopened, and would not examine new scores in the middle of an orchestral season.[76] Thirdly, he had no liking for serial music, which he considered "music of an experimental nature and doubtful value."[77]

In Chicago, Reiner conducted the world premieres of four pieces—Barber's *Souvenirs,* Copland's suite from *The Tender Land,* Robert Russell Bennett's Symphony, and Alexander Tcherepnin's Divertimento. The last two pieces were dedicated to Reiner, and the Tcherepnin work was composed at his suggestion. Reiner advised Barber to cut one movement from his piece, suggesting that fifteen minutes of dance music at a symphony concert was the maximum duration to retain an audience's attention.[78] He also persuaded Tcherepnin to cut a large part of the coda in the final movement of his work (which was originally conceived as a symphony).[79] Besides these compositions, three works received their American premiere under Reiner in Chicago: Milhaud's Symphony no. 7, Malcolm Arnold's Symphony no. 2, and Rolf Liebermann's Concerto for Jazz Band and Symphony Orchestra. The latter was a novelty, an unusual union of jazz band and symphony orchestra. It consisted of a twelve-tone concerto that incorporated three classical jazz forms—the jump, the blues, and boogie-woogie— and ended with a rousing mambo. It was played by the full Chicago Symphony Orchestra with the Sauter-Finegan Band and was recorded for RCA Victor. In performance, it required nineteen jazz players to take their place behind the orchestra. Reiner listened attentively to jazz records for months before conducting the score in public in order to make the performance as authentic as possible.[80] The only other twelve-tone pieces he conducted during his Chicago years were Stravinsky's ballet *Agon* and Webern's *Six Pieces* Op. 6—his first time conducting a work by Webern.[81] But these were not popular with the audience, even though they were well played. Furthermore, Reiner was unsympathetic to the style, thinking that it was wrong to use "musical expression to experiment with mathematical formulas." He therefore did not schedule any repeat performances of these works or undertake to conduct similar compositions.[82]

Despite an aversion to serial music, Reiner nevertheless conducted 111 works that had never appeared on Chicago Symphony Orchestra subscription programs. These were mainly contemporary pieces. They included American scores, such as Walter Piston's Violin Concerto no. 1 and Sixth Symphony, Thomson's Cello Concerto, Carl Eppert's *Speed,* Leo Sowerby's *Passacaglia, Interlude and Fugue,* Wallingford Riegger's *Dance Rhythms,* Ned Rorem's *Design* for Orchestra, Foss's Piano Concerto no. 2, Robert Russell Bennett's *Eight Etudes,* Hanson's *Elegy to the Memory of Serge Koussevitzky,* Randall Thompson's Symphony no. 2, Alan Hovhaness's Symphony no. 2 (*Mysterious Mountain*), Alexei Haieff's Symphony no. 2, and Barber's *Medea's Meditation and Dance of Vengeance* and *Prayers of Kierkegaard.* Of this group of pieces, only the Hovhaness symphony was recorded by Reiner. He did not find a place for all leading American composers on his programs, notably Charles Ives, Elliott Carter, and Roger Sessions. Reiner still did not program any works by Roy Harris, whose music did not impress him. He never scheduled anything by his friend William Schuman, though he had announced, on coming to Chicago, that he wanted to conduct the composer's Sixth Symphony, which he considered his best work.[83] David Diamond was keen to have a work conducted by Reiner, but the work he submitted (an *Elegy in Memory of Ravel*) was not to Reiner's taste.[84]

Among other contemporary composers, Reiner gave pride of place on his programs to Bartók, Stravinsky, and Hindemith. In Chicago he conducted fifteen works by Bartók, including the three piano concerti, the Concerto for Orchestra, the *Hungarian Sketches,* the Divertimento for Strings, the concert suite from *The Miraculous Mandarin,* and the Music for Strings, Percussion, and Celesta. His allegiance to Bartók was apparent in late 1956 when, upset by the Russian invasion of Hungary, he could not bring himself to play a piece by a living Russian composer. Accordingly, he dropped Shostakovich's Fifth Symphony from a concert and substituted Bartók's *Concerto for Orchestra* instead.[85] This was an appropriate gesture, since Bartók's concerto contains a pointed parody of Shostakovich's Symphony no. 7 (the *Leningrad*). Despite his operatic experience and links with Bartók, Reiner did not schedule the one-act opera *Duke Bluebeard's Castle* and only presented the concert suite from *The Miraculous Mandarin.*

Reiner's performances of Stravinsky, whom he had championed in Cincinnati and Pittsburgh, included the *Pulcinella* Suite, the divertimento from *Le Baiser de la fée,* the 1947 suite from *Petrushka,* an excerpt from *The Rake's Progress* (act 1 scene 3), the tone poem *Le chant du Rossignol,* the *Symphony of Psalms,* the 1919 suite from *The Firebird* ballet, *Mavra,* and the Chicago premiere of *Agon.* Notoriously, however, Reiner never conducted *Le Sacre du printemps,* which he had earlier named as the most important twentieth-century score. He now confessed privately that he found it coarse rather than erotic when compared with Bartók's *The Miraculous Mandarin.*[86] In fact, Reiner never conducted *Le Sacre* during his entire career (though he scheduled it for the 1960–61 Chicago season before having to cancel it due to illness). His performances of Hindemith included *Nobilissima Visione,* some songs from *Das Marienleben,* the Violin and Cello Concertos, and the Chicago premiere of the symphony *Die Harmonie der Welt.*

Reiner also conducted the Chicago premieres of an eclectic selection of scores by contemporary composers. These included Prokofiev's Cello Concerto and Seventh Symphony, Benjamin Britten's *Variations on a Theme of Frank Bridge* and *Variations and Fugue on a Theme of Purcell,* Dohnányi's Second Piano Concerto, Casella's Suite no. 1 from *La donna serpente,* Castelnuovo-Tedesco's Guitar Concerto no. 1, Ginastera's *Variaciones concertantes,* and three pieces by his friend and former teacher Leó Weiner—*Hungarian Folk Dances; Pastorale, Fantasy, and Fugue;* and the *Toldi* Suite. Some critics thought that Reiner should have scheduled more modern scores during his Chicago years; they regretted his lack of attention to contemporary American scores, especially since he had an orchestra at his command that could master new musical styles rapidly. But Reiner thought there were few young composers in the 1950s who had the stature of Hindemith or Stravinsky.[87] As we have seen, however, he still found a place in his programs for a varied diet of contemporary music.

Extensive programming of contemporary composers did not mean that older works were neglected. Far from it. Reiner's repertoire was still as varied and as comprehensive as that performed in earlier stages of his career. He did not attempt a great deal of baroque music except for some obviously popular pieces. These included a fair representation of Bach—several orchestral transcriptions of organ pieces, the Klavier Concertos nos. 1 and 2, the Suite no. 2 in B Minor, and four Brandenburg Concertos (nos. 2, 3, 4, and 5); Handel's Concerto Grosso, Op. 6 no. 5, *The Arrival of the Queen of Sheba* from *Solomon,* and three oratorios—*Israel in Egypt, Judas Maccabeus,* and *Messiah;* and Vivaldi's *Four Seasons.*

Reiner's classical repertoire was extensive. Several Haydn symphonies were performed (nos. 88, 94, 95, and 100–104). Mozart was liberally represented by three violin concertos (nos. 3, 4, and 5), five piano concertos (nos. 9, 20, 21, 23, and 25), eight symphonies (nos. 31, 32, 35, 36, and 38–41), two divertimenti (nos. 11 and 17), as well as *Eine kleine Nachtmusik,* several overtures, and the Chicago premiere of the Serenade no. 9 (the *Posthorn*). He conducted all the Beethoven symphonies, the five piano concerti, the Violin Concerto, the Triple Concerto, and six overtures.

Reiner also conducted repertoire by most well-known nineteenth-century composers. Schubert was represented by his fifth, eighth, and ninth symphonies and the *Rosamunde* Overture; Mendelssohn by his *Scotch* and *Italian* symphonies, the Violin Concerto, incidental music from *A Midsummer Night's Dream,* and four overtures; Schumann by all four symphonies; Berlioz by the

Symphonie fantastique, Harold in Italy, the dramatic symphony *Roméo et Juli-ette,* excerpts from *La Damnation de Faust,* and four concert overtures; Tchai-kovsky by symphonies nos. 4, 5, and 6 and *Manfred, Francesca da Rimini,* ex-cerpts from *The Nutcracker,* the Serenade for Strings, and the Piano Concerto no. 1; Dvořák by his eighth and ninth symphonies, the Cello Concerto, the Vi-olin Concerto, and the *Carnival* Overture; Bruckner by symphonies three and four; Liszt by his Piano Concerto no. 1, *Totentanz,* and *Mephisto* waltz no. 1; and Brahms by his four symphonies, two piano concertos, violin concerto, double concerto for violin and cello, Variations on a Theme of Haydn, and the *Academic Festival* and *Tragic* overtures.

Reiner programmed several other symphonies by late nineteenth- and twentieth-century composers. Sibelius was represented by his second, fourth, and fifth symphonies, the performance of the fifth symphony being scheduled, along with *Finlandia,* as a tribute to the recently deceased composer at the start of the 1957–58 season.[88] Two Mahler symphonies were programmed (nos. 1 and 4) and *Das Lied von der Erde.* Reiner also conducted Saint-Saëns's Sym-phony no. 3, Prokofiev's Symphonies nos. 1 and 5, Vaughan Williams's Sym-phony no. 3, and Shostakovich's Symphonies nos. 1 and 6.

Other music from the late romantic and early twentieth-century repertoire conducted by Reiner in Chicago is too extensive to mention here, but it was highly varied. Most national schools of composers were scheduled; only English and Scandinavian music did not find particular favor. Reiner conducted plenty of Wagner, notably excerpts from *The Ring* and other music dramas, and vir-tually all of the tone poems of Richard Strauss, together with excerpts from *Sa-lome* and *Elektra.* For the concert version of *Elektra* that ended the 1955–56 season, Reiner cut twenty-five minutes from the score, leaving seventy-two min-utes of playing time; he also insisted on sixteen rehearsals.[89] Lighter fare was not neglected. Chicago audiences were treated to many Viennese waltzes and polkas, Rossini overtures, Weinberger's polka and fugue from *Schwanda the Bagpiper,* orchestral transcriptions of Albéniz's piano pieces from *Ibéria,* Tchaikovsky's *1812* Overture, and Richard Rodgers's waltz from *Carousel.*

Reiner's initial concerts in Chicago drew universal praise from music crit-ics in the city. He was commended for his authority and excellence and for restoring clarity to the ensemble.[90] "All the evidence seems to be," wrote Irv-ing Kolodin, "that the years Reiner spent at the Metropolitan have renewed his zest for the orchestral literature, which is a fortunate thing for Chicagoans."[91] As his first season in Chicago progressed, Reiner was praised for the virtuoso playing he extracted from the orchestra, making it an ensemble second to none in the United States, and for putting on interesting programs.[92] The season ended with a sold-out concert of excerpts from *Der Rosenkavalier.* Reiner was the first conductor to please all parties—management, critics, and audience—

since the death of Stock. Subscription sales had soared; the orchestra appeared on television; and a recording contract with RCA Victor (lost to Chicago four years earlier) was restored.[93] Small wonder that Reiner, flushed with mid-season success, said that he had no objection to remaining in Chicago for forty years. He was pleased with the hard work put in by the orchestra, by the enthusiastic response from audiences, and by some brilliant performances.[94]

Reiner's successful start in Chicago continued during his second season. To mark the fiftieth anniversary of Orchestra Hall in December 1954, he was presented with the baton of Theodore Thomas, a gesture he regarded as a compliment and an honor.[95] Reiner rebuilt subscription concerts in Chicago to a pitch of excellence in performance that had not been heard consistently in the city since the death of Stock. Roger Dettmer, in the *Chicago American*, commented that Reiner did this with "a speed, efficiency and authority no other living conductor imaginably could have mustered." Such was Reiner's reputation for perfectly controlled orchestral performances that Herbert von Karajan, when visiting Chicago with the Berlin Philharmonic, called a special rehearsal before a concert, after hearing a virtuoso performance by Reiner, so that no ragged entrances would occur.[96]

The reputation of the Chicago Symphony in the 1950s was enhanced by television appearances, live broadcasts, and recordings. The first television appearance of the orchestra was at the Civic Theater, Chicago, on September 25, 1951, with Kubelik conducting. When Reiner arrived in Chicago, the orchestra was the only major symphony heard regularly on television. It appeared in a series of one-hour telecasts on WGN-TV. The series continued throughout Reiner's decade in Chicago, sometimes with him conducting, sometimes with guest conductors on the podium. From 1958 until 1963 the telecasts were featured in a weekly program called "Great Music from Chicago," from which kinescopes were marketed via independent stations throughout the world. The quality of these black-and-white films was variable; wide dynamic contrasts were not feasible with the microphones used; and usually the orchestra was cut down to sixty-five players (or fewer) to fit the studio space and the budget.[97] Reiner was not keen to do telecasts because of these musical compromises, but he knew the programs would enhance his reputation. They were also lucrative; by 1955–56, he earned fifteen hundred dollars per telecast. Despite limitations, these kinescopes are the best visual evidence of Reiner at work; some still survive with tolerable sound and picture quality.[98] Various radio broadcasts conducted by Reiner in the 1957–58 subscription season, but originally broadcast only in New York City, are preserved for posterity. More significant for the orchestra's reputation under Reiner was a series of recordings made for RCA Victor discussed in chapters 9 and 10.

Reiner's reputation spread widely, and he was very much in demand as a guest conductor during his years in Chicago. Yet he turned down far more offers than he accepted. His Chicago schedule was arduous, and he preferred to concentrate on building up his own orchestra, where he could establish standards of music making that satisfied him.[99] Extraneous noise and the difficulty in achieving acoustical balance and dynamic shading led him to no longer conduct open-air summer concerts.[100] Nor did he see the need, at this stage of his life, to guest conduct with little rehearsal time. This explains partly why, while music director, he did not appear at the Ravinia Festival with the orchestra until the summer of 1958.[101]

The offers Reiner received to serve as guest conductor were many and varied. He was asked to present two performances of *Salome* with Chicago's Lyric Theater in the Civic Opera House in 1954, but the price of the cast he suggested was staggering, and the project became untenable.[102] He was approached about conducting many notable European orchestras.[103] He was asked to direct concerts for Italian radio, to undertake a concert tour of Yugoslavia, to conduct opera and symphony concerts in Stockholm, to direct three cycles of the *Ring* in Venice, and to conduct *Don Giovanni* at La Scala, Milan, and La Fenice, Venice, and *Die Entführung aus dem Serail* at the Salzburg Festival.[104] He was invited to return to the Teatro Colón in Buenos Aires, where he had directed operas in the 1920s.[105] Closer to home, several American orchestras requested his services, including the Cleveland Orchestra—a direct invitation from Szell—and the Houston Symphony.[106] He refused these offers for various reasons—clashes with dates in his diary, the inconvenience of concerts during his winter or summer vacation, the demands of his schedule in Chicago, modest fees, lack of rehearsal time, the number of concerts offered, or the need to fly (he feared airplane travel).[107] Reiner expressed interest in conducting in the Soviet Union, however, especially after Stokowski had been invited to do so; but this never materialized.[108]

During his Chicago season Reiner made one or two interesting guest appearances, where he felt he could do justice to the engagement.[109] A planned exchange of orchestras between Reiner and Charles Munch was dropped because the Boston Symphony did not permit its music directors to guest conduct elsewhere in America.[110] But in 1958 a similar idea came to fruition when Reiner swapped podiums for a week with Eugene Ormandy. Reiner returned to Philadelphia to conduct the orchestra there, and Ormandy traveled to Orchestra Hall to direct the Chicago Symphony. This was one of the few occasions when the two Hungarians had direct contact following Ormandy's appointment as head of the Philadelphia Orchestra in 1938. It was also the last time that Reiner conducted the Philadelphians.

In 1960 Reiner returned to conduct the New York Philharmonic in two sets of concerts. Engaged at the suggestion of Leonard Bernstein, the Philharmonic's music director, Reiner told the players at their first rehearsal how nice it was to conduct his pupil's orchestra.[111] He scheduled Bartók's First Piano Concerto for the first concert, with Rudolf Serkin as soloist, along with the *Miraculous Mandarin* suite. This work had never been played by the Philharmonic and had received only a couple of performances in the United States since 1928, when Reiner introduced it to Manhattan concertgoers with the Cincinnati Symphony Orchestra and the composer as soloist. Kolodin thought that the New York Philharmonic had not sounded the same since Reiner last conducted it in 1943.[112]

Reiner took part in two prestigious European festivals during the late summer of 1956. In August he conducted the Vienna Philharmonic at Salzburg. In September he directed the Philharmonia Orchestra at the Lucerne Festival.[113] But his most important engagement in Europe at this time was an appearance at the reopening of the Vienna State Opera in 1955—his first visit to Vienna in twenty years.[114] Karl Böhm, the music director there at the time, was the instigator. Reiner was proud to be the only American-based conductor participating in the opening of the reconstructed opera house, which had been heavily bombed in the Second World War.[115] While in the Austrian capital, Reiner also conducted one concert by the Vienna Philharmonic in the Musikvereinsaal. This consisted of Stravinsky's *Symphony of Psalms* and Carl Orff's *Carmina Burana*. Reiner regarded this concert and his two performances of *Die Meistersinger* at the Vienna State Opera as highlights of his long career.[116] He was impressed with the first-rate playing of the Vienna Philharmonic, and he praised the acoustics of the Musikvereinsaal.[117] Viennese critics praised both the opera performances and the concert.[118]

Touring with his own orchestra proved more difficult for Reiner. This can be explained partly by his own temperament and partly by the attitude of various Chicagoans. When he came to Chicago, Reiner realized that planning and performing a complete season of orchestral concerts would take up much time and energy. He therefore had no definite plans to make music outside Chicago and its environs. He hated touring and made no secret of the fact.[119] But it was not entirely his fault that the orchestra did not tour: the Chicago Symphony had not traveled much outside the Midwest since World War I. It was the only major American orchestra that had not recently undertaken extensive tours in the United States or overseas.[120] In 1955 Mayor Richard J. Daley of Chicago announced that the city government could not fund a goodwill world tour by the orchestra; his call for public subscriptions to finance such a tour was unrealistic and halted the plans.[121] An invitation to give five European concerts in 1957 was declined because the Orchestral Association took a dim view of European touring.[122] Management turned down an offer to perform six concerts at the Brussels Fair in September 1958 because Chicago's mayor stated again that the city had no money to underwrite such a tour.[123]

The Chicago Symphony did not mount any kind of tour under Reiner's direction until 1958. Only then did Reiner feel sure that the orchestra was ready to impress music critics on the East Coast. A tour was scheduled for autumn 1958, consisting of ten concerts in a fortnight. The orchestra performed in Cleveland, Ann Arbor, Syracuse, Rochester, and Burlington, Vermont, while making its way eastward for major concerts in Boston, Philadelphia, New York, and Washington.[124] Critical praise was lavished on Reiner and his orchestra wherever they played. Paul Henry Lang, reporting on a concert in Carnegie Hall, pointed to Reiner's achievements as an orchestral builder. The orchestra played "with clockwork precision and a remarkably expressive and homogeneous tone," but the precision was subordinated to the requirements of the music and not presented for its own sake.[125]

The Boston concert proved to be the highlight of Reiner's tenure with the Chicago Symphony and one of the most notable achievements of his career. The program consisted of Berlioz's Overture *Le Corsaire*, Brahms's Third Symphony, and Richard Strauss's *Ein Heldenleben*. Local musical journalists commented on the memorable performances.[126] Reiner appeared in the dressing room after the concert with tears streaming down his face. He greeted each of the players, which was unheard of. "All my life I've waited for this moment: a perfect concert," he commented, "the only one I've ever experienced." This success can be attributed partly to the sheer form the orchestra accumulated as the tour proceeded; the playing just got better and better.[127] But there was another reason: at home in Orchestra Hall the players could not hear different sections well because of the acoustics. In Symphony Hall, Boston, it was different. As Reiner put it, "the men never really heard themselves until Boston."[128]

A touching footnote to the tour came when the Reiners returned to Chicago. Despite successful concerts and critical acclaim, there was no welcoming party for the conductor and his wife at LaSalle Street Station, no Chicago press reporters or photographers, and no civic reception. A few days later Reiner called Hendl into his office to show him the collected reviews of the tour, exuding pride at the critical approval. Hendl said that he and other pupils knew about Reiner's abilities twenty years ago. "How nice it would have been," Reiner remarked sadly, "if the world had known it twenty years ago."[129]

To demonstrate the achievements of the Chicago Symphony Orchestra under Reiner's direction, a major tour of Europe and the Near East was planned for 1959. It was intended to be the most prestigious tour ever set up for an American orchestra. In May 1958 the American National Theater and Academy (ANTA), backed by the U.S. State Department, announced that it was sponsoring a European tour by the orchestra for the late summer and early autumn of 1959. A nonprofit organization mainly concerned with the American theater, ANTA also administered overseas performance programs.

It acted as a liaison group between the orchestra and the State Department for the tour. The State Department then contacted overseas consular and embassy officials to promote the tour and work out a concert schedule. At this stage it was planned that the orchestra should play in Russia and all the major musical capitals of western Europe. A performance at the Lucerne Festival was included in the itinerary. Intensive preparation of the schedule took place in the second half of 1958.[130]

Unfortunately, the plans turned sour. Problems began to surface in February 1959. Reiner had set great store by the orchestra's appearing at the Lucerne Festival; he also expected to conduct in the major musical capitals of western Europe on a six-week tour. But the State Department wanted a longer tour of eight weeks, insisted that Lucerne would not fit the schedule, changed the itinerary to include cities in eastern Europe, and canceled planned appearances at the Edinburgh and Salzburg Festivals. Reiner cabled a telegram protesting at these changes, but Kuyper never explained Reiner's position in his discussions with ANTA and the State Department.[131]

Kuyper expressed surprise at Reiner's lack of detailed communication about the tour. For his part, Reiner wrote that he was still in the dark about the itinerary; during his midwinter vacation, he telephoned the orchestra's management to say that he would not go ahead with the tour.[132] A last-ditch attempt by ANTA to save the trip failed, even though lavish funding was promised.[133] On February 26, 1959, Oldberg, as president of the Orchestral Association, issued a press release saying that the proposed tour was canceled.[134] It quickly emerged that Reiner had pulled out of the tour at the eleventh hour after everything had been organized. No elaboration of the bare facts about the cancellation was made; nor was the Chicago public invited to ask such questions.[135] The orchestra was stunned; the press full of rumors about the reasons for cancellation; the musical pride of Chicago badly dented. Nothing could be done to save the tour after Reiner's veto. Some critics thought that Reiner was more concerned with his own comfort than with the livelihood of his players or the cultural pride of Chicago.[136]

Shock turned to anger among the orchestra after the announcement. Their disappointment was understandable, for the Chicago Symphony had never performed outside the United States. The Boston Symphony, New York Philharmonic, and Philadelphia Orchestras, by contrast, had all toured Europe more than once in the 1950s. Many of the Chicago musicians had never traveled in Europe. Moreover, they would lose two thousand dollars minimum in extra salary, which was galling for those who had spent money in connection with the trip, especially after income had just been lost owing to the cancellation of some recording sessions with Artur Rubinstein. Speculation was rife that the cancellation resulted from Reiner's health, from disagreement with the

State Department over the itinerary, from Reiner's refusal to share the podium with another conductor, and that he had already booked guest engagements elsewhere for the summer of 1959. Some even suspected that Reiner did not want to tour in eastern Europe lest he face retribution for his membership on an international Freedom for Hungarians committee that supported the Hungarian revolutionaries in 1956.[137]

When Reiner walked on stage to rehearse on the day the cancellation was announced, some hissing had to be silenced. He told the players that too many concerts had been scheduled for high quality to be maintained, and, besides, the tour had been planned for the rainy season in Russia. After a concert that evening, someone took an old dress suit out of a locker and placed a piece of cardboard on it with a sign reading, "Here lies our tour." The suit was placed on the floor of the locker room, and everyone had to step over it to get out.[138] This incident was reported in the national press. *Time* magazine embellished the story by stating that the sign on the dress suit said, "Farewell European tour—Thanks Fritz," and that several players had deliberately trampled on the garment. Reiner was furious about the incident and demanded an apology. He did not receive one.[139]

At the insistence of the orchestra's management, Reiner remained silent about the cancellation before any official announcement was made.[140] He did not issue a statement explaining his views until the April 1959 edition of the *Musical Courier*. "Our Chicago season contains a heavy schedule of rehearsals, concerts and recordings—every day but Sunday has its claims," Reiner commented. "A 10 to 12 week tour coming before the season is not feasible. After a trip of such duration it is not possible to guarantee the usual high standard of performances for the Chicago audiences, who have the right to expect their orchestra and their conductor to be in top form. ANTA refused to shorten this tour—to the length of previous trips made by Boston and Philadelphia, which were five to eight weeks. I have suggested a tour in the Spring of 1960, after our season." He continued: "The innuendoes of the Press regarding my health are not true, thank God, and the same goes for the behavior of my orchestra. There was no hissing or booing when I gave them the announcement. I realize that the news was disappointing, particularly to the younger men who have never been to Europe; but the majority recognize the inescapable fact that a tour of such duration is not a sightseeing pleasure trip. This decision was discussed with our president, Dr. Eric Oldberg, and has received his full approval. If it is unpopular with the Press I am very sorry, but I must follow the right path as I see it."[141]

The whole episode was a sorry one, and though Reiner appeared to be at fault, it was really poor management that should be blamed. The schedule for the tour would have been backbreaking: seventy-two concerts in fifty cities in eleven weeks was too much for the seventy-year-old Reiner. The tour was due to begin on August 7, the day after the end of the orchestra's six-week summer festival at Ravinia, and was scheduled to last until November 1, after which the orchestra faced twenty-eight weeks of subscription concerts in Chicago. Reiner thought that forty-six weeks of continuous concerts by the orchestra was too strenuous for the players to maintain musical standards.[142] Carlotta Reiner insisted that she and her husband had not been kept fully abreast of the tour itinerary and that the plans hatched by ANTA would have been a killing schedule just before the start of Reiner's regular Chicago season.[143] In an unpublished note Reiner jotted down various reasons for the tour's cancellation, including the fact that eleven weeks on tour was too much for his personal stamina. He added that "the original objection is still the most fundamental—Health, Health, Health," and that it would take too long to recuperate before the beginning of the season in Orchestra Hall.[144]

There were other problems, too. Reiner was expected to conduct all the concerts; attempts to engage a co-conductor fell through. The orchestra's management did not keep Reiner informed about the itinerary. Initially, the tour was supposed to last for six weeks, but the State Department decided that was too brief a period to make transportation expenses viable.[145] Eventually, the tour was scheduled for eleven weeks, including concerts in some of the lesser musical centers in Europe and the Middle East.[146] After the cancellation, Reiner told the State Department that he would not consider any tour that exceeded five weeks.[147] He should have made fuller enquiries about the extent of the tour, and no doubt many plans were hatched while he was on vacation in Connecticut. But the handling of the matter by the orchestra's management and the State Department was crass.

It has been suggested that the Chicago Symphony's management deliberately planned an exhausting tour, knowing that Reiner would not accept the itinerary and artistic compromises involved and would therefore find his authority in Chicago's musical life eroded.[148] That, of course, must remain pure speculation. There is little doubt, however, that relations between Reiner and the orchestra's management were strained before the tour was planned. In his diary for September and October 1957, Reiner jotted down some "grievances and aggravations." Expressing displeasure at the lack of publicity on his arrival in Chicago to begin the 1957–58 season, he bemoaned the absence of a rehearsal hall for the Chicago Symphony chorus, the lack of plans for the rehabilitation of Orchestra Hall, the failure to consult him on a public rehearsal to be conducted by his assistant conductor, and so on.[149] Cancellation of the 1959 tour only made his relations with the orchestral management more fractious. Kuyper felt drained by the debacle, became outspoken in criticizing Reiner's position, resented Oldberg's ineffectuality, and abruptly left his post as manager in November 1959 to take up a new position with the Los Angeles Philharmonic Orchestra.[150]

Reiner himself was under no illusions about the harm caused by the cancellation. He felt it left "scars for a lifetime."[151] Certainly it was a point of resentment among the players for a long time, and it is still recalled vividly by Chicago veterans today. But it did not affect the orchestra's professional standards. Chicago's loss was New York's gain, for the State Department quickly arranged for the New York Philharmonic to undertake the tour instead under the baton of Leonard Bernstein. It was ironic that Reiner's most illustrious pupil should inadvertently steal the limelight from him just at the point when Reiner's abilities as a conductor were at their peak. But Bernstein and his orchestra returned from the tour exhausted, having played fifty concerts in sixty-seven days; Reiner was right about the demands of the schedule.[152]

After the debacle of a canceled European tour, Reiner believed that the whole world was against him.[153] Some Chicago critics, it is true, tried to extract something positive from the situation. Donal Henahan criticized Reiner's stubbornness, mistakes, and frequent absences from the Windy City in the *Chicago Daily News* but concluded that Chicago had witnessed six good years of music making under Reiner. This undeniable fact, together with Reiner's worldwide reputation as a conductor, meant that he should be retained as music director. Dettmer, in the *Chicago American,* had earlier expressed concern about the botched tour yet still praised Reiner's tenure in Chicago for achieving "a singular quality of orchestral sound, rhythmic incisiveness," and "a pervading classicism that many have called cool." Despite volatility and organizational problems under Reiner, and the repetition of repertoire recently performed, concertgoing in Chicago while he was in charge of the orchestra was intense, memorable, and left no one unmoved.[154]

Cassidy, however, could find no such generosity in her heart. She began a relentless, destructive press campaign against Reiner. She criticized him for the cancellation of the 1959 tour, for leaving Chicago "absurdly orphaned" during the Christmas and New Year vacation, for being too preoccupied with making records, and for presenting concerts that no longer had the magnetic brilliance of his early Chicago years.[155] To her mind, Reiner's crime lay in not properly taking his place at the helm of Chicago's musical life: he only occasionally conducted Saturday-night popular concerts, had no interest in children's concerts, ignored the Civic Orchestra (Chicago's training ensemble), took little part in the Ravinia Festival, and showed no desire to conduct at the Chicago Lyric Opera, even though he was a renowned and highly experienced opera conductor. On top of this, he was now presenting dull programs and often scheduled soloists for concerts to coincide with a recording schedule. Cassidy also carped at some of Reiner's concerts. In particular, she alleged that concerts were being planned increasingly to suit RCA Victor's recording plans, leading to the repetition of repertoire.[156] There is some truth in this criticism, but it would have been played down if the tour debacle of 1959 had been avoided.

This volte-face by Cassidy, who had championed Reiner for most of his period in Chicago and remained on good terms with his wife, as dozens of mutual letters in Reiner's personal papers show, refutes Mark Grant's suggestion that Reiner had little trouble from Cassidy.[157] With hindsight, the bloodletting and aggression of her critical notices, and of those by some other critics, have an air of provincialism, a whiff of Chicago wanting to assert cultural superiority, to escape from its "second city" label. But the criticisms also reflected resentment at the Reiners' aloofness from social life in Chicago: Fritz and Carlotta enjoyed Chicago as a city but hated society functions. Reiner usually threw a party for the orchestra at the end of a season, but generally he and his wife did not attend social gatherings connected with the orchestra, least of all those at which members of the Orchestral Association were present.[158] Their exasperation at such gatherings was expressed by Carlotta just before Christmas 1954, when she referred to Fritz having to do a sustaining members' concert followed by "a lousy reception—which means at least an hour on our feet—once a year this is expected of us."[159] The cancellation of a similar concert for guarantors in 1956 was a relief, sparing Reiner from a rehearsal, a concert, and an hour's reception.[160]

Society ladies who carried out good works for the orchestra frequently complained that Reiner would not accept their invitations to dinner. Civic figures and trustees of the orchestra were disconcerted by the Reiners' removal from their Chicago apartment (at the Whitehall Hotel) to their Connecticut house during winter breaks, summer vacations, and whenever else Reiner's schedule allowed him to be absent from Chicago.[161] By maintaining such a low profile in Chicago, the Reiners failed to sustain many friendships there and remained relatively isolated. Reiner's frequent absence from Chicago proved a problem for the orchestra's management in raising funds from the local cultural community.[162]

Reiner commented that the Orchestral Association had rented his blood, not bought his privacy.[163] Music was a demanding love that took up all his time for work, and he could not understand why the orchestra's subscribers resented his inability to attend social functions with good grace. He rarely had a spare day in Chicago; there was a continuous round of rehearsals, concerts, television appearances, and recordings.[164] His schedule was far heavier than any music director would undertake with a major orchestra nowadays. Cassidy's criticisms of what he failed to do in Chicago overlooked the extent of his involvement in the city's musical life and the hours spent maintaining musical standards.

Censure from the press and mutterings of disapproval from the orchestral management came at a time when Reiner was planning the 1960–61 season in Chicago. He expected to accompany Sviatoslav Richter in his American debut and Dietrich Fischer-Dieskau in his orchestral debut and had scheduled for the season Liszt's *Mazeppa* and *Les Préludes,* Bruckner's Sixth and Mahler's Second Symphonies, Berg's *Three Pieces* Op. 6, Barber's *Toccata Festiva* for Organ and Orchestra, *Le Sacre du printemps,* and Carl Ruggles's *Sun Treader.*[165] Unfortunately, these plans were scrapped because Reiner was struck by serious illness. On October 7, 1960, a few days before the start of the season, he awoke feeling unwell and was taken to Presbyterian St. Luke's Hospital for medical tests. He had suffered a heart attack that led to serious circulatory collapse. Oldberg reported this to the board a few days later, though it was not announced publicly in Chicago until December.[166] The seizure was a shock; Reiner had previously enjoyed good health and had never been hospitalized. Initially he convalesced there for three weeks. His wife thought that too much strain on his heart had been caused by years of hard work.[167]

As a result of serious illness, Reiner immediately canceled concerts in Chicago, Los Angeles, and New York.[168] By January 1961 it was reported that he hoped to return to the podium in the final weeks of March, when, in fact, he did resume conducting the Chicago Symphony after his illness. He received a standing ovation from the players at the first rehearsal. At the concert following the rehearsal, on March 30, 1961, Reiner used a stool because he had not fully recovered. He conducted Mozart's Symphony no. 39 in E-flat, Wagner's *Siegfried Idyll,* and Beethoven's *Pastoral* Symphony. His appearance was greeted with a standing ovation from the orchestra and the audience. At the conclusion of the concert, he received a *tusch* from the orchestra (the first he had ever been given in Chicago).[169] Reiner nevertheless found conducting a physical strain, and his wife admitted privately that he was suffering from exhaustion and was struggling to get through the Chicago season.[170] Reiner informed Oldberg that he wanted to follow a more limited schedule in Chicago after the 1960–61 season and hoped that this would leave time for a successor to be found as music director.[171]

In spring 1961 Reiner's doctors advised him to curtail many of his musical activities so that he could make a fuller recovery. He spent a quiet summer in Connecticut recuperating and looked forward to conducting in the 1961–62 season. But in June 1961 his doctor recommended that he conduct only ten or eleven weeks of the following Chicago season. In the event, his continuing poor health meant that he did not return to conduct in Chicago until January 18, 1962.[172] His return to Chicago brought the 1961–62 season to a close with a performance of Handel's *Israel in Egypt.* The performance of the oratorio led to a standing ovation for Reiner's efforts in directing the orchestra to new heights of excellence over the past nine seasons. Reiner interrupted the applause to say, "just three words—I will be back."[173]

By summer 1962 Reiner's desire to return to his orchestra had diminished. This was occasioned not merely by his own health but by efforts made by the Chicago Symphony players' committee to secure better contracts from a management reluctant to grant such demands. While the powerful union boss James C. Petrillo dominated the Chicago local of the American Federation of Musicians (AFM), members of the orchestra were not allowed to form a committee. Negotiations over salaries were carried out at his national office in New York, where Kuyper would visit him. A few days after the cancellation of the 1959 European tour, however, a players' committee was formed to express dissatisfaction with such undemocratic arrangements.[174] The loss of income from the canceled tour had dramatized the players' weakness vis-à-vis management. They had formed a committee to provide a more vigorous negotiating group for the players' interests, and this helped to prevent summary dismissals without a season's notice.[175] In 1960 a new, inexperienced manager, Seymour Raven, a former journalist for the *Chicago Tribune* backed by Cassidy, tried to adopt a tough stance with militant players but became embroiled in petty conflicts with some orchestra members and found it difficult to change personnel because of Reiner's illness.[176] The players' committee started to make demands from management and Local 10 of the AFM to change the situation.

The committee, comprising four-fifths of the orchestra, requested a fifty-two-week working year, including two weeks' paid vacation, instead of the existing thirty weeks during the winter season with one week's paid holiday. They wanted six weeks' summer work under a separate contract at Ravinia and a minimum wage that doubled the existing six thousand dollars.[177] At the same time, sixty-one members of the orchestra filed unfair labor practices against Petrillo and Local 10, the first challenge in thirty years to Petrillo's presidency.[178] Players resented the need for his permission to secure freelance engagements and opposed his decision not to allow the orchestra members' committee to negotiate for conditions at the following summer's Ravinia Festival. The Orchestral Association regarded the demands as preposterous, and the dispute continued for months. The 1962–63 season began on time only because of an eleventh-hour compromise that gave the musicians more money and extended their yearly contracts. But the finer points of the settlement took a long time to resolve.[179] Reiner decided that he did not wish to return to direct an orchestra in such turmoil and relinquished his position as music director in August 1962.[180]

For the 1962–63 season, the Orchestra Association announced that Reiner would be retained as musical advisor and that a new music director would be appointed during the year. It was hoped that Reiner would return as laureate conductor.[181] The search for a new music director had begun early in 1961.

Offers were made to Erich Leinsdorf and Georg Solti, but Leinsdorf preferred to take up the music directorship of the Boston Symphony Orchestra, and Solti chose to extend a contract with the Royal Opera House at Covent Garden. Solti later admitted that he was wary of following in Reiner's footsteps, fearing comparison with his fellow compatriot and conductor. Apparently, the position at the Chicago Symphony was also offered to Markevitch, and possibly to Szell, but they declined.[182] Eventually the appointment fell to Jean Martinon, a French conductor and composer who already had a considerable reputation in Europe. Reiner refused to comment on his successor, but his own preference as a successor was Böhm, with whom he was on cordial terms.[183]

Reiner did not end his connection with the Chicago Symphony on a happy note. Only able to conduct six sets of subscription concerts in the 1962–63 season, he concluded his association with the orchestra on April 18 and 19, 1963, with a program consisting of Rossini's *Semiramide* Overture, Brahms's Second Symphony, and Beethoven's Fourth Piano Concerto, with Van Cliburn as soloist. The effort of preparing and conducting while still ill, together with a recording session with Cliburn, forced Reiner to withdraw from May concerts in Chicago.[184] There were, sadly, no celebrations before his departure from Chicago and no tribute to his achievements as an orchestra builder. A board member of the Orchestral Association summed up the rift that had arisen between Reiner and management: "We got rid of that son of a bitch out of Chicago without even giving him a farewell party."[185] This lack of civilities upset Reiner bitterly, and his wife never forgave the Windy City for its indifference.[186]

After conditional recovery from his illness and relief from the duties of music director in Chicago, Reiner wanted to share his time between guest conducting engagements and further recordings. In autumn 1962 he traveled to London to record Brahms's Fourth Symphony with the Royal Philharmonic Orchestra. And in September 1963, he recorded two Haydn symphonies (nos. 95 and 101) at Manhattan Center in New York with a handpicked ensemble of leading musicians, including many with whom he had worked in the course of his career. Some players turned up for the sessions with no idea who would be conducting them and were surprised when Reiner walked on stage from the wings and said a few personal words to players whom he had not seen since his days in Pittsburgh.[187] The Steel City must have occupied his thoughts at the time, for he had agreed to conduct the Pittsburgh Symphony for the first time in sixteen years at the beginning of the 1964–65 season.[188]

In spring 1963 Reiner was invited to be Distinguished Professor of Music at Florida State University in Tallahassee, but he declined because this would be too radical a change in his activities.[189] His stature as a musician was recognized by the award of an honorary degree from Northwestern University in 1959 and an honorary Doctor of Laws degree from Loyola University.[190] He turned down honorary D.Mus. degrees from the Chicago Conservatory of Music, the University of Hartford, and the Cincinnati Conservatory of Music because he could not attend the ceremonies and did not think that one should receive such awards in absentia.[191]

In October 1963, Reiner returned to the Met to prepare five performances of *Götterdämmerung* for a total fee of $7,500.[192] This was hardly a light task for a man in his condition of health, but he must have felt able—in one last effort of fiery determination—to conduct a work he had never performed at the Met (and had last conducted at the San Francisco Opera a quarter-century before). He admitted that *Götterdämmerung* was the Wagnerian music drama he loved most.[193] Preparing the production with the same score he had used in Dresden half a century before, Reiner worked for a couple of weeks and had gotten as far as dress rehearsals.[194] His conducting at the Met over a decade earlier was remembered avidly by opera buffs, and his projected performances of *Götterdämmerung* aroused great expectations. These were to be followed by four weeks of concerts with the Chicago Symphony in Orchestra Hall. He intended to celebrate his seventy-fifth birthday, on December 19, by returning to the two places where he felt he had gained his greatest recognition in the United States.[195] But on November 11, 1963, four days before the opening performance at the Met, he was stricken by bronchitis and was rushed the next day to Mount Sinai Hospital, New York. The bronchitis turned into pneumonia. He died the following Friday, November 15, aged seventy-four.[196]

Between two and three hundred people attended Reiner's funeral. They included many musicians, such as Licia Albanese, Lauritz Melchior, Robert Merrill, Leonard Bernstein, Van Cliburn, William Schuman, Morton Gould, Virgil Thomson, Norman Dello Joio, and Eugene Istomin; impresarios such as Rudolf Bing and Sol Hurok; and others connected with the music business, such as Bruno Zirato, Goddard Lieberson, George Marek, and Paul Henry Lang. But there was no representative from Chicago, either from the orchestra or from the city. Philip Hart, the former associate manager of the Chicago Symphony who was then working at Juilliard, worked hard in a self-effacing way to organize the funeral.[197]

Reiner had intimated privately that he would like Richard Strauss's *Tod und Verklärung* played at his funeral.[198] This, however, was clearly impracticable. Instead, the service began with the adagio section of Bach's Toccata and Fugue in C Major for organ. A short yet moving eulogy was given by the composer William Schuman, then president of the Lincoln Center for the Performing Arts. Schuman praised Reiner for being a teacher by example; not so much a classroom teacher but someone who taught all his orchestras, and the audiences who saw him, by the mastery of his art. Reiner earned respect for his craftsmanship, for his disciplined objectivity, for the catholic nature of his programs, and for nourishing music by presenting contemporary scores. To Schuman's mind, Reiner had the courage to adhere to the repertoire he wished to perform and to insist upon high standards of performance. He was also devoted to the art of conducting for a lifetime, and Schuman felt that his example would endure.[199] After the eulogy, the service concluded with a performance of the last movement of Bartók's Sixth String Quartet by the Juilliard Quartet.[200] Reiner's ashes were taken to Rambleside by Carlotta, where they remained below stairs, in his darkroom, until her death in 1983, when finally his and her ashes were interred in Willowbrook Cemetery near his home in Westport, Connecticut.

Tributes to Reiner soon appeared. Cassidy noted that he was never a Chicagoan but that Chicago would remain in his debt. In 1953 he was the conductor needed to restore the orchestra's fortunes, and this he did with music making that encompassed virtuosity, wit, incandescence, and tenderness. Under Reiner the Chicago Symphony took on a new life, attracted highly paid virtuoso players, and gained sufficient fame to lure distinguished guest conductors and soloists.[201] Henahan conceded that Reiner could be temperamental and difficult, but he was widely respected as a musician for his command of the opera and orchestral repertoire and for the clarity of his conducting. He was a perfectionist who settled for nothing less than the highest standards of musical re-creation. His decade in Chicago was marked by exceptional success in the recording field; the orchestra had acquired a worldwide reputation for its recordings of Bartók and Richard Strauss, among others.[202]

Dettmer took a broader view by summarizing Reiner's career as that of a genius dogged by frustration. He ran into conflict with the management in each of the cities where he held major appointments—Dresden, Cincinnati, Pittsburgh, New York, and Chicago. He never gained the three positions he would dearly have loved: to succeed Stokowski as head of the Philadelphia Orchestra in 1936, the music directorship of the New York Philharmonic in 1949, when Mitropoulos was favored instead, and to follow Koussevitzky as chief conductor of the Boston Symphony Orchestra in 1949. But his contribution to Chicago's musical life was substantial, as significant as that made by Thomas and Stock.[203] Stravinsky confirmed this when he stated that Reiner "made the Chicago Symphony into the most precise and flexible orchestra in the world."[204] Harold C. Schonberg praised Reiner's formidable musical knowledge, his precision and renowned baton technique, and his unrivaled ability to clarify the most complex scores.[205]

Of all the tributes to Reiner, those by the musicologist Paul Henry Lang were especially perceptive. In a private letter of condolence to Carlotta, Lang observed that most musicians who had great respect for Reiner did not really know him. They noticed, of course, the fabulously precise baton technique and the lack of exhibitionism but could not sense the extent of the mental processes that Reiner underwent before undertaking the first rehearsal of a piece. This became clear to Lang in private conversation with Reiner.[206] A few months later, on April 29, 1964, Lang gave an after-dinner speech at a meeting of the American Hungarian Studies Foundation where Reiner was posthumously awarded the foundation's George Washington Award. According to Lang, Reiner never succumbed to histrionic temptations; his conducting was always meaningful to the musicians playing under him. "What made his conducting so exciting to the musically knowledgeable," Lang noted, "was the bravado of his extraordinary if almost invisible virtuosity with the baton. Like a bullfighter, he was pirouetting within an inch of dangerous horns, but it was this inch that made for the unexampled precision and thrust of the orchestra under his direction." Lang praised Reiner for the opulent, sensuous sound he achieved in performances of Wagner and Richard Strauss but also commented on his receptivity to contemporary music of various styles, notably his championing of Bartók, Stravinsky, Hindemith, and Schoenberg. Above all, Reiner was a universal artist whose re-creative powers encompassed a wide repertoire that crossed all sorts of boundaries and tastes.[207] Fortunately, Reiner's extensive work in the recording studio, especially in his last decade, is a continuing legacy of those gifts.

9. THE RECORDED LEGACY

Until the age of fifty, Reiner's recording career consisted of false starts and dashed hopes. His debut as a recording artist came before the First World War when, at the age of eighteen, he played the piano into an acoustic horn to accompany a soprano singing German lieder for reproduction on a cylindrical record.[1] While he was *hofkapellmeister* in Dresden the singers of the Saxon State Opera House undertook some recordings, but they were made in Berlin with an anonymous orchestral backing and unnamed conductors: it is unlikely that Reiner was involved.[2] In 1925 and 1926 he took part in some piano-roll recordings in New York, for which he conducted and played one of the two piano parts. The works recorded included Beethoven's First and Fifth Symphonies, Haydn's Symphony no. 94 (the *Surprise*), Schubert's Symphony no. 8 (the *Unfinished*), and Tchaikovsky's Symphony no. 6 (the *Pathétique*).[3] After Reiner had conducted in Cincinnati for several seasons, Judson asked Columbia Records whether any recording opportunities were available; he was told that the firm had no definite plans to use Reiner's services.[4] This was around the time that electrical recording replaced acoustic horns, and no doubt Reiner and his manager thought it an opportune moment to take advantage of the new method of reproducing sound. In 1929 Judson reported that RCA Victor was interested in making records with Reiner. On this occasion, however, Reiner lacked interest in pursuing the matter. Toscanini had just made some discs for the company, and Reiner thought the Italian maestro's records would sell better, being issued first, and that there was no point in trying to compete.[5] In 1930 the Gramophone Company declined an interest in Reiner as a conductor for their records.[6] Thus no orchestral recordings emerged from Reiner's periods in Dresden and Cincinnati.

Reiner's first orchestral recordings date from the early thirties. Bell Laboratories, based in Camden, New Jersey, recorded a Wagnerian program that he conducted with the Philadelphia Orchestra in the Academy of Music on November 27 and 28, 1931. This was part of a series of experimental recordings that Leopold Stokowski arranged with the Electrical Research Products Corporation, affiliated with Western Electric. The surviving fragments have been remastered onto cassette from the original 33⅓ rpm discs. The orchestral passages preserved from *Tristan und Isolde, Die Meistersinger,* and *Parsifal* are eloquent harbingers of Reiner's later commercial recordings as well as an important documentary record.[7] Several extracts have abrupt endings, and the *Tristan* excerpts are affected by swish and pops, but the selections from *Parsifal* display the splendor of the Philadelphia Orchestra in its heyday, notably the virtuosity of the brass and strings. Bell Labs also recorded part of a Russian program in which Reiner conducted Tchaikovsky's First Piano Concerto, with Vladimir Horowitz as soloist, and substantial extracts from the *Lohengrin* performance that he led for the Philadelphia Grand Opera in February 1932.[8]

Reiner was fascinated by recording techniques then being developed; in 1931, he inspected a new double-faced record manufactured by RCA Victor that could play for thirty minutes.[9] Nevertheless, Reiner's recording career developed slowly. In the mid thirties, when he was a successful guest conductor with the Philadelphia Orchestra, he hoped to record two challenging contemporary works that he had performed in concert and that, at the time, were not represented in the record catalogs: Honegger's *King David* and Kodály's *Psalmus Hungaricus.* RCA Victor, however, rejected this proposition as too expensive to undertake; no doubt they were wary of the cost of hiring singers as well as paying for the orchestra.[10] The indifference of American recording companies to large-scale expensive projects meant that none of Reiner's opera conducting in Philadelphia or San Francisco in the midthirties was commercially recorded. All that survives of his work in Philadelphia are the Bell Labs recordings mentioned above. From his appearances with the San Francisco Opera, there is a version of act 2 of *Tristan und Isolde,* spoiled by very poor sound probably from an "in-house" recording at the Shrine Auditorium, Los Angeles, in autumn 1937, and a rather better aircheck of act 2 of *Die Walküre* taken from a performance on November 13, 1936. Performed with many cuts, this broadcast has recessed orchestral balance and ends with an announcer speaking insensitively over Wotan's broken words to Hunding at the end of the act. But the recording is worth hearing for its quartet of outstanding Wagnerian singers—Melchior, Flagstad, Lehmann, and Schorr—in splendid form and in their prime. It is Reiner's most extended extant recording of any part of the *Ring* cycle.[11]

By the late 1930s Reiner thought it was time for him to make records, since many of his colleagues, even lesser lights, were already doing so. RCA Victor did nothing to accommodate him: he was not then the chief conductor of a major orchestra and was unlikely to achieve sufficient record sales to be commercially viable.[12] Some of Reiner's Wagnerian performances at Covent Garden in the mid thirties were recorded live by HMV, but a few orchestral errors led to their not being released. Reiner disliked live recording because of distractions from errors and audience noise and was concerned about the illegal sale in other countries of transcriptions made in the United States.[13] Of the numerous radio performances he made at this time, a few have surfaced on disc. There was an LP issue of Reiner accompanying one of his favorite singers, Elisabeth Rethberg, in a 1937 radio performance of an aria from Gluck's *Alceste*, as well as radio recordings, also made in 1937, of Reiner conducting the Curtis Institute Orchestra in Brahms's *Academic Festival* Overture and Anton Rubinstein's Fourth Piano Concerto, with Josef Hofmann as soloist.[14]

Reiner's first commercial recordings were anonymous: neither orchestra nor conductor were named on the discs. On November 22, 1939, in Carnegie Hall he recorded four works for release as 78s. They appeared in a series entitled "The World's Greatest Music" that involved the collaboration of other leading conductors and singers. Reiner conducted a fairly rapid account (8 min., 57 sec.) of Wagner's prelude to act 1 of *Die Meistersinger* that emphasized the brilliance of the orchestral writing rather than the warmth of the leading motifs from the opera. The discs also included the prelude to act 1 of *Parsifal* and accounts of Debussy's "Nuages" and "Fêtes" from *Nocturnes* and the *Prélude à l'après-midi d'un faune* that offer clear definition of instrumental lines rather than an impressionistic haze. Unidentified on the records, the seventy-eight-strong orchestra was mainly drawn from the New York Philharmonic-Symphony Orchestra. The records, handled by RCA Victor, were distributed wholesale under the sponsorship of the *New York Post* in an effort to attract new subscribers; no royalties were paid. The issue of the discs led to an immediate reduction in the price of 78s.[15] When he realized the records were being issued generally, Reiner inquired of his lawyers whether he could sue for lack of royalties.[16] As it turned out, he decided to leave matters; he was not in a financial position to enter into legal expenses unless he could be certain of winning the case. He also did not wish to attract unfavorable publicity at a time when he had recently taken over the financially strapped Pittsburgh Symphony Orchestra, which was struggling to survive.[17]

By the time these recordings were made, Reiner had formulated his views on making records. He knew from experience that recorded sound was not the same as music heard in the concert hall. Fascinated by the technical aspects of recording, he nevertheless realized it was difficult to reproduce music satisfactorily on 78 rpm records. Shellac discs were scratchy and had to be changed every four minutes. Microphone placements could be a problem; they de-

pended very much on the type of score being recorded. An atmospheric Debussy composition, for instance, might work well with a single microphone
pickup; this could create "the shimmering, impalpable beauty of sound desired." But a complex score such as Stravinsky's *Le Sacre du printemps* required multiple microphones to encompass all the sonorities and counter-
rhythms. Attention needed to be paid to the recorded sound of different
orchestral instruments. Piccolos could be shrill and must therefore play less
vigorously than in the concert hall. Double basses could sound dull and
muddy; they needed to adjust their sound or use a special microphone for better focus. Overloud French horns could spoil a recording completely. All in all,
Reiner was in no doubt about the capricious nature of microphones. His experiences with making records before 1950 must have been trying; he once
said that it was not until then that records began to sound like music.[18]

Reiner's first significant recording activity arose with the revival of American Columbia's fortunes. After years of lagging behind the Victor Talking Machine Company and RCA Victor in recording classical music, Columbia trans-
formed itself rapidly. William Paley of CBS purchased Columbia at the end of
1938, and in the following year, under the energetic leadership of Edward
Wallerstein, Columbia reduced the retail price of classical records, made new
recordings, and began to compete effectively with RCA Victor for sales of classical records. RCA had established contracts with the Philadelphia, Boston
Symphony, and NBC Symphony Orchestras, so Columbia recorded with the
orchestras of Chicago, Cleveland, and Pittsburgh and with the Philharmonic-
Symphony of New York. Within three years all major American symphony orchestras were recording for one company or the other, and Reiner emerged as
a significant recording artist during this process.[19] After taking up the music
director's position with the Pittsburgh Symphony Orchestra, Reiner signed a
contract with Columbia for whom, during the 1940s, he recorded more than
forty works. These discs were all made with his Pittsburgh Orchestra until Reiner left his post there in 1948. His final records for Columbia, made between
1948 and 1950, were recorded with several groups based in New York.[20]

In Pittsburgh his first recording sessions were held in the Carnegie Music
Hall, but once that venue proved unsatisfactory the musicians decamped to
the nearby Syria Mosque, where recording conditions were better, though far
from ideal. For twenty-seven months, from August 1, 1942, until November
11, 1944, Reiner and his orchestra were unable to record because of the ban
imposed by James C. Petrillo, the powerful head of the AFM, over a dispute
with manufacturers about recording artists' payments. The ban was protracted
because two of the largest record manufacturers (RCA and Columbia) resisted Petrillo, fearing that their radio network contracts with NBC and CBS, respectively, would be whittled away. There was no hurry to resolve the dispute

because wartime brought an acute shortage of shellac from India, which was needed for making good records.[21] The recording ban ended with a compromise that gave Petrillo's organization 1 percent of the profits from record sales, a settlement that improved considerably the payment for musicians making recordings.[22]

When Reiner and the Pittsburgh Symphony began to record for Columbia in 1940, the first set of royalties was taken by the record company in lieu of several thousand dollars advanced to pay musicians' salaries. The conductor and the Pittsburgh Symphony Society received nothing until that amount was recovered.[23] After the Petrillo compromise, the Columbia Recording Corporation paid ten thousand dollars per session to the Pittsburgh Orchestra, with each musician earning fourteen dollars per hour.[24] A second recording ban occurred after the Taft-Hartley Act of 1947 made it illegal for the AFM to collect royalties from records. It lasted for almost the whole of 1948 but was resolved after labor and management agreed on a trustee to administer the Recording and Transcription Fund established in the wake of the first recording ban.[25]

For his Pittsburgh recordings, Reiner discussed with the producer (usually Goddard Lieberson) and technicians any cuts as well as the timings and breaks on each side before the recording took place. Only two microphones were used, set above and in front of the orchestra. They were so sensitive that Reiner was once asked to remove his shoes because they squeaked. The engineer balancing the recordings found the acoustics in the Syria Mosque difficult. Drapes and padding were used in the auditorium to improve sound quality, but this had only a limited effect on the acoustical deadness. The recordings were cut on sixteen-inch 33⅓ rpm lacquer or acetate discs. After the recordings were played back they were sent to New York, rerecorded on 78 rpm masters, and dispatched to the Columbia Laboratories at Bridgeport, Connecticut, where shellac discs were produced.[26] A lot of equipment was needed to make the recordings. For instance, in 1941 twenty-two trunkloads of equipment and two sound engineers were required to record the "Bacchanale" from *Tannhäuser*.[27] But Columbia always worked efficiently, since prolonged recording time was expensive. Thus in one afternoon and evening in November 1941, Reiner and his orchestra played thirty-four takes of works by five composers; only six takes were approved.[28]

Reiner's recordings in Pittsburgh featured music from the baroque and classical era. They included Bach's Suite no. 2 in B Minor for flute and strings and Lucien Cailliet's orchestration of the Fugue in G Minor, along with Mozart's symphonies nos. 35 (the *Haffner*) and 40 and Beethoven's Symphony no. 2 (but no Haydn). Most of his Pittsburgh recordings, however, consisted of orchestral music from the nineteenth and early twentieth centuries by Rossini, Brahms,

Wagner, Johann Strauss the younger, Richard Strauss, Mussorgsky, Debussy, Ravel, Gershwin, and Kabalevsky, among others. Four works recorded by Reiner in Pittsburgh received their premiere recordings—Mahler's *Lieder eines fahrenden gesellen,* Falla's *El amor brujo,* Robert Russell Bennett's suite from *Porgy and Bess,* and Bartók's *Concerto for Orchestra.* Reiner's recording of Shostakovich's Sixth Symphony was the second performance of the work on disc, the first being by Stokowski and the Philadelphia Orchestra in 1940.[29]

During initial discussions about recording for Columbia, Reiner expressed an interest in playing music by Wagner. The record company was worried that the Pittsburgh Symphony in 1939 could not sustain competition in this repertoire with more famous symphony orchestras in America and abroad. But the matter was left to Reiner's artistic discretion, and a selection of Wagnerian works was recorded.[30] For this occasion, marking the Pittsburgh Symphony's recording debut, Reiner took great care with the performances, recorded in the Carnegie Music Hall. Together with Moses Smith, the classical artists and repertoire (A&R) director at Columbia, he spent more than four hours listening to playbacks to ensure the recordings were well balanced.[31] Unfortunately, the result was a technical disaster. The recording engineers had problems with the electric current, and this slowed up the recording lathe. This meant that the 78 rpm masters had to be copied at the correct speed. Most test pressings were discarded because three rerecorded masters were damaged while being processed. Distortion and bad intonation affected the other discs so badly that Reiner referred to the recordings, with the exception of "The Ride of the Valkyries," as "actually an abortion." Most of these recordings have remained unreleased for these reasons.[32]

Another shelved recording was of Kodály's *Dances of Galánta,* withheld by Reiner because of dissatisfaction with his own account after he heard the composer conduct the work in Pittsburgh.[33] On hearing the test pressings, Reiner refused permission to release this performance because of "faulty execution" and poor intonation by the solo clarinet.[34] This performance has now been issued, fifty years later, on CD along with previously unreleased recordings of two of Bartók's brief *Hungarian Sketches* (recorded in April 1947) and Leó Weiner's *Divertimento* no. 1 for string orchestra (March 1945). These performances were acts of homage to compatriots who had made a deep impact on Reiner's early musical career. The refurbishment of the *Dances of Galánta* on CD suggests that Reiner was rather self-critical in rejecting the performance. The clarity of the demi-semiquavers at the opening of the *Dances* preserves a characteristic hallmark of his lucid conducting. The full, resonant sound of the strings at the appassionato at bar 135 indicates that the orchestra had a warmer timbre than was apparent when Reiner's Pittsburgh recordings were first released with variable sonics. And the synchronization of the headlong semiquavers between different instrumental lines from bar 445 onwards in the allegro vivace, coupled with the lift given to the first beat of the bar, provides an idiomatic yet tautly controlled rendering of the gypsy style upon which the composer originally based these dances.

Other recordings made by Reiner for Columbia were impaired, to some extent, by indifferent recording quality despite the use of lamination as a surfacing process to reduce needle noise. The performance of Brahms's First Piano Concerto, with Rudolf Serkin as soloist, received a shallow recording in which the piano tone was wooden and some of the instrumental details blurred. Upon its release, it was singled out as the worst recording of a major work over the past two years. The recording of Mozart's *Haffner* Symphony had coarsened tone in some ensembles.[35] Reiner was unhappy with the technical quality of the recording of *Don Quixote*, noting that there was no comparison between the original playbacks and the finished product: "the richness and mellowness of the orchestra is completely absent and only the precision of attacks remains something to be proud of."[36] The Mozart arias that Reiner recorded with Ljuba Welitsch with the Metropolitan Opera Orchestra in February 1950 had a weak and febrile tone and poor balance between the orchestra and the voice.[37]

Despite these recurrent technical flaws, many of Reiner's recordings in the 1940s enhanced his own reputation and that of the Pittsburgh Symphony Orchestra. They are artistically satisfying, they are in at least tolerable mono sound, and they include works that Reiner never rerecorded. They demonstrate the chief hallmarks of Reiner's conducting—rhythmic incisiveness, dramatic tension, a distinctive transparency of sound, and an uncanny ability to project the different styles of a varied repertoire. In Reiner's performance of music from the baroque and classical periods repeats are often ignored, unmarked ritardandos sometimes occur at the ends of movements, and there is sometimes lush legato phrasing from a large body of strings in slow movements—all characteristics of an older tradition of performance. Yet tempos are maintained without many significant gear changes, the playing is alert in quick movements and kept flowing in slower movements, and textures are light, which are all features of modern performance styles.

Reiner's accounts of Mozart's Symphonies no. 35, recorded in February 1946, and no. 40, recorded in April 1947, are marked by a classical sense of form and proportion, by lean yet firm string tone, by wind instruments playing as if a concertino, by crisp articulation, and by emphasis on sforzandos and contrapuntal effects. Ebullient allegros in the first movements—that of no. 40 a genuine allegro molto—coupled with flowing yet never cloying slow movements, steady minuets with trios taken at the same tempo, and very quick finales—stress the brilliance of the orchestral writing. The finale of the *Haffner*

Symphony, in particular, has an exhilarating propulsion. Reiner's recording of Beethoven's Second Symphony, made in March 1945, is one of robust articulation and sharp dynamic contrasts played by a sturdy ensemble, but with allowances made for the composer's dolce markings (as in the middle of the last movement). Throughout the symphony the frequent, abrupt sforzandos are highlighted, and the whole is given a forward impetus.

Among Reiner's Pittsburgh recordings of nineteenth-century repertoire are several devoted to shorter works such as Glinka's *Kamarinskaya*, Rossini's Overture *Il Signor Bruschino*, both recorded in February 1946, and a *A Night on the Bare Mountain*, made in March 1945. The latter piece, with harp and percussion nicely captured by the sound engineers, was recorded in one take when extra time was available at the end of a recording session.[38] Other shorter pieces recorded by Reiner included a selection of eight *Hungarian Dances* by Brahms in February 1946, full of shifting gypsy rhythms, subtle tempo fluctuations, and considerable panache in the vibrant, quick dances. Brahms did not write the word *rubato* in his score of the *Hungarian Dances*, but Reiner interpreted markings such as *ritenuto, stringendo, con passione*, and *espressivo* as implying such.[39] The gypsy style is especially captured in the middle of dance no. 12 in D Minor. Headlong tempi are the hallmark of the performance of no. 21 in E Minor.

Reiner also recorded warm-hearted, though never sentimental, accounts of three waltzes by Johann Strauss II: *Schatz-Walzer* (recorded in November 1941), *Rosen aus dem Süden* (recorded in February 1946), and *Wiener Blut* (recorded in January 1941). These recordings remind us of Reiner's innate grasp of the rapid changes of mood that are vital for performing music with a Hungarian flavor and his understanding of the lilt and variety of pace essential for playing Viennese waltzes in an authentic style. Dame Elisabeth Schwarzkopf has described Reiner's approach to Viennese waltz music as having "the perfect mixture of Hungarian dash, military exactitude and charm."[40] These recordings of shorter works also remind us that, at the time, Reiner was the equal of Beecham in the attentive musicianship and vivacious feeling he brought to bear on what other conductors considered mere trifles.

From his early days as a student and as an opera conductor in Budapest and Dresden, Reiner was a notable conductor of music by Wagner and Richard Strauss. Apart from the failed takes of music by Wagner referred to above, Reiner recorded other Wagner excerpts in January and November 1941: the preludes to acts 1 and 3 of *Lohengrin;* a cut version of the "Forest Murmurs" from act 2 of *Siegfried;* the bacchanale from *Tannhäuser's* "Venusberg Music"; and a concert suite from *Die Meistersinger*.

Reiner's personal friendship with Richard Strauss, and his penchant for conducting Strauss's music, led him to record four orchestral pieces in Pittsburgh:

Don Juan in January 1941, *Don Quixote* in November 1941, a suite from *Le bourgeois gentilhomme* in February 1946, and *Ein Heldenleben* in November 1947. Reiner had the gift of balancing all sections of the large orchestra required for performing Strauss so that nothing ever sounded muddy or overblown, even in heavily scored passages; clarity of texture was paramount. He provided thrilling climaxes aplenty in these scores, but in the quieter sections directed the music with an almost chamber-music, Mozartian delicacy. Particularly celebrated among these recordings is the account of *Don Quixote,* in which lush beauty of tone and dramatic impact are provided, and the three soloists, Gregor Piatigorsky (cello), Henri Temianka (violin), and Vladimir Bakaleinikoff (viola) are featured in the middle ground without the variations being turned into a triple concerto.[41] The other Strauss pieces are played with tremendous vitality and conviction, but they were surpassed in orchestral virtuosity by Reiner's rerecordings of these favorite works in Chicago in the 1950s (although listeners might prefer the accomplished, sweet violin playing by the orchestra's leader in the Pittsburgh *Heldenleben* rather than the somewhat angular playing of the same passages in the Chicago remake).

Apart from the Serkin version of Brahms's First Piano Concerto mentioned above, the only other Reiner Pittsburgh records that featured visiting soloists were performances from February 1946 of Mahler's *Lieder eines fahrenden Gesellen* and Falla's *El amor brujo,* both with Carol Brice as soloist. Brice had a smooth, even-textured voice that was almost that of a contralto in her powerful lower register, and she sings these two contrasting pieces with "vocal richness and emotional fervor."[42] When one considers that Pittsburgh Symphony concerts in the 1940s regularly included soloists of the caliber of Jascha Heifetz, Joseph Szigeti, Yehudi Menuhin, Vladimir Horowitz, Helen Traubel, and Lauritz Melchior, it is a pity that more recordings were not made to display Reiner's gifts as an accompanist in concertos and extracts from opera.

A few Pittsburgh discs remind us that Reiner was fully attuned to the sound world appropriate for performing impressionistic French music, which is unusual for a central European conductor. The pick of these recordings is a subtly molded *Ibéria,* made in November 1941. Reiner approached this music with an ear for careful gradations of different textures; transparency is combined with sensuality, and tempo fluctuations are fluent and well coordinated. Excellent solos by trumpet and cor anglais in "Le matin d'un jour de fête," along with clear percussion and rich strings throughout the recording, testify to the refinement and sonority of the orchestra that Reiner had fashioned within a few years. He also recorded Ravel's orchestration of Debussy's *Danse* with his Pittsburgh forces and a dynamic account of Ravel's *La valse* that provides agile brass playing but lacks a degree of warmth. These records were made in April 1947.

Reiner's interest in contemporary music led him to persuade Columbia to record several scores on which the ink had only just dried, as it were. The recording of Shostakovich's Sixth Symphony already mentioned was the first classical recording made in America after the Petrillo recording ban was lifted. When first released, it demonstrated an improvement on the quality of previous Columbia discs.[43] It sounds even more euphonious in its CD refurbishment. In the opening threnody, the heart of the symphony, Reiner is keenly observant of the composer's dynamic and rhythmic markings, and he imparts a continuous flow to this deeply introspective music by ensuring that the frequent changes of time signature are negotiated without hesitation or miscalculation. A live recording from 1943 of Reiner conducting the same symphony with the New York Philharmonic reveals a similar approach to the music.

In a lighter vein, Reiner recorded Robert Russell Bennett's orchestration of the waltz from Richard Rodgers's *Carousel* in February 1946, within a year of the musical's first production. Ethan Mordden regards this as the best version of the waltz on record, "a little fast but terribly exciting."[44] Reiner's recording of Robert Russell Bennett's "A Symphonic Picture" from Gershwin's *Porgy and Bess* includes an atmospheric cor anglais solo at the opening, some prominent banjo playing on "I Got Plenty of Nuttin'," and a deep string sound. Capturing the spirited energy and expressivity of the music, it is Reiner's tribute to Gershwin, who regarded the Hungarian maestro as the best conductor of his music.

Reiner's most significant recording of contemporary music in Pittsburgh was his account of Bartók's *Concerto for Orchestra,* made in February 1946, only fifteen months after the work's premiere. This was the first commercial recording of the work. It does not match the tonal luster of Reiner's famous October 1955 version with the Chicago Symphony Orchestra, nor does it have the raw excitement of Koussevitzky's live recording of the work; there are parts of the score where one is all too aware of musicians being fully stretched by the technical demands of the music. Nevertheless, the account intertwines fiery rhythmic playing and deeply felt expression in a fire-and-ice mixture that well suits Bartók's music, and which Reiner by temperament was so capable of providing.

Several of Reiner's Pittsburgh recordings received critical praise when they were first issued. His account of Richard Strauss's *Don Juan* demonstrated his flair for the romantic repertoire and achieved great clarity in presenting a complex score; many phrases and instrumental colors were heard with more transparency than on previous recordings of the work.[45] His performance of Berlioz's "Rakocky" march was considered the most thrilling then recorded, and his recording of Debussy's *Ibéria* captured its gaiety, brilliance, and color better than any previously recorded performance. His Wagnerian excerpts were praised as outstanding, and one reviewer hoped that the excellent recording would enhance

Reiner's fame; certainly they would not dim it in any way.[46] Reiner's version of the six Brandenburg concerti, made with his own handpicked chamber ensemble in 1949, suffered from rather recessed recording of the harpsichord continuo part, except in the cadenza of the Fifth Concerto, where it was prominent. There was also some strain in the playing of the high trumpet part in the Second Concerto. Despite these imperfections, the set was recommended as the first serious rival to the famous 1936 recording by the Busch Chamber Players.[47]

Reiner's plans to record other repertoire with Columbia never reached fruition. He wanted to tackle more music by Bartók and enquired, at the start of his association with Columbia, whether they would be interested in recording the composer's *Divertimento,* Second Piano Concerto, and *Roumanian Dances.* But the record company was not interested in pursuing these projects; it is likely that they thought contemporary works could only reach a limited consumer market.[48] The cost of recording large-scale works was prohibitive. Thus Reiner's discussions about recording Verdi's *Requiem* for Columbia came to nothing.[49] He wanted to record pieces that required smaller-scale forces, with a maximum of thirty-five players. One work that met these requirements was Richard Strauss's *Ariadne auf Naxos,* for which Reiner did not insist on star singers.[50] Columbia's Goddard Lieberson had definite plans to record an album of four sides from *Ariadne auf Naxos* with Reiner conducting the Metropolitan Opera Orchestra and singers, but the recording was never made.[51]

Apart from the Strauss opera, Reiner hoped to record the same composer's *Dance Suite after Couperin* and several other pieces, including Stravinsky's *Pulcinella* Suite, Schoenberg's Chamber Symphony no. 1, Wagner's *Siegfried Idyll,* Falla's Harpsichord Concerto, and several Mozart Divertimenti (K. 205 in D major, K. 209 in D major, K. 247 in F major, and K. 287 in B-flat major). These recordings never materialized, nor did a proposed recording of Schoenberg's *Verklärte nacht.*[52] It seems that Reiner's choice of repertoire with Columbia was pruned after the Philadelphia Orchestra was hired by the company from RCA Victor in 1943.[53]

Although there were some disagreements over repertoire to be recorded, Columbia gave Reiner and his orchestra full support by the mid-1940s. When Reiner led the Pittsburgh Symphony on a sponsored national tour in 1947, Columbia Records backed the tour with publicity kits and photographs of orchestral players in each of the cities where the orchestra played.[54] Reiner wanted to expand his horizons by making discs with other orchestras.[55] In 1947 Columbia offered him an exclusive personal contract for three years, and the executive committee of the Pittsburgh Symphony waived the exclusive recording provision in Reiner's contract to accommodate his making records with other orchestras. The understanding was that he would not record works elsewhere that his own orchestra could reasonably expect to make.[56] In the event, the only remaining records Reiner made for Columbia, after his departure from Pittsburgh in 1948, were the Brandenburg Concertos referred to above; Honegger's *Concertino*, with Oscar Levant as piano soloist and the Columbia Symphony Orchestra; and some Mozart arias and the closing scene from *Salome*, with Welitsch as soloist accompanied by the Metropolitan Opera Orchestra.

This last recording preserves Welitsch for posterity in her most famous role and Reiner in one of his most successful musical collaborations. The sensation that their joint debut in *Salome* created in February 1949 has already been discussed. This Columbia recording provides us with the horrific ending of the opera in its concert version, without the voices of Herod and Herodias.[57] Though plans to record a complete *Salome* with Reiner and Welitsch in 1949 for commercial release were abandoned owing to lack of funds,[58] we should be grateful for the sixteen-minute extract that was recorded. This is one of the few commercial discs emanating from Reiner's period at the Met between 1949 and 1953.

Reiner and Welitsch combine to impart force and passion to the final scene of the opera, in which Salome is killed after kissing the lips of John the Baptist's severed head. Reiner builds the tension of the music gradually, reveling in the lurid instrumental effects of Strauss's bold orchestration and laying bare every instrumental strand in the complex design. Welitsch's voice is lean, shimmering, full of brilliance and subtlety, with a cold smoothness of tone that captures the madness of the obsessed sixteen-year-old; it rings out over the full orchestra without stridence or shrillness. There have been many fine Salomes, but Welitsch's characterization has been a yardstick against which others are measured since the evening she burst on to the New York operatic scene. Reiner rerecorded the final scene from *Salome* in the mid 1950s with Inge Borkh—another renowned Salome—and the Chicago Symphony Orchestra. Superb though that recording is, both artistically and technically, it does not efface memories of Reiner's collaboration with the Bulgarian soprano.

These Columbia recordings were issued first (in most cases) on 78s. Some were later reissued on ten- or twelve-inch LPs in two budget-priced series—the "Columbia Entre" and, later, the "Columbia Harmony" labels. A number were made available again on discs with electronic stereo enhancement. Only recently have some of Reiner's Columbia recordings with the Pittsburgh Symphony Orchestra become available on CD. Live broadcasts of concerts conducted by Reiner during his years in Pittsburgh have also been issued on compact disc. The most valuable of these recordings include repertoire he never recorded commercially, such as Ravel's Second Suite from *Daphnis et Chloë* with the CBS Symphony Orchestra (recorded in September 1945) and a powerful account of Hindemith's *Mathis der Maler* Symphony with the NBC Symphony Orchestra from December 1946.

In 1950 Reiner left Columbia for RCA Victor, two years after 33⅓ rpm vinyl records began to replace 78 rpm shellac discs. The change occurred soon after his appointment at the Met, where several leading singers were contracted to RCA rather than to Columbia. Reiner was persuaded that it would benefit him to change companies, though he seems to have been unaware that he could record operatic extracts only with Met artists who lacked an exclusive arrangement with another recording company.[59] Reiner had been disappointed with the royalties earned from his Columbia discs—another reason for the change. RCA now regarded Reiner as a major conductor who could record a broad repertoire for them at a time when their most illustrious maestro, Toscanini, was over eighty years old and thinking of retiring, and when they had no other conductor on their books whose records could guarantee extensive sales. Reiner was more enthusiastic about recording than he had been in the 78 rpm era because Columbia's nonbreakable vinylite disc was "a conductor's dream come true" with "complete absence of surface noise and distortion."[60]

The beginning of the LP era encouraged major record companies to extend their roster of artists, as the commercial sales potential of the new technology became apparent.[61] RCA executives therefore offered Reiner a three-year contract in August 1950 to conduct complete operas and orchestral works with an ad hoc group called the RCA Victor Symphony Orchestra. This was a fine pickup ensemble consisting of the cream of musicians in Manhattan, drawn from the New York Philharmonic, the Met, and freelance players. Most of its recordings with Reiner were made in the Manhattan Center.[62]

For the next three years, while mainly conducting at the Met, Reiner made several recordings for his new company with the RCA Victor Symphony Orchestra, the NBC Symphony Orchestra, and the Robin Hood Dell Orchestra (the summer version of the Philadelphia Orchestra). Several of these records were issued on both 33⅓ and 45 rpm discs, for RCA was then engaged in a battle of the speeds with Columbia, the company that introduced the long-playing record in 1948; the contest was only resolved when RCA began issuing LPs in 1950.[63] The recordings were made with limited rehearsal time, though the orchestras concerned had high-quality personnel with quick sight-reading ability to offset this potential disadvantage.

Reiner was closely involved in decisions about the works he recorded for RCA. Some items he conducted were obviously put on disc because they were popular pieces that would sell well. This is true of a ten-inch disc, recorded in September 1950, that included a selection of Tchaikovsky's waltzes. Reiner recorded brief excerpts from operas without singers, including Wagner's "Festmarsch" from *Tannhäuser* and the prelude to act 3 of *Lohengrin* plus the "Dream Pantomine" from Humperdinck's *Hänsel und Gretel*.[64] These were all set down on October 19, 1950, as pieces suitable for the short playing time of 45 rpm discs. Reiner also recorded *Till Eulenspiegel* and *Tod und Verklärung* on successive days in September 1950. In the latter, the orchestra sounds technically stretched in meeting Reiner's conception of the music.

To follow up his Columbia recordings of the Brandenburg Concertos, Reiner turned his attention to Bach's four orchestral suites. The first, third, and fourth suites were recorded in October 1952; the second was recorded in April and May 1953. The performances display a mixture of styles: romantic accretions exist alongside a concern for chamber-music scale. The recordings, using a small string group and harpsichord continuo, had good instrumental balance. The contrapuntal lines can be easily heard in performances that were "clean, beautifully balanced, rhythmically alert, sensitive and spacious."[65] But as with his approach to the Brandenburgs, Reiner allowed legato phrasing where today it would be avoided and made a number of unmarked ritardandi. Such a mixture of styles has elicited differing critical comments. Reiner's opening movements of the two D major suites were, to some critics, full of breadth and nobility, whereas to others they had impossibly slow majestic tempi "once considered fitting for the great Bach."[66] Paul Henry Lang, while admiring the performances, wrote that the Second Suite (with Julius Baker as the flute soloist) was ponderous and big "with soulful crescendos that blow your hat off and ritards that give you asthma." He pinpointed the hybrid style of Reiner's Bach: the Third Suite sounded as if it were really chamber music, with subdued trumpets, whereas Bach had in mind something more festive; the fugue following the introduction was delightfully sprightly; the concluding gigue was played like the prestissimo furioso of a nineteenth-century symphony only to end with an exaggerated rallentando in the last two bars.[67]

In the early 1950s RCA Victor wanted to record opera, and Reiner was an obvious choice as conductor. In fact, his recording career for RCA began on September 20, 1950, with a disc of highlights from *Die Fledermaus* in English translation based on a production of this operetta that was the biggest box-office success in the Met's history. The singers were Patrice Munsel, Risë Stevens, Regina Resnik, Jan Peerce, and Robert Merrill, accompanied by the Robert Shaw Chorale. Unfortunately, the recording does not have a particularly Viennese atmosphere, and one suspects that the music moves more rapidly than usual in order to fit onto two sides of a disc.

Reiner turned down an offer to record *Der Rosenkavalier*, one of his favorite works, because it might take twenty-six sides of 45 rpm discs in a shortened version that would do no justice to the entire opera.[68] Yet he did record two extracts from the opera (the presentation of the silver rose and the closing scene) with Risë Stevens and Erna Berger and also accompanied Stevens in arias from *Le nozze di Figaro* and Gluck's *Orfeo et Euridice*. These recordings, made in March and April 1951, are worthy mementos of roles sung by Stevens many times at the Met. As in the live recording of *Der Rosenkavalier* discussed above, Berger's bright coloratura and Stevens' sensuous mezzo-soprano blend perfectly in projecting Strauss's taxing yet beautiful legato lines for his leading female singers.

Reiner's one full-length commercial opera recording consisted of *Carmen*. The sessions, held at the Manhattan Center in May and June 1951, were made in advance of a new Met production of the opera in January 1952. They catered to an expanding market for opera on disc. Using two hundred thousand feet, or about forty miles, of tape under a new recording system that allowed immediate and multiple playbacks for critical evaluation, the entire recording took fifteen days, including four days' rehearsal. But the soloists had rehearsed separately for weeks beforehand with Reiner. They included Risë Stevens in one of her celebrated starring roles; Jan Peerce as Don José, replacing the original choice for the role, Jussi Bjoerling; Robert Merrill as Escamillo; and Licia Albanese as Micaëla. Supporting the principals were a children's chorus, forty selected singers from the Robert Shaw Chorale, and the RCA Victor Orchestra, comprising eighty of the nation's virtuoso instrumentalists drawn from New York freelance players. Cast, chorus, and orchestra were assigned definite locations in the recording studio and tested singly and in combination, for motions of the arm and body had to be limited to avoid disturbing the recording balance.[69]

Stevens had restudied the role of Carmen for the recording and the Met production, and she projects a sultry, fascinating portrayal of the gypsy temptress. The rest of the principals are variable: Peerce is ardent but frequently sings at a heroic forte even when that is not called for; Albanese is spirited but has poor French diction and was obviously more at home in Italian opera; and Merrill is vocally stolid. The whole performance lacks an authentic French ring apart from the children's voices.[70] But the enterprise is redeemed by Reiner's subtle and fiery conducting of a favorite score and his partnership with Stevens in building up the tragedy with considerable momentum.[71] The well-disciplined orchestral playing represents the best collaboration between Reiner and this particular orchestra. RCA agreed that Reiner could record further works with the same players, including Tchaikovsky's *Hamlet* and *The Tempest*, Haydn's Symphony no. 100 in G Major (the *Military*), and Mahler's *Das Lied von der Erde*, but these plans did not materialize.[72]

In the early fifties, Reiner made a few discs for RCA with the NBC Symphony Orchestra and the Robin Hood Dell Orchestra. With NBC forces, he turned his attention in September 1954 to Mozart's Divertimento in D, K. 251, and *A Musical Joke,* K. 522, having previously undertaken Debussy's *Petite Suite* and Ravel's *Le tombeau de Couperin* with the same orchestra on January 21, 1952. Robert Bloom, the first oboist on the recording of K. 251, recalls that Reiner was a joy to work with during the sessions and that the ensemble playing was exceptionally good.[73] The Debussy and Ravel selections followed an NBC Symphony broadcast of the music. With the Robin Hood Dell Orchestra, Reiner recorded works he had scheduled for summer concerts in Philadelphia, and commercial considerations governed the selection to some extent. Thus excerpts from Mendelssohn's incidental music to *A Midsummer Night's Dream* were put onto disc rather than Haydn's *Military* Symphony because more royalties were likely to ensue.[74]

In these early years under contract to RCA, Reiner had a greater opportunity than during his stint in Pittsburgh to accompany leading soloists on disc. He resumed his partnership with the cellist Gregor Piatigorsky in Saint-Saëns's Cello Concerto no. 1, made with the RCA Victor Orchestra in December 1950, and Brahms's Double Concerto in A Minor, recorded in June 1951 with Nathan Milstein as the violin soloist and the Robin Hood Dell Orchestra. This performance is full of rhythmic zest, careful dovetailing of orchestral fragments in the accompaniment, and a high degree of unanimity and coordination between the soloists. With the same orchestra, Reiner accompanied William Kapell in a dazzling account of Rachmaninov's *Rhapsody on a Theme of Paganini* that combined stunning fingerwork by the young American pianist with sensitivity to the moods of individual variations.

With the RCA Orchestra Reiner partnered Alexander Brailowsky in another work that quoted the "Dies Irae" theme (Liszt's *Totentanz,* a disc made in March 1951) and accompanied Horowitz in Beethoven's Piano Concerto no. 5 (the *Emperor*) and Rachmaninov's Third Piano Concerto. The latter is one of Horowitz's finest performances of a work indelibly associated with him, and its rhythmic drive and color are matched by Reiner's direction. The other significant recording made with a soloist in the early 1950s was Brahms's *Alto Rhapsody,* sung by the African American contralto Marian Anderson accompanied by the Robert Shaw Chorale.

After he moved to Chicago, Reiner still hoped to conduct with the RCA Victor Symphony, an ensemble he regarded as appropriate for small-scale orchestral repertoire. Among works he wanted to record with them were Falla's Harpsichord Concerto, several Mozart Divertimenti, Wagner's *Siegfried Idyll,* Richard Strauss's Dance Suite after Couperin, and Stravinsky's *Pulcinella* Suite.[75] Reiner had failed to persuade Columbia to undertake several of these pieces under his direction in the late forties. The projects never got off the ground, however, probably because Reiner gave his full attention to recording with the Chicago Symphony Orchestra from the autumn of 1953 onwards.

On moving to Chicago, Reiner won back the RCA contract that the orchestra had lost four years previously to Mercury, with whom, during Rafael Kubelik's tenure, it had made some acclaimed mono recordings. For contractual reasons Mercury made two final recordings with the Chicago Symphony Orchestra, with Antal Dorati as conductor, during Reiner's first season. Then Reiner's first recordings with RCA got under way in March 1954. Mercury promptly transferred its attention to the Minneapolis Symphony Orchestra under Dorati and to the Detroit Symphony under Paul Paray.[76]

Over the next decade Reiner recorded 122 compositions with his new orchestra. He could now record works that had been given at least a couple of performances in the Chicago Symphony's regular subscription series.[77] He repeated some pieces he had put on to 78s in Pittsburgh, but he also included new works. Reiner's Chicago recordings took place in Orchestra Hall, which he regarded as the best recording venue in the world. When the hall was full the acoustics were very dry, but when empty it was quite reverberant and considered almost ideal for recording. Reiner was fortunate in making all of his Chicago recordings before 1966, when the hall was renovated to drastic effect, decreasing the reverberation time. He also benefited from many hours of recording time made possible by generous musicians' contracts.[78] Reiner quickly became a pinnacle of RCA's classical recording catalog and demanded many hours of recording time on the strength of his reputation.[79]

Reiner experienced some complications over repertoire when launching his RCA career. He wanted a significant piece to make a "splash" and demonstrate at once the quality of the music making emanating from Chicago under his direction. But he found it difficult to select something suitable. At the suggestion of RCA, he explored the possibility of recording Mahler's Sixth Symphony but abandoned the idea; he was bored by the music, and it required four long-playing sides and four recording sessions. Moreover, the expense of paying an orchestra of 116 musicians would make it difficult to recoup the initial investment. Reiner then thought of recording *Also sprach Zarathustra* but was worried that it would duplicate Rodzinski's Chicago recording of the work and that distortion might occur at the quiet ending of the tone poem if it was squeezed onto one side of a disc. He then proposed *Don Quixote*, with János Starker as cellist, but thought it too long for one long-playing side (even though Piatigorsky's 1953 recording with Charles Munch and the Boston Symphony Orchestra fit on one side). The possibility of extracts from *Elektra* was raised but discarded because Reiner insisted on vocal highlights rather than symphonic ones and thought an arrangement for instruments without voices would be justly criticized. The number of players needed was 110, which was a further consideration. (He later recorded extended excerpts from *Elektra*, however, including singers.) Reiner was unhappy with RCA's suggestion that he record Tchaikovsky's *Francesca da Rimini* or Sibelius's *Scènes Historiques* for his debut with the Chicago Symphony because he felt that both works contained too much weak music.[80]

At the beginning of his Chicago career, Reiner thought he was treated as "a negligible quantity as far as RCA promotion is concerned."[81] Upset by the changing whims of the company's recording executives, he complained to his agent that RCA gave priority to other conductors, notably Toscanini with his NBC Symphony and Munch with the Boston Symphony Orchestra. Toscanini's late recordings of operas and orchestral music were marketed aggressively by RCA in the late forties and early fifties.[82] This competition meant initially that Reiner did not record any Beethoven, Brahms, or Schumann symphonies and no works by Berlioz. RCA had their own priorities, of course. They distributed repertoire for recording among several illustrious orchestras and conductors, and the works they undertook with particular artists took account of practicalities as well as artistic considerations.[83] As late as 1953 RCA was insisting that they could only release one annual recording conducted by Reiner because he did not have his own orchestra. On taking over the Chicago Symphony, however, Reiner wanted a broader choice of repertoire to record; RCA, it seemed, was merely offering a "tie-up" contract to prevent him from recording for anyone else.[84]

As it happened, the debut recording of the Chicago Symphony under Reiner was *Also sprach Zarathustra* in March 1954, which created exactly the "splash" that the conductor wanted. One of the first LPs recorded in stereo, though not issued in that format until 1960, it has been acclaimed for forty years as one of the finest performances of the work ever recorded. On its first appearance the mono version was hailed as a performance without equal, one that was beautifully balanced, warm, and bright-toned. In its CD reincarnation, it has been praised in the *Gramophone* for presenting "a measure of raw passion and forward thrust unequalled on disc,"[85] and it is certainly a swifter, more intense reading of the score than Reiner's later remake of the same piece.

RCA soon became fully committed to recording in Chicago, partly because of the artistic and commercial success of the first discs Reiner made there and partly because of the expanding market for LPs. As a worldwide electronics company, RCA could offer state-of-the-art equipment and highly skilled technical personnel to facilitate recording. They supplied twenty-five thousand dollars' worth of the finest equipment, recruited some of the industry's best technicians, and invested two thousand dollars an hour in search of superior performance. By 1956 the chief RCA recording engineer, William H. Miltenburg, supervised most Chicago sessions with a three-man team. The equipment used in a makeshift studio in the basement of Orchestra Hall, Chicago, consisted of two Ampex dual-track tape recorders, a dual-channel mixer console, and a stereo speaker system for monitoring. Microphone placement varied a little from work to work, depending on the nature of a composition, the acoustics, and the soloists.[86]

Reiner's early recordings in Chicago were made separately in mono and stereo. RCA was already using stereo techniques in 1954, but the company's producers were unaware of the pioneering research on stereophony carried out by Bell Laboratories in the thirties.[87] By Christmas 1956, RCA began to issue expensive two-track open-reel stereo tapes for audiophiles, and within two years stereo discs became available after the Westrex Company successfully devised a method of putting two stereo channels into a single record groove.

An accomplished professional team supervised Reiner's RCA recordings. Richard Mohr was the senior A&R man for the recording sessions. He was aided by another producer, John Pfeiffer, and by the recording engineers Lewis Layton and Leslie Chase. From 1954 onwards, when stereo recording became common, Mohr and Layton took charge of mono recordings in Orchestra Hall while Pfeiffer and Chase produced concurrent two-track stereo tapes. Different consoles and microphone settings were used by both crews. The intention was for the mono recording to be released; the stereo recordings were experimental, and neither the engineers nor RCA knew what their quality would be. By planning the mono and stereo recordings simultaneously, using a three-channel recording on half-inch tape, RCA could budget for an expensive operation.[88]

Layton, a highly experienced recording engineer, experimented with different microphone settings. In 1956 and 1957, for recordings of *Pictures at an Exhibition* and Strauss waltzes, he used three microphones beyond the edge of the stage and one or two extra ones to highlight the woodwinds. By 1958 he added more microphones among the strings, often five in all, plus one or two among the winds, all of which helped him to balance the sound better. For mono recordings, Layton and his RCA colleagues followed the one omnidirectional microphone placement used by Mercury for recordings with the Chicago Symphony in the early fifties.[89]

Reiner could adjust the orchestra by ear after any playback to achieve the balance he wanted.[90] He admired RCA's technical resolution of potential recording problems and, in a brief statement presented on disc, cited the final movement of Beethoven's Seventh Symphony as an example of a recording that met this challenge.[91] Reiner demanded perfection of himself and of others, and few retakes occurred during his recording sessions. Always patient with the recording crew, making no unreasonable demands, he nevertheless became irritated if more than three takes of a particular passage were needed.[92] He preferred long takes so that recordings had the feel of a live performance. This was usually feasible, since he had a world-class orchestra at his disposal in Chicago and had usually performed works several times in concert prior to the recording sessions. Long takes were also favored because mistakes were expensive; musicians' fees for the recording sessions came from half of Reiner and the Chicago Orchestral Association's royalties. Thus Reiner also had a purely financial motive to ensure that recording sessions were efficient: his RCA contract stated that the shorter the recording session, the greater his fee would be.[93]

Starker recalled that many of Reiner's first takes were fine recordings but that he often wanted to touch up balances here and there and rerecord sections. Sometimes this practice drained the spontaneity out of performances; it was a legacy partly of the stop-and-start days of recording 78s. One well-known example of tinkering occurred when Reiner recorded the Brahms Violin Concerto with Heifetz in February 1955. The first take consisted of the entire work played straight through from beginning to end. But when Reiner and Heifetz started to "improve" upon it, the end result was only achieved seventeen hours later (and, in Starker's opinion, was inferior to the first take).[94] Heifetz was virtually the only solo virtuoso to whom Reiner deferred; he regarded him as the supreme professional.[95] But as the recording session dragged on, Reiner became tired and left the hall to go home, whereupon Heifetz shrugged his shoulders, packed up his violin, and announced that they would play the piece in concert tomorrow and record again on Monday.[96]

Occasionally Reiner passed a recording made in one take, despite some slips, when he thought the entire performance warranted it; this was the case with his second Chicago recording of *Don Juan*, made on February 6, 1960.[97] A similar situation occurred when *Scheherazade* was recorded two days later. Reiner had rarely performed this work, but he realized that it was ideal for displaying the virtuosity of his players. The finale was recorded in one take, without any splices, which amazed Mohr, the producer.[98] When Reiner recorded Brahms's Second Piano Concerto in February 1958, however, the soloist, Emil Gilels, had not yet memorized the music or played it in a public concert, so the piece was rehearsed and recorded simultaneously, and although the performance sounds spontaneous, the end result included extensive splicing.[99]

Perhaps the most difficult of all the pieces Reiner tackled, from the point of view of recording balance, was Respighi's *Pines of Rome* in sessions held in October 1959. The 109–piece orchestra required for this tone poem was augmented by twelve extra brass players for its final section, a depiction of the Roman legions marching along the Appian Way. The dynamic range of a live performance of the work was 40 percent greater than was possible on tape. The recording session began with a search for recording levels that could match the piano, mezzo-forte, and forte markings in the score, with Reiner selecting key passages, taping them, and listening to playbacks to check the balance. The recording session for the twenty-minute score took three hours and fifteen minutes.[100] The initial LP mastering was too dynamic for cartridges to track properly, and some fifteen hundred faulty test pressings had to be recalled after distribution. The original records were cut at too high a level, and an incorrect diameter equalization was used in the inner grooves. The distortion was not rectified until the performance was remastered for compact disc.[101]

Reiner's Chicago recordings included a number of discs in which he accompanied soloists in concertos and other concertante works. Among the leading soloists with whom he recorded were the pianists Gilels, Van Cliburn, Byron Janis, Artur Rubinstein, and André Tchaikowsky, the violinist Heifetz, and the cellist Antonio Janigro. These were usually amicable collaborations. RCA executives offered Gilels a choice of orchestra for his American debut recording of Tchaikovsky's First Piano Concerto in October 1955. He had no hesitation in specifying Reiner and the Chicago Symphony.[102] Gilels and Reiner spent much time in private going over the five hours of playing recorded for this performance, discussing which takes were best.[103] They forged a formidable partnership, combining vital, incisive music making with considerable poetry. Gilels and Reiner later made the acclaimed recording of Brahms's Second Piano Concerto mentioned above.

With Byron Janis, Reiner recorded staples from the romantic piano repertoire: Rachmaninov's First Piano Concerto and Richard Strauss's *Burleske*, both recorded in March 1957; Schumann's Concerto in A Minor; and Liszt's *Totentanz* (playing the autograph score, as published by Eulenberg, not the cut version by Alexander Siloti). The Schumann was recorded in February 1959 but not released at that time because RCA Victor had jumped on the bandwagon of the phenomenally successful Van Cliburn, whom they wanted to project as their leading pianist in this repertoire. Thus Janis's recording of the concerto was not released commercially until the 1980s. Janis recalls that Reiner undertook concerto recordings as a partnership between the soloist and conductor, slanting his podium to face the pianist and thus maintaining eye contact: "this podium placement was unique to Reiner, and it strongly facilitated communication."[104]

Reiner worked closely with Cliburn, with whom he recorded Brahms's Second Piano Concerto, Beethoven's Piano Concertos nos. 4 and 5, Schumann's Piano Concerto, and Rachmaninov's Piano Concerto no. 2. Their collaboration began soon after Cliburn's triumphant return from winning the Tchaikovsky piano competition in Moscow in 1958. Reiner recognized Cliburn's talent and treated him kindly. They established a fruitful rapport. Usually Cliburn visited Rambleside before a recording session was held; he and the conductor would go over piano scores to establish tempi and phrasing.[105] In the last few years before Reiner's death, Cliburn would only record with the Hungarian maestro (except when Reiner was ill).[106] The discs resulting from this partnership were all made between 1960 and 1963.

Reiner's collaboration with Rubinstein began well with a powerful account of Brahms's Piano Concerto no. 1, recorded concurrently in mono and stereo. This was released in January 1955 only in mono; the stereo recording was not issued until 1977 because Rubinstein, soon after the Chicago sessions, rerecorded the concerto in stereo for RCA with the Boston Symphony under Erich Leinsdorf. Reiner's other encounters with Rubinstein were more stormy. During a recording of Rachmaninov's Second Piano Concerto in January 1956, Rubinstein played some wrong notes and asked to repeat a certain passage. Reiner was furious. "Do you think we will stay here while you make your mistakes?" he asked. After a few silent seconds, Rubinstein replied, "Doesn't your orchestra ever make mistakes?" Reiner peered over his half-moon glasses and retorted, "Yes, but only once."[107] He turned to Rubinstein and said that if he had to correct all his mistakes, they would have to start the piece from the beginning. Rubinstein took offense at this comment and completed the session with Rachmaninov's *Rhapsody on a Theme by Paganini,* which he played faultlessly, and then canceled scheduled recordings of Grieg's Piano Concerto and Liszt's First Piano Concerto with Reiner and his orchestra.[108] Reiner and Rubinstein never worked together again. RCA was furious about the canceled sessions, as they had already assembled a recording crew in Chicago.[109] Orchestral players were also not amused: they lost several thousand dollars as a result of these cancellations.[110]

Reiner also became upset with André Tchaikowsky who confessed, during a February 1958 recording session for Mozart's Piano Concerto no. 25, that he had never played the work in public and had learned it just for that occasion. Reiner had been considerate towards Tchaikowsky until this point, but he was furious that the pianist should dare to record a concerto under such circumstances. The disc was released, but Tchaikowsky was never invited back to record in Chicago.[111] Tchaikowsky and Reiner recorded Bach's Concerto for Clavier no. 5 in F Minor (BWV 1056) in February 1958; this was unreleased at the time but later surfaced on a Chicago Symphony Orchestra fundraising LP in 1980.

A large number of works that Reiner planned to record with RCA never saw the light of day. In 1959 he wanted to make discs of Kodály's *Dances of Galánta,* Bartók's *Miraculous Mandarin,* Tchaikovsky's Fifth Symphony, Dukas's *The Sorcerer's Apprentice,* Saint-Saëns's *Danse Macabre,* Haydn's *Military* Symphony, Shostakovich's Sixth Symphony, Prokofiev's Fifth Symphony, Wagner's *Siegfried Idyll* and *Wesendonck* lieder, Ravel's Suites nos. 1 and 2 from *Daphnis et Chloë* and *La valse,* Satie's *Gymnopédies* nos. 1 and 3, and a selection of Mozart overtures. He also wanted to record some larger works with the Chicago Symphony Chorus, including Brahms's *German* Requiem, Berlioz's *Roméo et Juliette,* and Carl Orff's *Carmina Burana.*[112] He persuaded

RCA to record Bartók's *Music for Strings, Percussion, and Celesta* but failed to convince them of the need for a complete *Elektra*. By this stage of his career, however, he did not want to waste energy on prolonged tussles over repertoire to be recorded.[113]

Reiner had good financial sense; he wanted to record a stereo version of Ferde Grofé's *Grand Canyon* Suite, which he predicted would become a bestseller. But the trustees of the Chicago Symphony refused permission; they stated that such a popular piece was beneath the dignity of their orchestra. Instead, Arthur Fiedler and the Boston Pops Orchestra made the recording; it netted a million dollars in fifteen years.[114] RCA belatedly hoped to complete a cycle of Beethoven symphonies with Reiner and his Chicago forces,[115] but in 1961, when it was planned to fill the gaps, Reiner's illness forced him to curtail his conducting and this project. Reiner recorded six of the nine Beethoven symphonies in Chicago between December 1954 and May 1961 (all save numbers two, four, and eight); the fourth and eighth symphonies are available, however, in live mono recordings from his Chicago years. Videocassettes have been made of Reiner conducting his orchestra in telecasts of the second and seventh symphonies.

Given Reiner's long-standing association with the operas of Richard Strauss, it might be thought that these would be good choices for him to record. But this was not to be. In 1953 he canceled a proposed recording of *Salome* because, apart from Astrid Varnay, who was available and sang the title part well, first-class singers currently in the United States could not, in Reiner's opinion, be found for the other roles.[116] In 1956 George Marek, the A&R director of RCA Red Seal, vetoed a complete *Elektra* conducted by Reiner, arguing that the market for such an expensive project was too limited. Only excerpts from *Elektra* were recorded, with the soloists placed on a special platform behind the orchestra; the result was one of Reiner's most celebrated discs.[117] And though Reiner conducted the American premiere of *The Rake's Progress* at the Met, the complete recording of the opera fell to the composer, partly because Stravinsky recorded for Columbia, whereas Reiner was contracted to RCA.[118]

Reiner's recordings with the Chicago Symphony Orchestra display several of his hallmarks—his penchant for crisp, precise rhythms, for building up dramatic tension, for handling a varied and eclectic repertoire with conviction, and for perfecting the sound world appropriate for particular pieces. Reiner's recordings from the classical repertoire centered on Mozart and Beethoven symphonies. Agreeing with Tchaikovsky's observation that "Mozart is the sun around whom the rest of us revolve,"[119] Reiner took special care with his performances of Mozart. For recordings of Mozart's Symphonies nos. 36, 39, 40, and 41, made in April 1954 and April 1955, he used a fairly large string section and conducted direct, propulsive performances in a manner more akin to

Toscanini than to Furtwängler or Bruno Walter. Reiner's Mozart recordings maintain forward progress and display meticulous attention to minute details of phrasing and articulation; they also offer clear textures, especially in the balance between winds and strings in tuttis. Sometimes the finales are pressed precipitously, as if the main point were to display his orchestra's virtuosity: listen, for example, to the Chicago Symphony recording of the *Linz* Symphony, in which the speedy tempo for the last movement's *Presto* drains the music of grace and charm.[120] Yet even at speed Reiner never lost his technical command over the music's structure: his recording of the fugal finale of the *Jupiter* Symphony illustrates his ability to balance whirlwind speed and structural clarity.

Reiner's approach to Beethoven's symphonies was Olympian, with due regard to their structural cogency and sustained development of thematic material but also with an ability to convey their emotional depth and elemental dynamism. Reiner's Beethoven symphony recordings emphasize dramatic tensions in the music. This stemmed partly from his insistence on sharp articulation of notes and an intensity of attack in outer movements, his emphasis on dramatic sforzandi that pepper Beethoven's symphonies, and his ability to build up crescendi gradually where demanded by the score. In the opening movement of the Seventh Symphony, for example, Reiner emphasizes the string sforzandi in the *Poco Sostenuto* introduction and the crescendo poco a poco at bars 236–49. His projection of dramatic tension is shown especially well at bars 164–89 of the first movement of the Eighth Symphony, taken from a concert held on February 6, 1958. Here his beat emphasizes the second crotchet of each bar as the excitement increases up to the restatement of the symphony's opening theme in bar 190. The robust articulation and sharp dynamic contrasts of Reiner's Beethoven are displayed to good advantage in his account of the Storm in the *Pastoral* Symphony—a realization of the music praised for its vivid detail and impact.[121]

Reiner's Chicago Symphony recordings of music from the romantic repertoire included a fiery account of Dvořák's Symphony no. 9 (*From the New World*), made in November 1957; a powerful version of Tchaikovsky's *Pathétique* Symphony (from April 1957); a sparkling if rather symphonic set of numbers from *The Nutcracker* ballet (March 1959); grand, dramatic accounts of "bleeding chunks" from Wagner's *Die Meistersinger* and *Götterdämmerung* (April 1959); and a superbly characterized, sonorous performance of Mussorgsky's *Pictures at an Exhibition* in the familiar Ravel orchestration (December 1957). Reiner's conducting of "Bydlo" depicts the oxen at a lumbering tempo represented in the sonorous tuba solo. "Samuel Goldenburg and Schmuyle" includes a peerless account of the rapid, difficult trumpet part by Adolph Herseth, an object lesson in breath control, intonation, dynamics, and confident projection of the notes. The fishwives' gossip in the market in "Limoges" is brought to life with scampering virtuosity by the entire orchestra. "The Great Gate at Kiev" concludes the performance with cumulative power and vivid percussion.[122]

Reiner also made discs of overtures, tone poems, and lighter orchestral music, including Strauss waltzes. He lavished as much attention on these pieces as he did on more serious fare. The recordings of these items still sound fresh today because of Reiner's care in projecting their musical virtues and the superlative quality of the Chicago Symphony Orchestra. Reiner's stamp is set on such recordings as Smetana's Overture *The Bartered Bride*, dating from December 1955, where the scuttling opening is played with perfect articulation at a rapid tempo by the strings, and Liszt's *Mephisto Waltz no. 1*, where the cellos and double basses are encouraged to dig deep with their bows on the strings to characterize the sinister opening of the piece. Dvořák's *Carnival* Overture (January 1956) is dispatched with splendor and panache but with due respect to the atmospheric blending of the solo violin with the woodwinds in the *Andantino con Moto* section. Six Rossini overtures, recorded on a single day in November 1958, were conducted with verve and a concern for ensemble precision that made them "Toscaninian without the hypertension."[123]

Although it is uncommon for a central European conductor to show a marked affinity for French music, Reiner's recordings of Debussy's *Ibéria* and *La Mer* (from March 1957 and February 1960, respectively) and his accounts of Ravel's *Pavane pour une infante défunte* (March 1957), *Rapsodie espagnole* (November 1956), and *Valses nobles et sentimentales* (April 1957) reveal a highly sophisticated blend of delicate sonorities, fluid rhythms, and translucent orchestral textures that makes these performances special. Taking the middle movement of *La Mer* as an example, one hears the play of waves re-created in a reading that handles Debussy's frequently shifting tempo indications, key changes, and flecks of instrumental color in a highly atmospheric way where individual strands are dovetailed piquantly. The Chicago Symphony's ability to play with perfect synchronization in the animated staccato passages while taking time over the more languourous moments is highly impressive.

Reiner's career ended before the upsurge of interest in Mahler's music, but he recorded the Symphony no. 4 (December 1958), with the soprano Lisa della Casa singing the child's view of heaven in the last movement, and *Das Lied von der Erde* (November 1959), with Richard Lewis and Maureen Forrester as the tenor and contralto soloists. Reiner never had any personal contact with Mahler and admitted that during his long conducting career he had different reactions to that composer's music. Reiner found Mahler a variable composer, but he had finally learned to admire his works. "This recorded interpretation of the Fourth should represent a proof of my conversion," Reiner remarked in 1959, adding that the symphony was "an uneven work. Folksy tunes are mixed with olympic grandiloquence and noble pathos. Moods of heavenly peace are juxtaposed to diabolic sarcasm, the dissonant sounds of Death's fiddle. But there is no denying the fascination of this work's searching power, its naive religious feeling and subconscious revelation of many traits of the composer's enigmatic personality."[124] Reiner conducts Mahler in a cooler way than did his pupil Leonard Bernstein; he avoids sentimentality, illuminates the chamber-music elements in the music, and clarifies the complex strands of Mahler's scores by insisting on crystalline orchestral playing.

Reiner's finest recording achievement in Chicago lay in his series of discs devoted to Richard Strauss and Bela Bartók. He began his recording career in Chicago with sessions for Strauss's *Ein Heldenleben* and the "Dance of the Seven Veils" from *Salome* on March 6, 1954. With his Chicago forces over the next eight years he made two recordings of *Don Juan* (December 1954 and February 1960) and *Also sprach Zarathustra* (March 1954 and April–May 1962), to which he added the *Symfonia Domestica* (November 1956), *Don Quixote* with Antonio Janigro as the cello soloist (April 1959), a shortened suite from *Le bourgeois gentilhomme* (April 1956), an abbreviated version of the waltzes from *Der Rosenkavalier* (April 1957), the *Burleske* for piano and orchestra, the final scene from *Salome* with Inge Borkh in the title role (December 1955), and extended extracts from *Elektra* (April 1956). Reiner had recorded some of these pieces in Pittsburgh, but the later recordings benefit greatly from the superior recorded sound provided by RCA Victor.

Reiner brought out the opulence of Strauss's orchestration but never wallowed indulgently in the more episodic moments; instrumental textures were clarified so that transparency of sound was paramount; and climaxes were carefully prepared so that they did not appear bombastic. To successfully balance such a large orchestra while projecting seemingly spontaneous playing was a notable achievement. Critics have praised these Strauss recordings since the day they were first issued. The recording of the *Symfonia Domestica* in its reappearance on CD confirmed Reiner "as an outstanding Strauss interpreter. He obtains the utmost clarity from the huge orchestra's complex textures, with carefully considered balance throughout, meticulous observance of all the composer's rhythmic and dynamic nuances, and beautifully shaped phrasing."[125] *Ein Heldenleben,* to a critic for *Harper's Magazine,* confirmed Reiner as probably the greatest Strauss conductor alive: "the razor's edge combination of lean, hard clarity on a vast orchestral scale and perilously high tension emotionalism is exactly suited to his disciplined directing."[126] The heroic E-flat major opening of the tone poem begins with firm, riveting notes in the horns and lower strings; the section depicting the music critics snarls sarcastically; and the themes from Strauss's other symphonic poems are woven into the texture in a reflective, nostalgic way.

The recorded excerpts from *Salome* and *Elektra* have great depth, color, and intensity. Inge Borkh was a powerful, secure singer, and RCA's engineers provided rich and brilliant sound to ensure that she was never overwhelmed by the orchestra. She sang the final scene from *Salome* and joined Paul Schoeffler as Orest and Frances Yeend as Chrysothemis, along with the Chicago Lyric Theater chorus, in three extracts from *Elektra*. Reiner's direction is particularly telling in *Elektra:* a score that can sound merely noisy under lesser conductors is here presented with grandeur "from its psychotic quavering strings to the giant tam-tam strokes at the end."[127] Reiner's conducting maintained a suitably tense atmosphere, with fine coordination of the vocal and orchestral parts. "Reiner achieves power without excessive weight, maintaining quickish tempi and transparent textures," David McKee has written; "the death-dance is drawn on a grand and elegant scale, and the final pages achieve a massive gravitas that is quite unique, suggesting nothing so much as a curtain being majestically drawn over the tragic scene."[128]

Reiner championed the music of Bartók throughout his career and was instrumental in bringing a number of his works to the attention of the American public. Recording Bartók was not easy in the 1950s because RCA, and presumably other record companies, thought the records would not have a wide enough appeal to generate significant sales. Reiner's Chicago recordings of Bartók's music consisted of the *Concerto for Orchestra* (from sessions on October 22, 1955) and the *Music for Strings, Percussion, and Celesta* and *Hungarian Sketches*, recorded in December 1958. Reiner's tempos in the *Concerto for Orchestra* kept closely to the composer's markings in the score. Bartók's overall timing for the work came to 35 min., 36 sec.; Reiner takes 35 min., 38 sec. The performance has remained for over forty years a shining example of the impeccable execution of the Chicago Symphony—lean yet firm strings, plangent woodwinds, and agile brass playing with taut ensemble and exemplary intonation from all sections. "Most striking in Reiner's performance," Simon Trezise has written, "is his economy. Everything is perfectly focused on the expressive and musical point at hand. The introduction, which often falls apart, is given in one all-encompassing gesture with a sense of mystery and longing graphically conveyed. The first subject of the main *Allegro* has terrific energy, and Reiner doesn't allow the modest relaxation called for in the second subject to erode momentum. The other movements are every bit as impressive, with the whirlwind finale brought to a point of almost unbearable tension."[129]

Reiner's recordings in the early stereo era spread beyond Chicago. He wanted to record with European orchestras, but this was difficult to arrange because permission was needed from the AFM and the Chicago Symphony's board. In 1955 Reiner hoped to record *Die Meistersinger* with the Vienna Philharmonic when he conducted that opera as part of the postwar reopening of the

Vienna State Opera. He needed Petrillo's permission, which was not forthcoming;[130] a live recording of one performance of *Meistersinger* was nevertheless taped. Reiner wrote to the AFM about his hard work to increase the financial rewards of the Chicago Symphony Orchestra by agreeing to extra recording sessions (eighteen, for instance, in the 1955–56 season). The repertoire included several accompaniments for soloists, which were of no particular financial benefit to Reiner or the orchestra but which he complied with at the request of RCA Victor. Reiner and the Chicago Symphony had an exclusive contract with RCA; the Orchestral Association approved of his conducting and recording with other orchestras of equal reputation; and other conductors in the AFM had been granted permission to record in Europe. Reiner thought selective recordings in Europe would enhance his own reputation and that of his Chicago Orchestra.[131] Petrillo agreed that Reiner could make a limited number of recordings in Europe, but only one session with the Vienna Philharmonic took place.[132]

Reiner made further attempts to record in Europe. He hoped to record with the London Symphony Orchestra but was informed by the president of Chicago's Orchestral Association that he should desist from making discs with ensembles lacking the reputation of the Chicagoans.[133] Yet Reiner, aware of the ruling about conductors in the AFM recording with foreign orchestras, applied to record the Verdi *Requiem* and other works in Europe during the summer of 1960.[134] He was given permission to conduct the Verdi piece and some orchestral music, but the AFM would not allow him to record opera, a decision that scotched plans for him to assay Verdi's *Otello* with the Rome Opera House Orchestra and Chorus (it was eventually made under the baton of Tullio Serafin).[135]

Reiner only recorded in continental Europe with the Vienna Philharmonic in 1956 and 1960 when, with John Culshaw as producer, he conducted tone poems and dances by Brahms, Dvořák, and Richard Strauss and Verdi's *Requiem*. Reiner's reputation for rudeness preceded him, and that, coupled with his tiny beat, put the orchestra on its best behavior.[136] During his first recording session in the Sofiensaal with the Vienna Philharmonic, an orchestra he did not know well, Reiner sparred with the players for a quarter of an hour to win respect; their verdict was, "Reiner is granite." Reiner secured playing that was so precise and refined that hardly any recording adjustments were needed; he recorded *Till Eulenspiegel* in one take, and Culshaw noted that the performance was "a revelation."[137] These sessions were carried out by Decca under a reciprocal arrangement with RCA whereby Decca loaned some artists to RCA and were allowed to distribute their recordings throughout the British Isles and Europe, while RCA, who paid for the sessions, were given rights to release the discs in the United States.[138]

For the recording of Verdi's *Requiem,* Reiner had to change two of the

scheduled soloists. Leonie Rysanek cried off with a bad throat. Giulietta Simionato did not turn up. They were replaced by Leontyne Price and Rosalind Elias.
The male soloists were Jussi Bjoerling, in his last commercial recording, and
Giorgio Tozzi.[139] Reiner coached the singers in piano rehearsals in his hotel suite.
He continued the rehearsals there when the accompanist fell ill. Undeterred by
this problem, he displayed his sardonic humor about the situation. One morning after rehearsing three of the soloists in the "Lux aeterna," Reiner peered next
door into the accompanist's bedroom and said, "If we have given a good performance, you should be dead!"[140] On the recording Reiner began the *Requiem*
with a very slow account of the "Kyrie" and proceeded to offer a deliberate, do-
lorous account of Verdi's choral masterpiece that includes excellent singing from
the soloists.

Reiner's final recordings in Europe were made in London. In August 1962
he conducted Brahms's Fourth Symphony with the Royal Philharmonic Orchestra in sessions produced by Charles Gerhardt. This recording was released
by the *Reader's Digest* record club to mail-order subscribers in a series called
"Treasury of Great Music." On hearing the playback after the recording session, Reiner said that this was the most beautiful recording he had ever made.[141]
It was supposed to be followed by another disc, with the same orchestra, of
Tchaikovsky's Fifth Symphony, but Reiner canceled this assignment due to ill
health, and Jascha Horenstein substituted for him as conductor.

Reiner and his wife kept watchful eyes on the marketing of his records.
When he transferred allegiance from Columbia to RCA, he was worried that
his old company might reissue some of his early recordings at cheaper prices.
This would harm his current sales and establish a precedent for RCA to follow
suit with his future library.[142] Carlotta was initially worried about RCA's promotion of her husband's recordings. On a visit to Vienna she noticed that no
Reiner discs were available, but Columbia had plenty of Ormandy's recordings
for sale, and Angel had done likewise for Karajan's records.[143] But RCA soon
improved their marketing. In the seven years before 1960, the Reiner/Chicago
Symphony combination made thirty-five microgroove discs with an estimated
sale of 1.1 million copies.[144] Some of these discs won coveted awards. Reiner
received Grammys from the National Academy of Recording Arts and Sciences
for his second recordings of *Also sprach Zarathustra* and *Don Juan* and for
Haydn's Symphonies nos. 95 and 101, Beethoven's *Pastoral* Symphony, a selection of Rossini overtures, Schumann's Piano Concerto (with Cliburn), Debussy's *La Mer*, and Bartók's *Music for Strings, Percussion, and Celesta*.[145]

Yet Reiner's recording career in Chicago with RCA Victor ended on a sour
note. Once his position changed from music director to music adviser, effective
from the 1962–63 season, RCA lost interest in making records with the Chicago Symphony. Reiner's last two recordings for RCA with his orchestra date

from March and April 1963: Berlioz's song cycle *Nuits d'été* and Falla's *El Amor Brujo*, with Leontyne Price as soloist, on one disc and Beethoven's Fourth Piano Concerto, with Cliburn as soloist, on the other. RCA felt that the Chicago Symphony/Reiner combination was ineffective from a merchandising standpoint once another man had become music director. Initially they were not interested in making records with Reiner's successor Jean Martinon, claiming that there was no guarantee that orchestral standards would be maintained. RCA intended to record Reiner with European orchestras in the future.[146]

Reiner concluded his commercial recording career in the autumn of 1963 when, only a few months before his death, he conducted his own handpicked ensemble, billed as "Fritz Reiner and his Symphony Orchestra," in Haydn's Symphonies nos. 95 and 101 (the *Clock*). These recordings were made in the Manhattan Center. The players were selected from the best personnel locally available; they included musicians from the Met, the New York Philharmonic, the Symphony of the Air (formerly the NBC Symphony), and some freelancers.[147] Reiner was scheduled to record Mozart's Serenade in B-flat for thirteen wind instruments with a similarly expert handpicked ensemble, but the recording was never made.[148]

Reiner's recording career in Chicago coincided with the birth of the stereo era. In the autumn of 1958, several Reiner performances with the Chicago Symphony Orchestra were released as RCA "Living Stereo" recordings designed specifically for high-fidelity listening on a phonograph in an average living room. These discs ushered in the golden age of stereo.[149] Embodying RCA Victor's "New Orthophonic" recording technique, they were instantly recognizable by their covers, which featured the phrase "Living Stereo" in white capital letters enclosed between two speakers at the top of the record sleeve and a caption of a shaded dog peering into a gramophone in the top right corner (taken from the famous picture of Nipper used by HMV). *Also sprach Zarathustra* was the first Reiner disc released in the "Living Stereo" series. Several of his other stereo recordings made before 1958 were withheld from release at the time, though they later appeared on other RCA labels, because his record company wanted to promote their artists in fresh performances in the latest sound.[150]

"Living Stereo" discs were issued until the early 1960s, and, in the opinion of many audiophiles, they have never been surpassed in the quality of their music making and recorded sound.[151] Reiner and other RCA artists who graced that catalog had their performances released and rereleased on various labels, several of which had poor sound reproduction. "Living Stereo" discs were supplemented by the Dynagroove system, which aimed to improve the three major stages of record production—session, mix-down process, and disc cutting.[152] It proved a failure and was quietly dropped. From 1963 onwards many Reiner recordings were reissued as budget discs on RCA Victrola while others remained on full-price Red Seal. From late 1968 until 1976 some Reiner records appeared with new thinner Dynaflex pressings that were sonically inferior products.[153] RCA's spell in the doldrums of recording quality only ended in the early 1980s with the reissue of Reiner and other early stereo recordings in the 0.5 Series, which transferred the master tape to the master lacquer at half speed, thus ensuring better frequency response, lower distortion, and greater stereophonic separation.[154] In the late 1980s, Chesky Records obtained rights from RCA to reissue a selection of Reiner's stereo recordings. They released LPs that were as faithful as possible to the master tapes, using modern cutting lathes to restore frequency extremes and dynamics not fully captured on the original RCA issues.[155] Recently the fame and quality of Reiner's stereo recordings for RCA has led to special audiophile vinyl LPs in limited editions, with original sleeve designs and liner notes.[156]

With the arrival of compact discs in 1982, Reiner's stereo recordings were soon reissued in a new format that had the great advantage over LPs of uniform pressing quality, no scratches or pops, and much better channel separation at high frequencies (95 as opposed to 5 or 6 db). They were made with digital technology instead of the analog recording method used from Edison's time through the LP era. To begin with, Reiner CDs appeared only in the United States in digitally remastered analog recordings on RCA's Red Seal label. Not all issues were technically successful; the Brahms Second Piano Concerto with Gilels, for instance, was beset by poor frequency response, garish sound, and audible tape hiss.[157] In general, however, the CDs provide better overall satisfaction than the LP renderings of the recordings. They have been remastered from the original master tapes using state-of-the-art equipment.

Reiner's commercial recordings are supplemented by a large number of noncommercial tapes and discs, often taken from radio broadcasts. Some of these recordings are pirate editions of concerts and operas; others are legitimate broadcasts. Many are available for listening in the Music Division at the Library of Congress, at the Museum of Broadcasting in Chicago, and at the New York Public Library for the Performing Arts at Lincoln Center. Among the live recordings are two complete versions of *Salome* and *Der Rosenkavalier,* performances of *Le nozze di Figaro, Don Giovanni, Elektra, Der fliegende Holländer, Die Meistersinger,* and *Falstaff* (all from the Met), and some NBC Symphony and New York Philharmonic Orchestra concerts.[158]

The most sustained set of Reiner's live concert performances consists of broadcasts made during the 1957–58 season by Stephen F. Temmer for WBAI-FM; these were broadcast only in New York because the Chicago Symphony's trustees thought local broadcasts would reduce ticket sales. Temmer visited Chicago each week of that season to tape live subscription concerts, then flew back to New York; the concerts were broadcast on the following night. He used a single Neumann U 47 tube microphone, suspended over the third row of the orchestra, and sat backstage with a three-input Collins mixer. These broadcasts were in monaural sound. Several have been issued by the Chicago Symphony Orchestra on LP and CD from Temmer's master tapes.[159] Some works that Reiner included in telecasts for WGN-TV, with a reduced orchestra because of restricted studio space, have also been reissued on compact disc. The Fritz Reiner Society has issued cassettes of many of these performances.

These live recordings are particularly valuable for including works that Reiner never recorded commercially, such as Vaughan Williams's *Fantasia on a Theme by Thomas Tallis*, Schoenberg's *Verklärte Nacht*, Webern's *Six Pieces for Orchestra* Op. 6, Bartók's *Violin Concerto no. 2*, with Menuhin as soloist, and Satie's *Gymnopédies* nos. 1 and 2. Despite the dry acoustics, all these performances carry Reiner's characteristic textural transparency plus precise ensemble playing and idiomatic atmosphere.[160] The Webern performance reveals that Reiner could give a convincing reading of music in a highly concentrated, pared-down idiom that did not really appeal to him, "each movement a perfectly cut diamond."[161] The sound on these live recordings varies from muddy to acceptable to remarkably good, but the performances remind us vividly of Reiner's qualities as a musical interpreter—the subject of the remaining chapter of this book.

IO. REINER THE INTERPRETER

Reiner's quest for technical perfection in music making and his catholic taste meant that he was an exacting and significant interpreter of a wide range of music, from baroque concerti to Stravinsky's *Agon*. His insistence on thorough preparation, total knowledge of scores, and an awareness of different musical styles underpinned the re-creative methods he mastered. A book on Reiner would be incomplete without an examination of the skills he brought to musical interpretation and recording, and this chapter investigates his approach to these matters. Reiner's musical aesthetic can yield insights into his re-creative ability. This can be achieved by taking account of his comments on musical performance and through the evidence of his conducting scores and recorded legacy. My focus is thematic: the general features of Reiner's interpretative abilities are discussed, with pertinent musical examples from across his repertoire. No attempt is made to provide an encyclopedic analysis of Reiner's entire recorded output or to present an exhaustive survey of his discs according to chronological period of composers.[1]

To study Reiner's approach to musical interpretation and his recorded legacy is to provide a significant case study in the burgeoning research field of performance analysis. There is a well-established branch of musicology devoted to performance practice; this is perhaps most prominent in studies of early music, the use of original instruments, and the performing conventions of the preclassical era. Performance analysis is a newer field of study that casts a wider net than performance practice. As José A. Bowen has put it, performance analysis is "the study of how the music sounds, but it also considers performance attitudes, gesture, social context, and audience response."[2] While concentrating on the individuality of Reiner's musical aesthetic, my discussion takes account of different styles connected with geography, repertoire, genre, or specific periods; with traditions often manifested in the performance of particular works; and with the individual choices made by Reiner when conducting pieces.[3]

Such an analysis is needed because previous characterizations of Reiner's interpretative qualities have suffered from inaccurate, somewhat glib generalizations that are not borne out by his recorded legacy. For instance, Harold Schonberg, in an obituary notice for Reiner, held that the conductor was a literalist. He compared him with Arturo Toscanini for ridding performances of the cluttered performing characteristics of an earlier generation and for presenting them objectively in pristine form. By comparison, Hans Richter and Wilhelm Furtwängler expressed "podium romanticism" with their penchant for free rhythms, expressive devices such as ritardandos, slow tempi for feminine or soft themes, and quick tempi for masculine or loud themes.[4] Schonberg later referred to Reiner as "a modernist from the very beginning, able to resist the prevailing romanticisms."[5] In a similar vein, Joseph Horowitz has characterized Reiner as an antiromantic, as one of several European emigré conductors prominent in America whose interpretations were based on objectivity, precision, and linear tension and who imprinted Toscanini's "impersonal ideal" on musical performance—apart from Reiner, he mentions Artur Rodzinski, Erich Leinsdorf, George Szell, Guido Cantelli, Eugene Ormandy, and William Steinberg as torchbearers of this tradition.[6]

Writing independently but pursuing a similar line of analysis, Richard Taruskin, drawing on T. E. Hulme's ideas, has focused on Reiner's recording of Bach's Fifth Brandenburg Concerto to suggest that this represents a geometrical rather than a vitalist approach to music in performance. By "geometrical" he means something permanent and durable expressed in music with regular rhythmic patterns and a somewhat detached style. This contrasts with a vitalist or more overtly emotional approach to music making exemplified by more weighty expressive ideas and frequent use of crescendos and diminuendos, accelerandos and ritardandos, and tempo rubato. Generally speaking, the vitalist tradition of performing music gave way to the geometric during the first half of the twentieth century. Taruskin states that Reiner's approach to performing Bach was influenced by Stravinsky's neoclassicism. This suggestion is based on the unproven premise that conductors learn most from the music of their own time and on Reiner's conducting of Stravinsky's works in the United States.[7]

The true situation was more complex than these generalizations suggest. Reiner surely regarded himself as a re-creative artist, not as a creative interpreter following the style of Wagner's conducting.[8] Unlike one of Wagner's most significant conducting heirs, Furtwängler, Reiner did not write philosophical essays or diary jottings on the spiritual meaning of the music he conducted, nor did he regard musical performance as an act of creation using the score merely as the basis for the illumination of the moment.[9] Reiner did not apply a "Germanic emotive" style, with its emphasis on recurrent tempo and dynamic fluctuations, to all sorts of music.[10] But this does not mean that Reiner's conducting aesthetic was removed from romanticism. It seems to me that he was influenced both by the greater flexibility of music making current in the late romantic era, a style common until after the First World War, and by the more precise, detached, objective conducting styles favored by the mid-twentieth century. His rhythmic style lay exactly between the greater freedom of tempo advocated by Wagner, Hans von Bülow, Nikisch, Mahler, Mengelberg, and Richard Strauss (in his early years) and the stricter control of tempo exemplified by Felix Weingartner, Karl Muck, Richard Strauss (in his later years), and Toscanini—unsurprising given that his career broadly coincided with the decades when such a significant change in performing practice occurred.[11] Reiner would not have agreed with Stravinsky's dictum that "music should be transmitted and not interpreted,"[12] a reaction against romantic traditions of performance. Rather, he often displayed the flexibility in tempo, articulation, and accentuation that are found in the recordings and instrumental manuals of works prepared by his compatriot and teacher, Bartók.[13]

Reiner's recorded legacy illustrates some performing practices inherited from his predecessors. One recurrent matter to be decided by conductors of the baroque and classical periods concerns when to repeat passages, especially those with da capo markings. Reiner adhered to an older performing tradition that was inconsistent, one might say nonchalant, in observing repeats. This was common in many recordings made even up to the 1970s but is now found less often, perhaps because scholars have shown that instructions to repeat a passage of music by Mozart and his contemporaries were meant to be observed. As Hugh MacDonald has succinctly put it, "repeats in classical music are . . . what all textbooks say they are: instructions to repeat a passage of music, equivalent in force to the instructions which determine tempo, phrasing, dynamics and the notes themselves."[14] In short, there is little evidence to support the notion that Mozart and his contemporaries did not observe repeats.[15]

In Reiner's recordings of the first movements of Haydn's Symphonies nos. 88, 95, 101, and 104, no exposition repeats are observed. The same is true of his recordings of the first movement and finale of Mozart's Symphony no. 36 (the *Linz*) and the finale of Symphony no. 39. His recordings of Beethoven's Symphonies nos. 2, 7, and 8 and of Schubert's Symphony no. 8 (the *Unfinished*) all exclude exposition repeats in their first movements. Reiner's study scores have crossed-out markings for the exposition repeat of the first movement of Beethoven's *Eroica* Symphony, for the first time bars in the finale of Beethoven's

Fifth Symphony, and for the first time bars in the opening movement of Brahms's First Symphony.[16] In these instances, Reiner followed the practices of dozens of other conductors and probably the performing traditions of the orchestras he was conducting.

In the above cases, omission of the repeats does not eliminate any significant new music; in other instances, the situation was different. Reiner omitted repeats in the first movement of Mendelssohn's Symphony no. 4 (the *Italian*) and Brahms's Symphony no. 2. Yet Mendelssohn's second time marking in the first movement of the *Italian* Symphony includes twenty-three bars of felicitous music not heard elsewhere, and the first ending includes a coda theme played by the woodwinds at bar 157 that, if not heard at that point, would be played for the first time at bar 554 in the coda.[17] Brahms's first- and second-time bars include different phrases, with flute and oboe crotchets highlighted in the former but omitted in the latter in favor of phrases for clarinets and principal horn. It seems fair to conclude that if composers took the trouble to write different music over a series of bars for these repeats, they expected them to be played. Interestingly, the exposition repeat in the first movement of Brahms's Second Symphony was observed at the work's premiere, when Hans Richter conducted the Vienna Philharmonic in December 1877.[18]

In other instances where Reiner omitted repeats, the performance of a symphony can seem unbalanced if we make two assumptions: that the first movement of a symphony usually carried the weight of the musical argument, and that repeats were a crucial part of the proportions, "the balance of tonal areas, and of the interplay of harmonic tensions."[19] Reiner's recording of the first movement of Schubert's Fifth Symphony lasts for 4 min., 35 sec. and is followed by an Andante con Moto, made without repeats, that is over twice as long (9 min., 56 sec.). Arguably, this throws out the balance of the symphony's structure. A similar point could be made about Reiner's recording of Beethoven's Second Symphony, in which a time of 8 min., 42 sec. for the opening movement is followed by a Larghetto that plays for 11 min., 4 sec. Another example is the Chicago Symphony's rendering of Dvořák's Symphony no. 9 (*From the New World*), where a first movement lasting 8 min., 42 sec. is followed by a Largo that takes 12 min., 24 sec. Comparing the balance between symphonic movements simply in terms of their duration is not always helpful, however. In the case of the *New World* symphony, the composer did not want the exposition of the first movement repeated even though the repeat is marked in the score.[20] And so there is justification for Reiner following the usual practice of omitting the repeat.

The exposition of the first movement of Brahms's Third Symphony provides a good example of the complexity involved in choosing to make or omit repeats. It could be argued that this repeat prevents the movement from being too short compared with the other movements in the symphony. In addition, the rising thirds of bars 181–82 enlarge upon the first-time bars and therefore should not be left out. However, if the repeat is observed, the first two bars of the symphony "lose their raison d'être if they suddenly reappear, long after the symphony has been in full swing, merely as part of a formalized da capo. Moreover, the first-time bars are disconcertingly brief, as in Brahms's First Symphony, interrupting a particularly powerful propulsion of emotional excitement."[21] Clearly, there are valid arguments on both sides, and each case of a repeat needs to be judged on its merits.

Whether to repeat the exposition in a symphonic movement in sonata form was not a clear-cut decision. In his recording of Brahms's Symphony no. 3 Reiner omitted the exposition repeat in the opening movement, which plays for 9 min., 24 sec. Some of his illustrious contemporaries observed that particular repeat, seemingly giving a better balance to the symphony as a whole. Furtwängler played the repeat in some recorded performances but not in others.[22] By observing the repeat, Serge Koussevitzky's recording of the movement lasts twelve minutes, while Pierre Monteux's performance (13 min., 15 sec.) is almost half as long again as Reiner's.[23] Monteux, however, could vary his approach: he included the repeat of the first movement's exposition in his San Francisco Symphony and London Symphony Orchestra recordings of Brahms's Second Symphony but omitted it in his recording with the Vienna Philharmonic.[24]

Reiner had a similarly flexible attitude towards repeats. Two works that illustrate this are Mozart's Symphony no. 40 and Beethoven's Symphony no. 6 (the *Pastoral*). Reiner made two recordings of Mozart's great G minor symphony, one in Pittsburgh and one in Chicago, recorded eight years apart. Both reflect similar choices in the conductor's approach to the score. The first movements of both play for almost exactly the same time (7 min., 17 sec. and 7 min., 20 sec., respectively). Reiner repeated the exposition of the first movement; omitted the repeat of the first section of the Andante; observed all repeats in the minuet the first time around; and omitted the repeat of the first section of the finale. His performances of the symphony played for 24 min., 10 sec. (Pittsburgh) and 25 min., 1 sec. (Chicago). If he had included all the repeats, the symphony could have taken 37 min., 50 sec., as in Benjamin Britten's account with the English Chamber Orchestra (where the slow movement, including all repeats, takes sixteen minutes and lasts almost as long as the *marcia funèbre* of Beethoven's *Eroica*).[25] Reiner's recording of Beethoven's *Pastoral* Symphony left out the exposition repeat in the first movement and the repeat of the peasants' merrymaking. One review of the original RCA LP release criticized these omissions.[26] The missing sections were edited onto the British release of the RCA Victrola LP but excluded from a CD reissue; thus the timings of the two versions differ (10 min., 18 sec. and 13 min., 4 sec. for the first movement; 3 min., 20 sec. and 6 min., 4 sec. for the scherzo).

Another characteristic of recorded performances in the first half of the twentieth century was for some conductors to reorchestrate works, alter the printed score, and change instrumentation. Weingartner changed some of the instrumentation in Beethoven's symphonies, notably doubling the wind parts.[27] Leopold Stokowski made elaborate, romantic arrangements of Bach's organ music, made famous by his recordings with the Philadelphia Orchestra. He changed the ending of Tchaikovsky's Fantasy Overture *Romeo and Juliet,* with its timpani roll and grandiloquent accentuated chords, by substituting a pianissimo passage for strings. He included a bass soloist in some performances of Rimsky-Korsakov's *Russian Easter Festival* Overture.[28] In the early part of his career, Toscanini eliminated the bass drum and cymbals from the finale of Beethoven's *Choral* Symphony. He added notes to the timpani parts of several Beethoven symphonies in places where they were not conceivable in the early nineteenth century. Later he made minor instrumental changes to works by Beethoven, Schumann, Smetana, Ravel, and Tchaikovsky.[29]

Reiner performed transcriptions of Bach's organ music on many occasions, using versions by Reger, Respighi, Lucien Cailliet, Vittorio Gui, Frederick Stock, Riccardo Pick-Mangiagalli, and others. In the late 1930s he even gained exclusive rights to perform the transcription of Bach's Toccata and Fugue in D Minor for organ made by Leon Leonardi, a conductor and composer then residing in Hollywood.[30] Reiner tended to conduct these scores in the earlier part of his career; they were popular on orchestral programs in the 1920s and 1930s. By the time he was music director of the Pittsburgh Symphony Orchestra, he had changed his mind. He became irritated with the sheer number of lesser arrangers of Bach's organ and instrumental music and refused to play transcriptions except those written by composers of the stature of Schoenberg, Respighi, Hindemith, Webern, and Leó Weiner.[31]

Reiner was flexible in using reorchestrated versions of scores. When conducting Handel—a composer he never conducted on record—he used Franz Wüllner's version of the Overture in D and his collation of excerpts from the *Royal Fireworks* music. Reiner also conducted Sir Hamilton Harty's orchestration of suites from *The Water Music* and the *Royal Fireworks* music. Other standard arrangements used by Reiner favored repertoire that had colorful orchestration or were only otherwise available for piano, including Ravel's orchestration of Mussorgsky's *Pictures at an Exhibition,* Rimsky-Korsakov's realization of the same composer's *Night on a Bare Mountain,* Casella's version of Balakirev's exotic fantasy *Islamey,* the André Caplet orchestration of Debussy's *Children's Corner* Suite, Henri Büsser's arrangement of Debussy's *Pe-*

tite Suite, and Enrique Arbós's transcription of Albéniz's *Navarra, Fête-dieu à Seville,* and *Triana* (the latter two from *Ibéria*).[32]

Reiner conducted revised versions of music in cases where he considered that pieces originally conceived for chamber or operatic performance could be persuasively presented in the concert hall. He conducted Schoenberg's 1943 version of *Verklärte nacht* for string orchestra; took up Shostakovich's arrangement of excerpts from act 4 of Mussorgsky's *Boris Godunov* (the monologue, hallucination scene, and farewell of Boris); and collaborated with Robert Russell Bennett on the selection of numbers from Gershwin's *Porgy and Bess* for a concert suite he commissioned. The latter, premiered in Pittsburgh in 1943, differed in its selection of music from the opera from Gershwin's own suite *Catfish Row,* first performed by the Philadelphia Orchestra in 1936 but still unpublished as a score, and from the suite arranged by Morton Gould.[33] These three revised pieces are all represented in Reiner's discography.

The one major case where Reiner adjusted the orchestration of a composer was Schumann's symphonies, a matter that has vexed many conductors. Schumann's orchestration has often been described as clumsy and "thick" because of the unnecessary doubling of certain parts—something that Mahler attempted to rectify by extensive rescoring. Reiner's score of Schumann's Second Symphony includes plenty of changes that he made himself, especially in the first movement. At the opening of the symphony he crossed out the alto and tenor trombone parts in the first eight bars and cut the flute parts in various places (for example, in bars 9, 11, 15–16, and 18–22). He deleted the oboe parts in bars 26 and 28–30 and the flute, oboe, and clarinet parts in bars 38 and 39 of the first movement. These are only a few of the alterations.[34]

Reiner rarely changed instrumentation in other scores, however. In his recordings of the Bach Brandenburg Concertos, made in 1950, he used a harpsichord for the continuo throughout and as a solo instrument for the cadenza in the first movement of the Fifth Concerto. At the time, rival recorded sets by the Boston Symphony Orchestra under Koussevitzky and the Busch Chamber Players used a piano.[35] Thus Reiner included what would be the norm with period-instrument performances of Bach today. Though he avoided using other period instruments, as did most of his contemporaries, he did not include any novel instruments that would be stylistically inappropriate. Reiner included a solo trumpet in the Second Brandenburg Concerto, accepting the composer's intention that the part should be played by a "tromba." Others have found different solutions. In recordings Toscanini used a sopranino saxophone, Otto Klemperer divided the part between saxophone and clarinet, and, more recently, the Academy of St. Martin in the Fields have substituted a horn for the trumpet part.[36] Reiner did not use viola da gambas in the Sixth

Concerto, as the score directs; he included cellos instead. He preferred flutes to treble recorders in the second and fourth concertos.

Using different instruments for some parts in the Brandenburg Concertos reflects the ambiguities of what Bach originally intended. Scholars have yet to agree on which particular valveless trumpet the composer wrote for (whether in C, D, or F) in the second concerto, and whether it was transposed a fourth up or a fifth down. Bach stated that the fourth concerto had parts for the *fiauti d'echo,* and his use of this term has still to be explained (though most musicologists accept that he was writing for the treble recorder in F). There were various types of viola de gamba that Bach could have used for the Sixth Concerto, but no one is certain what he did use. Most of these debates about instrumentation in the Brandenburg Concertos have surfaced since Reiner recorded the works; some of the issues remain unresolved.[37]

Where legitimate alternatives about instrumentation were marked by composers, Reiner made a clear choice, but he did not always follow a composer's later thoughts. He used clarinets in the revised version of Mozart's Symphony no. 40 possibly because, as Richard Freed explains, "Reiner opted for the clarinets, as most of his contemporaries did, regarding the addition as Mozart's final thought on the work."[38] Since the clarinet was a relatively new instrument in Mozart's time, Reiner may have surmised that the composer would not include parts for it if he did not intend it to play. Other conductors—Furtwängler, Sándor Végh, and Christopher Hogwood, for instance—made recordings that use the original version with oboes rather than clarinets, though most recordings follow the composer's second thoughts.[39]

Reiner, however, did include the trumpet and horn fanfares in bars 237–44 of the third movement ("Dialogue du vent et de la mer") of Debussy's *La mer.* This was in accordance with the original 1905 version of the score.[40] It therefore ignored Debussy's deletion of these parts in his revised 1909 version. Other conductors have either kept the fanfares (Charles Munch, Ernest Ansermet) or omitted them (Toscanini, Piero Coppola, Szell). It is not known why Debussy deleted the trumpet fanfares, but he made no attempt to emulate their effect by other means.[41] Reiner retained them in part, one might suggest, because they emphasize a crucial climax with resounding brass chords; without the trumpets, the aural effect is less thrilling, and Reiner was a conductor who liked to use the full splendor of the Chicago Symphony Orchestra.

Sometimes Reiner made minor alterations in instrumentation to take account of practical difficulties. His study score indicates that he doubled the wind parts in Brahms's First Symphony, presumably to allow the texture and color of these instruments to be projected in tutti passages when playing with a full complement of strings.[42] When he recorded Richard Strauss's *Ein Heldenleben* at the beginning of his Chicago tenure, Reiner substituted a bass trombone for the tenor tuba because the euphonium player could not play softly enough.[43] For Mendelssohn's Overture to *A Midsummer Night's Dream,* there was (and is) the problem of what to do about the ophicleide part that depicts the uncouth Bottom; Reiner's solution was not to search for an obsolete brass instrument but to ask the tuba to play it.[44] Reiner preferred bells without cannon in Tchaikovsky's *1812* Overture, perhaps aiming to give this hackneyed work, which the composer himself regarded as little more than a pièce d'occasion, a more dignified atmosphere, but perhaps he was also mindful of the bass drum and full battery of percussion already included in the coda of the score.

Reiner went out of his way to find specific instruments for particular repertoire that were not normally used by a symphony orchestra. He always insisted on using *tuben* when conducting Wagner's *Ring,* even if they were difficult to get, because he thought they were a vital part of the sonority of *Die Walküre* and *Götterdämmerung.* He brought back from a visit to Vienna an authentic posthorn specifically for use in a Chicago Symphony Orchestra concert that included Mozart's *Posthorn* Serenade (available as a live recording on cassette).[45] He even went so far as to insist on the use of an authentic basque drum in his performances of *Carmen,* noting that it played a distinctive, albeit minor role in the opera's orchestration, in the gypsy dance in act 2 and during the prelude to act 4. The basque drum was larger than a tambourine, but it lacked jingles. After searching for such an instrument for fifteen years, Reiner was proud to have acquired one from Zarauz, a Spanish village in the Basque region where they were made.[46]

In performing orchestral music of the pre-1800 period, Reiner made choices about the number of performers that would be considered old-fashioned by today's purveyors of period playing. But he still recognized the need to conduct such music with a small number of players. The Chicago performances late in his career of two Handel oratorios, *Judas Maccabeus* and *Israel in Egypt,* both had small forces and a harpsichord.[47] Reiner's recordings of Bach's Brandenburg Concertos, made in 1950, include reduced numbers for some concerti and large groups for others. For example, he used six violins, six violas, six celli, two basses, and a harpsichord in the Third Brandenburg Concerto. For the First Concerto he used a solo violin, horn, and oboe, which were joined in the ripieno sections by four violins, two violas, two celli, two basses, one horn, two oboes, one bassoon, and a harpsichord. For the Second Concerto he included a solo trumpet, violin, flute, and oboe along with four other violins, two violas, two celli, two double basses, and a harpsichord. When he later conducted the work in Chicago, he used an augmented ensemble: thirteen first violins, ten second violins, six violas, four celli, and three double basses.[48] These are rather large groups of instruments by today's performing standards and at the opposite end of the instrumental spectrum from modern performances on period instruments using only one instrument to a part, as in Boston Baroque's recording of the Sixth Concerto.[49]

For his recording of the Sixth Brandenburg, however, Reiner included two solo violists, four additional violas, four celli, two bassoons, and a harpsichord. This ensemble is closer to modern performances in period style, save for the exclusion of viola de gambas (mentioned above) and the addition of bassoons (which Bach only specified for the first concerto). Yet even this change in instrumentation is not as inappropriate as it first seems, for it was common practice for bassoons to double a bass line in orchestral works until the time of Haydn.[50] In Reiner's recording of the Sixth Brandenburg Concerto, the bassoons play softly and blend well with the somber hues of other instruments.

Another performance choice lay in the number and distribution of string players in classical symphonies. For his 1955 Chicago Symphony recordings of Mozart's late symphonies Reiner used thirteen first violins, twelve second violins, eight violas, six celli, and four double basses; this was twenty-three fewer players than usual in the orchestra's string section.[51] Sometimes he altered this distribution of players, keeping the same forces but with two fewer second violins for Mozart's Symphony no. 36 (the *Linz*).[52] Reiner used a similar string distribution of 12:10:8:6:4 for Haydn's Symphony no. 88.[53] But he sometimes varied the number of string players within a symphony. His score of Mozart's *Haffner* Symphony has a string distribution of 14:12:8:6:4 for the first movement, but for the Andante this was reduced slightly to ten first violins, ten second violins, six violas, four cellos, and two double basses.[54]

Reiner was, relatively speaking, a purist in keeping to the composer's wishes as given in a score. He thought conductors should always adhere faithfully to the score in the great classics; otherwise, it would be unclear where to draw the line with adaptations. Individuality of interpretation in this repertoire should observe certain limits. To try something startlingly original with well-known scores might be to misquote great art, and that would be nothing short of criminal.[55] In his recording of Bach's Brandenburg Concerto no. 3 Reiner avoided the problem of what to play for the middle movement by eschewing the insertion of another movement from a Bach work or allowing the strings to play a few improvisatory bars with a chord progression; instead he adhered to the marking in the score, which consisted simply of a time signature and two minims. He may have thought this the best solution since we do not know what Bach intended or what the Margrave of Brandenburg's orchestra played at this place in the score.[56] Another conductor who, like Reiner, played only the bridge chords at this point in the score and omitted a cadenza was Furtwängler in both of his recordings of the work.[57] Clearly, however, there are various interpretative possibilities here. An old recording by the Boston Symphony Orchestra under Koussevitzky inserted the Sinfonia of Bach's Cantata no. 4 at this point.[58]

Philip Pickett's New London Consort includes a short violin improvisation at the phrygian cadence linking the two allegros.[59] Robert Haydon Clark and the Consort of London insert the Adagio from the Trio Sonata in G (BWV 1038).[60] Roy Goodman and the Brandenburg Consort play a Largo from the Sonata in G Major (BWV 1021).[61]

Because he avoided an embellishment of the middle movement of the Third Brandenburg Concerto, one might think that Reiner was opposed to any other possible solution. This was not the case; his reasoning seems to have been, rather, that if Bach had wanted something more substantial inserted at that point he would have indicated it in the score. Reiner was not opposed to additions to the score where stylistically appropriate, but he included such material sparingly. In his NBC Symphony Orchestra recording of Mozart's Divertimento in D, K. 251, he allowed the first violin to improvise a cadenza passage lasting for well over a minute at bar 231 of the fifth movement. This is not stylistically inappropriate, given that the violin often had a solo concertante role in such works.[62]

Interestingly, Reiner avoided some minor changes to the performing practice of Beethoven's symphonies that were often made by his contemporaries. Many of these are familiar from rescorings by Bülow, Mahler, and Weingartner.[63] A few examples of how Reiner avoided these retouchings will illustrate the point. In conducting the thunderstorm of Beethoven's *Pastoral* Symphony, Toscanini played the first timpani roll for four more bars than was marked in the score and added timpani to the first beats of bars 53 and 54; he also introduced a third drum in E at bar 78.[64] Reiner eschewed all these additions. In the Allegretto of Beethoven's Seventh Symphony some conductors, notably Klemperer, Richard Strauss, Erich Kleiber, and his son Carlos, played the final string phrase as a pizzicato.[65] Though the movement contains much pizzicato writing for the strings, especially for the cellos and double basses, Beethoven indicated that in bars 275–76, shortly before the end of the movement, the strings should resume playing arco, and that is what Reiner did in his Chicago Symphony recording of the symphony.[66] One minor element of retouching that Reiner did observe, however, was to allow the trumpets to complete the main theme at bars 655–62 of the first movement of the *Eroica* Symphony, a practice followed by many modern conductors.[67] In Beethoven's day the trumpets did not have all the available notes on their instruments to play the theme in these bars, so the composer let them begin the passage and then allowed the woodwinds to finish it alone.[68]

There were some other instances where Reiner deviated from the composer's wishes. A minor example occurs in his recording of *Carmen*, where he inserted the "Danse bohémienne" from Bizet's *La Jolie fille de Perth* and the "Farandole" from the second suite of *L'Arlésienne* in succession just after the beginning of act 4. These brief orchestral extracts add extra color to a score already replete with imaginative instrumental writing. Nevertheless, Reiner always tried to observe the conductor's wishes when specific instructions were written down. In his full score of Berlioz's *Roméo et Juliette*, Reiner followed the composer's advice that the entire body of strings should not be used for the "Queen Mab" scherzo by indicating the need for reduced strings only for this short movement of his dramatic symphony.[69] This was presumably intended to project the gossamer lightness of the music.

When scores did not provide the key to the performance of a piece, Reiner followed his instincts about the composer's wishes. For instance, he thought the offstage trumpet fanfares in Beethoven's *Leonore* Overtures nos. 2 and 3 should not be rushed or played at first in the distance and then nearer. He wanted a firm, secure, loud, dramatic sound from the trumpet and argued that the various calls should be played from the same spot; this was the case in *Fidelio*, and Beethoven made no indication that one trumpet call should be louder than another.[70] Where scores were incomplete, such as Schubert's *Unfinished* Symphony, Reiner made no attempt to seek out completed versions or to add extra pieces from Schubert's other orchestral music to add to the work. In this particular case, he felt the work was perfect in itself and needed no apology as an incomplete torso; it was presumptuous to suggest that improvements to the score could be made.[71] In conducting Bartók's *Concerto for Orchestra*, Reiner followed the revised longer ending normally used today. This can be heard on his Pittsburgh Symphony and Chicago Symphony recordings. The new ending added nineteen bars, culminating in upward Lydian F scales, and was appended by the composer at Koussevitzky's suggestion after the premiere of the work on December 1, 1944.[72]

Only once did Reiner seriously rearrange a composer's wishes. In the 1930s he played Beethoven's *Eroica* with the Philadelphia Orchestra by reversing the order of the *marcia funèbre* and the scherzo and trio. Outlining his reasons for the alteration, Reiner argued that the funeral march was composed two years before the rest of the symphony and had no mental connection with the other movements. Beethoven had changed the order of several compositions, including some of his later piano sonatas, the Ninth Symphony, and various chamber works. The proportions of the *Eroica* were better as a result of the change because two long movements, of about fifteen minutes each, did not have to follow one another. There were other considerations. According to Reiner, the E-flat major of the finale sounded fresher after the C minor of the funeral march, and, for psychological reasons, it did not seem reasonable to have all the rejoicing after the hero's death. To play the finale after the *marcia funèbre* was to present a general apotheosis of the hero's life and deeds of valor. Although this unusual rearrangement is testimony to Reiner's open mind about presenting the classics, the change shocked some listeners. Reiner never repeated the experiment; he did not attempt it for his Chicago Symphony recording.[73]

The only other occasions where Reiner sanctioned rearrangements were in some recordings of vocal music, where there was the need to fit a certain amount of music onto one disc. The duets he recorded from *Der Rosenkavalier*, with Risë Stevens and Erna Berger, were featured on a compilation disc. Presumably for commercial reasons, the parts of Faninal and the Marschallin in excerpts from act 3 were omitted. Similarly, in his recording of excerpts from *Elektra*, three scattered sections were recorded (Elektra's "Allein! Weh, gag allein" soliloquy, the recognition scene, and the finale) but the voices of Aegisthus and the Preceptor were omitted. The original version of these excerpts placed the monologue and final scene on side one and the Recognition scene on side two in order to fit the side-lengths of a long-playing record. (The correct order is reinstated on the CD version.) In these performances Reiner sanctioned cuts and rearrangements for recording purposes. He made some excisions on discs of Johann Strauss waltzes, generally omitting repeats and shortening the coda in the *Emperor* waltz; he offered his own abbreviated version of the *Der Rosenkavalier* waltzes rather than the familiar concert suite. Reiner's omission of the passage for flute, horn, and cello in the postlude of the *Emperor* waltz may have reflected the orchestral parts he used, for the same cut was made in Frederick Stock's earlier recording of the piece with the same orchestra.[74] Reiner's Chicago Symphony recording omitted three of the sixteen sections of Falla's ballet *El amor brujo*. His Pittsburgh Symphony recording of Richard Strauss's *Le bourgeois gentilhomme* included all eight movements of the suite, but his Chicago Symphony remake of the same piece omitted two movements (the Lully minuet and the courante). He also followed the standard cuts in Rachmaninov's Third Piano Concerto in his recording with Vladimir Horowitz and in Tchaikovsky's Violin Concerto with Jascha Heifetz. These cuts presumably followed the preferences of the soloists (and, in the case of the Heifetz disc, included some rewriting of the solo violin part). For his Chicago Symphony recording of the *1812* Overture, Reiner cut a whopping seventy-two bars.

Reiner's scores show that he occasionally made adjustments to dynamic levels and expressive markings. This was particularly true of the baroque and classical repertoire, where there was naturally a greater space between what was marked on paper—sometimes little more than notation, pitch, and tempo—and what was necessary to realize the music in performance.[75] His scores of Bach's Brandenburg Concertos and four orchestral suites include a large number of penciled dynamic markings, added crescendi and diminuendos, and indications of legato and staccato phrasing.[76] His markings of Beethoven's symphonies are too numerous to cite here. But they included an inserted "pianissimo" over the pizzicato crotchets in the strings in bar 46 of the first movement of the Eighth

Symphony, a change in dynamics that presumably allowed the "p dolce" melody on the flute, oboe, and bassoon to be heard.[77] Reiner's markings in his score of the *Eroica* Symphony included several sets of crescendo and diminuendo markings over brief spans of bars in the first movement.[78] For the opening of Haydn's Symphony no. 104 (the *London*), Reiner marked "pp" over bar 4 and "p" over bar 5, followed by "pp espressivo" at bar 12 and "cantabile" at bars 14 and 15.[79]

These minor alterations to phrasing and dynamics indicate Reiner's sensitivity to slight adjustments to the written score that were needed to perform the music satisfactorily. He also had a scenario in mind for particular works. Not all of his conducting scores have such markings, particularly the miniature scores from later in his career; but some mention extramusical associations that Reiner had in mind for different repertoire. Over the head of the second movement of Haydn's Symphony no. 88 Reiner wrote, "Praise God from whom all blessings flow" and "Sunday morning church atmosphere." This is followed by "chorus" over bars 9–11 and "organ interlude" over bars 26–28. Inscribed at the head of the third movement's trio are the phrases "handlicher Tanz" and "bagpipes."[80]

In his score of Mozart's *Haffner* symphony, Reiner inserted several separate phrases over the head of the minuet—"hoopskirts, courtsies, powdered wigs, crinolins" and "Watteau," associational references to the lifestyle and art of the upper classes in ancien-régime Europe.[81] For Mahler's Fourth Symphony, there are again some inscriptions. Reiner marks the beginning of the second movement "Danse macabre" followed by "sharp & piercing, ghostly, creepy, weird," which he presumably conveyed to the solo violinist, playing a whole tone higher, whose music largely depicts these feelings. Then for the beginning of the third movement Reiner wrote "composed like a prayer . . . peacefully," and at the first entry of the soprano in the finale, "childishly gay."[82]

The best surviving example among Reiner's scores of these handwritten notations is the leather-bound, gold-embossed copy of Brahms's Symphony no. 2. Opposite the first page Reiner penciled in that this was the "Pastoral synfonie" of Brahms and that the first movement represented "the sparkling air & water & the spicy wood smell of Pörtschach [where Brahms composed the work]. The best medicine against fear, anger, anxiety, sadness or similar plagues." In the first movement he wrote "Sunset" across empty bars for low brass in bars 2–5; at bars 11 and 12, "Night"; and the phrase "der junge Morgen" at letter A. The markings continue until bar 514, where he wrote "ein sommernachtraum" at the conclusion of the movement. The jottings continue less heavily throughout the rest of the symphony. At the opening of the third movement Reiner wrote "al modo antico" and "mit kinderaugen" over bars 2–5 and "elfen und kobolde tanzen" over bars 7–12.[83] In his miniature score of the same symphony Reiner duplicated many of these jottings and added "Mendelssohnisch" at letter C in the first movement, the phrase "Queen Graziosa saying farewell" at the end of the third movement, and, for the tranquillo section of the finale, "Forest Murmurs of Brahms."[84] Thus the notations merge imaginative and pictorial jottings with references to passages reminiscent of the style of other composers'.

Crucial to any consideration of Reiner's interpretative abilities is his handling of tempo, for this is the musical decision that "links the performer's appreciation of expressive content with his perception of formal structure."[85] Robert Philip's examination of many recordings made in the first half of the twentieth century led him to conclude that tempos became slower during that period.[86] More extensive listening has established, however, that there was no clear trend towards slower tempi.[87] On the contrary, conductors throughout the twentieth century chose variable tempi: there was no dichotomy between strict time beating and free expression.[88]

Reiner's recordings indicate that he became a little more expansive in his interpretations over time. The appendix presents data on the timing of performances where Reiner made more than one recording. There are a few instances where tempo durations remained relatively constant in the same works recorded at different times. This is the case with the Pittsburgh and Chicago recordings of Bartók's Concerto for Orchestra (36 min., 1 sec. and 37 min., 15 sec., respectively). It is also true of the Pittsburgh Symphony version and the 1954 Chicago Symphony recording of Richard Strauss's *Don Juan* (15 min., 44 sec. and 15 min., 56 sec., respectively). The 1960 remake of the piece with the Chicago Symphony, however, is a little more expansive (16 min., 15 sec.). In Reiner's two recordings of Shostakovich's Sixth Symphony, the opposite occurs. The live New York Philharmonic recording from 1943 is 3 min., 29 sec. longer than the studio recording made in Pittsburgh two years later, a result due almost entirely to a longer opening Largo (21 min., 22 sec. as opposed to 18 min., 27 sec.).

In most cases, however, the later recording of a work conducted by Reiner took longer. A glance at the timings in the appendix for recordings of Richard Strauss's *Also sprach Zarathustra, Tod und Verklärung,* Mozart's Symphony no. 40, and Wagner's Prelude to act 1 of *Die Meistersinger,* among other works, will confirm this. Two recordings of Brahms's Hungarian Dances show significant fluctuations in timings. Reiner recorded the same selection of eight of these pieces in Pittsburgh in 1946 and with the Vienna Philharmonic in 1960. The Vienna performances are considerably more expansive. This fits in with the general trend towards longer performances in repertoire where Reiner made more than one recording. The slower tempi in Vienna may also reflect the traditions of that orchestra. The only case where Reiner's later recording of a work was shorter than his earlier one comes with Richard Strauss's *Don Quixote.* The earlier recording of 1941 lasts for 46 min., 1 sec.; the later one, made in

1959, for 43 min., 2 sec. But one suspects that the exception to the rule is caused by the preference of the respective soloists, Gregor Piatigorsky and Antonio Janigro, over tempos and Reiner's deference to their wishes. Thus in terms of tempi Reiner falls exactly between the subjectivity enshrined in the exaggerations and pulling around of scores by major conductors such as Willem Mengelberg and Furtwängler and the clean, often metronomic approach to rhythm more characteristic of modern recordings.

Reiner did not use a metronome; he relied in setting tempi on his taste, experience, and attention to different musical styles. When conducting Bach, he had to decide the main tempo for individual movements because most of the composer's instrumental works have no indications about speed other than a simple Allegro.[89] Words for tempo modification in scores only began to appear in the second half of the eighteenth century in works by Haydn, Mozart, and their contemporaries.[90] Some of Reiner's conducting scores include his jottings about the appropriate tempi to be adopted. Taking Brandenburg Concerto no. 1, for instance, he indicated a speed of $\quarternote$ = 76 for the first movement, $\quarternote$ = 100 for the minuet, and $\quarternote$ = 60 for the Adagio. He wrote "un poco pesante" over the first movement of the third Brandenburg Concerto.[91]

In conducting music from the classical period, Reiner did not significantly adjust the main tempo established unless there were clear indications in the score. Such indications were rare in music of the classical period, as indeed were expressive accentuation and dynamic nuance: "expressive playing" depended more on "subtleties of touch and dynamics" than on tempo changing.[92] In Reiner's recording of the second movement of Beethoven's Eighth Symphony, the witty and alert allegretto scherzando ticks along like a clock without any change to the tempo set at the outset ($\quarternote$ = 88). Maintenance of the chosen tempo has almost the effect of a metronome, and indeed this movement was associated with Dr. Johann Nepomuk Maelzel, the inventor of that device.[93] Similarly, in Reiner's recording of Mozart's Symphony no. 36 (the *Linz*), the allegro spiritoso in the first movement is maintained at the same basic tempo throughout. Reiner's account of the double bass recitative near the start of the finale of Beethoven's *Choral* Symphony is played in strict tempo, not slowly as Wagner and several other conductors before him were wont to do.[94]

Three other facets of Reiner's handling of tempo deserve mention. First, he did not follow the practice of necessarily slowing up for the second subject in a sonata form movement. In Mendelssohn's *Italian* Symphony, the sprightly tempo that forms the basis of the first movement is maintained with no reduction in speed for the lyrical material. Reiner's live performance of Schubert's Great C Major Symphony does not relax the tempo for the woodwind theme that leads into the second subject of the first movement (bar 134 onwards).[95] Secondly, Reiner did not include unmarked accelerandi to raise the musical tension of a movement. This is well illustrated by comparing his recording of the opening of Mozart's Symphony no. 39 (where there is no marked accelerando) with a version of the same symphony conducted by Furtwängler (which does include the accelerando).[96] Similarly, Reiner's account of Schubert's Symphony no. 9 eschews an accelerando in the first movement's transition from Andante to Allegro ma non troppo, whereas Furtwängler's Berlin Philharmonic performance of 1942 includes such a sudden rush.[97] Thirdly, where composers marked tempo changes clearly in a score, Reiner observed them without usually adding interpretative amendments of his own. A good example is the first movement of his 1960 Chicago Symphony recording of Mahler's Fourth Symphony, where the composer's dynamic and tempo markings are closely observed. At the opposite pole is Mengelberg's interpretation with the Concertgebouw Orchestra of Amsterdam in 1939, which makes extreme, unmarked adjustments to the tempo markings.[98]

Nevertheless, Reiner's handling of tempi did include some variations. Treatises of the classical and romantic period considered that it was aesthetically appropriate to hold back some notes and quicken others, within certain regular parameters, in order to fit the music's expressive content.[99] In conducting classical music Reiner sometimes held back the tempo ever so slightly to emphasize structural aspects of scores. His recording of Mozart's *Jupiter* Symphony illustrates these points: he slows up fractionally at bars 210–11 of the first movement, just before the bridge passage of the recapitulation, and includes a ritardando at bar 223 in the finale, where the main theme is reintroduced at the end of the development of a sonata form movement with fugal portions. In a symphony with so much counterpoint, he may have felt that such discreet nudges helped listeners to follow the structural logic of the score. In his live recording of Beethoven's Fourth Symphony with the Chicago Symphony Orchestra, Reiner paused very briefly at bar 98 of the slow movement just before the upward arpeggios on violin, horn, and clarinet. Reiner's tempi throughout both movements of Schubert's *Unfinished* Symphony were steady. In that work he made slight, almost imperceptible tempo adjustments at bars 274–79 in the first movement, where the second subject reappears pianissimo with a decrescendo just before a fortissimo outburst in the last part of the recapitulation; and at bars 253–54 in the second movement, a couple of quieter bars sandwiched between fortissimo statements. These fastidious tempo adjustments all occur at natural transition points in their respective scores.

Reiner did not intervene to modify tempi where the structural development of a passage was already indicated in the music, however. Thus in his Chicago Symphony recording of Mozart's Symphony no. 40 Reiner conducted bars 158–66 of the first movement, where the development fuses into the recapitulation, without any "articulative intervention." A more didactic approach to the same passage is found in Szell's recording with the Cleveland Orchestra. This included a ritenuto within bar 165, just before the fourth beat of the bar, as well as a pause before the downbeat of bar 166.[100] In his live broadcast with the Chicago Symphony of Schubert's Great C Major Symphony Reiner played the end of the first movement a tempo, with no slowing down for the brass reprise of the opening chorale-like tune. In his score he marked "tempo" at this point.[101] His performance, like recent commercial recordings conducted by Carlo Maria Giulini and Sir Charles Mackerras, followed a proportionate tempo relationship. It equated a minim in the opening Andante with the semibreve of the ensuing Allegro, following Schubert's reintroduction of the Andante theme at the end of the first movement with its note values twice the length.[102]

Reiner modified tempi more where movements included the development of complex symphonic arguments on a scale pointing more towards nineteenth-century romanticism than eighteenth-century order and decorum. In the first movement of Beethoven's *Eroica,* for instance, Reiner adjusted the pulse to reflect the changing moods of the music. He slowed up slightly at bars 84–100, presumably regarding this as the beginning of the second group of the exposition (whereas others have located this at either bar 45 or bar 57).[103] He reduced the tempo again at the beginning of the development and again later after bar 330 and at measures 486–501. Yet despite these fluctuations in speed, nothing sounded unnatural or forced, and forward momentum was maintained. It may be that Reiner wanted to reduce the intensity at certain points in the trajectory of the music by relaxing tempo only to quicken it later; certainly these tempo modifications occur at natural transition points in the score.

In a work conceived on an even larger scale, Beethoven's *Choral* Symphony, Reiner introduced a greater number of tempo changes. His reading of the symphony's first movement maintained a genuine maestoso tempo but then slowed down suddenly at bars 138, 158, and 407. Reiner changed tempo to emphasize the woodwind figurations (it is not known whether Beethoven intended this). The first of these bars—sometimes referred to as the "third subject" by older writers—contains some "strangely intricate woodwind writing" that "demands a slight relaxation of tempo." Indeed, Wagner recommended that, for these reasons, this should occur in performance precisely at this point in the movement.[104] Reiner also pulled back the speed in two passages of proclamation near the end of the third movement's adagio, in the first complete statement of the theme of the finale (the D in the twelfth and twentieth bars) and at bar 195 in the finale. These tempo modifications are not as prevalent, however, as they are in the several recordings of the symphony by Furtwängler.[105]

One tempo change that Reiner incorporated from a previous generation consisted of a pair of *luftpausen* inserted in the trio of Beethoven's Fifth Symphony. These occur in the cello and double bass solo just after the second time bar. Reiner paused slightly after the last crotchet of bar 161 before the quavers beginning on the downbeat of bar 162 and repeated the effect where the same passage reappears in bars 163–64. Gunther Schuller has taken Reiner to task for this "bizarre idea" that "drastically" recomposes Beethoven's music.[106] (Lukas Foss, by contrast, regards this passage as an example of Beethoven's humor: the cellos and double basses make a number of false starts, as if they were practicing in public.)[107] Reiner omitted the fermata after the opening statement of the same symphony, presumably because it held up the onward flow of the music. For a contrasting approach, one can cite Furtwängler's observation of the same fermata in his recordings of Beethoven's Fifth Symphony, where the silence after the held minims in the first five bars is longer than the quaver rest indicated.[108] This latter approach separates the motto from the elaboration of it that follows. Toscanini and Herbert von Karajan conducted the opening bars in a similar fashion to Reiner and maintained the quick tempo throughout the movement. By contrast, Stokowski's first two recordings of the symphony are nearer to Furtwängler's, playing the opening four notes slowly and then speeding up.[109]

One aspect of tempi in baroque and classical music where Reiner was idiosyncratic lay in the deployment of ritardandos. His recordings of the Brandenburg Concertos illustrate the point. The third movements of the First and Fourth Concertos end with a large rallentando, yet the first movement of the Fourth Concerto does not; a big ritardando occurs at the end of the Fifth Concerto. Reiner occasionally added ritardandos for effect when conducting classical music, but not consistently. He slowed up in the final two bars of the andante of the *Linz* Symphony and in the last two bars of the finale of Haydn's *Clock* Symphony. The effect rounds off the symphonies almost in a courtly style, but it now sounds old-fashioned. Reiner also included an unmarked ritardando in the last three bars of the introduction to the first movement of Dvořák's *New World* Symphony. But in other cases he avoided ritardandi—witness his recordings of Mozart's Divertimento no. 11, K. 251, and Haydn's Symphony no. 88, where none occur.

In conducting music of the post-Beethoven era, Reiner was more willing to use rubato to fluctuate tempi, and not only in lighter music such as Dvořák's *Slavonic Dances* where, in his recording with the Vienna Philharmonic, he used rubato sensitively (in Op. 46 no. 8 and Op. 72 no. 2, for example). In his recording with the Robin Hood Dell Orchestra of Mendelssohn's Overture *A Midsummer Night's Dream*, Reiner gave just a hint of rubato to accompany the lyrically warm string playing in bars 138–67 and 458–94. Reiner's live recording of Schumann's Second Symphony includes a third movement—the emotional center of the music, marked *adagio espressivo*—that deploys rubato in bars 1, 4, and 5, used sensitively for the string cantabile. This establishes the mood for a spacious interpretation of the movement that sustains a rapt atmosphere; rubato is used again later in the movement.

By the second half of the nineteenth century tempo flexibility, whether marked in a score or by use of rubato, was used widely by composers and performers; it was probably "the chief element in the service of musical expression."[110] A good example of Reiner's extensive use of rubato in music of that era occurs in the languorous approach to the violin melody at the beginning of the third movement of Rimsky-Korsakov's *Scheherazade* ("The Young Prince and Princess") and again after letter I, where the main theme returns on the violins (marked *dolce e cantabile* in the score). Reiner's tempo for these sections is much slower ($\downarrow$. = 40) than the composer's indication ($\downarrow$. = 52). His pocket score includes his markings "rubato" and "pp" over the cello semiquavers in bars 27 and 35.[111] The extent of rubato employed is daring, but the basic pulse of the music is kept flowing without any loss of forward impetus. By contrast, the account of the same passage by Pierre Monteux in his recording with the San Francisco Symphony Orchestra is played for the most part at the composer's preferred tempo ($\downarrow$. = 52) with some speeding up in places (to $\downarrow$. = 60); characterization of the melody is left entirely to instrumental color and phrasing rather than to rubato. Monteux makes no rubato in the bars marked by Reiner.[112] Yet another way of playing this music is represented by Artur Rodzinski's account with the Cleveland Orchestra, where the first few statements of the main melody are played *a tempo* (the nearest of the three recordings to the composer's specified tempo), with no rubato in the bars marked by Reiner. Later in the movement, however, Rodzinski invests the recall of the main theme with various degrees of rubato, as one can hear when listening to the section between letters I and K in the score.[113]

Reiner's conducting and his recorded legacy also displayed his concern for drawing a distinctive sound from an orchestra. The sound he drew from the Chicago Symphony Orchestra was as instantly recognizable as, though different from, Stokowski's sound with the Philadelphia Orchestra or Koussevitzky's with the Boston Symphony Orchestra. Stokowski cultivated what became known as "The Philadelphia Sound." This had a rich, almost voluptuous string tone, based on the players changing bows at different times to create a seamless sound. Supported by characterful woodwind and brilliant brass playing, it was a homogeneous, sustained sound established on a powerful bass sounding like an organ.[114] Stokowski's transcriptions of instrumental and organ music by Bach project this sound particularly well. Koussevitzky's sound texture with the Boston Symphony comprised "triumphant brass with a hint of rubato, delicate but expressive woodwinds, a strong yet malleable sheet of violin tone, richly yielding lower strings (the double basses being predictably prominent), and a weighty—if not always ideally focused—arsenal of percussion."[115] Many of Koussevitzky's brass and woodwind players performed on French-style instruments, adding a distinctive, fruity sound to the overall orchestral texture; and the strings, in tutti passages, played with a pristine yet torrential sonority. A representative recording of the Bostonians' sound under Koussevitzky would be their performance of Tchaikovsky's Fourth Symphony.[116]

By contrast, the string sound Reiner cultivated was firm, lean at times and rich at others, never quite lush, yet never thin either. It had sufficient vibrato in the strings to sound warm. Early in his Chicago tenure, Reiner stopped the orchestra during rehearsal and said to the first violins, "I don't like cold tone. No neutral tone. Warmth. Warm sounds I want."[117] He did not elaborate on the point, but it seems he wanted more pressure on the strings coupled with more vibrato. The woodwind players in Reiner's Chicago Symphony orchestra were highly articulate and well blended; the brass were agile in quicker passages and played with a deep, Germanic sound that had long been cultivated in the orchestra from the days when Stock was chief conductor. The overall sound Reiner drew from the orchestra meshed effectively. Peter J. Rabinowitz has remarked that "no other conductor in my experience achieved such solidity of orchestral tone. It's perfectly balanced from top to bottom, with clearly articulated inner voices and an exceptionally solid bass—a sound that's far leaner, tighter, and more precise than, say, the Furtwängler sound (which tends to mush orchestral timbres), but also fuller and weightier than the clean sound of Szell, which is comparatively light and airy."[118] Irving Kolodin thought Reiner's conducting of the Chicago Symphony had "just the right admixture of European and American values to realize its players' potentialities best. Thus, the fundamental coloration comes from deep and sonorous basses and cellos, to which upper strings are added, rather than vice-versa: mellowness rather than brilliance characterizes the brass, resulting in a tonal mass of wonderful consistence rather than mere surface sheen."[119]

Reiner's concern for transparency of sound is well captured on a CD entitled *The Reiner Sound* that includes Liszt's *Totentanz*, Weber's *Invitation to the Dance*, Rachmaninov's tone poem *The Isle of the Dead*, and Ravel's *Pavane pour une infante défunte* and *Rapsodie espagnole*. The performance of *The Isle of the Dead* illustrates the different types of string tone Reiner could coax from his Chicago forces. Based on Arnold Bocklin's painting depicting Charon rowing the dead across the Styx, this somber orchestral piece is highly atmospheric; sound projection is crucial for its success in performance. The orchestra begins the piece with careful dynamic shadings for the 5/8 rocking theme. Plangent violin and oboe solos intersperse the dark-hued texture of the music. The players sustain a level of lean, icy string tone from much of the central part of the score, an expressive string cantilena intended by Rachmaninov to represent a life theme and separate from the imaginative stimulus provided by Bocklin's picture. Greater tension is applied to the playing at the meno mosso (page 53), with an impressive, almost Wagnerian depth of string tone, leading up to the *fff* climax at letter 22. The building up and release of tension is handled subtly throughout the twenty-minute piece with close observation of the sound and dynamic levels appropriate for different sections of the score. Reiner's combination of precision and drama and his concern for crystalline orchestral texture and vitality of rhythm are hallmarks not only of this recording but of "The Reiner Sound" in general. The combination of these qualities informs his recorded legacy and testifies to his superior re-creative abilities as a performing musician.

Appendix
Timings of Recordings by Reiner

Composer	Piece	Orchestra	Year	Timing
Bartók	Concerto for Orchestra	Pittsburgh Symphony	1946	36.10
		Chicago Symphony	1955	37.15
Beethoven	Piano Concerto no. 5	RCA Victor Symphony	1952	37.04
		Chicago Symphony	1961	37.19
Brahms	Hungarian Dances nos.	Pittsburgh Symphony	1946	17.13
	1, 5, 6, 7, 12, 13,	Vienna Philharmonic	1960	19.02
	19, and 21			
	Piano Concerto no. 1	Pittsburgh Symphony	1946	43.43
		Chicago Symphony	1954	45.68
	Piano Concerto no. 2	Chicago Symphony	1958	44.53
		Chicago Symphony	1961	48.21
Debussy	*Ibéria* from *Images*	Pittsburgh Symphony	1941	19.07
		Chicago Symphony	1957	20.22
	"Nuages" from	New York Philharmonic	1939	8.36
	Nocturnes	Chicago Symphony	1957	10.09
Kabalevsky	Overture *Colas*	Pittsburgh Symphony	1945	4.16
	Breugnon	Chicago Symphony	1959	4.45
Kodály	*Dances from Galánta*	Pittsburgh Symphony	1945	15.09
		Chicago Symphony	1959	15.50
Mozart	Symphony no. 40	Pittsburgh Symphony	1947	24.10
		Chicago Symphony	1955	25.01
Mussorgsky	*A Night on a Bare*	Pittsburgh Symphony	1945	8.38
	Mountain	Chicago Symphony	1959	10.13
Rachmaninov	Piano Concerto no. 2	Chicago Symphony	1956	33.11
		Chicago Symphony	1962	33.18
Ravel	*La valse*	Pittsburgh Symphony	1947	11.21
		Chicago Symphony	1960	12.54
Rossini	Overture,	Pittsburgh Symphony	1946	4.26
	Il Signor Bruschino	Chicago Symphony	1959	4.31
Schumann	Piano Concerto	Chicago Symphony	1959	29.82
		Chicago Symphony	1960	30.32

Shostakovich	Symphony no. 6	New York Philharmonic	1943	35.10
		Pittsburgh Symphony	1945	30.32
Johann Strauss	*Schatz* waltz	Pittsburgh Symphony	1941	7.13
		Chicago Symphony	1960	7.31
	Wiener Blut waltz	Pittsburgh Symphony	1941	7.27
		Chicago Symphony	1960	8.50
	Rosen aus der	Pittsburgh Symphony	1946	7.38
	Süden waltz	Chicago Symphony	1960	8.38
Richard Strauss	*Till Eulenspiegel*	RCA Victor Symphony	1950	14.19
		NBC Symphony	1952	14.52
		Vienna Philharmonic	1956	14.57
		Chicago Symphony	1957	15.08
	Tod und Verklärung	RCA Victor Symphony	1950	21.58
		Vienna Philharmonic	1956	24.00
	Also sprach	Chicago Symphony	1954	31.52
	Zarathustra	Chicago Symphony	1962	33.55
	Ein Heldenleben	Pittsburgh Symphony	1947	39.14
		Chicago Symphony	1954	43.27
	Don Quixote	Pittsburgh Symphony	1941	46.10
		Chicago Symphony	1959	43.02
Wagner	Prelude to Act 1	New York Philharmonic	1939	8.57
	of *Die*	Pittsburgh Symphony	1941	8.29
	Meistersinger	Chicago Symphony	1959	9.55
	Prelude to Act 3, Dance	Pittsburgh Symphony	1941	13.03
	of the Apprentices	Chicago Symphony	1959	12.03
	and Procession of the			
	Masters from *Die*			
	Meistersinger			
	Prelude to Act 1 of	Pittsburgh Symphony	1941	7.52
	Lohengrin	Chicago Symphony	1960	8.32

Notes

Abbreviations

ARG	*American Record Guide*
CA	*Chicago American*
CCT	*Cincinnati Commercial Tribune*
CDN	*Chicago Daily News*
CE	*Cincinnati Enquirer*
CHS	Cincinnati Historical Society
CP	*Cincinnati Post*
CS-T	*Chicago Sun-Times*
CT	*Chicago Tribune*
CtiSO Arch	Cincinnati Symphony Orchestra Archives
CT-S	*Cincinnati Times-Star*
CU	Butler Library, Special Collections, Columbia University
DLC	Library of Congress
MA	*Musical America*
MC	*Musical Courier*
MOA	Metropolitan Opera Archives
NN	New York Public Library for the Performing Arts
NU	Deering Library, Northwestern University
NYH-T	*New York Herald-Tribune*
NYPA	New York Philharmonic Archives
NYT	*New York Times*
PBI	*Pittsburgh Bulletin Index*
PEB	*Philadelphia Evening Bulletin*
PI	*Philadelphia Inquirer*
PP	*Pittsburgh Press*
PP-G	*Pittsburgh Post-Gazette*
PS-T	*Pittsburgh Sun-Telegraph*
SFPALM	San Francisco Peforming Arts Library and Museum
SR	*Saturday Review*

Chapter 1: The Man and the Musician

1. Humphrey, *Eye for Music,* 51.
2. Galkin, *History of Orchestral Conducting,* 753; Wright, "Great Conductors," 61.
3. Antheil, *Bad Boy of Music,* 351.

4. Daniels, *Conversations with Menuhin,* 91.

5. Quoted in Ewen, *Living Musicians,* 293.

6. Kozma, "Ave Atque Vale," 11.

7. Quoted in *PEB,* Oct. 5, 1927.

8. Dettmer, "Fritz Reiner," 63; Eugene Weintraub to Olin Downes, June 19, 1944, and Erno Balogh to Reiner, Oct. 12, 1960, Reiner Collection, files for 1943–45 and 1959, NU.

9. Page and Page, eds., *Selected Letters of Virgil Thomson,* 206.

10. Isaac Stern in Papp, "Reiner."

11. Bernstein, *Findings,* 200.

12. David Diamond, interview with the author.

13. János Starker, interview with the author.

14. See chapter 8 for details of these awards.

15. Merrill with Dody, *Once More from the Beginning,* 166; Rubinstein, *My Many Years,* 486.

16. *NYH-T,* Nov. 24, 1963.

17. Max Rudolf, interview with the author.

18. *CDN,* Nov. 23, 1963.

19. George Gaber and Robert Mayer, interviews with the author.

20. Quoted in Gould, "Artist's Life," 21.

21. Philip Farkas, interview with the author.

22. *CT,* Feb. 16–22, 1957.

23. John Pfeiffer, interview with the author.

24. Speech by Paul Henry Lang at a meeting of the American Hungarian Studies Foundation, Apr. 29, 1964, Reiner Collection, loose files, NU.

25. Ewen, *Musicians since 1900,* 672.

26. Max Rudolf, interview with the author; "Interview between Edward Downes and Fritz Reiner," radio broadcast, n.d. (the audiocassette has no date, but the interview probably occurred during the intermission of a Metropolitan Opera broadcast in the early 1960s); *New York Post Home News,* Dec. 8, 1948, Fritz Reiner scrapbooks (1948–57), NN (quotation).

27. Potter, "Fritz Reiner," 13–14, 16–17; Hart, *Fritz Reiner,* 19–20.

28. "Reiner Centenary Scrapbook," 16; *PEB,* Sept. 12, 1927; Hart, *Fritz Reiner,* 20–21.

29. Tuśy to Reiner, Apr. 5, Dec. 12, 1929; Tuśy to Carlotta Reiner, Apr. 19, 1958; Carlotta Reiner to Eva Bartenstein, Mar. 9, 1962, and to Tuśy, Nov. 6, 1962; Reiner to S. E. Bremer, May 7, 1946, and to Tuśy, Nov. 15, 1947; all in Reiner Collection, files for 1945–46, 1947, 1962, loose files, NU; "Reiner Centenary Scrapbook," 14.

30. "Reiner Centenary Scrapbook," 14.

31. *CP,* June 30, 1922; *Philadelphia Public Ledger,* Nov. 22, 1929; Roger Dettmer, interview with the author.

32. Eva Bartenstein, interview with the author.

33. Roger Dettmer, interview with the author.

34. *CP,* June 30, 1922; *MC* 91.9 (Aug. 27, 1925): 5.

35. Eva Bartenstein, interview with the author.

36. *CE,* Jan. 21, 1930; *Philadelphia Bulletin,* Jan. 21, 1930.

37. Goldovsky, *My Road to Opera,* 153.

38. Dana S. Hawthorne to Rev. Ralph S. Thom, Jan. 25, 1945, Reiner Collection, file for 1943–45, NU.

39. Max Rudolf, interview with the author. Berta's death was announced in the *NYT,* Aug. 8, 1951.

40. *PP,* Sept. 23, 1938, Mar. 28, 1939; Roger Dettmer, interview with the author; *Philadelphia Bulletin,* Aug. 28, 1931.

41. Helmbrecht, "Carlotta Reiner," 28–30; *PP,* Sept. 23, 1938; *Philadelphia Bulletin,* Aug. 28, 1931; *CT,* Mar. 1, 1955; Roger Dettmer, interview with the author. The Theater section of NN has plenty of information on the Stuart Walker Company plus photographs of Carlotta Reiner as an actress.

42. *Brooklyn Daily Eagle,* Oct. 25, 1936; *NYT,* Nov. 16, 1963; Sablosky, "Trial and Triumph of Fritz Reiner," 30; *The Podium* (Spring/Summer 1983): 28.

43. Personal communication with Gina Pia Cooper, Feb. 13, 1991.

44. *New York Post,* Nov. 15, 1938.

45. Roger Dettmer, interview with the author.

46. *CE,* Sept. 27, 1926 (quotation), May 29, 1928.

47. Saerchinger, "Fritz Reiner," 9.

48. *New York World Telegram,* July 28, 1931; *Brooklyn Daily Eagle,* Oct. 25, 1936.

49. Dettmer, "Kaviar für Volk," 18; Willis, "Reiner Library a Gift to N.U."

50. Mayer, "Dr. Reiner's Orchestra," 111; *PS-T,* Jan. 14, 1947.

51. Sablosky, "Trial and Triumph of Fritz Reiner," 29.

52. All of these scores are in the Reiner Collection at NU.

53. Briggs, *Leonard Bernstein,* 98.

54. *MA* 40.15 (Aug. 2, 1924): 2, 23; Paul Henry Lang to Carlotta Reiner, Dec. 7, 1963, Reiner Collection, loose files, NU.

55. Leonard Sharrow in Papp's documentary *Reiner: The Great Leveller;* John de Lancie, interview with the author.

56. *Musical Leader* 50.3 (July 6, 1925): 51–52.

57. Samuel Thaviu, interview with the author (quotation); "Reiner Symposium in Bloomington/I," 10.

58. David Walter and David Diamond, interviews with the author.

59. *NYT,* Nov. 24, 1963; *NYH-T,* Dec. 16, 1946.

60. Victor Aitay in Papp, *Reiner.*

61. Levin, "Reiner and Stokowski," 10.

62. Reiner, "Secrets of the Conductor," 25.

63. "Pittsburgh's Principal Flutist Recalls Dr. Reiner," 9.

64. *CT-S,* Feb. 24, 1926.

65. *PEB,* Oct. 5, 1927.

66. *New York Post Home News,* Dec. 8, 1948, Fritz Reiner scrapbooks (1948–57), NN.

67. David Diamond, interview with the author; "Interview with George Gaber," 22.

68. Reiner to Bruno Zirato, n.d., Reiner Collection, file for 1948, NU.

69. *New York Evening Post,* Aug. 6, 1924.

70. "Reminiscences of Saul Goodman," 79–81, Columbia Oral History Collection, CU.

71. *Hi-Fi and Stereo Review* 12.2 (Feb. 1964): 74.

72. *CE,* Apr. 20, 1930; *PP,* Aug. 3, 1941.

73. Norton, *Music in My Time,* 177–78; *Cincinnati Fine Arts* 1.3 (Sept. 1928): 1; personal communication with Fred Lerdahl, Oct. 14, 1999.

74. Samuel Thaviu, interview with the author.

75. Potter, "Fritz Reiner," 141, table 1.

76. Reiner to Edward Specter, May 8, 1938, Reiner Collection, loose files, NU.

77. David Diamond, interview with the author.

78. Lukas Foss in Papp, *Reiner.*

79. Kolodin, "Fritz Reiner."

80. *CE,* Mar. 10, 1929.

81. John de Lancie, interview with the author; Lancie, "Im Gesprach mit Richard Strauss."

82. Jablonski and Stewart, *Gershwin Years,* 275; Marjory Fisher to Carlotta and Fritz, Mar. 7, 1937, Reiner Collection, file for December 1936–Spring 1937, NU; Aaron Copland to Reiner, Apr. 18, 1945, Reiner Papers, CU; Gould, "Artist's Life," 21.

83. *New York World Telegram,* July 28, 1931.

84. Harrison, "Return of Reiner."

85. *CA,* Oct. 11, 1953.

86. *PEB,* Oct. 5, 1927.

87. Hitchcock and Sadie, eds., *New Grove Dictionary of American Music,* vol. 4, 27–28; personal communication with Fred Lerdahl, Oct. 1, 1999.

88. Harrison, "Return of Reiner," 12–13.

89. Kolodin, "Fritz Reiner."

90. *New York Sun,* Feb. 23, 1938.

91. *MA* 42.18 (Aug. 22, 1925): 14.

92. Reiner, "Wagner."

93. Reiner, "Your Chances with the Symphony"; *Chicago Sunday Tribune,* Mar. 19, 1950; *NYT,* Aug. 5, 1962.

94. Reiner to Serge Koussevitzky, July 25, 1944, Koussevitzky Collection, DLC.

95. Victor Aitay, interview with the author.

96. *CT-S,* Feb. 12, 1927.

97. Marek, *Toscanini,* 169, 173; Sachs, *Toscanini,* 209, 214.

98. Roger Dettmer, interview with the author.

99. Schonberg, *Horowitz,* 140; Dettmer, "Fritz Reiner," 62.

100. John Pfeiffer, interview with the author.

101. *CA,* Nov. 24, 1963.

102. Dettmer, "Fritz Reiner," 62.

103. Goddard Lieberson to Reiner, Dec. 1, 1942, and Reiner to Goddard Lieberson, Dec. 4, 1942 (quotation), Reiner Collection, file for 1942, NU.

104. *MA* 86.12 (Oct. 1956): 4, 14; Smith, *Worlds of Music,* 16, 35–36; Ezra Rachlin, interview with the author.

105. Leinsdorf, *Cadenza,* 89. For an account of Judson's career see Hart, *Orpheus in the New World,* chap. 4, and Lebrecht, *When the Music Stops,* 93–131.

106. Personal communication with Eugene Weintraub, July 16, 1991.

107. See correspondence between Schulhof and Reiner in Reiner Collection, loose files, NU.

108. Sol Hurok to Reiner, Mar. 23, 1948, and contract between Reiner and Sol Hurok, 1949, Reiner Collection, loose files, NU; Roger Dettmer, interview with the author.

109. Reiner to Michel Kachouk, Aug. 31, 1948, Reiner Collection, loose files, NU; Smith, *Worlds of Music,* 13, 19.

110. Reiner to Arthur Judson, Mar. 16, 1941, and to Mae Frohman, Dec. 5, 1953, Reiner Collection, loose files, NU.

111. "Interview with George Gaber," 25.

112. Arnold Jacobs in Papp, *Reiner.*

113. Leinsdorf, *Cadenza,* 84; *PBI,* Oct. 9, 1941.

114. Arnold Jacobs, cited in the *Chicago Reader,* June 1, 1984.

115. *CE,* May [?], 1949.

116. Philip Sieburg, cited in *Fritz Reiner Society Newsletter* 14, 3–4.

117. Philip Farkas, interview with the author.

118. Furlong, *Season with Solti,* 55–56.

119. Sargeant, *Geniuses, Goddesses, and People,* 259.

120. Furlong, *Season with Solti,* 52; Sablosky, "Trial and Triumph of Fritz Reiner," 35–36.

121. János Starker, interview with the author.

122. Edward Specter to Reiner, Apr. 6, 1942, Reiner Collection, loose files, NU.

123. Reiner to Edward Specter, Mar. 16, 1946, Reiner Collection, loose files, NU; Levant, *Memoirs of an Amnesiac,* 207.

124. Max Rudolf, interview with the author.

125. Quoted in Mayer, "Dr. Reiner's Orchestra," 40.

126. Quoted in Stern with Potok, *My First Seventy-Nine Years,* 301.

127. Francine Blum to Reiner, Oct. 18, 1944, with a typed reply, n.d.; Reiner to Norman Pellegrini, Aug. 22, 1957, and to Paul Karody Jr., May 17, 1963; all in Reiner Collection, files for 1943–45, 1957, and 1963–January 1964, NU.

128. Victor Aitay, interview with the author; *NYT,* Nov. 16, 1963; Papp, "Hindsight."

129. "János Starker Speaks about His Reiner Years/II," 17; "János Starker Speaks about His Reiner Years," 31; János Starker in Papp, *Reiner;* Marek, *Toscanini,* 10–11.

130. John de Lancie, interview with the author.

131. "János Starker Speaks about His Reiner Years," 13.

132. Stoddard, "Fritz Reiner," 14.

133. Lukas Foss cited in Burton, ed., *Conversations about Bernstein*, 7.

134. Ezra Rachlin, interview with the author.

135. Merrill with Dody, *Once More from the Beginning*, 246.

136. Igor Kipnis, interview with the author.

137. Stoddard, "Fritz Reiner," 13.

138. *Fritz Reiner Society Newsletter* 1 (1975): 4; Slonimsky, *Music since 1900*, 564.

139. *Buffalo Evening News,* Feb. 8, 1944.

140. Reiner to Edward Specter, Sept. 29, 1942, Reiner Collection, loose files, NU.

141. *South Bend (Ind.) News-Times,* Aug. 23, 1936; *Boston Evening Transcript,* July 22, 1937; *New York Post Home News,* Dec. 8, 1948, in Fritz Reiner scrapbooks (1948–57), NN.

142. *CT-S,* June 4, 1925; Ewen, *Musicians since 1900,* 672; *Bridgeport (Conn.) Sunday Post,* July 25, 1943.

143. *NYT,* Aug. 5, 1962.

144. *CP,* Mar. 24, 1925; Goldovsky, *My Road to Opera,* 255; *CT-S,* Jan. 28, 1927.

145. *CT-S,* Mar. 8, 1924; *PBI,* Mar. 10, 1938; "Biography of Fritz Reiner" (typescript ca. 1937–38), Reiner Collection, loose files, NU.

146. Reiner to Marvin D. Rosenberg, Feb. 21, 1956, Reiner Collection, file for 1955–56, NU; *CT-S,* Dec. 12, 1922, Sept. 28, 1925; *CP,* Mar. 25, 1925; *CS-T,* Oct. 15, 1953.

147. *PBI,* Mar. 10, 1938. The August 1937 issue of *Country Life* includes some photographs of Nantucket by Reiner.

148. *Bridgeport (Conn.) Sunday Post,* Apr. 19, 1953; typescript of interview with Reiner, KDKA radio network, Mar. 26, 1938, Reiner Collection, loose files, NU.

149. *NYT,* Nov. 16, 1963.

150. *PEB,* Oct. 5, 1927.

151. *NYT,* Aug. 16, 1931.

152. Fritz Reiner, "Music for the Greatest Audience."

153. *New York Telegraph,* July 20, 1924.

154. *CCT,* Sept. 11, 1929; *PBI,* Mar. 10, 1938; *PS-T,* Aug. 14, 1943; Fritz Reiner, "Last Time I Saw Sicily," unidentified newspaper clipping, Reiner Collection, loose files, NU.

155. Roger Dettmer, interview with the author.

156. Carlotta Reiner to Claudia Cassidy, Aug. 8, 1955, Reiner Collection, file for 1955–56, NU.

157. Thomson, *Musical Scene,* 43.

158. Lancie, "Orchestral Malaise."

Chapter 2: Early Years in Europe

1. A fair amount of material in this chapter is based on Dettmer, "Reiner," 60–69; Potter, "Fritz Reiner," 9–18; Stoddard, "Fritz Reiner," 13–14; Guthrie-Treadway, "Fritz Reiner"; Cassidy, "Fritz Reiner and His Magic Baton"; Saerchinger, "Fritz Reiner"; Carlotta Reiner, typescript on the career of Fritz Reiner, Reiner Collection, file for 1953, NU; and "Interview between Edward Downes and Fritz Reiner."

2. Cassidy, "Fritz Reiner and His Magic Baton."

3. *Xaverian News,* Nov. 3, 1929.

4. Reiner described his first meeting with Weiner in a booklet on Wagner that he wrote for Columbia Records. Reiner, "Wagner."

5. "János Starker Speaks about His Reiner Years," 12.

6. *New York Post-Home News,* Dec. 8, 1948, Fritz Reiner scrapbooks (1948–57), NN.

7. For Reiner's musical education in Hungary, see Bónis, "Fritz Reiner," 218–20.

8. *Christian Science Monitor,* Apr. 10, 1924; Guthrie-Treadway, "Fritz Reiner."

9. "Interview with Gordon Peters," 10.

10. *Az Országos M. Kir. Zeneakadémia Évkönyve* (Budapest, 1903–9).

11. *A Liszt Ferenc Zenemuvészeti Foiskola oktatói: 1875–1975,* 279.

12. *Az Országos M. Kir. Zeneakadémia Évkönyve* (Budapest, 1906–7), 114.

13. Hart, *Fritz Reiner,* 4.

14. Demény, "Bartók Béla és a Zeneakadémia," 143.

15. Gillies, "Teacher," 80.

16. *Az Országos M. Kir. Zeneakadémia Évkönyve* (Budapest, 1906–7), 92, and (1904–5), 105, 185.

17. Los Angeles Philharmonic Orchestra program, Aug. 17, 1937, Los Angeles Philharmonic Association.

18. Klinger, "Memories of Fritz Reiner as a Young Man."

19. Szigeti, "Making Music with Bartók," 10.

20. Hart, *Fritz Reiner,* 5.

21. Botstein, "Out of Hungary," 16–17.

22. Fritz Reiner baptismal certificate, Nov. 10, 1908, Reiner Collection, NU.

23. Eva Bartenstein, interview with the author.

24. For commentary on the musical atmosphere of Budapest on the eve of World War I, see Suchoff, ed., *Béla Bartók Essays,* 460; Eosze, *Zoltán Kodály,* 7–8, 14, 16; and Lukacs, *Budapest 1900,* esp. 45, 75, 177.

25. "János Starker Speaks about His Reiner Years," 11–12. These artists can be identified in the large collection of concert posters and recital programs in the Graphics and Prints Department of the National Széchényi Library, Budapest.

26. *CT-S,* Oct. 10, 1923. The American premiere of Reiner's *Vónosnégyes* for string quartet was given by the Chicago Symphony string quartet at an annual gala held by the NU Library Council in October 1988.

27. Caratelli, *Musician's Odyssey,* 102.

28. Quoted in Bónis, "Fritz Reiner," 219.

29. Reiner commented on this in "Making of a Conductor," 23.

30. Saerchinger, "Fritz Reiner," 9.

31. A vivid sketch of Leó Weiner is included in Dorati, *Notes of Seven Decades,* 39–42.

32. *NYT,* Nov. 16, 1963.

33. Poster for the Népszínhaz Vígopera, June 24, 1908, National Széchényi Library, Budapest.

34. Quoted in Rothe, "Fritz Reiner," 7.

35. Dorati, *Notes of Seven Decades,* 39.

36. "Fritz Reiner," Associated Press Biographical Service, sketch no. 4145, Mar. 1, 1963, Reiner Collection, NU.

37. *PBI,* Oct. 22, 1942.

38. Stoddard, *Symphony Conductors of the USA,* 175.

39. Spendal, "Ljubljana"; Grange, *Mahler,* 83–86.

40. *Repertoar Slovenskih Gledali 1867–1967,* 647.

41. Ibid.

42. Hart, *Fritz Reiner,* 6.

43. Details on Reiner's conducting at the Budapest Népopera are based on information in *Magyar Szinpad* plus the surviving Népopera playbills in the National Széchényi Library, Budapest. Hart failed to consult *Magyar Szinpad,* and his account of Reiner's conducting is therefore incomplete: he only covers 1913 and 1914 (*Fritz Reiner,* 7).

44. Hart erroneously states that Reiner only conducted one Hungarian opera, *Radda* (ibid., 8).

45. *A Zene,* July 1912, 160.

46. *A Zene,* Nov. 1912, 240.

47. Beckett, *Richard Wagner,* 94.

48. Quoted in Bónis, "Fritz Reiner," 219.

49. Hart wrongly states that Jadlowker was a German tenor (*Fritz Reiner*, 8).

50. Key, *Music Yearbook 1925–26*, 342.

51. Turnbull, *Opera Gazetteer*, 197.

52. *Staatskapelle Dresden*, 28. Hart states, on the contrary, that Muck turned down the offer of the post, but he provides no citation to support this statement (*Fritz Reiner*, 12).

53. Details of these conductors and residences are taken from *TageBuch der königlich Sächsischen hoftheater fur Das Jahr* (Dresden, 1914–21).

54. Krause, "Im Glauze der Strauss-Oper," 73.

55. Reiner, "Wagner."

56. For good essays on the musical traditions of Dresden see Bauman and Härtwig, "Dresden," 1246–53; and Steude, Landmann and Härtwig, "Dresden," 612–26.

57. *New York Mirror*, July 26, 1936.

58. Potter, "Fritz Reiner," 14–15.

59. *CP*, June 30, 1922.

60. The theater in which Reiner conducted the Dresden Opera was gutted in 1945. It has been restored to its former glory and was reopened in 1985.

61. Details of the symphonic and operatic repertoire conducted by Reiner in Dresden are taken from *Königlich Sächsische Hoftheater zu Dresden: Rückblick* (Dresden, 1914–21) and the *Theaterzettel* (1914–21). Copies of these publications are available at the Dresden Stadtarchiv and at the Semperoper, Dresden. Hart's account of Reiner's operatic repertoire in Dresden states that Reiner conducted "more than eight hundred performances of forty-seven operas" (*Fritz Reiner*, 15). He seems to have wrongly counted performances at the Semperoper conducted by Kutzschbach, Striegler, and Pembaur in his totals, failing to separate them from those under Reiner's baton.

62. Hart wrongly states that Reiner conducted *Carmen* forty-one times in Dresden (*Fritz Reiner*, 15).

63. Laux, *Dresden Staatskapelle*, 73.

64. Ibid.

65. *New York Evening Post*, Aug. 6, 1924.

66. "Interview between Edward Downes and Fritz Reiner."

67. *Brooklyn Daily Eagle*, July 11, 1937; *NYT*, Feb. 25, 1948.

68. Reiner to "Herr Professor," July 28, 1919, Letters from Fritz Reiner to Jean-Louis Nicodé, Manuscripts Department, Sächsische Landesbibliothek, Dresden.

69. Kolodin, "Fritz Reiner."

70. Jefferson, *Life of Richard Strauss*, 156.

71. Mann, *Richard Strauss*, 173; Schuh, ed., *Richard Strauss*, 166; Hartmann, *Richard Strauss*, 124.

72. Krause, "Im Glauze der Strauss-Oper," 73.

73. *Staatskapelle Dresden*, 28.

74. *The News* (Mexico), Oct. 9, 1951, Fritz Reiner scrapbooks (1948–57), NN.

75. Dettmer, "Reiner," 61.

76. Levant, *Memoirs of an Amnesiac*, 207.

77. Hart's account of these operas misspells the titles of the operas by Franckenstein and Schreker and lists a Hugo Kann, which should be Kaun (*Fritz Reiner*, 15). For the Schreker performance, see Hailey, *Franz Schreker*, 308.

78. *CE*, Mar. 4, 1926; Kolodin, *Musical Life*, 236; Key, *Pierre Key's Musical Who's Who*, 272, 360; Henschel und Friedrich, *Elisabeth Rethberg*, 16.

79. *Dresdner Nachtrichten*, Feb. 10 and Mar. 20, 1918. Copies of this newspaper are available at the Sächsische Landesbibliothek, Dresden.

80. *Dresdner Nachtrichten*, Nov. 24, 1919.

81. *Dresdner Nachtrichten*, Aug. 23, 1916, Nov. 24, 1921, Apr. 30, 1917.

82. *Dresdner Nachtrichten*, Jan. 8, 1917.

83. *Dresdner Nachtrichten,* Aug. 24, 1919.

84. *Dresdner Nachtrichten,* Jan. 26, 1918.

85. *Dresdner Nachtrichten,* Jan. 28, 30, and Feb. 3, 1918.

86. Busch, *Pages from a Musician's Life,* 133, 144; Joseph Szigeti to Jean-Do. Mondoloni, May 13, 1971, *The Podium,* 1.1 (1976): 3.

87. Laux, *Dresden Staatskapelle,* 73.

88. All details on Reiner's symphonic conducting in Dresden are gleaned from the *Programmhefte* of the Dresden Opera's *Sinfoniekonzerte,* available at the Sächsische Landesbibliothek, and from the playbills of the Sächsische Staatstheater Opernhaus, available at the Semperoper and the Stadtarchiv, Dresden.

89. Krause, "Im Glauze der Strauss-Oper," 73.

90. Slonimsky, *Baker's Biographical Dictionary of Musicians,* 613, 1608.

91. Hart, who has not consulted all the available material, wrongly states that Reiner conducted forty concerts in Dresden (*Fritz Reiner,* 13, 17).

92. Boult, *Boult on Music,* 101.

93. Thomas, "History of the Cincinnati Symphony Orchestra to 1931," pt. 2, 539 n.149.

94. Quoted in Earl G. Talbott, "Fritz Reiner—One of the World's Great Conductors," *NYH-T,* Nov. 16, 1963.

95. Reiner, "Technique of Conducting," 9–11.

96. Respighi, *Ottorino Respighi,* 78.

97. Biographical File on Fritz Reiner, San Francisco Opera Archives, SFPALM.

98. Hart, *Fritz Reiner,* 19–20; Potter, "Fritz Reiner," 16–17.

99. Laux, *Dresden Staatskapelle,* 73.

100. Hart, *Fritz Reiner,* 22.

101. Reiner to unknown, Sept. 16, 1920, Reiner Collection, loose files, NU.

102. *Dresdner Nachtrichten,* Dec. 19, 1920.

103. Busch, *Pages from a Musician's Life,* 132.

104. For the Hamburg engagement, see Stephenson, *Hundert Jahre Philharmonische Gesellschaft in Hamburg,* 240.

105. Hart, *Fritz Reiner,* 22.

106. Muck, *Einhundert jahre Berliner Philharmonisches Orchester,* vol. 3, 166, 175, 191, 192, 196. Muck shows, contrary to Hart (*Fritz Reiner,* 22), that Reiner conducted concerts in Berlin before 1921.

107. Saleski, *Famous Musicians of Jewish Origin,* 274–76; Frajese, *Dal Costanzi All'-Opera,* 141–42.

108. Reiner to George Marek, Apr. 3, 1951, Reiner Collection, file for 1951, NU.

109. Respighi, *Ottorino Respighi,* 86.

110. Hart, *Fritz Reiner,* 23.

111. Ibid.; Biographical file on Fritz Reiner, San Francisco Opera Archives, SFPALM; Saleski, *Famous Musicians of Jewish Origin,* 274–76.

112. *CE,* May 27, 1922.

113. Milton Diamond to Reiner, Oct. 13, 1921, Reiner Collection, file for 1920–21, NU.

114. Schonberg, *Great Conductors,* 342.

115. Saleski, *Famous Musicians of a Wandering Race,* 142.

Chapter 3: Cincinnati

1. Thomas, "History of the Cincinnati Symphony Orchestra to 1931," pt. 2, 498.

2. *CE,* May 27, 1922; *CCT,* May 27, 1922. Most of the Cincinnati newspaper references cited below are available in the Cincinnati Symphony Orchestra scrapbooks, vols. 27–28, 30, and 32–39, at CHS.

3. *CP,* June 30, 1922; *CT-S,* Sept. 26 and 30, 1922.

4. See Henry Wadsworth Longfellow's poem "Catawba Wine" (1854).

5. Hart, *Fritz Reiner*, 25; Sheblessy, *One Hundred Years of the Cincinnati May Festival.*
6. Thomas, "History of the Cincinnati Symphony Orchestra to 1931," pt. 1, chap. 1.
7. Ibid., pt. 2, 498.
8. Foster, "Cincinnati Symphony Orchestra," 299–301.
9. Thomas, "History of the Cincinnati Symphony Orchestra to 1931," pt. 2, 507, 514, 524, 533 n.135, 578–79, 606, 613, 616, 626, 646–48.
10. *Argentisches Tageblatt,* June 22, 1926.
11. CE, Mar. 6, 1923.
12. Reiner to Arthur Judson, December 27, 1930, Reiner Collection, loose files, NU.
13. CT-S, Mar. 12, 1925.
14. Hart, *Fritz Reiner*, 31–32.
15. Reiner to Mrs. Charles P. Taft, Apr. 26, 1927, Reiner Collection, file for 1926–27, NU.
16. CE, Oct. 15, 1922.
17. CT-S, Dec. 1922.
18. CP, Oct. 1, 1923.
19. CT-S, Oct. 9, 1922.
20. Thomas, "History of the Cincinnati Symphony Orchestra to 1931," pt. 2, 503. For Ysaÿe's tenure as music director of the Cincinnati Symphony Orchestra, see ibid., pt. 2, chap. 7.
21. Roger Dettmer, interview with the author. Compare the examples cited in Hart, *Fritz Reiner,* 32.
22. Roger Dettmer, interview with the author.
23. Quoted in Thomas, "History of the Cincinnati Symphony Orchestra to 1931," pt. 2, 537–39; *Christian Science Monitor,* Apr. 10, 1924.
24. Reiner to Reuben Lawson, Mar. 8, 1927, Reiner Collection, file for 1926–27, NU.
25. Potter, "Fritz Reiner," 27–28; Thomas, "History of the Cincinnati Symphony Orchestra to 1931," pt. 2, 745–51, appendix 3; CT-S, Sept. 28, 1927.
26. Thomas, "History of the Cincinnati Symphony Orchestra to 1931," pt. 2, 540.
27. Ibid., pt. 2, 548.
28. CT-S, Jan. 20, 1926.
29. Reiner to Frank Kelemen, Nov. 5, 1927, Reiner Collection, file for 1927, NU.
30. Details of soloists and programs for the Reiner era in Cincinnati are taken from Hillyer, "Cincinnati Symphony Orchestra Programs."
31. CE, Oct. 14, 1928.
32. Cincinnati Symphony Orchestra program book, Oct. 23–24, 1925, CtiSO Arch.
33. Cincinnati Symphony Orchestra program book, Nov. 26–27, 1926, CtiSO Arch.
34. CT-S, Mar. 15 and Apr. 22, 1924.
35. Reiner to Robert A. Simon, Feb. 2, 1925, Reiner Collection, file for 1925, NU.
36. CE, Dec. 21, 1929.
37. CCT, Nov. 5, 1923.
38. CE, Oct. 28, 1928.
39. Pollack, *Skyscraper Lullaby,* 241.
40. MC 89.24 (Dec. 11, 1924): 29.
41. CCT, Sept. 4, 1928.
42. Potter, "Fritz Reiner," 141, table 1.
43. CCT, Oct. 1, 1923.
44. *Christian Science Monitor,* Sept. 27, 1922.
45. Quoted in CE, June 10, 1928.
46. CE, June 10, 1928.
47. *Christian Science Monitor,* Sept. 27, 1922.
48. Wachman, "Guest Conductor."
49. Cincinnati Symphony Orchestra program book, Apr. 17–18, 1925, CtiSO Arch; CE, Sept. 15, 1927.

50. *CT-S,* Sept. 9, 1923; *CE,* Mar. 13, 1927; Reiner to Arthur Bliss, Feb. 23, 1925, Reiner Collection, file for 1925, NU.

51. *CCT,* Feb. 16, 1929.

52. Quoted in Thomas, "History of the Cincinnati Symphony Orchestra to 1931," pt. 2, 529–30, 631.

53. Cincinnati Symphony Orchestra program book, Nov. 21–22, 1924, Feb. 6–7, 1925, CtiSO Arch.

54. *CP,* Nov. 13, 1930; *CT-S,* Nov. 11, 1930.

55. *CCT,* Oct. 12, 1930.

56. Thomas, "History of the Cincinnati Symphony Orchestra to 1931," pt. 2, 629.

57. Ibid., 556–57.

58. Reiner to G. C. Ricordi, Jan. 8, 1925, Reiner Collection, file for 1925, NU; *CE,* Mar. 9, 1930.

59. *CT-S,* Sept. 28, 1922.

60. Thomas, "History of the Cincinnati Symphony Orchestra to 1931," pt. 2, 592.

61. Shanet, *Philharmonic,* 251.

62. Reiner to Alexander Smallens, Feb. 1928, Alexander Smallens Papers, series 1, folder 47, NN.

63. Béla Bartók to Reiner, Oct. 29, 1928, in Demény, ed., *Béla Bartók Letters,* 190.

64. Quoted in *MA* 38.24 (Oct. 6, 1923): 32.

65. *CT-S,* July 22, 1924.

66. *CCT,* Dec. 6, 1924.

67. *CT-S,* Feb. 27, 1925; *Christian Science Monitor,* Mar. 9, 1925.

68. *MA* 40.17 (Aug. 16, 1924): 4.

69. Roy Hornikel to Reiner, Dec. 16, 1926, Reiner Collection, file for 1926–27, NU.

70. Thomas, "History of the Cincinnati Symphony Orchestra to 1931," pt. 2, 569–71.

71. Quoted in *Newsweek,* 44.22 (Nov. 29, 1954): 47; *CT-S,* Nov. 26, 1926.

72. Reiner to Ora Talbot, Mar. 11, 1929, Reiner Collection, file for 1929, NU.

73. Thomas, "History of the Cincinnati Symphony Orchestra to 1931," pt. 2, 569–71; Jablonski, *Gershwin,* 184.

74. Olmstead, *Roger Sessions and His Music,* 27.

75. *CE,* Nov. 30, 1930; Olmstead, ed., *Correspondence of Roger Sessions,* 127, 157–58.

76. Aaron Copland to Roger Sessions, Oct. 17, 1927, in Olmstead, ed., *Correspondence of Roger Sessions,* 86–87.

77. Percy Grainger to Reiner, Dec. 6, 1930, and Reiner to Percy Grainger, Dec. 9, 1930, Percy A. Grainger Correspondence, Music Division, DLC.

78. Reiner to Herbert French, Feb. 21, 1929, Reiner Collection, file for 1929, NU.

79. *CCT,* Oct. 28, 1922.

80. *New York World,* Feb. 12, 1923.

81. *CE,* Oct. 23, 1926.

82. Thomas, "History of the Cincinnati Symphony Orchestra to 1931," pt. 2, 556–57.

83. Quoted in *CT-S,* Feb. 12, 1927.

84. Quoted in *CT-S,* Jan. 14, 1926.

85. Fritz Reiner, "Some Remarks on the Principles of Ensemble Playing," Reiner Collection, loose files, NU.

86. Thomas, "History of the Cincinnati Symphony Orchestra to 1931," pt. 2, 508.

87. Itinerary of the Cincinnati Symphony Orchestra season, 1926–27, Reiner Collection, file for 1927, NU; program of a tour by the Cincinnati Symphony Orchestra, 1923–24, Cincinnati Symphony Orchestra scrapbook, vol. 32, CHS.

88. Reiner to Ernest Lunt, Feb. 10, 1927, Reiner Collection, file for 1926–27, NU.

89. Hart, *Fritz Reiner,* 28, 39; Roger Dettmer, interview with the author.

90. *CE,* Mar. 6, 1923.

91. Hart, *Fritz Reiner,* 30.

92. Thomas, "History of the Cincinnati Symphony Orchestra to 1931," pt. 2, 508, 521–22, 551–55, 557–60, 571, 591–92, 617, 629–30, 638–39; *CCT*, Oct. 1, 1925.

93. Hart, *Fritz Reiner,* 39.

94. Prospectus for the 1927–28 season of the Cincinnati Symphony Orchestra, Cincinnati Symphony Orchestra scrapbook, vol. 29, CHS; *Ambridge (Pa.) Citizen,* Dec. 14, 1943; *Greater Pittsburgh,* Jan. 1944.

95. Palmer, *Composer in Hollywood,* 69.

96. *CE,* June 25, 1927.

97. Reiner to Béla Bardos, Nov. 5, 1927, Reiner Collection, file for 1927, NU.

98. Wachman, "Guest Conductor."

99. *CE,* Aug. 10, 1924.

100. *MA* 40.17 (Aug. 16, 1924): 4; *New York Evening Post,* Aug. 6, 1924; Wachman, "Guest Conductor."

101. Mrs. Artie Mason Carter to Reiner, Feb. 21, 1925, Reiner Collection, file for 1925, NU; Jones, *Hollywood Bowl,* 100–101.

102. Hollywood Bowl concert programs, July 7–Aug. 1, 1925, Los Angeles Philharmonic Association; Koopal, *Miracle of Music,* 94.

103. Thomas, "History of the Cincinnati Symphony Orchestra to 1931," pt. 2, 536 (source of information); *Musical Leader* 50.3 (July 6, 1925): 51–52.

104. Stravinsky, *An Autobiography,* 122.

105. Hart, *Fritz Reiner,* 44–45. Details of Reiner's concerts with the Philadelphia Orchestra are taken from the orchestra's program books at the Curtis Institute of Music.

106. Prospectus for the 1927–28 season of the Cincinnati Symphony Orchestra, CHS.

107. Philadelphia Orchestra to Reiner, Feb. 29, 1928, Reiner Collection, file for 1927–28, NU.

108. Kupferberg, *Those Fabulous Philadelphians,* 70.

109. *PI,* Apr. 24, 1926.

110. Thomas, "History of the Cincinnati Symphony Orchestra to 1931," pt. 2, 589.

111. Kolodin, "Fritz Reiner."

112. *CT-S,* Feb. 12, 1927.

113. Erskine, *Philharmonic-Symphony Society of New York,* 97, 100, 101, 107–8.

114. *CP,* June 30, 1922; *CE,* May 6, Aug. 29, Oct. 1, 1923; *CT-S,* Sept. 21, 1923.

115. *MA* 40.4 (May 17, 1924): 6; *New York World,* May 11, 1924; Wachman, "Guest Conductor"; poster for the Queen's Hall concert, Reiner Collection, NU.

116. Szigeti, *With Strings Attached,* 105; Foreman, *Bax,* 206.

117. *CT-S,* July 22, 1924; *CE,* Apr. 18, 1926.

118. Beranek, *Music, Acoustics, and Architecture,* 181.

119. Caamaño, *La historia del Teatro Colón,* vol. 2, 132–33.

120. *CT-S,* Nov. 14, 1928.

121. *Deutsche La Plata Zeitung,* July 9, 1926.

122. *CE,* Apr. 21, 1926; Thomas, "History of the Cincinnati Symphony Orchestra to 1931," pt. 2, 562.

123. Ciampelli, *Ente Concerti Orchestrali Sei Anni di Vita Milano,* 29; *MC* 95.7 (Aug. 18, 1927): 25.

124. Reiner to H. A. Frisker, May 3, 1927, and to Marjorie Harwood, Apr. 19, 1927, Reiner Collection, files for 1926–27 and 1927, NU; *CCT,* Sept. 15, 1927; *New York Telegraph,* May 29, 1927.

125. *CT-S,* Aug. 19, 1928.

126. Selvini, "Maestri," 95.

127. *CCT,* Sept. 11, 1929.

128. Quoted in *CCT,* Oct. 1, 1923.

129. *CT-S,* Oct. 1, 1923 (quotation), Apr. 21, 1925.

130. *CCT,* Oct. 1, 1923.

131. Wachman, "Guest Conductor."

132. *MA* 40.17 (Aug. 16, 1924): 4.

133. *CCT,* Sept. 29, Oct. 1, 1923; *CE,* Oct. 1, 1923.

134. Quoted in *CCT,* Oct. 1, 1923.

135. Quoted in *CT-S,* July 22, 1924.

136. *CCT,* Oct. 1, 1923, Sept. 15, 1927; *CE,* Oct. 1, 1923.

137. *CCT,* Sept. 15, 1927.

138. Reiner to Olga Samaroff, n.d., Reiner Collection, file for 1926–27, NU.

139. Edward Miller to Reiner, Dec. 31, 1926, Reiner Collection, file for 1926–27, NU. The Reiners had previously tried to become U.S. citizens in 1922 (*CT-S,* Nov. 6, 1922).

140. Reiner to Edwin F. Kalmus, Dec. 20, 1926, Reiner Collection, file for 1926–27, NU.

141. Reiner to Arthur Judson, Mar. 23, 1927, Reiner Collection, file for 1926–27, NU.

142. Reiner to Louis T. More, Dec. 23, 1926, Jan. 7, 1927, and to Arthur Judson, Jan. 18, 1928, Reiner Collection, files for 1926–27 and 1927, NU.

143. Reiner to [Herbert G. French], n.d. [late 1928/early 1929], Reiner Collection, file for 1928–29, NU.

144. Herbert G. French to Reiner, Feb. 2, 1929, Reiner Collection, file for 1929, NU.

145. Reiner to Moses Strauss, Nov. 21, 1927, Reiner Collection, file for 1927, NU.

146. Reiner to Arthur Judson, Feb. 11, 1929, Reiner Collection, file for 1929, NU.

147. Roger Dettmer, interview with the author.

148. *CCT,* Jan. 21, 1930; Thomas, "History of the Cincinnati Symphony Orchestra to 1931," pt. 2, 628; Potter, "Fritz Reiner," 33 (quotation).

149. *CCT,* Apr. 29, 1930; Dettmer, "Reiner," 62.

150. Rosen, *Goossens,* 143; Hart, *Fritz Reiner,* 41.

151. Thomas, "History of the Cincinnati Symphony Orchestra to 1931," pt. 2, 632–33.

152. Reiner to Herbert G. French, June 19, 1930, Reiner Collection, file for 1930, NU.

153. J. Herman Thuman, "Reminiscences," May Festival scrapbook, vol. 2 (1932–42), CHS.

154. Thomas, "History of the Cincinnati Symphony Orchestra to 1931," pt. 2, 635.

155. Dettmer, "Reiner," 62; Rosen, *Goossens,* 109–10.

156. *CP,* Dec. 1930.

157. Reiner to Arthur Judson, Dec. 13, 1930, Reiner Collection, loose files, NU.

158. *Columbus (Ohio) Dispatch,* Oct. 2, 1946.

159. Eugene Goossens to Reiner, Nov. 2, 1934, Reiner Collection, file for 1934, NU.

160. Goossens, *Overture and Beginners,* 264.

161. Rosen, *Goossens,* 142.

162. César Saerchinger to Reiner, Dec. 15, 1930, Reiner Collection, file for 1928–29, NU.

163. Thomas, "History of the Cincinnati Symphony Orchestra to 1931," pt. 2, 645, 648.

164. Reiner to Mr. Schmoeger, Mar. 21, 1931, and Arthur Judson to Reiner, Apr. 2, 1931, Reiner Collection, file for 1928–29 and loose files, NU.

165. Reiner to Miss Weise, Apr. 3, 1931, loose files, NU.

Chapter 4: Teaching at Curtis

1. Hart, *Orpheus in the New World,* 139, 158; Goldovsky, *My Road to Opera,* 193; Broder, *Samuel Barber,* 13–14; *Overtones* 11.1 (1974): 13. For a detailed appraisal of Mary Curtis Bok, see Viles, "Mary Louise Curtis Bok Zimbalist."

2. Hart, *Fritz Reiner,* 59.

3. Reiner to M. C. Bok, Dec. 18, 1927, George Antheil Collection, box 2, DLC; Stoddard, "Fritz Reiner," 13.

4. Goldovsky, *My Road to Opera,* 153–54.

5. Galkin, *History of Orchestral Conducting,* xxxvi n.1.

6. Hart, *Fritz Reiner,* 60; Josef Hofmann to Reiner, Mar. 11, 1935, Mar. 28, 1936, and Mary Curtis Bok to Reiner, May 2, 1938, Reiner Collection, loose files and file for 1937–38, NU.

7. N. W. Ayer and Son, Inc., to Reiner, July 22, 1940, Reiner Collection, file for 1940–41, NU.

8. Briggs, *Leonard Bernstein*, 47.

9. *CT*, Oct. 11, 1959.

10. These views are outlined in two articles by Reiner: "The Secrets of the Conductor" and "The Technique of Conducting." Compare Reiner, "Your Chances with the Symphony" and typescript of interview with Reiner, Mar. 26, 1938, KDKA radio network, Reiner Collection, loose files, NU.

11. Reiner, "Technique of Conducting," 10; Reiner, "Secrets of the Conductor," 24; Reiner, "Making of a Conductor," 23.

12. Reiner, "Outline for a Course in Conducting," typescript, Reiner Collection, file marked "Curtis Institute," NU.

13. Stoddard, "Fritz Reiner," 10.

14. Caratelli, *Musician's Odyssey,* 90.

15. Kozma, "Ave Atque Vale," 11.

16. Reiner, "Outline for a Course in Conducting," typescript, Reiner Collection, file marked "Curtis Institute," NU.

17. Reiner, "Secrets of the Conductor," 23.

18. Reiner, "Technique of Conducting," 10.

19. Reiner, "Secrets of the Conductor," 23–24.

20. Ibid., 25; Raven, "Reiner Tells Views on Art of Conducting" (quotation), 2.

21. Reiner, "Making of a Conductor," 23.

22. Kupferberg, "Lukas Foss," 13; "Interview with Morton Gould," 9.

23. Reiner, "Secrets of the Conductor," 24–25.

24. Reiner to Mary Bok, Sept. 14, 1938, Reiner Collection, loose files, NU; Reiner, "Your Chances with the Symphony."

25. Kupferberg, "Lukas Foss," 14; "Interview with Lukas Foss" (quotation), 5.

26. Stoddard, "Fritz Reiner," 13.

27. Walter Hendl and Ezra Rachlin, interviews with the author.

28. Walter Hendl, interview with the author.

29. Stanley, "Baton," 133.

30. Reiner, "Technique of Conducting," 11.

31. Ezra Rachlin, interview with the author; "Conductors' Guild Holds 'Reiner Retrospective,'" 9; Reiner, "Outline for a Course in Conducting"; Potter, "Fritz Reiner," 41.

32. Reiner, "Secrets of the Conductor," 25; Lukas Foss, interview with the author.

33. Reiner, "Technique of Conducting," 17; David Diamond, interview with the author.

34. Reiner, "Technique of Conducting," 11.

35. Ibid., 16.

36. "Conductors' Guild Holds 'Reiner Retrospective,'" 9.

37. Reiner, "Outline for a Course in Conducting," typescript, Reiner Collection, file marked "Curtis Institute," NU.

38. Potter, "Fritz Reiner," 41.

39. Walter Hendl, interview with the author.

40. Clark, "Frank Miller," 21.

41. Ezra Rachlin, interview with the author.

42. "Conductors' Guild Holds 'Reiner Retrospective,'" 9; Reiner, "Outline for a Course in Conducting," typescript, Reiner Collection, file marked "Curtis Institute," NU.

43. Dorati, *Notes of Seven Decades,* 313; "Conductors' Guild Holds 'Reiner Retrospective,'" 13.

44. Max Rudolf, interview with the author.

45. Levine, "Behind the Downbeat," 1–2.

46. "Interview between Edward Downes and Fritz Reiner."

47. Victor Aitay in Papp, *Reiner.*

48. "Conductors' Guild Holds 'Reiner Retrospective,'" 9.

49. Potter, "Fritz Reiner," 41; "Interview with Walter Hendl," 12.

50. Reiner, "Secrets of the Conductor," 25.

51. Reiner, "Technique of Conducting," 10.

52. Ezra Rachlin and Lukas Foss, interviews with the author; "Conductors' Guild Holds 'Reiner Retrospective,'" 9.

53. Goldovsky, *My Road to Opera*, 163.

54. "Conductors' Guild Holds 'Reiner Retrospective,'" 9; Reiner, "Technique of Conducting," 10.

55. Reiner, "Technique of Conducting," 16; Goldovsky, *My Road to Opera*, 155, 163; Walter Hendl, interview with the author.

56. Ezra Rachlin, interview with the author; *PBI,* Oct. 9, 1941.

57. Walter Hendl, interview with the author; Potter, "Fritz Reiner," 41.

58. Ezra Rachlin, interview with the author; Briggs, *Leonard Bernstein*, 46.

59. Quoted in Potter, "Fritz Reiner," 40. Compare Chesterman, ed., *Conversations with Conductors,* 56.

60. Goldovsky, *My Road to Opera*, 157, 161.

61. "Conductors' Guild Holds 'Reiner Retrospective,'" 9.

62. Reiner to Deborah Niklad, Dec. 1, 1935, Reiner Collection, file for 1935, NU.

63. Bernstein, "Memories of the Curtis Institute," 9, 11.

64. Goldovsky, *My Road to Opera*, 161–63.

65. Ezra Rachlin, interview with the author.

66. Potter, "Fritz Reiner," 41; Reiner, "Outline for a Course in Conducting," typescript, Reiner Collection, file marked "Curtis Institute," NU.

67. Goldovsky, *My Road to Opera*, 154.

68. Reiner, "Technique of Conducting," 10–11.

69. Ibid., 9; Potter, "Fritz Reiner," 41.

70. John de Lancie, interview with the author.

71. Peyser, *Bernstein,* 69.

72. Reiner, "Secrets of the Conductor," 25.

73. Goldovsky, *My Road to Opera*, 154.

74. Sablosky, "Trial and Triumph of Fritz Reiner," 36–38.

75. Potter, "Fritz Reiner," 46; John de Lancie and Ezra Rachlin, interviews with the author.

76. Freedland, *Leonard Bernstein,* 38.

77. Potter, "Fritz Reiner," 43–45.

78. Personal communication with Leonard Slatkin, June 5, 2000.

79. Leonard Sharrow, interview with the author.

80. *PI,* Dec. 17, 1931, Dec. 25, 1932.

81. *Philadelphia Ledger,* Dec. [?], 1932.

82. Hart, *Fritz Reiner,* 61; Benko, "Incomparable Josef Hofmann," 21.

83. *Overtones* 2.2 (1931): 20. Details of many but not all of the Curtis Symphony Orchestra's concerts under Reiner's direction are given in different issues of *Overtones.*

84. Lukas Foss, interview with the author; Burton, *Leonard Bernstein,* 63.

85. Hart, *Fritz Reiner,* 66.

86. *Overtones* 4.1 (May 1936): 61–62.

87. Lawrence, *World of Opera,* 140.

88. *Overtones* 7.2 (May 1937): 81; Gruen, *Menotti,* 33–34.

89. Reiner to Josef Hofmann, July 23, 1937, Reiner Collection, loose files, NU.

90. Burton, *Leonard Bernstein,* 87.

91. For career details of Reiner's conducting students, see *Overtones* 11.1 (1974): 79–80; Slonimsky, ed., *Baker's Biographical Dictionary of Musicians;* and Sadie, ed., *New Grove Dictionary of Music and Musicians.* Morton Gould won a scholarship to study conducting with Reiner at Curtis but withdrew for family reasons ("Interview with Morton Gould," 10).

92. Broder, *Samuel Barber,* 15; Heyman, *Samuel Barber* (quotation), 311.
93. Heyman, *Samuel Barber,* 90–91, 195.
94. Hillyer, "Barber as Conductor."
95. Gradenwitz, *Leonard Bernstein,* 29; Burton, *Leonard Bernstein,* 59.
96. Potter, "Fritz Reiner," 39; Bernstein, *Findings,* 201–3; Briggs, *Leonard Bernstein,* 19–21; Secrest, *Leonard Bernstein,* 63, 66.
97. Gradenwitz, *Leonard Bernstein,* 8, 29, 30.
98. Freedland, *Leonard Bernstein,* 38, 42.
99. David Diamond, interview with the author.
100. Matheopoulos, *Maestro,* 13; Gruen, *Private World of Leonard Bernstein,* 53.
101. Eckman, "Leonard Bernstein Story," 35.
102. Briggs, *Leonard Bernstein,* 98–99.
103. Kupferberg, *Tanglewood,* 136.
104. *The Podium* 1.2 (1977): 34.
105. Gradenwitz, *Leonard Bernstein,* 31.
106. Burton, *Leonard Bernstein,* 90.
107. Serge Koussevitzky to Randall Thompson, Sept. 27, 1940, Koussevitzky Collection, box 61, folder 7, DLC.
108. Leonard Bernstein to Reiner, n.d. [1940], Reiner Collection, file for 1956–57, NU; "Conductors' Guild Holds 'Reiner Retrospective,'" 10.
109. Leonard Bernstein to Reiner, Aug. 27, 1940, Reiner Collection, file for 1956–57, NU.
110. Reiner to Leonard Bernstein, Aug. 29, 1940, Springate Corporation, New York City.
111. Leonard Bernstein to Reiner, n.d. [late 1942], and Reiner to "To Whom It May Concern," Oct. 12, 1942, Reiner Collection, file for 1956–57, NU; Reiner to Leonard Bernstein, Sept. 4, 1943, Springate Corporation, New York City; Burton, ed., *Conversations about Bernstein,* xx.
112. Chesterman, ed., *Conversations with Conductors,* 56.
113. Briggs, *Leonard Bernstein,* 55.
114. See, for example, Eckman, "Leonard Bernstein Story," 35; and Freedland, *Leonard Bernstein,* 47.
115. David Diamond, interview with the author; Burton, ed., *Conversations about Bernstein,* 23.
116. Potter, "Fritz Reiner," 48; Lukas Foss to Reiner, June 4, 1940, and July 5, 1957, Reiner Collection, files for 1940–41 and 1956–57, NU; "Conductors' Guild Holds 'Reiner Retrospective,'" 9; Ezra Rachlin, interview with the author.
117. Potter, "Fritz Reiner," 46.
118. This was Leonard Bernstein's view. See *The Podium* (Spring/Summer 1986): 26.
119. Bernstein, "Memories of the Curtis Institute," 9.
120. John de Lancie, interview with the author.
121. Mary Bok to Reiner, Feb. 7, 1941, Reiner Collection, loose files, NU.
122. Reiner to Mary Louise Bok, Feb. 18, 1941, Reiner Collection, file for 1941, NU.
123. Benser and Urrows, *Randall Thompson,* 27.
124. Mary Bok to Reiner, Feb. 19, 1941, Reiner Collection, file for 1941, NU.
125. Reiner to William Schuman, Sept. 18, 1945, Reiner Collection, file for 1948, NU.
126. "Interview with William Schuman," 10; Reiner to William Schuman, Nov. 15, 1947, Reiner Collection, file for 1947, NU.
127. Reiner to Donald A. Pask, Jan. 9, 1946, Reiner Collection, file for 1945–46, NU.
128. Carlotta Reiner to Joseph Kreines, Oct. 3, 1958, Reiner Collection, file for 1958, NU.
129. Reiner to Ernest Hutcheson, Aug. 22, 1947, Reiner Collection, file for 1947, NU.
130. *NYT,* Aug. 5, 1962.
131. Bernstein, *Findings,* 20–25.
132. Reiner to Leonard Bernstein, Nov. 14, 1959, Springate Corporation, New York City.
133. For further details on the funeral oration, see chapter 8.

Chapter 5: A Guest Conductor in the 1930s

1. Albrecht with Davis-Millis, "Philadelphia," 991–92.
2. Graf, *Opera for the People*, 84.
3. Hart, *Fritz Reiner*, 69.
4. Philadelphia Grand Opera programs, 1931–32, Curtis Institute of Music, from which details of the casts given below are taken. Gerson states that Stokowski allowed Reiner to direct a performance of Berg's *Wozzeck* on Nov. 19, 1931, but the Philadelphia Grand Opera's programs and reviews in the Philadelphia press indicate that Stokowski was the conductor. Gerson, *Music in Philadelphia*, 238.
5. Dettmer, "Reiner," 62; Potter, "Fritz Reiner," 68–69; *Overtones* 11.1 (1974): 15.
6. Sargeant, "Future of Opera in America," 390.
7. *PEB*, Oct. 23, 1931.
8. *PI*, Dec. 11, 1931.
9. Hart, *Fritz Reiner*, 70.
10. *Philadelphia Record*, Oct. 27, 1931.
11. *PI*, Oct. 30, 1931.
12. Goldovsky, *My Road to Opera* (quotation), 164; Ashbrook, "Nelson Eddy's Career in Opera," 15. Hart wrongly states that Ingrid Bjoerner sang Chrysothemis (*Fritz Reiner*, 70).
13. Hart, *Fritz Reiner*, 70.
14. Goldovsky, *My Road to Opera*, 157, 192.
15. Ashbrook, "Nelson Eddy's Career in Opera," 16.
16. *New York Evening Post*, Nov. 9, 1932.
17. Reiner to Paul Longone, Oct. 16, 1933, Reiner Collection, file for 1933–34, NU.
18. Hart, *Fritz Reiner*, 71; Kupferberg, *Those Fabulous Philadelphians*, 94; Daniel, *Stokowski*, 320–21.
19. Arthur Judson to Reiner, July 24, 1934, Reiner Collection, file for 1934–35, NU; Daniel, *Stokowski*, 319.
20. Daniel, *Stokowski*, 321–22.
21. Goldovsky, *My Road to Opera*, 193.
22. Arthur Judson to Reiner, May 24, 1934, Reiner Collection, file for 1934, NU.
23. Graf, *Opera and Its Future in America*, 247, 264–65; Graf, *Opera for the People*, 206. Plates 90, 91, and 93 in *Opera and Its Future in America* illustrate the revolving stage.
24. Kupferberg, *Those Fabulous Philadelphians*, 95; Graf, *Opera for the People*, 6; Graf, *Producing Opera for America*, 92; *PI*, Apr. 28, 1935.
25. Reiner to Miss Pringle, Aug. 26, 1934, Reiner Collection, file for 1934–35, NU (quotation); Kolodin, "Opera, American Plan," 419.
26. Hart, *Fritz Reiner*, 72.
27. Memorandum, Mar. 22, 1935, Reiner Collection, file for 1935, NU.
28. Potter, "Fritz Reiner," 71; Kupferberg, *Those Fabulous Philadelphians*, 95; Kolodin, "Opera, American Plan," 419.
29. Quoted in Goldovsky, *My Road to Opera*, 212.
30. Speech given by Reiner, n.d. [ca. 1932], Reiner Collection, file for 1932–33, NU.
31. *PEB*, Oct. 4, 1934; Kolodin, "Opera, American Plan," 415.
32. Reiner, "The Philadelphia Opera," Reiner Collection, file for 1934–35, NU (partly reproduced in *NYH-T*, Sept. 16, 1934).
33. *PEB*, Nov. 30, 1934.
34. *Oakland Tribune*, Nov. 1, 1936.
35. Graf, *Opera for the People*, 7.
36. Reiner, "The Philadelphia Opera," Reiner Collection, file for 1934–35, NU; Goldovsky, *My Road to Opera*, 196–97.
37. Reiner to Miss Pringle, Aug. 28, 1934; Reiner, "The Philadelphia Opera," Reiner Col-

lection, file for 1934–35, NU; Graf, *Opera for the People,* 8; Kupferberg, *Those Fabulous Philadelphians,* 95.

38. Reiner to Mr. Archipenko, Aug. 17, 1934, Reiner Collection, file for 1934–35, NU.

39. Graf, *Opera for the People,* 8.

40. *New York Post,* Oct. 20, 1934.

41. Goldovsky, *My Road to Opera,* 197–98.

42. *Time,* Oct. 29, 1934; *New York Sun,* Oct. 22, 1934.

43. Vogt, *Flagstad,* 96–97.

44. *PEB,* Oct. 20, 1934.

45. *PR,* Oct. 20, 1934; *New York Sun,* Oct. 22, 1934.

46. *NYH-T,* Oct. 20, 1934.

47. Reiner to Elizabeth L. Anderson, Mar. 4, 1951, Lawrence Gilman Collection, Beinecke Library, Yale University.

48. Quoted in Goldovsky, *My Road to Opera,* 198–99.

49. Ibid., 199.

50. Ibid., 199–202; Reiner to Edward Dent, Dec. 3, 1934, Reiner Collection, file for 1934, NU.

51. *PI,* Mar. 16, 1935.

52. Kolodin, "Opera, American Plan," 421.

53. Goldovsky, *My Road to Opera,* 202–3.

54. Ibid., 203–5.

55. *PR,* Dec. 1, 1934; Goldovsky, *My Road to Opera,* 205–6; Glass, *Lotte Lehmann,* 156–57; Graf, *Opera for the People,* 9.

56. Goldovsky, *My Road to Opera,* 194–96, 217.

57. *PI,* Feb. 2, 1935.

58. Reiner to Mr. Simon, Apr. 29, 1935, Reiner Collection, file for 1935, NU.

59. Graf, *Opera for the People,* 9.

60. Kolodin, "Opera, American Plan," 421–23.

61. Ibid., 419; Graf, *Opera for the People,* 8–9; Goldovsky, *My Road to Opera,* 220–21; Kupferberg, *Those Fabulous Philadelphians,* 96.

62. Kupferberg, *Those Fabulous Philadelphians,* 96; Graf, *Opera for the People,* 9; Graf, *Opera and Its Future in America,* 247.

63. Dizikes, *Opera in America,* 469; Commanday, "San Francisco," 164–65. Details of Reiner's opera performances in San Francisco are based on Bloomfield, *San Francisco Opera,* 331–35, and on the San Francisco Opera Company programs at SFPALM.

64. Dizikes, *Opera in America,* 469; Smith, *Worlds of Music,* 206; Hart, *Fritz Reiner,* 93.

65. *Time,* Nov. 9, 1936, 35.

66. Reiner to Ilya Schkolnik, Oct. 29, 1936, Reiner Collection, file for Sept. 1936, NU.

67. *Oakland Tribune,* Nov. 1, 1936; Hart, *Fritz Reiner,* 94.

68. Reiner to Arthur Judson, July 17, 1936, Reiner Collection, file for Sept. 1936, NU.

69. *Time,* Nov. 30, 1936, 30; *Oakland Tribune,* Nov. 1, 1936; Hart, *Fritz Reiner,* 93–94.

70. McArthur, *Flagstad,* 23.

71. Charles O'Connell to Reiner, Mar. 23, 1938, Reiner Collection, file for 1939, NU.

72. *Time,* Nov. 30, 1936, 30.

73. *San Francisco Chronicle,* Nov. 9, 1936; *San Francisco Newsletter,* Nov. 14, 1936; *San Francisco News,* Nov. 9, 1936.

74. Leinsdorf, *Cadenza,* 89.

75. *Time,* Nov. 30, 1936, 30; Stoddard, "Fritz Reiner," 14.

76. The provenance of this in-house recording is discussed by David McKee in the *Opera Quarterly* 13.2 (1997): 179.

77. *San Francisco Newsletter,* Nov. 5, 1937.

78. *Boston Evening Transcript,* July 22, 1937.

79. Bloomfield, *San Francisco Opera,* 333–35.

80. *San Francisco Newsletter,* Oct. 28, 1938.

81. Reiner to Edward Specter, Oct. 11, 1938, Reiner Collection, loose files, NU.

82. Seinfelt, "Reiner as Conductor of Opera," 5; Hart, *Fritz Reiner,* 90.

83. Telegram from Carlotta Reiner to Reiner, Jan. 29, 1936, Reiner Collection, file for 1936, NU.

84. Rosenthal, *Two Centuries of Opera at Covent Garden,* 785–89.

85. Savage, *Voice from the Pit,* 45.

86. *Providence (R.I.) News-Tribune,* Sept. 9, 1936.

87. Rosenthal, *Two Centuries of Opera,* 506, 785–86, 788–89; Seinfelt, "Reiner as Conductor of Opera," 7.

88. *Daily Telegraph,* June 18, 1937. Compare Ernest Newman's notice in the *Sunday Times,* June 20, 1937.

89. Newman quoted in Seinfelt, "Reiner as Conductor of Opera," 7; Sanders, ed., *Walter Legge,* 36.

90. Seinfelt, "Reiner as Conductor of Opera," 5.

91. Personal communication with Mary Ellen Evans, Aug. 9, 1993.

92. Quoted in Seinfelt, "Reiner as Conductor of Opera," 6.

93. Wright, ed., *Cardus on Music,* 127.

94. Quoted in Seinfelt, "Reiner as Conductor of Opera," 6.

95. Ibid; *Sunday Times,* Apr. 25, 1937.

96. Rosenthal, *Two Centuries of Opera,* 508; Altman, "*Tristan und Isolde* at Covent Garden."

97. Seinfelt, "Reiner as Conductor of Opera," 6; Rosenthal, *Two Centuries of Opera,* 508.

98. *Morning Post,* June 8, 1937.

99. A collation from the *Tristan* performances of May and June 1936 is available on three digitally remastered CDs (VAIA 1004–3). Act 1 and most of act 3 of Reiner's performance of *Tristan* at Covent Garden on June 11, 1936, were mistakenly issued by EMI as a performance conducted by Beecham (EMI Classics CHS 7–64037–2, 3 CDs, mono). See Hamilton, "Recordings." The exceptional intensity of the performance is discussed in Marinelli, *Opere in Disco da Monteverdi a Berg,* 152.

100. F. W. Gaisberg to Reiner, June 10, 1936, and Reiner to Lawrence Gilman, Apr. 30, 1937, Reiner Collection, files for 1937 and 1937–38, NU. Another copy of the latter is available at NN, Mss. filed under "MNY."

101. F. W. Gaisberg to Reiner, July 20, 1936, Reiner Collection, file for 1937, NU.

102. The Gramophone Company Ltd. to Reiner, June 23, 1937, Reiner Collection, file for 1937, NU. Reiner's contract for the recording is included in Miss Gibbs to Mr. Bicknell, June 22, 1937, EMI Music Archives, Hayes, Middlesex, England.

103. Reiner to F. W. Gaisberg, July 24, 1936, Reiner Collection, file for 1937, NU.

104. Carlotta Reiner to Kleinchen Melchior, July 27, 1936, Reiner Collection, files for 1936 and 1937, NU.

105. Mordden, *Guide to Opera Recordings,* 9.

106. Biancolli, *Flagstad Manuscript,* 204; Gramophone Co. Ltd. to Henry Johansen, July 16, 1937, EMI Music Archives, Hayes, Middlesex, England.

107. F. W. Gaisberg to Reiner, July 30, 1936, Reiner Collection, file for 1937, NU; Reiner to Lawrence Gilman, April 30, 1937, Mss. filed under "MNY," NN.

108. Savage, *Voice from the Pit,* 45.

109. Kolodin, *Musical Life,* 254; Slonimsky, *Music since 1900,* 553.

110. *Philadelphia Bulletin,* Feb. 19, 1932; *Philadelphia Public Ledger,* Feb. 21, 1932.

111. *Overtones* 4.1 (May 1933): 21.

112. *Pester Lloyd,* May 11 and 16, 1933; *Budapesti Hirlap,* May 11 and 16, 1933; *Nemzeti Ujsag,* May 16, 1933.

113. *Overtones* 5.1 (May 1934).

114. Reiner to Henry Bare, Jan. 24, 1937, Reiner Collection, file for December 1936–Spring 1937, NU; Craven, ed., *Symphony Orchestras of the World,* 308.

115. Organisation Artistique Internationale Marcel de Valmalete to Fritz Reiner, June 9, 1936, Reiner Collection, loose files, NU.

116. BBC contract, January 1, 1937, and Reiner to Hilda Bennett, February 1, 1937, Reiner Collection, file for Dec. 1936–Spring 1937, NU.

117. *La Tribuna,* Jan. 12, 1937; *Il Popolo di Roma,* Jan. 11, 1937; *Il Messagero,* Jan. 11, 1937.

118. Henry Bare to Carlotta Reiner, July 3, 1937, and Reiner to Mrs. Bare, May 25, 1938, Reiner Collection, files for Dec. 1936–Spring 1937 and 1937–38, NU.

119. Hart, *Fritz Reiner,* 82–83.

120. *PI,* Dec. 25, 1932; Reiner to Max Heinrici, Jan. 23, 1935, Reiner Collection, file for 1934, NU.

121. Details of Reiner's concerts with the Philadelphia Orchestra are taken from the orchestra's programs at the Curtis Institute of Music.

122. The seasons were 1931–32, 1932–33, 1933–34, and 1935–36. Information on Reiner's concerts with the Rochester Philharmonic is based on the orchestra's program books.

123. The Rochester Civic Music Association to Reiner, Nov. 11, 1932, and Jan. 13, 1933, Reiner Collection, file for 1932–33, NU.

124. Fritz Reiner Diary, 1935, Reiner Collection, NU. Details of Reiner's appearances with the Detroit Symphony Orchestra are taken from the orchestra's program books.

125. Reiner to Kurt Seman, June 23, 1938, Reiner Collection, file for 1938, NU.

126. Reiner to Serge Koussevitzky, Dec. 23, 1938, Reiner Collection, file for 1939, NU.

127. Serge Koussevitzky to Reiner, Jan. 2, 1939, Reiner Collection, file for 1939, NU.

128. *PI,* Aug. 13, 1931; typescripts of programs for the Robin Hood Dell, Aug. 1934, Reiner Collection, file for 1933–34, NU.

129. San Francisco Symphony Orchestra programs, SFPALM; *San Francisco News,* July 9, 1934.

130. Reiner to Arthur Judson, Aug. 4, 1937, Reiner Collection, file for 1937–38, NU.

131. Hollywood Bowl programs, Aug. 1937, Los Angeles Philharmonic Association.

132. Details of Reiner's concerts at Lewisohn Stadium are taken from the Stadium Concerts Review, NYPA.

133. *NYT,* Feb. 25, 1948.

134. *MA* 57.13 (Aug. 1937): 21; *Brooklyn Daily Eagle,* July 11, 1937.

135. Reiner to Arthur Judson, Aug. 4, 1937, Reiner Collection, file for 1937–38, NU.

136. Hart, *Fritz Reiner,* 81.

137. Reiner to Arthur Judson, Oct. 3, 1937, Reiner Collection, file for 1937–38, NU.

138. Axelrod, *Heifetz,* 366.

139. Hart, *Fritz Reiner,* 87.

140. Barnouw, *Golden Web,* 34; "Ford Sunday Evening Hour Features Standard Repertoire," *MC* 133.8 (Apr. 15, 1946): 13. Details of Reiner's appearances on the Ford Sunday Evening Hour are taken from the Detroit Symphony Orchestra's program books.

141. Fritz Reiner Diary, May 1, 1938, Reiner Collection, NU; *NYH-T,* July 22, 1935.

142. Reiner to J. E. Otterson, n.d. [ca. 1937], Reiner Collection, file for Dec. 1936–Spring 1937, NU.

143. Typescript of Music Guild Productions, Inc., and Reiner to Mr. Cruger, Aug. 22, 1935, Reiner Collection, file for 1935, NU.

144. Reiner to Arthur Judson, Mar. 8, 1938, Reiner Collection, file for 1937–38, NU.

145. Bertha Svedofsky to Reiner, Dec. 16, 1934, Aug. 4, 1936, Reiner Collection, files for 1934 and Sept. 1936, NU.

146. Marjory [Fisher] to Carlotta and Fritz, Mar. 7, 1937, Reiner Collection, file for Dec. 1936–Spring 1937, NU.

147. Carlotta Reiner to Mrs. Goldstein, n.d. [ca. 1932], Reiner Collection, file for 1932–33, NU.

148. César Saerchinger to Reiner, Nov. 6, 1933, Reiner Collection, file for 1933–34, NU.

149. Hart, *Fritz Reiner*, 90.

150. Carlotta Reiner to Elizabeth Sprague Coolidge, Feb. 24, 1936, Coolidge Collection, DLC; Hart, *Fritz Reiner*, 79–80.

151. Reiner to Arthur Judson, Aug. 21, 1933, Reiner Collection, loose files, NU.

152. Reiner to Mr. Scholnik, Nov. 5, 1936, Reiner Collection, file for Sept. 1936, NU.

153. Arthur Judson to Charles Triller, Mar. 24, 1936, Executive Committee and Board minutes, NYPA.

154. Hart, *Fritz Reiner*, 77.

155. Dettmer, "Reiner," 62.

156. Charles O'Connell to Reiner, Mar. 23, 1938, Reiner Collection, file for 1939, NU.

Chapter 6: Pittsburgh

1. For background on the Pittsburgh Symphony Orchestra, see Mueller, *American Symphony Orchestra*, 174–75; Stephens, "Pittsburgh Symphony Orchestra"; Dorian and Meibach, *History of the Pittsburgh Symphony Orchestra;* and Schmalz, "Paur and the Pittsburgh."

2. *PP-G*, Mar. 2, 1938 (quotation); Heyworth, *Otto Klemperer*, 91–92.

3. Contract between Reiner and the Pittsburgh Symphony Orchestra, 1938, Reiner Collection, loose files, NU.

4. Heyworth, ed., *Conversations with Klemperer*, 97–98; *Time*, Mar. 14, 1938; Potter, "Fritz Reiner," 53.

5. *PP*, Mar. 2, 1938.

6. *PP-G*, Feb. 11 and Mar. 16, 1942.

7. *PP-G*, Sept. 12, 1945; *PBI*, May 11, 1946.

8. Thomson, *Art of Judging Music*, 196.

9. Hart, *Fritz Reiner*, 101.

10. Dorian and Meibach, *History of the Pittsburgh Symphony Orchestra*, 9.

11. Samuel Thaviu, interview with the author; *PP-G*, Apr. 2, 1945.

12. Typescript of interview with Reiner, KDKA radio network, Mar. 26, 1938, Reiner Collection, loose files, NU; *Ambridge (Pa.) Citizen*, Oct. 5, 1938.

13. Bruno Zirato to Reiner, Jan. 12, 1945, Reiner Papers, CU.

14. Potter, "Fritz Reiner," 60; *Greater Pittsburgh*, Apr. 1944; *PP-G*, Mar. 29, 1944; *PS-T*, Oct. 31, 1945.

15. Typescript of interview with Reiner, KDKA radio network, Mar. 26, 1938, Reiner Collection, loose files, NU.

16. Reiner quoted in *PP*, Feb. 3, 1944.

17. Details about conductors, soloists, and repertoire for the Pittsburgh Symphony Orchestra are taken from Hillyer, "Pittsburgh Symphony Concerts."

18. *PP*, Apr. 8, 1947; *PS-T*, Apr. 8, 1947.

19. Reiner to Edward Specter, Aug. 14, 1942, Reiner Collection, loose files, NU.

20. "Pittsburgh's Principal Flutist Recalls Dr. Reiner," 9; Samuel Thaviu, interview with the author.

21. "Conductors' Guild Holds 'Reiner Retrospective,'" 13.

22. Quoted in ibid., 9–10.

23. Lukas Foss to Reiner, Apr. 5, 1945, Reiner Papers, CU.

24. *PP-G*, Jan. 5, 1940.

25. Personal communication with Gardner Read, Feb. 6, 1991.

26. Caratelli, *Musician's Odyssey*, 87.

27. Quoted in ibid., 88.

28. Quoted in ibid., 88–89.

29. Quoted in "Reiner Symposium in Bloomington/1," 14.

30. Irving Sarin, interview with the author.

31. Ewen, *Dictators of the Baton,* 223; *PBI,* Nov. 21, 1940, Oct. 22, 1942; "Interview with John S. Edwards," 18–19.

32. Irving Sarin, interview with the author.

33. Dorian and Meibach, *History of the Pittsburgh Symphony Orchestra,* 10.

34. Irving Sarin and Samuel Thaviu, interviews with the author.

35. Typescript of interview with Reiner, KDKA radio network, Mar. 26, 1938, Reiner Collection, loose files, NU.

36. David Walter, interview with the author.

37. Pittsburgh Symphony Orchestra programs, 1939–44, Pittsburgh Symphony Orchestra; *PBI,* Nov. 27, 1941; *Musical Forecast,* Sept. 1942.

38. Typescript of interview with Reiner, KDKA radio network, Mar. 26, 1938, Reiner Collection, loose files, NU; *PP,* Nov. 7, 1944.

39. Potter, "Fritz Reiner," 54; *PP,* Mar. 31, Nov. 7 and 11, 1944, Oct. 18, 1946.

40. *PP,* Sept. 15, 1941.

41. "Interview with John S. Edwards," 18.

42. Bruno Zirato to Edward Specter, n.d., Reiner Papers, CU.

43. Potter, "Fritz Reiner," 54.

44. David Walter, interview with the author; *PS-T,* June 6, 1948.

45. John de Lancie, interview with the author.

46. *Musical Forecast,* May 1939, 13.

47. Caratelli, *Musician's Odyssey,* 89.

48. Reiner to Edward Specter, Oct. 8, 1945, Reiner Collection, loose files, NU.

49. "Reiner Symposium in Bloomington/II," 18–19, 21–22.

50. Samuel Thaviu, interview with the author.

51. "Reiner Symposium in Bloomington/I," 10.

52. "Interview with George Gaber," 35.

53. Levant, *Smattering of Ignorance,* 36–37.

54. Dorian and Meibach, *History of the Pittsburgh Symphony Orchestra,* 11.

55. David Walter, interview with the author.

56. "Conductors' Guild Holds 'Reiner Retrospective,'" 11.

57. John de Lancie, interview with the author.

58. Walter Damrosch to Reiner, Dec. 14, 1939, Damrosch Collection, NN.

59. *PP-G,* Nov. 11, 1939, Nov. 13, 1943. Compare *PBI,* Nov. 16, 1944.

60. *MC* 123.3 (Feb. 1, 1941): 68.

61. *Cleveland Plain Dealer,* Jan. 22, 1947; *Toledo Blade,* Feb. 28, 1946.

62. *Toledo Times,* Jan. 23, 1947.

63. Potter, "Fritz Reiner," 58.

64. Mahlon Lewis to Reiner, June 14, 1945, Reiner Collection, file for 1943–45, NU; *PP,* Nov. 6, 1947.

65. Irving Sarin, interview with the author.

66. Reiner to Edward Specter, June 18, 1945, Reiner Collection, loose files, NU.

67. Reiner to Edward Specter, July 28, 1945, Reiner Collection, loose files, NU.

68. *Greater Pittsburgh,* June 1941.

69. *East Liberty Tribune* (Pittsburgh), Feb. 16, 1940.

70. *PP-G,* Feb. 24, 1940.

71. *PS-T,* Nov. 24, 1939.

72. *NYH-T,* Oct. 12, 1947; Potter, "Fritz Reiner," 142, table 1.

73. Reiner to Olin Downes, Mar. 27, 1938, Reiner Collection, file for 1938, NU.

74. Reiner to Arnold Schoenberg, n.d., Reiner Papers, CU.

75. Arnold Schoenberg to Reiner, July 15, 1944, Reiner Papers, CU.

76. Reiner to Arnold Schoenberg, Oct. 25, 1944, Reiner Collection, file for 1943–45, NU.

77. Arnold Schoenberg to Reiner, Oct. 29, 1944, in Stein, ed., *Arnold Schoenberg Letters,* 221.

78. Arnold Schoenberg to Reiner, Apr. 24, 1939, Reiner Collection, file for 1939, NU.

79. Reiner to Nicolai Berezowsky, Jan. 24, 1940, Spec MS Correspondence Berezowsky, CU.

80. Reiner to Howard Hanson, Aug. 11, 1945, Reiner Collection, file for 1943–45, NU.

81. "Interview with William Schuman," 10; Reiner to George Antheil, Oct. 24, 1944, MS Collection Antheil, CU.

82. Reiner to Edward Specter, Aug. 31, 1946, Reiner Collection, loose files, NU.

83. Reiner to Charles Wakefield Cadman, Jan. 30, 1941, Reiner Collection, file for 1941, NU.

84. Arthur Judson to Reiner, Oct. 20, 1941, Reiner Collection, file for 1941, NU.

85. Reiner to Edward Specter, Oct. 9, 1942, Reiner Collection, loose files, NU.

86. Reiner to Darius Milhaud, Oct. 6, 1942, Reiner Papers, CU (quotation); Reiner to Victor Babin, Jan. 10, 1942, Babin Papers, DLC.

87. Darius Milhaud to Reiner, Dec. 1, 1942, Reiner Papers, CU.

88. Igor Stravinsky to Hans Heinsheimer, Feb. 19 and Mar. 14, 1947, and to Bean, Jan. 26, 1948, in Craft, ed., *Stravinsky: Selected Correspondence,* vol. 2, 255, vol. 3, 313–14, 321.

89. Reiner to Goddard Lieberson, Aug. 8, 1942, Reiner Collection, file for 1941–42, NU; "Interview with Morton Gould," 13.

90. Jablonski, *Gershwin,* 295–96.

91. *NYT,* Apr. 1, 1943; *Brooklyn Daily Eagle,* Apr. 1, 1943.

92. Reiner to Goddard Lieberson, Dec. 4, 1942, Reiner Collection, file for 1942, NU.

93. Robinson, *Bernstein,* 12; Peyser, *Bernstein,* 121.

94. Leonard Bernstein to Reiner, n.d., Reiner Papers, CU; Gruen, *Private World of Leonard Bernstein,* 108.

95. "Interview with George Gaber," 20; *PP,* Feb. 6, 1944.

96. "Reiner Symposium in Bloomington/II," 20.

97. Bruno Zirato to Arthur Judson, Sept. 29, 1942, Executive Committee and Board minutes, NYPA; Slonimsky, *Music since 1900,* 663.

98. Fassett, *Béla Bartók's Last Years,* 260–61; Griffiths, *Bartók,* 173–74; Stevens, *Life and Music of Béla Bartók,* 97–98.

99. Fassett, *Béla Bartók's Last Years,* 264, 293.

100. Reiner to Ernest Hutcheson and to Glendenning Keeble, both June 7, 1942, Reiner Collection, file for 1941–42, NU.

101. Griffiths, *Bartók,* 173–74; Stevens, *Life and Music of Béla Bartók,* 99.

102. H. W. Heinsheimer to Reiner, Apr. 17, 1945, Reiner Collection, file for 1943–45, NU.

103. Joseph Szigeti to Reiner, Oct. 5, 1945, Reiner Collection, file for 1945–46, NU.

104. *PP-G,* Nov. 8, 1940; *Pittsburgh Journal,* Oct. 14, 1941.

105. Pittsburgh Symphony Orchestra scrapbook, 1943–44, Hillman Library, University of Pittsburgh; *PBI,* May 11, 1946.

106. *MA* 62.2 (Jan. 25, 1947): 27.

107. Dorian and Meibach, *History of the Pittsburgh Symphony Orchestra,* 11–12; Potter, "Fritz Reiner," 61–62.

108. Carlotta Reiner, "Here Comes the Band!" Reiner Collection, file for 1948, NU.

109. Hart, *Fritz Reiner,* 113–14.

110. Fritz Reiner Diary, 1946, Reiner Collection, NU; Dorian and Meibach, *History of the Pittsburgh Symphony Orchestra,* 11.

111. Hart, *Fritz Reiner,* 113–14.

112. Samuel Thaviu, interview with the author; "Interview with John S. Edwards," 20, 22.

113. Citation made by the Provost of the University of Pennsylvania, June 19, 1940; Ralph Lewando to Reiner, July 2, 1940, June 24, 1941, Reiner Collection, files for 1940–41 and 1941, NU.

114. Martin G. Dumler to Reiner, Feb. 13, 1945, Reiner Collection, file for 1945–46, NU; *PP-G,* Mar. 10, 1945.

115. *PS-T,* Mar. 27, 1939, Dec. 11, 1940.

116. *PS-T,* Mar. 27, 1939; Ernest Bloch to Douglas Moore, May 20, 1939, Reiner Collection, loose correspondence, NU.

117. *PS-T,* Nov. 25, 1940.

118. Pittsburgh Symphony Orchestra programs, 1940–41, Pittsburgh Symphony Orchestra; Davis, *Opera in Chicago,* 217, 361.

119. "Fritz Reiner: Biography," Oct. 1946; N. W Ayer and Son to Reiner, July 22, 1940, and John Anderson to Reiner, Nov. 20, 1940, Reiner Collection, file for 1940–41 and loose files, NU.

120. Reiner to Arthur Judson, Jan. 7, 1941, Reiner Collection, loose files, NU.

121. William J. Reddick to Reiner, Mar. 17 and Oct. 23, 1941, Reiner Collection, file for 1941, NU.

122. "Fritz Reiner: Biography," Oct. 1946, Reiner Collection, loose files, NU; Executive Committee and Board to Reiner, Apr. 18, 1944, Executive Committee and Board minutes, NYPA.

123. Hart, *Fritz Reiner,* 120; Fritz Reiner Diary, 1946; William J. Reddick to Reiner, Oct. 23, 1941; and Samuel Chotzinoff to Reiner, July 19, 1946, Reiner Collection, files for 1941 and 1945–46, NU.

124. *Cleveland Plain Dealer,* Dec. 29, 1944; Bruno Zirato to Reiner, Mar. 15, 1945, Reiner Collection, file for 1945–46, NU.

125. Irving Sarin, interview with the author.

126. *Boston Herald,* Dec. 22, 1945. Compare *Boston Evening Globe,* Dec. 22, 1945.

127. Daniel, *Stokowski,* 513; Schickel, *World of Carnegie Hall,* 352–53; Bloom, ed., *Year in American Music,* 13–14. The making of the film is discussed in *Film Daily,* Oct. 28, 1946.

128. *Parkersburg (W.V.) News,* Sept. 12, 1946.

129. Reiner to Mrs. Charles Swift, Jan. 12, 1943; Mrs. C. H. Swift to Reiner, Jan. 15, 1943, Reiner Collection, file for 1943, NU.

130. Arthur Judson to Reiner, Mar. 17, 1941, Reiner Collection, loose files, NU.

131. Hart, *Fritz Reiner,* 118–19.

132. Carlotta Reiner to Serge Koussevitzky, May 30, 1944; Bruno Zirato to Reiner, n.d. [1944]; Reiner to Bruno Zirato, Oct. 23, 1944, Reiner Collection, file for 1943–45, NU.

133. Yasda Fishberg to Reiner, July 25, 1945; Reiner to Arthur Judson, Oct. 4, 1945, Reiner Collection, files for 1943–45 and 1945–46, NU.

134. Edward Specter to Reiner, Feb. 15, 1938, Reiner Collection, file for 1937–38, NU.

135. Potter, "Fritz Reiner," 62; *Oakland News,* July 29, 1943; *PBI,* Apr. 5, 1945.

136. Potter, "Fritz Reiner," 63.

137. Hart, *Fritz Reiner,* 124.

138. Reiner, undated typescript [ca. 1943], Reiner Collection, loose files, NU.

139. Irving Sarin, interview with the author.

140. Reiner to Harry Ellis Carter, Apr. 11, 1948, and to Liliane and Edgar Kaufman, n.d. [1948], Reiner Collection, file for 1948, NU; Krokover, "Pittsburgh Symphony," 36.

141. Reiner to John J. McKee, Nov. 15, 1947, and to Harry Ellis Carter, Apr. 10, 1948, Reiner Collection, files for 1947 and 1948, NU.

142. *PBI,* Oct. 9, 1941; *Newsweek,* Mar. 8, 1948.

143. Reiner to Bruno Zirato, n.d. [ca. 1946], Reiner Collection, file for 1945–46, NU.

144. Thruston Wright to Reiner, May 1, 1947, Reiner Collection, file for 1947, NU.

145. Potter, "Fritz Reiner," 62–63; Krokover, "Pittsburgh Symphony," 36; Caratelli, *Musician's Odyssey,* 103.

146. Sebastian Caratelli to Reiner, Feb. 28, 1948, Reiner Collection, file for 1948, NU.

147. Personal communication with David Walter, July 15, 1999.

148. Speech by Reiner to the Pittsburgh Symphony Orchestra, 1948, Reiner Collection, file for 1948, NU.

149. Irving Sarin, interview with the author.

150. Pittsburgh Symphony Orchestra program, Apr. 24, 1948, Pittsburgh Symphony Orchestra.

151. Stephens, "Pittsburgh Symphony Orchestra," 352.

Chapter 7: At the Met

1. Schonberg, *Facing the Music*, 291.

2. Smith, *Worlds of Music*, 173.

3. Artists' contract forms for Fritz Reiner, 1948–52, MOA.

4. Undated memorandum, Reiner Collection, file for 1948, NU.

5. Leonard Bernstein to Reiner, Feb. 25, 1948, Reiner Collection, file for 1948, NU; Rothe, "Fritz Reiner," 6; *NYT*, Jan. 30, 1949 (quotation).

6. *Newsweek*, Feb. 14, 1949, 75.

7. *New York Post*, Jan. 23, 1943.

8. Mayer, *The Met*, 236–37.

9. Mercer, *Tenor of his Time*, 269.

10. Potter, "Fritz Reiner," 73; Seltsam, *Metropolitan Opera Annals*, 11–64.

11. Jackson, *Saturday Afternoons at the Old Met*, 487–88.

12. Smith, *Worlds of Music*, 174–75; Bing, *Five Thousand Nights at the Opera*, 135–38; Crichton, *Subway to the Met*, 143; Beranek, *Music, Acoustics, and Architecture*, 162.

13. Mayer, *The Met*, 240; Crichton, *Subway to the Met*, 151; Jacobson, *Magnificence on Stage at the Met*, 12.

14. Smith, *Worlds of Music*, 182–83; Dizikes, *Opera in America*, 489.

15. Bing, *Five Thousand Nights at the Opera*, 142; Lawrence, *Rage for Opera*, 69.

16. *NYT*, Jan. 30, 1949.

17. *NYH-T*, Mar. 22, 1953.

18. Ezra Rachlin, interview with the author.

19. *NYT*, Apr. 11, 1953.

20. *NYT*, Jan. 30, 1949.

21. *NYT*, Jan. 30, 1949.

22. Quoted in Rothe, "Fritz Reiner," 7.

23. Quoted in "Conductors' Guild Holds 'Reiner Retrospective,'" 17.

24. Victor Aitay, interview with the author.

25. Abraham Marcus and Risë Stevens, interviews with the author.

26. Max Rudolf, interview with the author.

27. Victor Aitay, interview with the author.

28. Quoted in "János Starker Speaks about His Reiner Years/II," 16.

29. Risë Stevens, interview with the author.

30. Quoted in Potter, "Fritz Reiner," 75–76. See also McGovern and Winer, *I Remember Too Much*, 31–32, 254.

31. *NYT*, Jan. 30, 1949; Scherer, "Maxims," 20.

32. Levy, *Bluebird of Happiness*, 205–6.

33. Steber with Sloat, *Autobiography*, 97.

34. McGovern and Winer, *I Remember Too Much*, 33.

35. Risë Stevens, interview with the author.

36. "Conductors' Guild Holds 'Reiner Retrospective,'" 18.

37. Risë Stevens, interview with the author.

38. *Newsweek*, Feb. 14, 1949, 75.

39. Full details of repertoire, soloists, and dates for Reiner's performances at the Met are supplied in Seltsam, *Metropolitan Opera Annals*, 11–64; Eaton, *Opera Caravan*, 364–79; and Fitzgerald, *Annals of the Metropolitan Opera*, vol. 2, 592–632. This material is summarized in Totels, "Reiner at the Met, Part II," 28.

40. Mayer, *The Met*, 225; Eaton, "*Der Rosenkavalier* Is Viewed by Vast Television Audience," 4.

41. *PI*, Dec. 12, 1952; *NYH-T*, Dec. 11, 1952.

42. Seinfelt, "Reiner as Conductor of Opera," 4.

43. Quoted in *NYH-T*, Mar. 22, 1953.

44. *NYH-T*, Feb. 4, 1950.

45. Jackson, *Sign-Off for the Old Met*, 20.

46. *NYT*, Jan. 5, 1950; *MA* 70.2 (Jan. 15, 1950): 63.

47. Hamilton, "*Le nozze di Figaro* at the Met," 16.

48. See Jackson, *Sign-Off for the Old Met*, 49–51.

49. *NYT*, Nov. 10, 1950.

50. *NYH-T*, Nov. 10, 1950.

51. Jackson, *Sign-Off for the Old Met*, 12.

52. Victor Aitay, interview with the author; Kolodin, *Metropolitan Opera*, 479; *MA* 69.5 (Apr. 1, 1949): 9.

53. Seinfelt, "Reiner as Conductor of Opera," 6.

54. Quoted in "Reiner at the Met/I," 7.

55. *MA* 70.2 (Jan. 15, 1950): 79; Jackson, *Sign-Off for the Old Met*, 78–79.

56. Reiner to Elizabeth L. Anderson, Mar. 4, 1951, Lawrence Gilman Collection, Beinecke Library, Yale University.

57. Kolodin, *Metropolitan Opera*, 504.

58. Sheean, *First and Last Love*, 282–83.

59. *NYH-T*, Dec. 2, 1950.

60. *NYH-T*, Jan. 23, 1951.

61. Lawrence, *Rage for Opera*, 113; Lawrence, *World of Opera*, 139–40; Max Rudolf, interview with the author.

62. *NYH-T*, Nov. 22, 1949.

63. *SR*, Dec. 28, 1963; Jackson, *Saturday Afternoons at the Old Met*, 457–59.

64. Smith, "Strauss' *Der Rosenkavalier* Opens Metropolitan Season," 13.

65. Ibid.; Jackson, *Sign-Off for the Old Met*, 112–13.

66. Jacobson, "Notes on the Singers," 38, 40; Morgan, "Risë Stevens," 13–14.

67. Quoted in Totels, "Reiner at the Met, Part I," 6.

68. Ibid.

69. Smith, *Worlds of Music*, 186.

70. *ARG* 46.1 (Oct. 1982): 68; Jackson, *Sign-Off for the Old Met*, 67 (quotation); Luten, "Astrid Varnay"; Marinelli, *Opere in Disco da Monteverdi a Berg*, 467–68.

71. Smith, "Strauss's *Elektra* Revived with Varnay and Hoengen."

72. Eaton, "Opera Production in the Making."

73. *Cue*, Jan. 29, 1949.

74. Jackson, *Saturday Afternoons at the Old Met*, 445.

75. *NYH-T*, Feb. 5, 1949.

76. Eaton, *Miracle of the Met*, 299; Peyser, "Reiner Leads Brilliant *Salome* Revival," 27.

77. Dettmer, "Fritz Reiner."

78. Jackson, *Saturday Afternoons at the Old Met*, 445; *Newsweek*, Feb. 14, 1949, 35 (quotation); Peyser, "Reiner Leads Brilliant *Salome* Revival," 262.

79. Peyser, "Reiner Leads Brilliant *Salome* Revival," 27.

80. *Newsweek*, Feb. 14, 1949, 35 (quotation); Lawrence, *Rage for Opera*, 68; Kolodin, *Metropolitan Opera*, 478; Totels, "Reiner at the Met, Part I," 6.

81. Briggs, *Requiem for a Yellow Brick Brewery*, 274.

82. *ARG* 46.1 (Oct. 1982): 68. For further analysis of the performance, see Morgan, "*Salome* at the Met," 46–50; and Green, "Welitsch's Salome," 405–7.

83. Jacobson, ed., *Reverberations*, 305.

84. Ljuba Welitsch to Reiner, May 3, 1949, Reiner Collection, file for 1948–49, NU; *NYH-T,* Jan. 10, 1952 (quotation); Jackson, *Sign-Off for the Old Met,* 65–67.

85. *MA* 72.2 (Jan. 15, 1952): 4, 24.

86. Telegram from Reiner, Sept. 18, 1949, Reiner Collection, file for 1948–49, NU.

87. *NYH-T,* Jan. 28, 1952.

88. Quoted in *NYH-T,* Jan. 28. 1952.

89. "János Starker Speaks about His Reiner Years," 32; Crichton, *Subway to the Met,* 169.

90. Jones, liner notes.

91. Bing, *Five Thousand Nights at the Opera,* 185–86; *NYH-T,* Jan. 28, 1952; *The New Yorker,* Feb. 9, 1952; Crichton, *Subway to the Met,* 166.

92. Bing, *Five Thousand Nights at the Opera,* 185–86.

93. Guthrie, *Life in the Theatre,* 253.

94. Crichton, *Subway to the Met,* 170; Morgan, "Risë Stevens," 16.

95. Jones, liner notes.

96. Smith, "*Carmen.*"

97. *St. Louis Post-Dispatch,* May 24, 1952.

98. Jackson, *Sign-Off for the Old Met,* 52.

99. Risë Stevens, interview with the author.

100. Reiner, "My Favorite Opera," 7.

101. Kolodin, *Metropolitan Opera,* 478.

102. Jackson, *Saturday Afternoons at the Old Met,* xiv–xv, 439, 444.

103. Smith, "*Falstaff* and *Pelléas* at Metropolitan," 5.

104. *NYT,* Feb. 13, 1953; Victor Aitay, interview with the author.

105. Craft, *Stravinsky: Chronicles of a Friendship,* 93, 100.

106. *SR,* Feb. 28, 1953; Thomson, *Virgil Thomson Reader by Virgil Thomson,* 356.

107. Seltsam, *Metropolitan Opera Annals,* 61–62.

108. Bing, *Knight at the Opera,* 168.

109. Stravinsky and Craft, *Stravinsky in Pictures and Documents,* 417–18.

110. Dettmer, "Fritz Reiner"; János Starker, interview with the author.

111. Max Rudolf, interview with the author.

112. McGovern and Winer, *I Remember Too Much,* 18–19, 22–23; Rudolf Bing to Reiner, Mar. 28, 1950, File on Fritz Reiner, MOA.

113. Reiner to Rudolf Bing, Mar. 30, 1950, File on Fritz Reiner, MOA.

114. Reiner to Garson Kanin, Oct. 31, 1950, File on Fritz Reiner, MOA.

115. Rudolf Bing to Reiner, Nov. 1, 1950, File on Fritz Reiner, MOA.

116. Garson Kanin to Reiner, Nov. 7, 1950, File on Fritz Reiner, MOA.

117. Drake, *Richard Tucker,* 124–25.

118. Bing, *Knight at the Opera,* 13–14.

119. Roger Dettmer, interview with the author.

120. Mayer, *The Met,* 248–49; *NYH-T,* Sept. 21, 1950; Rudolf Bing to Reiner, Sept. 29, 1950, File on Fritz Reiner, MOA.

121. Rudolf Bing to Reiner, Nov. 23, 1950, File on Fritz Reiner, MOA.

122. McGovern and Winer, *I Remember Too Much,* 29–31.

123. Mayer, *The Met,* 248–49.

124. Eaton, *Miracle of the Met,* 320.

125. Max Rudolf, interview with the author; Bing, *Knight at the Opera,* 14.

126. Press release, Nov. 24, 1950, MOA; Crichton, *Subway to the Met,* 154; Briggs, *Requiem for a Yellow Brick Brewery,* 287.

127. Sherman, *Music and Maestros,* 260.

128. Details of these concerts are given in the Stadium Concerts Review, NYPA.

129. Details of these broadcasts can be gleaned from NBC microfilms deposited in the Recorded Sound Division at DLC.

130. Copland and Perlis, *Copland since 1943,* 94, 96.

131. Reiner to George A. Kuyper, May 18, 1951, Reiner Collection, file for 1951, NU. Details of Reiner's Robin Hood Dell concerts are printed in *PI*, June 1951.

132. Reiner to Madame Beek, May 19, 1951, Reiner Collection, file for 1951–52, NU.

133. Ralph Hawkes to Reiner, Dec. 28, 1948, Reiner Collection, file for 1948–49, NU.

134. *Cronache del Teatro di S. Carlo 1948–1968*, 67; Reiner to Max Rudolf, Aug. 9, 1953 (postcard in the possession of Max Rudolf).

135. Telegram, Aug. 22, 1951; Reiner to Madame Beek, Jan. 29 and Feb. 2, 1952, Reiner Collection, files for 1951 and 1951–52, NU.

136. Marjory M. Fisher to Reiner, Feb. 6, 1952; Reiner to Marjory Fisher, Feb. 19, 1952, Reiner Collection, file for 1952, NU.

137. Sol Hurok to Arthur Judson, Dec. 1, 1951, Executive Committee and Board minutes, NYPA.

138. Arthur Judson to Sol Hurok, Dec. 5, 1951, Executive Committee and Board minutes, NYPA.

139. Reiner to Howard R. Will, Mar. 31, 1951, Reiner Collection, file for 1951, NU.

140. Bing, *Five Thousand Nights at the Opera*, 172.

141. Eaton, *Miracle of the Met*, 320.

142. Max Rudolf, interview with the author.

143. Risë Stevens, interview with the author.

144. *The News* (Mexico), Oct. 9, 1951.

145. Quoted in *CDN*, Nov. 21, 1963.

146. Ewen, *Musicians since 1900*, 671.

147. Mayer, *The Met*, 240; Abraham Marcus, interview with the author.

148. Bing, *Five Thousand Nights at the Opera*, 171.

149. Telegram from Rudolf Bing, n.d., Reiner Collection, file for 1953, NU; William Schuman to Reiner, Dec. 19, 1952, box 36, folder 4, William Schuman Papers, NN.

150. Reiner to Mrs. Belmont, Apr. 12, 1953, Reiner Collection, file for 1953, NU, with a duplicate copy in Spec MS Collection Belmont, CU; Reiner to John Mundy, Oct. 25, 1953, Reiner Collection, file for 1953–54, NU.

151. "Interview between Edward Downes and Fritz Reiner."

152. *NYT*, Apr. 11, 1953.

153. Reiner to Rudolf Bing, Apr. 8, 1953, File on Fritz Reiner, MOA.

154. Kolodin, *Metropolitan Opera*, 539, 566; Eaton, *Miracle of the Met*, 320.

155. Lawrence, *World of Opera*, 139.

156. *MA* 69.7 (May 1949): 4; *MA* 70.7 (June 1950): 4; *MA* 72.8 (June 1952): 4.

Chapter 8: Chicago

1. Statement of Fritz Reiner on the Furtwängler–Chicago Symphony Orchestra controversy, n.d., Reiner Collection, file for 1948–49, NU. Compare Gillis, *Furtwängler and America*, 97–126.

2. For background material on the Chicago Symphony Orchestra, see Schabas, *Theodore Thomas;* Mayer, "Dr. Reiner's Orchestra," 40; Mueller, *American Symphony Orchestra,* 101–13; Hart, *Fritz Reiner,* chap. 11; Freed, "Golden Age Deferred"; and Craven, ed., *Symphony Orchestras of the United States,* 110–16. The reasons behind Kubelik's departure from Chicago are outlined in *CDN*, Dec. 10, 1952; and *CS-T*, Dec. 21, 1952. Most of the newspaper references below can be found in the Chicago Symphony Orchestra's scrapbooks at the Newberry Library, Chicago.

3. *Chicago Symphony Orchestra: The First 100 Years*, CSO 90/2.

4. Roger Dettmer, interview with the author.

5. Mayer, "Dr. Reiner's Orchestra," 112; Hart, *Orpheus in the New World*, 45–46; Asbell, "Claudia Cassidy," 26, 28–29; Rosenberg and Rosenberg, *Music Makers*, 165–66; Hart, *Fritz Reiner*, 153, 166; Grant, *Maestros of the Pen*, 258–60; Wendt, *Chicago Tribune*, 615;

Hitchcock and Sadie, eds., *New Grove Dictionary of American Music,* vol. 1, 377. Cassidy's scrapbooks are in the Special Collections of the Chicago Public Library.

6. Potter, "Fritz Reiner," 86.

7. Hart, *Fritz Reiner,* 156.

8. *Chicago Daily Tribune,* Mar. 15 and 24, 1950.

9. *CDN,* Dec. 10, 1952.

10. *CT,* Nov. 24, 1963; *Chicago Daily Tribune,* Aug. 16, 1953.

11. Roger Dettmer, interview with the author.

12. Hart, "How Fritz Reiner Came to Chicago," 10; "Interview between Edward Downes and Fritz Reiner."

13. Sablosky, "Trial and Triumph of Fritz Reiner," 36.

14. *CT,* Dec. 10, 1952.

15. Hart, "How Fritz Reiner Came to Chicago," 8–9.

16. *CS-T,* Nov. 16, 1963.

17. *CDN,* May 22, 1953.

18. Mayer, "Dr. Reiner's Orchestra," 41.

19. Agreements between the Orchestral Association and Fritz Reiner, Dec. 1952 and May 3, 1958, and CSO Minutes, June 17, 1955, May 2, 1958, Rosenthal Archives; *NYT,* Dec. 10, 1952; *CS-T,* Dec. 10, 1952.

20. Mayer, "Dr. Reiner's Orchestra," 39, 41.

21. Undated note by Fritz Reiner, Reiner Collection, file for 1953–54, NU.

22. Papp, *Reiner.*

23. Victor Aitay, interview with the author.

24. Quoted in "Reiner Symposium in Bloomington/I," 12.

25. Sablosky, "Trial and Triumph of Fritz Reiner," 25.

26. "Interview with Edward Druzinsky," 21.

27. Quoted in "Conductors' Guild Holds 'Reiner Retrospective,'" 30.

28. Isaac Stern in Papp, *Reiner.*

29. Potter, "Fritz Reiner," 110; "Interview with Donald Peck/II," 19.

30. "Adolph Herseth Interviewed," 11.

31. Papp, *Reiner.*

32. Jerry Sirucek in Papp, *Reiner;* "János Starker Speaks about His Reiner Years/II," 13; "Interview with Victor Aitay," 10.

33. "Fritz Reiner Remembered," 15–16; "Interview with Donald Peck/II," 19.

34. *Time,* Mar. 24, 1958, 49, 90.

35. Jerry Sirucek in Papp, *Reiner;* Jerry Sirucek, interview with the author; Furlong, *Season with Solti,* 53.

36. Mayer, "Dr. Reiner's Orchestra," 39–40; Hart, *Fritz Reiner,* 159.

37. János Starker, interview with the author.

38. *CT,* Oct. 5, 1953.

39. Sablosky, "Trial and Triumph of Fritz Reiner," 38 (quotation); Hart, "Reiner in Chicago," 44.

40. "Adolph Herseth Interviewed," 12.

41. Leonard Sharrow in Papp, *Reiner.*

42. Hart, "Reiner in Chicago," 43; Victor Aitay, interview with the author.

43. "Interview with Donald Peck/I," 13; "Interview with Clark Brody," 11.

44. Ray Still to Reiner, Jan. 1957, Reiner Collection, file for 1956–57, NU.

45. CSO Minutes, Dec. 19, 1958, Rosenthal Archives.

46. "Interview with Clark Brody," 12.

47. "Fritz Reiner Remembered," 15.

48. Mayer, "Dr. Reiner's Orchestra," 39; "János Starker Speaks about His Reiner Years/II," 14; "Interview with Donald Peck/I," 12.

49. "Frank Miller (1912–1986)," 13; "Interview with Gordon Peters," 19–20; "Interview with Edward Druzinsky," 21.

50. "Fritz Reiner Remembered/II," 17; Potter, "Fritz Reiner," 117.

51. Sablosky, "Trial and Triumph of Fritz Reiner," 28.

52. Sammons, "Chicago Symphony Orchestra," 146.

53. "Reiner Symposium in Bloomington/I," 12; "Fritz Reiner Remembered," 13; "Interview with Victor Aitay," 13.

54. "Fritz Reiner Remembered/II," 19; "Interview with Donald Peck/I," 13; Furlong, *Season with Solti*, 53.

55. Roger Dettmer, interview with the author.

56. Beranek, *Music, Acoustics, and Architecture*, 120–21.

57. *CT*, Oct. 5, 1953.

58. Hillyer, "Sound and Sense of Divided Seating," 22–24.

59. Dettmer, liner notes to *Chicago Symphony Orchestra: From the Archives, Vol. 1*.

60. *CDN*, Feb. 4, 1955.

61. *CT*, Feb. 13, 1955.

62. Samuel Antek to Reiner, Feb. 26, 1957, Reiner Collection, file for 1956–57, NU; *CDN*, Mar. 17, 1956.

63. Kupferberg, "Lukas Foss," 15; Lukas Foss, interview with the author.

64. Dettmer, liner notes to *Chicago Symphony Orchestra: From the Archives, Vol. 1*.

65. "Interview with Walter Hendl," 20; Carlotta Reiner to Claudia Cassidy, Jan. 31, 1958, Reiner Collection, file for 1957, NU; *CDN*, Mar. 4, 1961.

66. "Interview with Clark Brody," 13.

67. Material on the guest conductors and repertoire of the Chicago Symphony Orchestra is drawn from Hillyer, "Chicago Symphony Orchestra Subscription Concerts 1953–1963"; and Gwiasda, "Chicago Symphony Orchestra Popular and Special Concerts 1953–1962."

68. *CDN*, Feb. 21, 1953.

69. Potter, "Fritz Reiner," 91.

70. "Interview with Margaret Hillis—Part 1," 15–16.

71. Carlotta Reiner to Lukas Foss, Apr. 26, 1956, Reiner Collection, file for 1956–57, NU.

72. "Interview with Margaret Hillis—Part 1," 15–17; Rosenberg and Rosenberg, *Music Makers*, 165–66.

73. Reiner to Nelson Fuqua, Apr. 18, 1958, Reiner Collection, file for 1957, NU.

74. Fritz Reiner Diary, 1953, Reiner Collection, NU. These plans were reported in the *CDN*, May 22, 1953.

75. *Newsweek*, May 3, 1954, 48.

76. *CDN*, Feb. 21 and May 2, 1953; Reiner to Leonard Kastle, Dec. 22, 1957, Reiner Collection, file for 1957, NU.

77. *CA*, Oct. 11, 1953; Potts, "Chicago Symphony Orchestra," 53.

78. Reiner to Samuel Barber, Sept. 18, 1953, Reiner Collection, file for 1953, NU.

79. Craven, ed., *Symphony Orchestras of the United States*, 114.

80. *Newsweek*, Nov. 29, 1954, 47.

81. Hart, *Fritz Reiner*, 160.

82. Mayer, "Dr. Reiner's Orchestra," 116 (quotation); Craven, ed., *Symphony Orchestras of the United States*, 114.

83. *CDN*, Feb. 21, 1953.

84. David Diamond to Reiner, Sept. 14, 1956, and Reiner to David Diamond, Oct. 29, 1956, Reiner Collection, file for 1956–57, NU.

85. *CT*, Nov. 14, 1956. Reiner's anger at the Hungarian Revolution of 1956 is evident in correspondence: see [Carlotta Reiner] to Eva Bartenstein, Nov. 8, 1956, and Carlotta Reiner to Stevan Dohanos, Nov. 25, 1956, Reiner Collection, files for 1955–56 and 1956–57, NU.

86. Roger Dettmer, interview with the author.

87. *MA* 75.7 (May 1955), 12; *CA*, Apr. 24, 1955, May 18, 1959; *Milwaukee Journal,* Oct. 7, 1956.

88. *CS-T,* Oct. 18, 1957.

89. *CS-T,* Apr. 8, 1956.

90. Potter, "Fritz Reiner," 87–88.

91. *SR,* Dec. 12, 1953.

92. Palmer, "Chicago Symphony Rapidly Becoming Virtuoso Ensemble under Fritz Reiner"; Palmer, "Chicago Symphony Shows Gains as 63rd Season Comes to a Close."

93. *Newsweek,* May 3, 1954, 80.

94. *Time,* Jan. 4, 1954, 48; Reiner to Jim Keller, Dec. 9, 1953, Reiner Collection, file for 1953–54, NU.

95. *CT,* Dec. 12, 1954.

96. *CA,* Apr. 24, 1955 (quotation); *CDN,* Nov. 21, 1963.

97. Willis, "Reiner on TV," 3–4; Hart, *Fritz Reiner,* 169–70.

98. Roger Dettmer, interview with the author; George A. Kuyper to Reiner, Oct. 10, 1955, Rosenthal Archives.

99. Sammons, "Chicago Symphony Orchestra," 81.

100. Victor Aitay, interview with the author.

101. *CT,* June 29, 1958.

102. Lawrence V. Kelly to Reiner, May 5, 1954, Reiner Collection, file for 1954, NU.

103. Extensive material on these invitations is contained in Reiner Collection, files for 1953–54, 1955–56, 1957, 1958, 1960, 1962, and 1963–64, NU.

104. Reiner to Veljko Bijedic, Mar. 24, 1956; Lacy L. Herrman to Carlotta and Fritz Reiner, Dec. 28, 1954; Reiner to Elsa Respighi, June 21, 1955; Carlotta Reiner to Claudia Cassidy, Sept. 6, 1956; William L. Stein to Reiner, May 2, 1958; Ada Finzi to Reiner, Jan. 5, 1960; all in Reiner Collection, files for 1955–56, 1956–57, 1958, and 1960, NU; *CT,* Oct. 1, 1955.

105. Alfonso de Quesada to Reiner, Nov. 15, 1956, Reiner Collection, file for 1955–56, NU.

106. Reiner to George Szell, n.d. [Jan. 1957], and to Leopold Stokowski, Dec. 6, 1958, Reiner Collection, files for 1956–57 and 1958, NU.

107. Carlotta Reiner to Lacy Herrman, Jan. 5, 1955, Reiner Collection, file for 1955–56, NU.

108. Reiner to Sol Hurok, May 7, 1958, Reiner Collection, file for 1958, NU.

109. Reiner to Norman Connell, July 12, 1959, Reiner Collection, file for 1960, NU.

110. Henry B. Cabot to Eric Oldberg, June 14, 1956, Reiner Collection, loose files, NU.

111. Alan Shulman to Stephen C. Hillyer, *The Podium* (Fall/Winter 1986): 5.

112. *SR,* Mar. 26, 1960.

113. Carlotta Reiner to Edith and Bill [Ragland], Jan. 17, 1956, Reiner Collection, file for 1955–56, NU.

114. *CT,* Nov. 26, 1955.

115. Note by Reiner, 1955, Reiner Collection, file for 1955–56, NU; "Karl Böhm (1894–1981)," 5.

116. Fritz Reiner, memorandum, n.d., Reiner Collection, file for 1955–56, NU.

117. *CT,* Nov. 26, 1955.

118. *Violins and Violinists* 17 (Jan.–Feb. 1956): 17.

119. *CT,* Dec. 19, 1954; Reiner to Carlotta Reiner, May 8, 1953, Reiner Collection, file for 1952–53, NU.

120. Marsh, "Recluse on the Road"; Hart, *Fritz Reiner,* 184.

121. *CT,* Nov. 26, 1955.

122. *CA,* Jan. 1, 1956; Carlotta Reiner to Claudia Cassidy, Sept. 6, 1956, Reiner Collection, file for 1956–57, NU.

123. Reiner to Wilfred Van Wyck, Nov. 16, 1957, Reiner Collection, file for 1957, NU; CSO trustees' minutes, Nov. 15, 1957, Rosenthal Archives.

124. Hart, *Fritz Reiner*, 185; Potter, "Fritz Reiner," 92.

125. *NYH-T*, Oct. 17, 1958.

126. See press notices in the *Boston Globe*, Oct. 14, 1958, and the *Boston Herald*, Oct. 14, 1958.

127. Quoted in "Reiner Symposium in Bloomington/II," 22.

128. Quoted in Mayer, "Dr. Reiner's Orchestra," 39.

129. Quoted in "Interview with Walter Hendl," 21.

130. Potter, "Fritz Reiner," 93–94; Hart, *Fritz Reiner*, 205–6.

131. Hart, *Fritz Reiner*, chap. 14.

132. George A. Kuyper to Reiner, Feb. 4, 1959, and Reiner to Eric Oldberg, Feb. 14, 1959, Reiner Collection, loose files, NU.

133. *CT*, Mar. 8, 1959.

134. *MC* 159.5 (Apr. 1959): 24.

135. Mayer, "Dr. Reiner's Orchestra," 111; Marsh, "Recluse on the Road," 4.

136. *CT*, Feb. 26, 1959; *CA*, Mar. 15, 1959.

137. *CA*, Feb. 27, 1959; "Reiner Symposium in Bloomington/II," 25; Walter Hendl in Papp, *Reiner;* Swain, "Reputations," 42.

138. "Reiner Symposium in Bloomington/II," 25.

139. *Time*, Mar. 19, 1959, 52; Furlong, *Season with Solti*, 110–11.

140. Hart, "Reiner in Chicago," 42.

141. *MC* 159.5 (Apr. 1959): 24. Compare Reiner to Ross Parmenter, Mar. 16, 1959, Reiner Collection, file for 1959, NU.

142. *CS-T*, Mar. 8, 1959.

143. Carlotta Reiner to Eva Bartenstein, Mar. 16, 1959, Reiner Collection, file for 1959, NU.

144. Note by Fritz Reiner, n.d., loose files, NU.

145. *CS-T*, Mar. 8, 1959.

146. Dettmer, "Fritz Reiner"; Potter, "Fritz Reiner," 94; Reiner to Ross Parmenter, Mar. 16, 1959, Reiner Collection, file for 1959, NU; "Interview with Donald Peck/II," 16; *CS-T*, Feb. 27, 1959.

147. Carlotta Reiner to Ada Finzi, Apr. 17, 1959, Reiner Collection, file for 1959, NU.

148. Dettmer, "Fritz Reiner."

149. Fritz Reiner, Diary, Dec. 31, 1957, Reiner Collection, NU.

150. CSO Minutes, Nov. 20, 1959, Rosenthal Archives; Hart, *Fritz Reiner*, 214, 222.

151. Carlotta Reiner to Ada Finzi, Apr. 17, 1959, Reiner Collection, file for 1959, NU.

152. Dettmer, "Fritz Reiner"; Hart, *Fritz Reiner*, 212.

153. Furlong, *Season with Solti*, 225.

154. *CDN*, Mar. 14, 1958; *CA*, April 28, 1961 (quotation), June 1, 1960, and May 5, 1963.

155. *CT*, Dec. 27, 1959.

156. *CT*, Mar. 8, 1959, and May 15, 1960.

157. Grant, *Maestros of the Pen*, 259.

158. Carlotta Reiner to Bud, Feb. 10, 1962, Reiner Collection, file for 1960, NU; "Interview with Victor Aitay," 12.

159. Carlotta Reiner to Muddy, Dec. 5, 1954, Reiner Collection, file for 1954, NU.

160. Carlotta Reiner to Ann [?], Dec. 8, 1956, Reiner Collection, file for 1955–56, NU.

161. *CA*, May 5, 1963.

162. Hart, *Fritz Reiner*, 168, 180.

163. Dettmer, liner notes to *Chicago Symphony Orchestra: From the Archives, Vol. 1.*

164. *CT*, Feb. 16–22, 1957; Hart, "Reiner in Chicago," 42.

165. Carlotta Reiner to Hanna [?], Jan. 7, 1956, and to Muddy, Mar. 25, 1956, Reiner Collection, file for 1955–56, NU; Hillyer, "NU Launches Reiner Collection," 8.

166. CSO Minutes, Oct. 11, 1960, Rosenthal Archives; Dettmer, "Fritz Reiner, 1888–1963," 273.

167. Carlotta Reiner to Paul Lang, Oct. 31, 1960, to Lacy L. Herrman, Oct. 31, 1960, to F. Bernasian, Jan. 7, 1961, and to Tuśy, Oct. 29, 1960, Reiner Collection, files for 1960 and 1961, NU.

168. Carlotta Reiner to Pali and Erika, Nov. 3, 1960, Reiner Collection, file for 1960, NU.

169. Roger Dettmer, "Return of Reiner," 20.

170. Carlotta Reiner to Eva Bartenstein, Apr. 18, 1961, Reiner Collection, file for 1961, NU.

171. Reiner to Eric Oldberg, n.d., Reiner Collection, file for 1960, NU.

172. Reiner to James F. Maguire, Apr. 14, 1961, Reiner Collection, file for 1961, NU; CSO Minutes, June 16, 1961, Rosenthal Archives; Potter, "Fritz Reiner," 98.

173. Quoted in Dettmer, "Symphonic Strife," 12; Potter, "Fritz Reiner," 98.

174. Hart, *Fritz Reiner*, 159, 228.

175. *CA*, Mar. 15, 1959; Furlong, *Season with Solti*, 111.

176. Hart, *Orpheus in the New World*, 112–13; Wendt, *Chicago Tribune*, 615.

177. Dettmer, "Symphonic Strife."

178. Seltzer, *Music Matters*, 68–69.

179. *CA*, Sept. 8, 1962; *CS-T*, Sept. 28, 1962.

180. Carlotta Reiner to Edith and Bill [Ragland], Aug. 6, 1962, Reiner Collection, file for 1962, NU.

181. Carlotta Reiner to Eva Reiner Bartenstein, Oct. 21, 1962, Reiner Collection, file for 1962, NU; Potter, "Fritz Reiner," 98.

182. *CA*, Dec. 17, 1961, Apr. 1, 1962; Furlong, *Season with Solti*, 96.

183. *NYT*, Aug. 5, 1962; *CS-T*, Apr. 14, 1963; Dettmer, liner notes to *Chicago Symphony Orchestra: From the Archives, Vol. 1*.

184. Dettmer, "Reiner Retires," 12–13; *CT*, Nov. 16, 1963.

185. Quoted in Osborne, *Herbert von Karajan*, 560.

186. Victor Aitay in Papp, *Reiner*; Roger Dettmer, interview with the author.

187. David Walter, interview with the author.

188. Charles Denby to Carlotta Reiner, Jan. 29, 1964, Reiner Collection, file for 1963–64, NU.

189. K. O. Kuersteiner to Reiner, Mar. 19, 1963, and Reiner to K. O. Kuersteiner, Mar. 26, 1963, Reiner Collection, file for 1963–64, NU.

190. Reiner to Seymour Raven, May 12, 1959, and Carlotta Reiner to Tuśy, Feb. 10, 1962, Reiner Collection, files for 1959 and 1962, NU.

191. Vincent F. Malek to Reiner, Feb. 9, 1960; Nathan Gottschalk to Reiner, Mar. 6, 1963; W. S. Naylor to Reiner, Apr. 27, 1955; Reiner to W. S. Naylor, May 2, 1955; all in Reiner Collection, files for 1955–56, 1960, 1963, and January 1964, NU.

192. Rudolf Bing to Reiner, June 4, 1963, File on Fritz Reiner, MOA.

193. Klinger, "Memories of Fritz Reiner as a Young Man."

194. Hart, "Reiner in Chicago," 46.

195. *CDN*, Nov. 16, 1963; *CS-T*, Nov. 16, 1963.

196. Ewen, *Musicians since 1900*, 672.

197. Roger Dettmer, interview with the author.

198. Cited by Robert C. Marsh in *High Fidelity*, May 1964, 82.

199. Schuman, "Reiner in Memoriam."

200. *NYT*, Nov. 19, 1963.

201. *CT*, Nov. 16 and 24, 1963.

202. *CDN*, Nov. 16 and 23, 1963.

203. *CA*, Nov. 24, 1963.

204. Stravinsky, *Themes and Conclusions*, 225.

205. *NYT*, Nov. 24, 1963.

206. Paul Henry Lang to Carlotta Reiner, Dec. 7, 1963, Reiner Collection, file for 1963, NU.

207. Quoted in Willis, liner notes.

Chapter 9: The Recorded Legacy

1. Fritz Reiner, "Recording," Reiner Collection, file for 1951–52, NU; Reiner, "From Cylindrical to Long Playing Records."

2. Hart, "Toward a Reiner Discography," 66.

3. Ibid.; *Library of Welte-Mignon Music Records*, 183.

4. J. MacDonald to Arthur Judson, Nov. 10, 1926, Reiner Collection, file for 1927, NU.

5. Arthur Judson to Reiner, Feb. 9, 1929, and Reiner to Arthur Judson, Mar. 4, 1929, Reiner Collection, file for February 1929, NU.

6. The Gramophone Company Ltd. to Electrola Gesellschaft, July 11, 1930, EMI Archives.

7. Hart, "Toward a Reiner Discography," 66; "FRS Centenary Tape Features Reiner's Earliest Recordings."

8. Hart, *Fritz Reiner*, 86, 258 n.12.

9. *Business Week*, Oct. 14, 1931, 9.

10. Reiner to Charles O'Connell, Dec. 6, 1935, and Charles O'Connell to Reiner, Dec. 10, 1935, Reiner Collection, file for 1938, NU.

11. For commentary on these recordings, see Hart, "Underground Reiner," 209–11.

12. Reiner to James E. Sauter, Oct. 23, 1937, Reiner Collection, file for 1937–38, NU.

13. Reiner to Kirsten Flagstad, Nov. 11, 1938, Reiner Collection, file for 1939, NU.

14. Glendale Records (GL 8003), cited in Blyth, ed., *Opera on Record 2*, 64; Hart, *Fritz Reiner*, 278, 284; Benko, "Incomparable Josef Hofmann," 21.

15. O'Connell, *Other Side of the Record*, 330; Gelatt, *Fabulous Phonograph*, 273; Emmons, *Tristanissimo*, 164; *Fritz Reiner Society Newsletter*, no. 1 [n.d.]; *Fanfare* 15.4 (Mar./Apr. 1992): 427.

16. Maurice J. Speiser and Herbert A. Speiser to Reiner, Nov. 25, 1940, Reiner Collection, file for 1940–41, NU.

17. Reiner to Maurice Speiser, Dec. 4, 1940, Reiner Collection, file for 1940–41, NU.

18. Reiner, "Recording," Reiner Collection, file for 1951–52, NU; Marsh, "Kubelik and the Thomas Tradition."

19. Gelatt, *Fabulous Phonograph*, 274–75; Hart, *Fritz Reiner*, 108–9.

20. Reiner's Columbia recordings are discussed in Morgan, "Reiner in Pittsburgh."

21. Hart, *Orpheus in the New World*, 106; Leiter, *Musicians and Petrillo*, 137; Seltzer, *Music Matters*, 39, 42, 44.

22. *PS-T*, Mar. 27, 1945.

23. *PBI*, Oct. 9, 1941.

24. *PS-T*, Mar. 27, 1945.

25. Leiter, *Musicians and Petrillo*, 166–68; Seltzer, *Music Matters*, 52–53; Gelatt, *Fabulous Phonograph*, 279–81.

26. *PP*, Dec. 21, 1941; Hart, *Fritz Reiner*, 110.

27. *PS-T*, Mar. 23, 1941.

28. Hart, "Recent Fritz Reiner Compact Discs," 253.

29. Hart, "Toward a Reiner Discography," 67 (Hart wrongly states that this was the first recording of Shostakovich's Sixth Symphony); Morgan, "Reiner in Pittsburgh," 30.

30. Moses Smith to Reiner, Sept. 7, 1939, Reiner Collection, file for 1939–40, NU.

31. *PP-G*, Feb. 29, 1940.

32. Reiner to Arthur Judson, Apr. 4, 1940, and Reiner to Edward Specter, Apr. 16, 1940 (quotation), Reiner Collection, file for 1939–40 and loose files, NU.

33. "Interview with Victor Aitay," 11.

34. Reiner to Goddard Lieberson, Dec. 26, 1946, Goddard Lieberson Papers, Sterling Memorial Library, Yale University.

35. *EMG Monthly Letter* 19.4 (Apr. 1949): 5; *ARG* 15.11 (July 1949): 343.

36. Reiner to Goddard Lieberson, Nov. 13, 1942, Reiner Collection, file for 1942, NU.

37. *EMG Monthly Letter* 22.4 (Apr. 1952): 12.

38. John de Lancie, interview with the author.

39. See Hudson, *Stolen Time*, 302.

40. *Records and Recording* 23.8 (May 1980): 18.

41. *Gramophone Shop Record Supplement* 5.12 (Dec. 1942): 6.

42. Kolodin, *New Guide to Recorded Music*, 237.

43. Ibid., 388.

44. Mordden, *Broadway Babies*, 228.

45. *PBI*, Nov. 13, 1941.

46. *The New Records* 10.1 (Mar. 1942), 4, and 12.6 (Aug. 1944), 2.

47. *ARG* 16.9 (May 1950): 287; *Library Journal*, June 15, 1950, 1060.

48. Reiner to Andrew Schulhof, Nov. 20, 1940, and Moses Smith to Edward Specter, Nov. 25, 1940, Reiner Collection, loose files, NU.

49. Moses Smith to Reiner, Sept. 7, 1939, Reiner Collection, loose files, NU.

50. Reiner to Edward Specter, June 13, 1945, Reiner Collection, loose files, NU.

51. Goddard Lieberson to Reiner, Sept. 10, 1947, Goddard Lieberson Papers, Sterling Memorial Library, Yale University.

52. Reiner to Edward Wallerstein, June 10, 1945, and Reiner to Edward Specter, July 8, 1947, Reiner Collection, loose files, NU.

53. Hart, "Recent Fritz Reiner Compact Discs," 253.

54. *Radio and Television Retailing* (New York), Feb. 1947.

55. Reiner to Thruston Wright and Edward Specter, Sept. 25, 1946, Reiner Collection, loose files, NU.

56. Reiner to Thruston Wright, Apr. 25, 1947, Reiner Collection, file for 1947, NU, and in Goddard Lieberson Papers, Sterling Memorial Library, Yale University.

57. *Gramophone* 27.318 (Nov. 1949): 103; *ARG* 15.9 (May 1949): 282.

58. Liner notes to live recording of *Salome*, 1952 (Myto 2MCD 952.125).

59. Totels, "Reiner at the Met, Part I," 9.

60. Quoted in the Minneapolis Symphony Orchestra program, Oct. 30, 1948.

61. Hart, *Fritz Reiner*, 111, 139; Gronow and Saunio, *International History of the Recording Industry*, 113.

62. John Pfeiffer, interview with the author; Gray, "Recording Reiner," 47.

63. Rooney, "Life and Death of the LP," 10; Millard, *America on Record*, 205–7.

64. Robert C. Marsh wrongly speculates that Reiner conducted this opera in his early career (see liner notes to *Reiner Conducts Wagner*, BMG Classics CD 09026 61792 2).

65. *ARG* 20.5 (Jan. 1954): 158; *MA* 74.1 (Jan. 1, 1954): 17.

66. *MA* 74.1 (Jan. 1, 1954): 17; *Harper's Magazine*, Mar. 1954, 12 (quotation).

67. *SR*, Feb. 27, 1954, 57.

68. Reiner to Alan Kayes, July 3, 1950, Reiner Collection, loose files, NU.

69. RCA press release on *Carmen*, Reiner Collection, file for 1951, NU.

70. Compare *Gramophone* 31.370 (Mar. 1954): 398.

71. *SR*, Oct. 27, 1951, 48.

72. Recording contract between Reiner and RCA, July 20, 1950, Reiner Collection, loose files, NU.

73. Robert Bloom cited in the liner notes to *Divertimento No. 11 en ré majeur, K. 251, pour cordes, hautbois et deux cors*, RCA France GM 43558.

74. Richard Mohr to Reiner, Feb. 28, 1951, Reiner Collection, loose files, NU.

75. Reiner to George Marek, Jan. 18, 1954, Reiner Collection, loose files, NU.

76. *CS-T*, July 10, 1960.

77. Hart, *Fritz Reiner*, 173; Gronow and Saunio, *International History of the Recording Industry*, 147.

78. Semple, "History of the Chicago Symphony Orchestra's Recording Career," 132.

79. "Fritz Reiner Remembered/II," 17.

80. Reiner to Alan Kayes, Nov. 22, 1953, Reiner Collection, loose files, NU.

81. Ibid.

82. Horowitz, *Understanding Toscanini*, 275.

83. Gray, "Recording Reiner," 53.

84. Reiner to Sol Hurok, Nov. 24, 1953, Reiner Collection, loose files, NU.

85. *ARG* 21.2 (Oct. 1954): 61; *Gramophone* 70.835 (Dec. 1992): 89 (quotation). An alternate take of the first seven minutes of *Zarathustra* has recently been issued on *A Tribute to John Pfeiffer* (BMG/RCA 68524, 2 CDs).

86. *CS-T*, July 10, 1960.

87. Gray, "Recording Reiner," 49; Valin, *RCA Bible*, 29.

88. John Pfeiffer, interview with the author.

89. Gray, "Recording Reiner," 48–49, 52; Henderson, "Golden Age of Recording," 103.

90. Sammons, "Chicago Symphony Orchestra," 146; Beranek, *Music, Acoustics, and Architecture*, 120–21.

91. Reiner's brief remarks are given on an RCA disc entitled *Showcase in Sound* (SRL 12–28).

92. Reich, *Van Cliburn*, 229; John Pfeiffer and Victor Aitay, interviews with the author.

93. Gray, "Recording Reiner," 53; Hart, "Reiner in Chicago," 46; Gronow and Saunio, *International History of the Recording Industry*, 147.

94. "János Starker Speaks about His Reiner Years/II," 12–13.

95. Roger Dettmer, interview with the author.

96. Chapin, *Musical Chairs*, 89–90.

97. Hart, "Reiner in Chicago," 46.

98. *Fanfare* 6.4 (Mar.–Apr. 1983): 229–30.

99. Hart, "Reiner in Chicago," 46.

100. *CS-T*, Nov. 1, 1959.

101. Roger Dettmer, interview with the author; Gray, "Pines of Rome."

102. *CDN*, Oct. 21, 1955.

103. *NYT*, Nov. 20, 1955.

104. Byron Janis, liner notes to the Reiner/Janis/Chicago Symphony recording of Rachmaninov's Piano Concertos nos. 1 and 3.

105. Reich, *Van Cliburn*, 209–10; Richard Mohr, liner notes to the Reiner/Cliburn/Chicago Symphony recording of Beethoven's Piano Concerto no. 4.

106. *CT*, Nov. 24, 1963.

107. Leonard Sharrow, interview with the author.

108. "Interview with Donald Peck/I," 8; John Pfeiffer, interview with the author.

109. János Starker, interview with the author.

110. Philip Farkas, interview with the author.

111. "János Starker Speaks about His Reiner Years," 12; *CS-T*, Mar. 21, 1956.

112. Reiner to George Kuyper, Feb. 7, 1959, Reiner Collection, loose files, NU.

113. Schlachtmeyer, "Interview with Carlotta Reiner," 7.

114. Dettmer, "Kaviar für volk," 18; Roger Dettmer, interview with the author.

115. George Kuyper to Seymour Raven, May 3, 1960, Reiner Collection, loose files, NU.

116. Reiner to Eric Oldberg, Mar. 21, 1953, Reiner Collection, loose files, NU.

117. Dettmer, "Kaviar für Volk," 18; Schlachtmeyer, "Interview with Carlotta Reiner," 7; Hart, *Fritz Reiner*, 175.

118. "Interview with Margaret Hillis—Part 2," 34.

119. *CDN*, Nov. 21, 1963.

120. *ARG* 22.6 (Feb. 1956): 86; *The New Records* 23.12 (Feb. 1956): 2.

121. *EMG Monthly Letter* 32.11 (Nov. 1962): 2; *Hi-Fi and Stereo Review* 12.2 (Feb. 1964): 74.

122. Compare Steven J. Haller's review in *ARG* 45.9 (July/Aug. 1982): 9.

123. Dettmer, "Reiner," 68.

124. Reiner, "Mahler."

125. *Gramophone* 68.811 (Dec. 1990): 1276.

126. *Harper's Magazine,* Nov. 1954, 110.

127. *Gramophone* 70.840 (May 1993): 106; *High Fidelity* 6.11 (Nov. 1956): 92 (quotation).

128. McKee, "Recordings," 491–92.

129. *Classic CD,* July 1995, 39.

130. Reiner to Sol Hurok, Mar. 10, 1955, Reiner Collection, loose files, NU.

131. Reiner to Clair Meeder, June 20, 1956, Reiner Collection, file for 1956–57, NU.

132. James C. Petrillo to Reiner, June 21, 1956, Reiner Collection, file for 1956–57, NU.

133. Reiner to Alan Kayes, Nov. 2, 1957, Reiner Collection, loose files, NU.

134. Reiner to Herman D. Kenin, Feb. 7, 1960, Reiner Collection, file for 1960, NU.

135. Henry Zaccardi to Reiner, Feb. 29, 1960; Carlotta Reiner to Ada Finzi, Mar. 6, 1960; Richard Mohr to Reiner, Oct. 28, 1959, all in Reiner Collection, file for 1960 and loose files, NU.

136. Culshaw, *Putting the Record Straight,* 143.

137. Ibid.; Culshaw, *Ring Resounding,* 60 (quotation); "Conductor's Guild Holds 'Reiner Retrospective,'" 24; Roger Dettmer, interview with the author.

138. Valin, *RCA Bible,* 29.

139. Hart, *Fritz Reiner,* 219–20.

140. Quoted in Culshaw, *Putting the Record Straight,* 238.

141. Svejda, *Record Shelf Guide to the Classical Repertoire,* 87.

142. Reiner to Sol Hurok, Aug. 8, 1953, Reiner Collection, file for 1952–53, NU.

143. Carlotta Reiner to Karl F. Bauer, Dec. 19, 1954, Reiner Collection, file for 1954–55, NU.

144. *CA,* Oct. 1, 1960.

145. O'Neil, *The Grammys,* 38, 47, 58, 70, 81, 94; Richard Mohr to Reiner, Apr. 1 and Oct. 23, 1963, Reiner Collection, file for 1963–64, NU.

146. Reiner to Bud and Mary, June 30, 1962, Reiner Collection, file for 1962, NU.

147. Richard Mohr to Reiner, June 10, 1963, Reiner Collection, file for 1963–January 1964, NU.

148. Peter Dellheim to Reiner, June 14, 1963, Reiner Collection, file for 1963–January 1964, NU.

149. Valin, *RCA Bible,* 26; Gelatt, *Fabulous Phonograph,* 314, 316–17.

150. Valin, *RCA Bible,* 26.

151. Ibid., 26, 100.

152. Cowan, "Living Stereo."

153. Valin, *RCA Bible,* 15–16.

154. Pfeiffer, "Superiority of a Fraction."

155. Gray, "Reiner."

156. Pfeffer, "Michael Hobson of Classic Records and the Rebirth of Quality Vinyl."

157. Rooney, "Fritz Reiner on CD," 13.

158. Hart, "Underground Reiner," 209–13.

159. Temmer, liner notes for *Chicago Symphony Orchestra: From the Archives, Vol. 1;* Hart, "Chicago Symphony Orchestra, from the Archives, Volumes I and II," 129–30.

160. *CT,* Apr. 14, 1996.

161. Linkowski, "Chicago Symphony in Concert," 228.

Chapter 10: Reiner the Interpreter

1. Reiner's recordings on CD are listed in the discography. Details of his recordings on 78s and LPs and all recordings by other conductors are footnoted below.

2. Bowen, "Performance Practice versus Performance Analysis," 19.

3. Ibid., 21–22.

4. *NYT,* Nov. 24, 1963.

5. Schonberg, *Great Conductors,* 337.

6. Horowitz, *Understanding Toscanini*, 377.

7. Taruskin, *Text and Act*, 108–15.

8. On creative interpretation, see Bowen, "Mendelssohn, Berlioz, and Wagner as Conductors."

9. Ardoin, *Furtwängler Record*; Whiteside and Tanner, eds., *Wilhelm Furtwängler.*

10. Taruskin, "Golden Age of Kitsch," 33–34.

11. Philip, "1900–1940," 471–72; Hudson, *Stolen Time.*

12. Quoted in Taruskin, *Text and Act*, 360–61. Compare Hudson, *Stolen Time*, 382.

13. Hudson, *Stolen Time*, 376–79.

14. MacDonald, "To Repeat or Not to Repeat?"

15. Zaslaw, *Mozart's Symphonies*, 501.

16. Beethoven, Symphony no. 3 (Eulenburg miniature score); Beethoven, Symphony no. 5 (Philharmonia pocket score); Brahms, Symphony no. 1 (Simrock miniature score); all in Reiner Collection, NU.

17. Canarina, "Conductor for All Repertoire," 8.

18. Brinkmann, *Late Idyll*, 16.

19. Rosen, *Classical Style*, 395.

20. *Gramophone* 77.920 (Nov. 1999): 6.

21. Del Mar, *Conducting Brahms*, 47.

22. Ardoin, *Furtwängler Record*, 251. Ardoin notes of Furtwängler's 1949 recording with the Berlin Philharmonic (EMI CD CZS 252 3212) that he "inexplicably decided to take the first movement repeat." In his 1949 recording of the same piece with the same orchestra, Furtwängler omitted the repeat (Music and Arts CD 941).

23. Boston Symphony Orchestra, Koussevitzky, Pearl GEMM CD 9237; Concertgebouw Orchestra of Amsterdam, Monteux, Tahra CD, TAH 175-178.

24. Canarina, "Conductor for All Repertoire," 8. The London Symphony, Monteux, Philips CD, 442 547-2; Vienna Philharmonic, Monteux, Decca Eclipse LP, ECS 96.

25. English Chamber Orchestra, Britten, Decca CD 444 323-2DF2.

26. *EMG Monthly Letter* 32.11 (Nov. 1962): 2.

27. Pickett, "Comparative Survey of Rescorings in Beethoven's Symphonies," 217–19; Weingartner, *On the Performance of Beethoven's Symphonies.*

28. Robinson, *Stokowski*, 53, 116. Some of Stokowski's orchestrations of Bach's organ music are played by the Philadelphia Orchestra on a Sony Masterworks Heritage CD (MH2K 62345). Stokowski's performance of *Romeo and Juliet* with the New York City Symphony Orchestra is on a CALA CD (CA CD 0502). His account of the *Russian Easter Festival* Overture, with the Leopold Stokowski Symphony Orchestra and bass soloist Nicola Moscona, appeared on an RCA LP (LM 1816).

29. Ardoin, *Furtwängler Record*, 36; Horowitz, *Understanding Toscanini*, 330–31; Shanet, *Philharmonic*, 261–63; Pickett, "Comparative Survey of Rescorings in Beethoven's Symphonies," 221.

30. Hollywood Bowl program, August 1937, Los Angeles Philharmonic Association.

31. Reiner to Vladimir Bakaleinikoff, Sept. 25, 1945, Reiner Collection, loose files, NU.

32. Hart, *Fritz Reiner*, 291–98.

33. For a modern recording of *Catfish Row*, see BBC Philharmonic Orchestra, Yan Pascal Tortelier, Chandos CD 9325. Gould's suite can be heard on an RCA LP (LMF 2002).

34. Based on the score in Reiner Collection, NU.

35. *Gramophone Shop Record Supplement* 13.6 (June 1950): 2. For details of these recordings, see the appendix.

36. Boyd, *Bach*, 30; Academy of St. Martin in the Fields, Marriner, Philips, 2 CDs, 4260882; Pro Musica Orchestra, Paris, Klemperer, Vox LP, set 619.

37. Boyd, *Bach*, 30; Marrissen, *Social and Religious Designs of J. S. Bach's Brandenburg Concertos*, 58–59, 64–65.

38. Freed, liner notes.

39. Ardoin, *Furtwängler Record*, 95–96; Vienna Philharmonic, Furtwängler, EMI CD, CDH 763 1932; Berlin Philharmonic, Furtwängler, Fonit Cetra CD, CDE 1015; Academy of Ancient Music, Hogwood, L'Oiseau-Lyre CD, 443 180-20M; Salzburg Mozarteum Camerata, Vegh, Decca CD, 448 062-2DH.

40. A Durand miniature copy of this score can be found in Reiner Collection, NU.

41. Trezise, *Debussy*, 16–17, 29; Boston Symphony, Munch, BMG/RCA CD, 09026 61956 2; Suisse Romande Orchestra, Ansermet, Decca CD, 4337112; BBC Symphony, Toscanini, Grammofono 2000 CD, AB 78613; Paris Symphony Orchestra, Coppola, Lys CD 295/7; Cleveland Orchestra, Szell, CBS Classics LP, 61075.

42. Brahms, Symphony no. 1 (Simrock miniature score), Reiner Collection, NU.

43. Frederiksen, *Arnold Jacobs*, 37–38.

44. Mendelssohn, Overture to *A Midsummer Night's Dream* (Philharmonia miniature score), Reiner Collection, NU. Reiner's recording with the Robin Hood Dell Orchestra is on an RCA LP (LM 1724).

45. *CDN*, Sept. 7, 1956.

46. *NYH-T*, Jan. 28, 1952; Abraham Marcus, interview with the author.

47. Roger Dettmer, interview with the author.

48. Bach, Brandenburg Concerto no. 2 (Broude Brothers score), Reiner Collection, NU.

49. Boston Baroque, Martin Pearlman, Telarc CD 80354. Scholarly support for one player per line is given in Marrissen, "Performance Practice Issues That Affect Meaning in Selected Bach Instrumental Works."

50. Zaslaw, *Mozart's Symphonies*, 464.

51. Hart, *Fritz Reiner*, 202.

52. Mozart, Symphony no. 36 (Philharmonia miniature score), Reiner Collection, NU.

53. Haydn, Symphony no. 88 (Eulenburg miniature score), Reiner Collection, NU.

54. Mozart, Symphony no. 35 (Philharmonia miniature score), Reiner Collection, NU.

55. Reiner, "Making of a Conductor"; *CT-S*, Feb. 24, 1926.

56. Boyd, *Bach*, 26–30.

57. Ardoin, *Furtwängler Record*, 75–76; Berlin Philharmonic, Furtwängler, Symposium CD 1043; Vienna Philharmonic, Furtwängler, Refrain [Japan] CD, DR 920018.

58. HMV 78 rpm set DB 6455/6.

59. L'Oiseau-Lyre CD, 440 675-20H2.

60. Collins Classics CD, CO11 3054-2.

61. Hyperion CD, CDA 66711/2.

62. NBC Symphony, Reiner, RCA LP, LM-1952.

63. Pickett, "Comparative Survey of Rescorings in Beethoven's Symphonies," 207–25.

64. Hughes, *Toscanini Legacy*, 70. These alterations can be heard on Toscanini's 1952 recording with the NBC Symphony Orchestra, BMG/RCA, GD 60254.

65. Concertgebouw Orchestra of Amsterdam, Erich Kleiber, Decca CD, 425 9872; Vienna Philharmonic, Carlos Kleiber, DGG CD, 415 862 2; Philharmonia, Klemperer, rec. 1957, Angel LP 35330; Berlin State Opera Orchestra, Richard Strauss, Koch CD 3-7115-2.

66. Compare Schuller, *Compleat Conductor*, 258.

67. Pickett, "Comparative Survey of Rescorings in Beethoven's Symphonies," 210.

68. Robinson, *Solti*, 88.

69. Berlioz, *Roméo et Juliette* (Broude Brothers full score), Reiner Collection, NU.

70. Irving Sarin, interview with the author.

71. Reiner to Olin Downes, Oct. 26, 1927, Reiner Collection, file for 1927, NU.

72. Cooper, *Bartók*, 25, 65.

73. *Philadelphia Public Ledger*, Jan. 25, 1936.

74. Freed, "Feast of Reiner CDs from RCA," 33. Stock's performance was issued on an RCA Victor 78 rpm disc (V-7653).

75. Bowen, "History of Remembered Innovation," 160 n.56.

76. Bach, Brandenburg Concerti (Broude Brothers scores), Reiner Collection, NU.

77. Beethoven, Symphony no. 8 (Eulenburg miniature score), Reiner Collection, NU.

78. Beethoven, Symphony no. 3 (Eulenburg miniature score), Reiner Collection, NU.

79. Haydn, Symphony no. 104 (Eulenburg miniature score), Reiner Collection, NU.

80. Haydn, Symphony no. 88 (Eulenburg miniature score), Reiner Collection, NU.

81. Mozart, Symphony no. 35 (Philharmonia miniature score), Reiner Collection, NU.

82. Mahler, Symphony no. 4 (Universal edition miniature score), Reiner Collection, NU.

83. Brahms, Symphony no. 2 (gold-embossed score), Reiner Collection, NU. See also Dettmer, "Kaviar für Volk," 19–21.

84. Brahms, Symphony no. 2 (Simrock miniature score), Reiner Collection, NU.

85. Cone, "Pianist as Critic," 253.

86. Philip, *Early Recordings and Musical Style,* 35–36.

87. Bowen, "Tempo, Duration, and Flexibility."

88. Schuller, *Compleat Conductor,* 70–71.

89. Marshall, *Music of Johann Sebastian Bach,* chap. 15.

90. Hudson, *Stolen Time,* 4.

91. Bach, Brandenburg Concertos nos. 1 and 3 (Broude Bros. score), Reiner Collection, NU.

92. Brown, *Classical and Romantic Performing Practice,* 59; Hudson, *Stolen Time* (quotations), 156.

93. Hughes, *Toscanini Legacy,* 82.

94. Levy, "Contrabass Recitative in Beethoven's Ninth Symphony Revisited," 15–16.

95. Schubert Ninth Symphony, Chicago Symphony, Reiner, live performance from 1957, available on a cassette from the Fritz Reiner Society.

96. Berlin Philharmonic, Furtwängler, DGG CD, 427 7762/427 7732.

97. Berlin Philharmonic, Furtwängler, DGG CD, DG427 7812/427 7732.

98. Kozinn, "Willem Mengelberg," 10.

99. Brown, *Classical and Romantic Performing Practice,* 375.

100. Levy, "Beginning-Ending Ambiguity," 165; Cleveland Orchestra, Szell, Sony Classical CD, SBK 46333.

101. Schubert, Symphony no. 9 (Eulenburg miniature score), Reiner Collection, NU.

102. Newbould, *Schubert and the Symphony,* 218; Bavarian Radio Symphony Orchestra, Giulini, Sony Classical CD, SK 53971; Orchestra of the Age of Enlightenment, Mackerras, Virgin CD, VC 759669-2.

103. Broyles, *Beethoven,* 85.

104. Cook, *Beethoven,* 29 (quotation), 53; Cook, "Conductor and the Theorist."

105. Ardoin, *Furtwängler Record,* 144–49. A representative Furtwängler recording is his 1951 version with the Bayreuth Festival Orchestra (EMI CD 7243 5 66218 2 4).

106. Schuller, *Compleat Conductor,* 190 n.56.

107. Thomas, "Conversation with Lukas Foss," 2–3.

108. Ardoin, *Furtwängler Record,* 127.

109. Robinson, *Stokowski,* 93–95; NBC Symphony, Toscanini, BMG/RCA CD, GD 60255; Berlin Philharmonic, Karajan, Teldec CD, 4509-95038-6; The Philadelphia Orchestra: The Centennial Collection, CD 1, POA 100–1; All American Youth Orchestra, Stokowski, Music and Arts CD, MACD-857.

110. Hudson, *Stolen Time,* 143.

111. Rimsky-Korsakov, *Scheherazade* (Belaieff pocket score), Reiner Collection, NU.

112. San Francisco Symphony, Monteux, BMG/RCA CD, 09026 61893-2.

113. Cleveland Orchestra, Rodzinski, Lys CD, 161.

114. Compare Robinson, *Stokowski,* 23–24.

115. Cowan, liner notes.

116. Boston Symphony, Koussevitzky, Biddulph CD, WHL 034.

117. Quoted in *CA,* Oct. 15, 1953.

118. *ARG* 50.1 (Jan./Feb. 1987): 87.

119. *SR,* Nov. 1, 1958.

Discography
Reiner on Compact Disc

This discography includes all performances conducted by Fritz Reiner that were issued on CD before the end of 2001. Excerpts from works on compilation discs and items of limited circulation are excluded.

Abbreviations

ARPCD	Archipel
ARL and ARLA	Arlecchino
BIDDULPH	Biddulph
RCA	BMG/RCA Victor
CHESKY	Chesky
CSO	Chicago Symphony Orchestra
DECCA	Decca
EMI	EMI
GALA	Gala
GEBHARDT	Gebhardt
GM	Golden Melodram
GRA	Grammofono 2000
GHCD	Guild Historical
LGD and LCD	Legend
LONDON	London
LYS	Dante-Lys
MEL	Melodram
MET	Metropolitan Opera Association
M&A	Music & Arts
MCD	Myto
PEARL	Pearl
PHILIPS	Philips
PSS	Pittsburgh Symphony Society
SONY	Sony
SRO	Standing Room Only
VAIA	VAI Records

CBS Symphony Orchestra

Ravel, *Daphnis et Chloë*. Suite no. 2. LYS 165, LYS 259-260

Chicago Symphony Orchestra

Albeniz, *Navarra*, "Fête-Dieu à Seville," and "Triana" from *Iberia*. RCA RCD1-5404, RCA 09026-62586-2
Auber, Overture *Masaniello*. CSO-CD-96B-2
Bartók, Concerto for Orchestra. RCA 5604, RCA 09026-61504-2
Bartók, Hungarian Sketches. RCA 60206, RCA 09026-61504-2
Bartók, Violin Concerto no. 2. (Y. Menuhin) CSO-CD-96B-2
Bartók, Divertimento for Strings. ARLA-83
Bartók, Music for Strings, Percussion, and Celesta. RCA 5604, RCA 09026-51504-2
Beethoven, Piano Concerto no. 4 (V. Cliburn) RCA 7943
Beethoven, Piano Concerto no. 5. (V. Cliburn) RCA 7943, RCA 09026-61961-2
Beethoven, Overture, *Leonore* no. 2. CSO 96B-2
Beethoven, Overture, *Coriolan*. CSO CD 03-2, EMI 7243 5 62866 2
Beethoven, Overture, *Coriolan*. RCA RCD-5403, RCA 09026-689762-2, RCA 09026-60962-2
Beethoven, Overture, *Egmont*. CSO CD 03-2.
Beethoven, Overture, *Fidelio*. RCA RCD1-5403, RCA 09026-68976-2, RCA 09026-60962-2
Beethoven, Symphony no. 1. RCA GD 60002
Beethoven, Symphony no. 3. RCA 09026-60962-2, RCA 74321 886 812, ARPCD 0212
Beethoven, Symphony no. 4. CSO 88/2, ARL-A44
Beethoven, Symphony no. 5. RCA RCD1-5403, RCA 09026-68976-2, RCA 74321 886 812
Beethoven, Symphony no. 6. RCA GD 60002, RCA 74321 886 812
Beethoven, Symphony no. 7. RCA GD 86532, RCA 09026-68976-2, RCA 6376-2-RC, RCA 74321 886 812
Beethoven, Symphony no. 8. CSO-CD-96B-2
Beethoven, Symphony no. 9. (P. Curtin, F. Kopleff, J. McCollum, D. Gramm, CSO Chorus) RCA GD 86532, RCA 09026-61795-2
Berlioz, Overture, *Benvenuto Cellini*. CSO 96A-2
Berlioz, Overture, *Le carnaval romain*. CSO 88/2
Berlioz, *Les nuits d'été* (L. Price) RCA 09026-61234-2
Berlioz, *Roméo et Juliette*, two exc. CSO-CD-96B-2
Borodin, Polovtsian March from *Prince Igor*. RCA 5602-2-RC, RCA 09026-61958-2
Brahms, Piano Concerto no. 1. (A. Rubinstein) RCA 5668
Brahms, Piano Concerto no. 2. (E. Gilels) RCA 60536-2-RV, EMI 7243 5 62866 2
Brahms, Piano Concerto no. 2. (V. Cliburn) RCA 5406, RCA 09026-68480-2, RCA GD 87942
Brahms, Violin Concerto. (J. Heifetz) RCA 5402, RCA 09026-61495-2
Brahms, Symphony no. 3. RCA 09026-61793-2
Brahms, Tragic Overture. RCA 5406, EMI 7243 5 62866 2
Copland, Suite, *The Tender Land*. CSO-CD-90-07
Debussy, "Nuages" from *Nocturnes*. CSO-CD-96B-2
Debussy, "Ibéria" from *Images*. RCA 5720, RCA 74321 886 922
Debussy, *La mer*. RCA RCD1-7018, RCA 09026-68079-2, RCA 74321 886 922
Delius, Prelude to *Irmelin*. CSO 96B-2
Dvořák, *Carnival* Overture. RCA 5606, RCA 09026-62587-2, RCA 61716
Dvořák, Symphony no. 9. RCA 5606, RCA 09026-62587-2
Falla, *El amor brujo*. (L. Price) RCA RCD1-5404, RCA 09026-62586-2
Falla, *El sombrero de tres picos*, three dances. RCA RCD1-5404, RCA 09026-62586-2
Falla, *La vida breve*, Interlude and Dance. RCA RCD1-5404, RCA 09026-62586-2
Glinka, *Ruslan and Ludmila* Overture. RCA 5605, RCA 09026-61958-2
Granados, Intermezzo from *Goyescas*. RCA RCD1-5404, RCA 09026-62586-2
Haydn, Symphony no. 88. RCA 09026-60729-2
Haydn, Symphony no. 104. CSO 88/2, ARL-A44
Hindemith, Cello Concerto. (J. Starker) CSO 88/2

Hovhaness, Symphony no. 2 ("Mysterious Mountain"). RCA 5733-2-RC, RCA 09026-61957-2

Kabalevsky, *Colas Breugnon* Overture. RCA 5602-2-RC

Kodály, Dances of Galánta. CSO-CD-90-07

Liszt, *Totentanz*. (B. Janis) RCA 09026-61250-2

Liszt, *Mephisto* Waltz no. 1. RCA 09026-61246-2

Mahler, Symphony no. 4. (L. Della Casa) RCA 5722-2-RC, RCA 74321-21286-2, RCA 74321 84599-2(2)

Mahler, *Das Lied von der Erde*. (M. Forrester, R. Lewis) RCA 5248, RCA 74321 84599-2(2)

Mendelssohn, Symphony no. 4. ARLA-83

Mendelssohn, Overture, *The Hebrides*. RCA 09026-61793-2

Mozart, Overture, *Don Giovanni*. RCA 6521

Mozart, *Eine kleine Nachtmusik*. RCA 09026-62585-2

Mozart, Symphony no. 31. CSO-CD-91-2

Mozart, Symphony no. 36. EMI 7243 5 62866 2

Mozart, Symphony no. 39. RCA 09026-62585-2

Mozart, Symphony no. 40. RCA 090326-62585-2

Mozart, Symphony no. 41. RCA 6376-2-RC

Mussorgsky, *A Night on a Bare Mountain*. RCA 5602-2-RC, RCA 09026-61958-2

Mussorgsky, *Pictures at an Exhibition*. RCA RCD1-5407, RCA 09026-61401-2, RCA 09026-61958-2

Mussorgsky, Prelude to *Khovanschina*. CSO-CD-96B-2

Prokofiev, Suite, *Lieutenant Kijé*. RCA 5605, RCA 09026-61957-2

Prokofiev, Symphony no. 5. CSO-CD-90-06

Prokofiev, *Alexander Nevsky*. (R. Elias, CSO Chorus) RCA 5605

Rachmaninov, Piano Concerto no. 1. (B. Janis) RCA 09026-68762-2

Rachmaninov, Piano Concerto no. 2. (V. Cliburn) RCA 4934, RCA 09026-61961-2, RCA RD 85912

Rachmaninov, Piano Concerto no. 2. (A. Rubinstein) RCA 09026-61851-2

Rachmaninov, *The Isle of the Dead*. RCA 61250, RCA 09026-61250-2

Rachmaninov, Rhapsody on a Theme of Paganini. (A. Rubinstein) RCA 4934, RCA 09026-68886-2, RCA 09026-61851-2

Ravel, *Alborada del gracioso*. RCA 5720, RCA 74321 886 922

Ravel, *Pavane pour une infante défunte*. RCA 5720, RCA 09026-61250-2, RCA 74321 886 922

Ravel, *Rapsodie espagnole*. RCA 5720, RCA 09026-61250-2, RCA 74321 886 922

Ravel, *La valse*. CSO-CD-90-06

Ravel, *Valses nobles et sentimentales*. RCA 5720, RCA 74321 886 922

Respighi, *Fountains of Rome*. RCA RCD1-5407, RCA 09026-61401-2, RCA 09026-68079-2

Respighi, *Pines of Rome*. RCA RCD1-5407, RCA 09026-61401-2, RCA 09026-68079-2

Rimsky-Korsakov, *Scheherazade*. RCA RCD1-7018, RCA 09026-68168-2

Rossini, Overture, *Il barbiere di Siviglia*. RCA GD 60387

Rossini, Overture, *La Cenerentola*. RCA GD 60387

Rossini, Overture, *La gazza ladra*. RCA GD 60387

Rossini, Overture, *Guillaume Tell*. RCA GD 60387

Rossini, Overture, *La scala di seta*. RCA GD 60387

Rossini, Overture, *Il Signor Bruschino*. RCA GD 60387

Rossini, Overture, *L'Italiana in Algeri*. RCA GD 60387

Satie, *Gymnopédies* nos. 1 and 3. CSO-CD-90-06

Schoenberg, *Verklärte nacht*. CSO 96A-2, ARL ARL 199

Schubert, Symphony no. 5. RCA 09026-61793-2

Schubert, Symphony no. 8. RCA RCD1-5403, RCA 74321 84607-2(2)

Schumann, Symphony no. 2. CSO 96A-2 ARL ARL 199

Schumann, Piano Concerto. (V. Cliburn) RCA 60420-2-RG, RCA 09026-62691-2

Smetana, Overture, *The Bartered Bride*. RCA 5606, RCA 09026-62587-2

Strauss, Johann the younger, *Kaiser Waltzer.* RCA 5405, RCA 09026-68160-2
Strauss, Johann the younger, Waltz, *Kunstlerleben.* RCA 5405
Strauss, Johann the younger, Waltz, *Auf dem schönen blauen Donau.* RCA 5405, RCA
09026-68160-2
Strauss, Johann the younger, Waltz, *Morgenblätter.* RCA 5405, RCA 09026-68160-2
Strauss, Johann the younger, Waltz, *Rosen aus der Süden.* RCA 5405, RCA 09026-68160-2
Strauss, Johann the younger, *Schatzwaltzer.* RCA 5405, RCA 09026-68160-2
Strauss, Johann the younger, Polka, *Donner und Blitzen.* RCA 5405, RCA 09026-68160-2
Strauss, Johann the younger, Waltz, *Wiener Blut.* RCA 5405, RCA 09026-68160-2
Strauss, Josef, Waltz, *Dorfschwalben aus Österreich.* RCA 5405, RCA 09026-68160-2
Strauss, Josef, Waltz, *Mein Lebenslauf ist Lieb und Lust.* RCA 5405
Strauss, Richard, *Till Eulenspiegels lustige Streiche.* CSO-CD-96B-2
Strauss, Richard, *Also sprach Zarathustra,* rec. 1954. RCA 09026-68638-2, RCA 5721-2-
RC, RCA 6722, RCA 09026-61494-2, RCA 09026-60930-2, RCA 7432184608-2(2),
ARPCD 0212
Strauss, Richard, *Also sprach Zarathustra,* rec. 1962. RCA CML 082, RCA 09026-68638-2
Strauss, Richard, Suite, *Le bourgeois gentilhomme.* RCA 5721-2-RC, RCA 09026-60930-
2, RCA 09026-68637-2
Strauss, Richard, *Burleske* for piano and orchestra. (B. Janis) RCA 09026-61796-2, RCA
09026-68638-2, RCA RD 85734, RCA 74321-21286-2
Strauss, Richard, *Ein Heldenleben.* RCA 09026-61494-2, RCA RD 85408, RCA
7432184608-2(2)
Strauss, Richard, *Don Juan,* rec. 1954. RCA 5722-2-RC, RCA 5408, RCA 09026-68170-2
Strauss, Richard, *Don Juan,* rec. 1960. RCA RD 85408, RCA 09026-63301-2, RCA 09026-
68170-2
Strauss, Richard, *Don Quixote.* (A. Janigro) RCA 09026-61796-2, RCA RD 85734, RCA
09026-68170-2
Strauss, Richard, *Elektra,* three exc. (I. Borkh, F. Yeend, P. Schoeffler) RCA 5603-2-RC, RCA
09026-68636-2
Strauss, Richard, *Der Rosenkavalier,* waltzes. RCA 09026-60930-2, RCA 5721-2-RC, RCA
09026-68160-2, RCA 09026-68638-2
Strauss, Richard, "Dance of the Seven Veils" and final scene from *Salome.* (I. Borkh) RCA
5603-2-RC, RCA 09026-68636-2
Strauss, Richard, *Symphonia Domestica.* RCA GD 60388, RCA 09026-68637-2
Stravinsky, Divertimento from *The Fairy's Kiss.* RCA 5733-2-RC, RCA 09026-61957-2,
RCA 7432184609-2(2)
Stravinsky, *Le chant du Rossignol.* RCA 5733-2-RC, RCA 09026-68168-2, RCA
7432184609-2(2)
Tchaikovsky, "Marche miniature" from Suite no. 1. RCA 09026-61958-2, RCA 5602-2-RC
Tchaikovsky, Violin Concerto. (J. Heifetz) RCA 1011, RCA 09026-61495-2, RCA 5602
Tchaikovsky, *1812* Overture. RCA 56542-2-RC, RCA 09026-61958-2
Tchaikovsky, *Marche slave.* RCA 5642-2-RC, RCA 09026-61958-2
Tchaikovsky, *The Nutcracker,* exc. RCA 5642-2-RC, RCA 09026-68530-2
Tchaikovsky, Piano Concerto no. 1. (E. Gilels) RCA 09026-68530-2
Tchaikovsky, Symphony no. 4. CSO-CD-3
Tchaikovsky, Symphony no. 6. RCA 5602-2-RC, RCA 09026-61246-2
Vaughan Williams, Fantasia on a Theme of Thomas Tallis. CSO 96A-2, RCA ARLA-83
Wagner, Prologue, Siegfried's Rhine Journey, and Siegfried's Funeral Music from *Götter-
dämmerung.* RCA 4738, RCA 09026-61792-2, EMI 7243 5 62866 2
Wagner, Prelude to Act 1 of *Lohengrin.* CSO 96B-2
Wagner, Overture, *Rienzi.* CSO 96A-2, ARL ARL-45
Wagner, Preludes to Acts 1 and 3, Dance of the Apprentices, and Entry of the Masters from
Die Meistersinger von Nürnberg. RCA 4738, RCA 09026-61792-2, RCA 09026-63301-2

Wagner, Good Friday Spell from Act 3 of *Parsifal*. CSO 88/2, ARL ARL-45
Wagner, Prelude and Liebestod from *Tristan und Isolde*. CSO 88/2, ARL-45
Weber, *Invitation to the Dance*. RCA 09026-61250-2, RCA 5606
Webern, Six Pieces for Orchestra, Op. 6. CSO-CD-96B-2
Weinberger, Polka and Fugue from *Schwanda the Bagpiper*. RCA 5606, RCA 090926-62587-2

Covent Garden Opera

Wagner, *Der fliegende Holländer*, exc. (K. Flagstad, H. Janssen, M. Lorenz, L. Weber) LYS 159-160, SRO-808-1, GM 1.0064
Wagner, *Parsifal*, exc. (T. Ralf, H. Janssen, L. Weber, chorus) LYS 159-160
Wagner, *Tristan und Isolde*. (K. Flagstad, S. Kalter, L. Melchior, E. List, H. Janssen) VAIA 1004-3 [Most of acts 1 and 3 of this performance are also available on EMI CHS7-64077-2], NAXOS 8.110068-70, RADIO YEARS RY 3941

Curtis Institute of Music Symphony Orchestra

Beethoven, Violin Concerto, first movement only. (O. Shumsky) BIDDULPH LAB 137
Brahms, Overture, *Academic Festival*. VAIA 1020, LYS LYS 259-260
Hofmann, Josef, *Chromaticon*. (J. Hofmann) VAIA 1020
Rubinstein, Anton, Piano Concerto no. 4. (J. Hofmann) VAIA 1020, ARCHIPEL ARPCD 0012(2CD)

Ensemble of Soloists

Bach, Brandenburg Concertos nos. 1–6. LYS 464-465

Fritz Reiner and His Symphony Orchestra

Haydn, Symphony no. 95. RCA 09026-60729-2
Haydn, Symphony no. 101. RCA 09026-60729-2

Metropolitan Opera

Bizet, *Carmen*, rec. 1953. (M. Del Monaco, F. Guarrera, F. Barbieri, H. Gueden) MCD 032.H074
Mozart, *Le nozze di Figaro*. (V. De los Angeles, N. Conner, C. Siepi, G. Valdengo) AS 1108/9, ARL-A68/70, WALHALL WLCD 0013
Mozart, *Don Giovanni*, rec. 1951. (P. Silveri, R. Resnik, L. Welitsch, E. Conley, S. Baccaloni) ARL-A75/76, WALHALL WLCD 0013
Mozart, *Don Giovanni*, exc. (L. Welitsch) SONY MH2K 62866, PREISER 90476
Strauss, Richard, *Der Rosenkavalier*, rec. 1949. (E. Steber, R. Stevens, E. Berger, G. Di-Stefano, E. List) ARL-A37/39, LYS 425-427
Strauss, Richard, *Der Rosenkavalier*, rec. 1953, exc. (A. Varnay, R. Stevens, N. Conner, E. Koreh) GALA GL 100.512 ADD
Strauss, Richard, *Elektra*, rec. 1952 (A. Varnay, S. Svanholm, E. Höngen, P. Schoffler) GHCD 228586, ARPCD 01492
Strauss, Richard, *Salome*, final scene. (L. Welitsch) SONY MH2K 62866, PREISER 90476
Strauss, Richard, *Salome*, rec. 1949. (L. Welitsch, K. Thorborg, H.'Janssen, F. Jagel) MEL CDM 27042, GEBHARDT JGCD 0013
Strauss, Richard, *Salome*, rec. 1952. (L. Welitsch, E. Hoengen, H. Hotter, S. Svanholm) MYTO MCD 952.125, H 073 (This is another Myto release.)
Verdi, *Falstaff*. (L. Albanese, R. Resnik, C. Elmo, L. Warren, G. Valdengo, G. Di Stefano) ARL 85/86, WALHALL WLCD 0012

Wagner, *Der fliegende Holländer,* rec. 1950 (A. Varnay, H. Hotter, S. Svanholm, S. Nilsson) ARL-A35/36, NAXOS 8.11018990, ARKADIA GA2041

Wagner, *Die Meistersinger von Nürnberg,* rec. 1952 (P. Schoeffler, H. Hopf, H. Janssen) ARL-A40/43, ARCHIPEL ARPCD 0065 (4CD)

NBC Symphony Orchestra

Bartók, Two Roumanian Dances. M&A 292

Copland, Clarinet Concerto. (B. Goodman) AS 628, LGD 122

Debussy, Petite Suite. M&A 292

Hindemith, *Mathis der Maler* Symphony. LYS 158

Ravel, *Le tombeau de Couperin.* M&A 292, EMI 7243 5 62866 2 (This is a studio performance of the work; the one already listed, with the same orchestra, was a broadcast— i.e., different—performance.)

Strauss, Richard, *Till Eulenspiegels lustige Streiche.* M&A 292

Strauss, Richard, "Dance of the Seven Veils" from *Salome.* LYS 259-260

New York Philharmonic–Symphony Orchestra

Bartók, Piano Concerto no. 1. (R. Serkin) AS 526, ARL-198

Bartók, *The Miraculous Mandarin Suite.* AS 526, ARL-198

Brahms, Symphony no. 2. ARL-131, NEW YORK PHILHARMONIC 9708/09

Debussy, *Prélude à l'après-midi d'un faune.* LYS 083

Debussy, "Nuages" and "Fêtes" from *Nocturnes.* PEARL 9922, LYS 083

Kodály, Variations on a Hungarian Folksong (*Peacock*) AS 526

Mussorgsky (orch. Shostakovich), *Boris Godunov,* exc. (A. Kipnis) AS 628, M&A CD-4867(1), PREISER 89166

Shostakovich, Symphony no. 6. AS 628, LGD 122

Wagner, Prelude to Act 1 of *Die Meistersinger von Nürnberg.* LYS 083

Wagner, Prelude to Act 1 of *Parsifal.* PEARL 9922, LYS 083

Philadelphia Orchestra

Wagner, Transformation music from act 1 of *Parsifal.* PHILADELPHIA ORCHESTRA CENTENNIAL COLLECTION

Pittsburgh Symphony Orchestra

Bach, Suite no. 2. (S. Caratelli) LYS 464-465, LYS 126

Bach, Fugue in G Minor. ("Little") BIDDULPH BID83069/70

Bartók, Hungarian Sketches. SONY MHK 62343

Bartók, Concerto for Orchestra. LYS 093, PEARL GEM0173

Beethoven, Symphony no. 2. LYS 126, SONY MHK 62344

Berlioz, "Rackocky" March from *Le Damnation de Faust.* LYS 259-260

Brahms, Hungarian Dances. LYS 127, PSS ARL-131

Brahms, Piano Concerto no. 1. (R. Serkin) LYS 127, PIANO LIBRARY PL 237

Debussy, "Ibéria" from *Images.* LYS 083

Falla, *El amor brujo.* (C. Brice) LYS 148, EMI 7243 5 62866 2

Gershwin, *Porgy and Bess,* a Symphonic Picture. SONY MH2K 60648, PSS LYS 259-260

Glinka, *Kamarinskaya.* SONY MHK 62343, LYS 259-260

Kabalevsky, *Colas Breugnon* Overture. SONY MHK 62343, LYS 259–260

Kodály, *Dances of Galánta.* SONY MHK 62343

Mahler, *Lieder eines fahrenden gesellen.* (C. Brice) LYS 148, BIDDULPH BID83067/8

Mozart, Symphony no. 35. SONY MHK 62344, LYS 165

Mozart, Symphony no. 40. SONY MHK 62344, LYS 165
Mussorgsky, *A Night on a Bare Mountain*. LYS 259-260
Ravel, *La valse*. LYS 259-260
Rodgers, Waltz from *Carousel*. LYS 259-260
Rossini, Overture, *Il Signor Bruschino*. LYS 259-260
Shostakovich, Symphony no. 6. LYS 093, SONY MHK 62343
Strauss, Johann the younger, Waltz, *Rosen aus der Süden*. LYS 259-260
Strauss, Johann the younger, *Schatzwalzer*. LYS 44-45
Strauss, Johann the younger, *Wiener Blut* waltz. LYS 44-45 PSS
Strauss, Richard, *Don Juan*. LYS 44-45 PSS, BIDDULPH BID83067-8
Strauss, Richard, *Don Quixote*. (G. Piatigorsky) LYS 44-45, BIDDULPH BID83067-8
Strauss, Richard, *Le bourgeois gentilhomme* suite. LYS 148, BIDDULPH BID83067-8
Strauss, Richard, *Ein Heldenleben*. LYS 158, BIDDULPH BID83067-8
Wagner, "Ride of the Valkyries" from *Die Walküre*. LYS 44-45
Wagner, Prelude to Act 1 of *Lohengrin*. LYS 44-45
Wagner, Prelude to Act 3 of *Lohengrin*. LYS 44-45 PSS
Wagner, "Forest Murmurs" from *Siegfried*. LYS 44-45
Wagner, Preludes to Acts 1 and 3, Dance of the Apprentices, and Procession of the Masters from *Die Meistersinger von Nürnberg*. LYS 44-45
Wagner, Bacchanale from *Tannhäuser*. LYS 44-45
Weiner, Divertimento no. 1 for String Orchestra. SONY MHK 62343

RCA Victor Symphony Orchestra

Beethoven, Piano Concerto no. 5. (V. Horowitz) RCA 7992, PHILIPS 456841-2, URANIA SP-4217
Bizet, *Carmen*. (R. Stevens, J. Peerce, L. Albanese, R. Merrill, Shaw Chorale) RCA 7981-2-RG
Bizet, *Carmen*, exc. MET 114CD
Gluck, *Orfeo ed Euridice*, exc. (R. Stevens) MET 114CD
Humperdinck, Dream Pantomine from *Hänsel und Gretel*. RCA 09026-61792-2
Mozart, *Le nozze di Figaro*, exc. (R. Stevens) MET 114CD
Rachmaninov, Piano Concerto no. 3. (V. Horowitz) RCA 7754, PHILIPS 456841-2
Strauss, Richard, *Der Rosenkavalier*, exc. (R. Stevens, E. Berger) MET 114CD
Strauss, Richard, *Till Eulenspiegels lustige Streiche*. EMI 7243 5 62866 2
Strauss, Richard, *Tod und Verklärung*. RCA GD 60388, RCA 74321 84608-2(2)
Wagner, Prelude to Act 3 of *Lohengrin*. RCA 09026-61792-2
Wagner, Festmarsch from Act 2 of *Tannhäuser*. RCA 09026-61792-2

Robin Hood Dell Orchestra

Brahms, Double Concerto for Violin and Violincello. (N. Milstein, G. Piatigorsky) RCA 09026-61485-2
Mendelssohn, *A Midsummer Night's Dream* (Scherzo) EMI 7243 5 62866 2
Rachmaninov, Rhapsody on a Theme of Paganini. (W. Kapell) RCA 09026-61485-2, RCA 74321 84595-2(2), RCA 68992, NAXOS 8.110692

Royal Philharmonic Orchestra

Brahms, Symphony no. 4. CHESKY CD-6

San Carlo Opera, Naples

Bizet, *Carmen*, rec. 1953 (G. Simionato, F. Corelli, U. Saverese, P. De Palma, E. Rizzieri) ARCHIPEL ARPCD 0130

San Francisco Opera

Wagner, *Die Walküre,* Act 2. (K. Flagstad, L. Lehmann, K. Meisle, L. Melchior, F. Schorr) GRA AB 78545, M&A CD 1048

Wagner, *Tristan und Isolde,* Act 2. (K. Flagstad, L. Melchior, K. Meisle) LCD-145-1

Vienna Philharmonic Orchestra

Brahms, Hungarian Dances nos. 1, 5, 6, 7, 12, 13, 19, and 21. LON 417 696, DECCA 448 568-2

Dvorak, Slavonic Dances nos. 1, 3, 8, and 10. LON 417 696-2, DECCA 448 568-2

Strauss, Richard, *Till Eulenspiegels lustige Streiche.* DECCA 448 568-2

Verdi, *Messa da Requiem.* (L. Price, R. Elias, J. Bjoerling, G. Tozzi, Gesellschaft der Musik-freunde Chorus) LON 421608, DECCA 444833, DECCA 467119

Vienna State Opera

Wagner, *Die Meistersinger von Nürnberg.* (I. Seefried, R. Anday, H. Beier, P. Schoeffler, G. Frick, M. Dickie, E. Kunz) MEL CDM-47083

Bibliography

The documentation available for Fritz Reiner's career is copious. He left extensive personal papers that include memoranda and diaries, scores and books, press clippings of his concerts, and thousands of letters. These items are mainly deposited at the Deering Music Library at Northwestern University, where they are kept in a climate-controlled Fritz Reiner Room. Some papers are included in ring binders, others in loose manila folders. The papers in ring binders usually follow a rough chronological order, sometimes with several binders available for particular years. The loose material is completely unsorted. The bulk of this material covers Reiner's years in the United States after 1922. For some reason, little is available here on his teaching at the Curtis Institute and his years at the Met. The pre-1931 papers are much thinner than those that follow Reiner's departure from Cincinnati. It seems likely that either Berta Gerster-Gardini or Carlotta Reiner removed some of this material. Very little manuscript evidence has survived from Reiner's years in Budapest, Laibach, and Dresden.

To date, the Reiner Papers at Northwestern are uncataloged. Thus material of musical significance is accompanied by all sorts of trivia—laundry bills, recipes, holiday postcards, and so on, which means that the researcher has to delve deeply to extract the nuggets of gold. Despite this limitation, this archive of personal papers is more extensive than those available for any other major conductor who worked in the United States (with the exception of the Toscanini Papers at the New York Public Library for the Performing Arts and the Koussevitzky Papers at the Library of Congress). The Deering Library at Northwestern, incidentally, has a helpful typescript list of the more than seven hundred music scores in the Reiner Collection.

The other main collection of Fritz Reiner correspondence is a much smaller set of papers housed in the Special Collections Department of Columbia University's Butler Library. It consists of approximately eighty letters written to or from composers such as Bartók, Richard Strauss, Respighi, Malipiero, and Schoenberg. There are several other smaller collections of Reiner's papers, notably at the Curtis Institute of Music in Philadelphia and in the Metropolitan Opera's archives. Correspondence concerning Reiner is also available in the Oldberg Papers at the Deering Music Library and in the Moldenhauer Archives. I have not been able to see these materials. The Oldberg Papers are currently sealed from use. The Moldenhauer Archives, which used to be housed together, are now split among various depositories: the Reiner material appears to be inaccessible. A few items in manuscript relating to Reiner have surfaced in other archives:

these are listed under the primary sources below. Some of Reiner's letters and scores were bought by private collectors after Carlotta Reiner's death in 1983.

Despite the existence of thousands of letters by or to Reiner, scholarly study of his career needs to cast its net more widely. The repertoire that he conducted can be reconstructed from programs of his concerts, which are available in the archives of the orchestras and opera companies listed under primary sources. The most difficult of these sources to research are the files of the NBC Symphony Orchestra concerts, available on microfilm at the Library of Congress, for which one needs to know the date and time of a broadcast to confirm the program information. The minutes of orchestral boards, trustees, and associations often provide incidental information. For Reiner's period in Cincinnati, there is a thorough and reliable citation of orchestral association minutes in Louis R. Thomas's "A History of the Cincinnati Symphony Orchestra to 1931" (Ph.D. dissertation, University of Cincinnati, 1972). Similar minutes are available for the New York Philharmonic and Chicago Symphony Orchestras, but comparable material for the Pittsburgh Symphony Orchestra for Reiner's period has been destroyed.

Sifting through the vast number of press notices of Reiner's career is a herculean task, but one made a little easier by the existence of scrapbooks. For Reiner's years in Cincinnati, a set of Cincinnati Symphony Orchestra scrapbooks includes the four main newspapers that covered musical events in the Queen City. These records are kept at the Cincinnati Historical Society. There is consistent coverage for the period 1922–30, but the scrapbook for 1930–31 is missing. Thomas's dissertation states that it was available at the Cincinnati Symphony Orchestra's Archives, but when I checked the holdings there the staff could not locate it. The Chicago Symphony Orchestra has deposited scrapbooks of press clippings at the Newberry Library (also available on microfilm); these are invaluable. The New York Philharmonic Archives has extensive scrapbook material, including press clippings. Reiner's papers at Northwestern University include scrapbooks with miscellaneous clippings, which are particularly useful for notices from European and South American papers when he guest conducted in cities such as Rome, Venice, Barcelona, and Buenos Aires. Though no comprehensive set of press clippings exists for the Met, a selection of such material is available on microfilm.

The location and state of press notices for other stages of Reiner's career are varied. Newspaper clippings from the *Philadelphia Record* are filed under "Reiner" at the Urban Archives Center at Temple University. The other Philadelphia newspapers are best consulted on microfilm in the city's Free Library. Material from various American newspapers can often be located among the microfilms at the Library of Congress's Newspaper Division; the coverage, though extensive, is not systematic. The Pittsburgh Symphony Orchestra does not hold scrapbooks of press clippings. However, several large boxes of completely unsorted press notices relating to the orchestra are held at the Archives of Industrial Society in the Hillman Library, University of Pittsburgh. Newspaper reports of Reiner's infrequent appearances in England can be checked at the British Library's Newspaper Division, Colindale, London.

Searching through back issues of record magazines and periodicals for critiques of Reiner's recordings would be even more time-consuming were it not for the existence of Kurtz Myers's *Index to Record Reviews*. These hefty volumes cite reviews under several headings—conductors, composers, and soloists. They cover records issued from the 78 rpm era up to 1987. For reviews of Reiner recordings reissued on CD since that date, the *CD Review Digest* is the most helpful. Culling opinions from record reviews is worthwhile even if, as with newspaper articles, one finds more dross than silver. The annual entries in *The Reader's Guide to Periodical Literature* provide helpful leads to other writings about Reiner. Articles in periodicals such as *Etude, Musical America,* and the *Mu-*

sical Courier print frequent assessments of Reiner's concert and opera performances. A wealth of relevant material is included in *The Podium: The Magazine of the Fritz Reiner Society*. Issued once or twice a year between 1976 and 1988, this magazine published appreciations of Reiner's artistry, consideration of his recordings, and biographical information as well as many interviews with musicians who performed with Reiner. A six-part radio series entitled "Reiner: The Great Leveller," independently produced by David Papp, includes a number of perceptive remarks by musicians associated with Reiner.

Interviews

Conducted and recorded by the author

Victor Aitay, Chicago, July 3, 1991
Eva Bartenstein, Zurich, June 26, 1994
Roger Dettmer, Annapolis, Md., September 11, 1993
David Diamond, New York City, July 9, 1994
Philip Farkas, Bloomington, Ind., July 15, 1992
Lukas Foss, New York City, November 10, 1994
George Gaber, Bloomington, Ind., July 15, 1992
Walter Hendl, Erie, Pa., July 11, 1992
Igor Kipnis, West Redding, Conn., July 16, 1991
Joseph Kovacs, Bloomington, Ind., July 15, 1992
John de Lancie, Paris, October 22, 1993
Abraham Marcus, Scarsdale, N.Y., August 18, 1992
Robert Mayer, Bloomington, Ind., July 15, 1992
John Pfeiffer, New York City, August 18, 1992
Ezra Rachlin, London, October 6, 1993
Max Rudolf, Philadelphia, September 10, 1993
Irving Sarin, Livonia, Mich., July 13, 1992
Leonard Sharrow, Bloomington, Ind., July 15, 1992
Jerry Sirucek, Bloomington, Ind., July 15, 1992
János Starker, Bloomington, Ind., July 15, 1992
Risë Stevens, New York City, November 9, 1994
Samuel Thaviu, Evanston, Ill., June 29, 1991
David Walter, Princeton, N.J., August 2, 1991

Manuscript Collections

Beinecke Library, Yale University
    Lawrence Gilman Collection
Boston Symphony Orchestra
    Boston Symphony Orchestra programs
Butler Library, Special Collections, Columbia University
    Columbia Oral History Collection: Saul Goodman interview
    Special Collections: Fritz Reiner Papers; Spec MS Collection Belmont; Spec MS Collection
        Spanish Refugee; Spec MS Correspondence Berezowsky; MS Coll Antheil
Cincinnati Historical Society
    Cincinnati Symphony Orchestra scrapbooks
Cincinnati Symphony Orchestra Archives
    Cincinnati Symphony Orchestra program books
Cleveland Orchestra
    Cleveland Orchestra programs

Curtis Institute of Music, Philadelphia
  File on Fritz Reiner
  Philadelphia Grand Opera programs, 1931–33
  Philadelphia Orchestra programs
Deering Library, Northwestern University
  Fritz Reiner Collection: files, scrapbooks, memoranda, diaries, recording contracts, press
    releases, correspondence
Detroit Symphony Orchestra
  Detroit Symphony Orchestra programs
  Ford Sunday Evening Hour programs
Dresden Semperoper
  Theaterzettel
Dresden Stadtarchiv
  Königlich Sächsische Hoftheater zu Dresden: Ruckblick
    Theaterzettel
EMI Archives, Hayes
  Artists' contract forms and correspondence
Hillman Library, University of Pittsburgh
  Archives of Industrial Society: boxes of Pittsburgh Symphony Orchestra scrapbooks, press
    clippings, and programs
Library of Congress
  Babin Papers
  Coolidge Collection
  George Antheil Collection
  Koussevitzky Collection
  NBC Symphony Orchestra programs (microfilm)
  Percy A. Grainger Correspondence
Los Angeles Philharmonic Association
  Hollywood Bowl programs
  Los Angeles Philharmonic Orchestra programs
Metropolitan Opera Archives, New York City
  Artists' contract forms
  File on Fritz Reiner
  Press releases
National Széchényi Library, Budapest
  Magyar Szinpad
  Népopera playbills
  Posters of concerts, recitals, and operas
The Newberry Library, Chicago
  Chicago Symphony Orchestra scrapbooks
New York Philharmonic Archives
  Executive Committee and Board minutes
  Fritz Reiner letters
  Stadium concerts review programs
New York Public Library for the Performing Arts, Lincoln Center
  Alexander Smallens Papers
  Arturo Toscanini Collection
  Artur Rodzinski Papers
  Fritz Reiner scrapbooks, 1948–57 (microfilm)
  Mss filed under "MNY"
  Walter Damrosch Papers
  William Schuman Papers

Pittsburgh Symphony Orchestra
  Pittsburgh Symphony Orchestra programs
Rochester Philharmonic Orchestra
  Rochester Philharmonic Orchestra programs
Rosenthal Archives, Chicago Symphony Orchestra
  Agreements between Fritz Reiner and the Orchestral Association
  Correspondence with Fritz Reiner
  Orchestral Association minutes
Sächsische Landesbibliothek, Dresden
  Dresden Semperoper's programmhefte
  Sinfoniekonzerte programs at the Dresden Semperoper
San Francisco Performing Arts Library and Museum
  Biographical file on Fritz Reiner
  San Francisco Opera Archives
  San Francisco Opera Company programs
  San Francisco Symphony Orchestra programs
Springate Corporation, New York City
  Correspondence between Fritz Reiner and Leonard Bernstein
Sterling Memorial Library, Yale University
  Goddard Lieberson Papers
Teatro dell'Opera, Rome
  Concert programs
Urban Archives Center, Temple University, Philadelphia
  Philadelphia newspaper clippings

Published Sources

"Adolph Herseth Interviewed." *The Podium: Magazine of the Fritz Reiner Society* (Fall/Winter 1981): 7–15.

Albrecht, Otto E., with Nina Davis-Miller. "Philadelphia." In *The New Grove Dictionary of Opera.* Vol. 3. Ed. Stanley Sadie. London: Macmillan, 1992. 991–42.

Altman, Allan. "*Tristan und Isolde* at Covent Garden, 1936." Liner notes for Richard Wagner, *Tristan und Isolde.* VAIA 1004-3.

Antheil, George. *Bad Boy of Music.* Garden City, N.Y.: Doubleday, Doran, and Co., 1945.

Ardoin, John. *The Furtwängler Record.* Portland, Ore.: Amadeus Press, 1994.

Arias, Enrique Alberto. "The Chicago Symphony Orchestra." In *Symphony Orchestras of the United States: Selected Profiles.* Ed. Robert R. Craven. Westport, Conn.: Greenwood, 1986. 110–18.

Arkatov, James. *Masters of Music: Great Artists at Work.* Santa Barbara, Calif.: Capra Press, 1990.

Asbell, Bernard. "Claudia Cassidy: The Queen of Culture and Her Reign of Terror." *Chicago* 3 (June 1956): 22–29.

Ashbrook, William. "Nelson Eddy's Career in Opera." *Opera Quarterly* 13.3 (Spring 1997): 7–18.

Axelrod, Herbert R. *Heifetz.* 2d rev. ed. Neptune City, N.J.: Paganiniana Publications, 1981.

Az Országos M.Kir. Zeneakadémia Évkönyve. Budapest: Franz Liszt Academy of Music, 1903–9.

Balogh, Erno. "Bartók in America." *Long Player* 2 (October 1953): 18–23.

Barnouw, Erik. *The Golden Web: A History of Broadcasting in the United States.* Vol. 2, *1933 to 1953.* New York: Oxford University Press, 1968.

Bauman, Thomas, and Dieter Härtwig. "Dresden." In *The New Grove Dictionary of Opera.* Vol. 1. London: Macmillan, 1992. 1246–53.

Beckett, Lucy. *Richard Wagner: Parsifal.* Cambridge: Cambridge University Press, 1981.

Benko, Gregor. "The Incomparable Josef Hofmann." *International Piano Quarterly* 2.7 (1999): 12–22.

Benser, Caroline Cepin, and David Francis Urrows. *Randall Thompson: A Bio-Bibliography.* Westport, Conn.: Greenwood Press, 1991.

Beranek, Leo L. *Music, Acoustics, and Architecture.* New York: Wiley, 1962.

Berlász, Melinda. "Néhany dokumentum Weiner Leó tanári muködésének utolsó Idoszakából." In *A Liszt Ferenc Zenemuveszeti Foiskola 100 Éve.* Ed. József Ujfalussy. Budapest: Zenemukiadó, 1977. 222–38.

Bernstein, Leonard. *Findings.* London: MacDonald and Co., 1982.

———. "Memories of the Curtis Institute." *The Podium: Magazine of the Fritz Reiner Society* (Spring/Summer 1983): 6–12.

Biancolli, Louis. *The Flagstad Manuscript.* New York: Putnam, 1953.

Bing, Sir Rudolf. *Five Thousand Nights at the Opera.* Garden City, N.Y.: Doubleday and Co., 1972.

———. *A Knight at the Opera.* New York: J. P. Putnam's Sons, 1981.

Bloom, Julius, ed. *The Year in American Music, 1946–1947.* New York: Allen, Towne, and Heath, 1947.

Bloom, Robert. Liner notes for *Divertimento No. 11 en ré majeur, K. 251, pour cordes, hautbois et deux cors.* RCA France GM 43558.

Bloomfield, Arthur. *The San Francisco Opera, 1922–1978.* Sausalito, Calif.: Comstock Editions, 1978.

Blyth, Alan, ed. *Opera on Record 2.* London: Hutchinson, 1983.

———. *Opera on Record 3.* London: Hutchinson, 1984.

Bónis, Ferenc. "Fritz Reiner—An Early Bartók Conductor." *New Hungarian Quarterly* 17 (1976): 218–20.

Botstein, Leon. "Out of Hungary: Bartók, Modernism, and the Cultural Politics of Twentieth-Century Music." In *Bartók and His World.* Ed. Peter Laki. Princeton, N.J.: Princeton University Press, 1995. 3–63.

Boult, Adrian C. *Boult on Music: Words from a Lifetime's Communication.* London: Toccata Press, 1983.

———. *Thoughts on Conducting.* London: Phoenix House, 1963.

Bowen, José A. "Finding the Music in Musicology: Performance History and Musical Works." In *Rethinking Music.* Ed. Nicholas Cook and Mark Everist. Oxford: Oxford University Press, 1999. 424–51.

———. "The History of Remembered Innovation: Tradition and Its Role in the Relationship between Musical Works and Their Performances." *Journal of Musicology* 11 (1993): 139–73.

———. "Mendelssohn, Berlioz, and Wagner as Conductors: The Origins of the Ideal of 'Fidelity to the Composer.'" *Performance Practice Review* 6 (1993): 77–88.

———. "Performance Practice versus Performance Analysis: Why Should Performers Study Performance?" *Performance Practice Review* 9 (1996): 16–35.

———. "Tempo, Duration, and Flexibility: Techniques in the Analysis of Performance." *Journal of Musicological Research* 16.2 (July 1996): 111–56.

Boyd, Malcolm. *Bach: The Brandenburg Concertos.* Cambridge: Cambridge University Press, 1993.

Briggs, John. *Leonard Bernstein: The Man, His Work, and His World.* Cleveland: World Publishing Co., 1961.

———. *Requiem for a Yellow Brick Brewery: A History of the Metropolitan Opera.* Boston: Little, Brown, 1969.

Brinkmann, Reinhold. *Late Idyll: The Second Symphony of Johannes Brahms.* Trans. Peter Palmer. Cambridge, Mass.: Harvard University Press, 1995.

Broder, Nathan. *Samuel Barber.* New York: Schirmer, 1954.

Brown, Clive. *Classical and Romantic Performing Practice, 1750–1900.* Oxford: Oxford University Press, 1999.

Brown, Jonathan. *Parsifal on Record: A Discography of Complete Recordings, Selections, and Excerpts of Wagner's Music Drama.* Westport, Conn.: Greenwood Press, 1992.

Broyles, Michael. *Beethoven: The Emergence and Evolution of Beethoven's Heroic Style.* New York: Excelsior Music Publishing Co., 1987.

Burton, Humphrey. *Leonard Bernstein.* New York: Faber, 1994.

Burton, William Westbrook, ed. *Conversations about Bernstein.* New York: Oxford University Press, 1995.

Busch, Fritz. *Pages from a Musician's Life.* London: Hogarth Press, 1953.

Caamaño, Roberto. *La historia del Teatro Colón, 1908–1968.* 3 vols. Buenos Aires: Editorial Cinetea, 1969.

Canarina, John. "A Conductor for All Repertoire." Liner notes for *The Pierre Monteux Edition.* 15 CDs. RCA 09026 618932.

Caratelli, Sebastian. *A Musician's Odyssey.* New York: Vantage Press, 1983.

Cassidy, Claudia. "Fritz Reiner and His Magic Baton."

Chapin, Schuyler. *Musical Chairs: A Life in the Arts.* New York: Putnam, 1977.

Chesterman, Robert, ed. *Conversations with Conductors.* London: Robson Books, 1976.

Ciampelli, G. M. *Ente Concerti orchestrali Sei Anni di Vita Milano, 1924–1929.* Milan: Arti Grafiche dino Grossi, 1929.

Clark, Sedgwick. "Frank Miller: Inspiring Presence of the Chicago Symphony." *Keynote* 9.3 (May 1985): 18–23.

Cohn, Arthur. *Recorded Classical Music: A Critical Guide to Compositions and Performances.* New York: Schirmer, 1981.

Commanday, Robert. "Philadelphia." In *The New Grove Dictionary of Opera.* Vol. 4. Ed. Stanley Sadie. London: Macmillan, 1992. 164–67.

"Conductors' Guild Holds 'Reiner Retrospective.'" *The Podium: Magazine of the Fritz Reiner Society* (Spring/Summer 1988): 7–31.

Cone, Edward T. "The Pianist as Critic." In *The Practice of Performance: Studies in Musical Interpretation.* Ed. John Rink. Cambridge: Cambridge University Press, 1995.

Cook, Nicholas. *Beethoven: Symphony no. 9.* Cambridge: Cambridge University Press, 1993.

———. "The Conductor and the Theorist: Furtwängler, Schenker, and the First Movement of Beethoven's Ninth Symphony." In *The Practice of Performance: Studies in Musical Interpretation.* Ed. John Rink. Cambridge: Cambridge University Press, 1995. 105–25.

Cooper, David. *Bartók: Concerto for Orchestra.* Cambridge: Cambridge University Press, 1996.

Copland, Aaron, and Vivian Perlis. *Copland since 1943.* New York: St. Martin's Press, 1989.

Cowan, Robert. Liner notes for *Koussevitzky Conducts Schubert, Mendelssohn, Schumann.* Pearl GEMM CD 9037.

———. "Living Stereo." *Gramophone* 70.839 (April 1993): 20–21.

Craft, Robert. *Stravinsky: Chronicle of a Friendship.* Rev. and expanded ed. Nashville: Vanderbilt University Press, 1994.

———, ed. *Stravinsky: Selected Correspondence.* Vols. 2 and 3. London: Faber and Faber, 1984–85.

Craven, Robert R. *Symphony Orchestras of the World: Selected Profiles.* New York: Greenwood Press, 1987.

Crichton, Kyle. *Subway to the Met: Risë Stevens' Story.* Garden City, N.Y.: Doubleday, 1959.

Cronache del Teatro di S. Carlo 1948–1968. Naples: Edizioni del San Carlo, 1969.

Csáth, Géza. *Éjszakai Esztetizálás: 1906–1912 Zenei Évadjai.* Ed. János Demény. Budapest: Zenem kiado, 1971.

Culshaw, John. *Putting the Record Straight.* London: Secker and Warburg, 1981.

———. *Ring Resounding.* New York: Viking Press, 1967.

Daniel, Oliver. *Stokowski: A Counterpoint of View.* New York: Dodd, Mead, and Co., 1982.

Daniels, Robin. *Conversations with Menuhin.* New York: St. Martin's Press, 1980.

Davis, Ronald L. *Opera in Chicago.* New York: Appleton-Century, 1966.

Del Mar, Norman. *Conducting Beethoven.* Vol. 1, *The Symphonies.* Oxford: Oxford University Press, 1992.

———. *Conducting Brahms.* Oxford: Clarendon Press, 1993.

Demény, János, ed. "Bartók Béla és a Zeneakadémia." In *A Liszt Ferenc Zenemuvészeti Foiskola 100 Éve.* József Ujfalussy. Budapest: Zenemukiadó, 1977. 130–43.

———. *Bartók Béla Levelei.* Budapest: Zenemukiadó, 1951.

———. *Béla Bartók Letters.* Trans. Péter Balabán and István Farkas; trans. rev. Elisabeth West and Colin Mason. New York: St. Martin's Press, 1971.

Dettmer, Roger. "Fritz Reiner."

———. "Fritz Reiner, 1888–1963." *Musical America* 83.12 (December 1963): 272–73.

———. "Kaviar für Volk." *The Podium: Magazine of the Fritz Reiner Society* (Spring 1981): 18–21.

———. Liner notes for Bela Bartók, *Music for Strings, Percussion, and Celesta* and *Hungarian Sketches.* Chicago Symphony Orchestra. Fritz Reiner. RCA LSC-2374.

———. Liner notes for *Chicago Symphony Orchestra: From the Archives, Vol. 1: The Reiner Era.* CSO 86/2.

———. Liner notes for Ottorino Respighi, *The Fountains of Rome* and *The Pines of Rome* RCA SB-2103.

———. "The Reign of Reiner." *Chicago Sunday Tribune,* September 11, 1994.

———. "Reiner." *Fanfare* 5.2 (November–December 1981): 60–69; reprinted with amendments as the liner notes for *The Art of Fritz Reiner.* M&A CD-292.

———. "Reiner Remembered." *Chicago Tribune,* November 27, 1988, Arts Section, 12–13, 27.

———. "Reiner Retires." *Musical America* 83.7 (July 1963): 12–13.

———. "Return of Reiner." *Musical America* 81.6 (June 1961): 20–21.

———. "Symphonic Strife." *Musical America* 82.7 (July 1962): 12–13.

Dizikes, John. *Opera in America: A Cultural History.* New Haven, Conn.: Yale University Press, 1993.

Dorati, Antal. *Notes of Seven Decades.* Rev. ed. Detroit: Wayne State University Press, 1981.

Dorian, Frederick, and Judith Meibach. *A History of the Pittsburgh Symphony Orchestra.* Pittsburgh: Music and Art Department, Carnegie Library, 1987.

Drake, James A. *Richard Tucker: A Biography.* New York: Dutton, 1984.

Eaton, Quaintance. "*Der Rosenkavalier* Is Viewed by Vast Television Audience." *Musical America* 69.15 (December 1949): 4.

———. *The Miracle of the Met: An Informal History of the Metropolitan Opera, 1883–1967.* New York: Meredith Press, 1968.

———. *Opera Caravan: Adventures of the Metropolitan on Tour, 1883–1956.* New York: Farrar, Straus, and Cudahy, 1957.

———. "An Opera Production in the Making: How Strauss' *Salome* Grew from Early Rehearsals to Successful Performance at the Metropolitan." *Musical America* 69.3 (February 1949): 4–5, 138, 156, 160, 298–99.

Eckman, Fern Marja. "The Leonard Bernstein Story." *New York Post,* June 3, 1960.

Emmons, Shirlee. *Tristanissimo: The Authorized Biography of Heroic Tenor Lauritz Melchior.* New York: Schirmer Books, 1990.

Eosze, Laslo. *Zoltán Kodály: His Life and Work.* Boston: Crescendo Publishing Co., 1962.

Erskine, John. *The Philharmonic-Symphony Society of New York: Its First Hundred Years.* New York: Macmillan, 1943.

Ewen, David. *Dictators of the Baton.* Chicago: Alliance Book Corporation, 1943.

———. *Living Musicians.* New York: H. W. Wilson Co., 1940.

———. *Musicians since 1900: Performers in Concert and Opera.* New York: H. W. Wilson Co., 1978.

Fassett, Agatha. *Béla Bartók's Last Years: The Naked Face of Genius.* Boston: Houghton Mifflin, 1958.

Fellers, Frederick P. *The Metropolitan Opera on Record: A Discography of the Commercial Recordings.* Westport, Conn.: Greenwood Press, 1984.

Fitzgerald, Gerald. *Annals of the Metropolitan Opera.* 2 vols. Boston: G. K. Hall, 1989.

Foreman, Lewis. *Bax: A Composer and His Times.* London: Scolar Press, 1983.

Foster, Donald H. "Cincinnati Symphony Orchestra." In *Symphony Orchestras of the United States: Selected Profiles.* Ed. Robert R. Craven. Westport, Conn.: Greenwood Press, 1986. 299–305.

Frajese, Vittorio. *Dal Costanzi All'Opera.* Rome: Capitolium, 1977.

"Frank Miller (1912–1986)." *The Podium: Magazine of the Fritz Reiner Society* (Spring/Summer 1986): 7–16.

Frederiksen, Brian. *Arnold Jacobs: Song and Wind.* Ed. John Taylor. [United States]: Wind Song Press, 1996.

Freed, Richard. "A Feast of Reiner CDs from RCA." *Opus* 2 (1986): 32–33, 61.

———. "A Golden Age Deferred." *Classic Record Collector* 24 (Spring 2001): 12–21.

———. Liner notes for Wolfgang Amadeus Mozart, *Symphony no. 40.* Chicago Symphony Orchestra. Fritz Reiner. RCA CD 09026 62585 2.

Freedland, Michael. *Leonard Bernstein.* London: Harrap, 1987.

"Fritz Reiner." *Current Biography* 2.4 (April 1941): 74–76.

"Fritz Reiner Remembered." *The Podium: Magazine of the Fritz Reiner Society.* 1.1 (1976): 12–16.

"Fritz Reiner Remembered/II." *The Podium: Magazine of the Fritz Reiner Society.* 1.2 (1977): 15–20.

"FRS Centenary Tape Features Reiner's Earliest Recordings." *The Podium: Magazine of the Fritz Reiner Society* (Spring/Summer 1988): 5–6.

Furlong, William Barry. *Season with Solti: A Year in the Life of the Chicago Symphony.* London: Macmillan, 1974.

Galkin, Elliott W. *A History of Orchestral Conducting.* New York: Pendragon Press, 1988.

Gelatt, Roland. *The Fabulous Phonograph, 1877–1977.* 2d rev. ed. New York: Macmillan, 1977.

Gerson, Robert A. *Music in Philadelphia.* Philadelphia: Theodore Presser Co., 1940.

Gillies, Malcolm. "The Teacher." In *The Bartók Companion.* Ed. Malcolm Gillies. London: Faber, 1994. 79–88.

Glass, Beaumont. *Lotte Lehmann: A Life in Opera and Song.* Santa Barbara, Calif.: Capra Press, 1988.

Goldovsky, Boris. *My Road to Opera.* Boston: Houghton Mifflin Co., 1979.

Goossens, Eugene. *Overture and Beginners: A Musical Autobiography.* London: Methuen, 1951.

Gould, Morton. "Artist's Life." *Keynote* 12.10 (December 1988): 21.

Gradenwitz, Peter. *Leonard Bernstein: The Infinite Variety of a Musician.* New York: St. Martin's Press, 1987.

Graf, Herbert. *The Opera and Its Future in America.* New York: W. W. Norton, 1941.

———. *Opera for the People.* Minneapolis: University of Minnesota Press, 1951.

———. *Producing Opera for America.* New York: Atlantis Books, 1961.

Graffman, Gary. *I Really Should Be Practicing.* Garden City, N.Y.: Doubleday, 1981.

Grange, Henry-Louis de la. *Mahler.* Vol. 1. London: Victor Gollancz, 1976.

Grant, Mark N. *Maestros of the Pen: A History of Classical Music Criticism in America.* Boston: Northeastern University Press, 1998.

Gray, Michael H. "The Pines of Rome: A Pressing Story." *The Absolute Sound* 12.49 (1987): 64.

———. "Recording Reiner—RCA and the First Stereo Years." *The Absolute Sound* 12.49 (1987): 46–63.

———. "Reiner: The Sound of the Chesky Re-issues." *The Absolute Sound* 12.49 (1987): 64–65.

Green, London. "Weitsch's Salome, Lehmann's Marschallin, Pauly's Elektra." *Opera Quarterly* 15.3 (Summer 1999): 401–13.

Griffiths, Paul. *Bartók*. London: J. M. Dent, 1984.

Gronow, Pekka, and Ilpo Saunio. *An Illustrated History of the Recording Industry*. London: Cassell, 1998.

Gruber, Paul, ed. *The Metropolitan Opera Guide to Recorded Opera*. New York: W. W. Norton, 1993.

Gruen, John. *Menotti: A Biography*. New York: Macmillan, 1978.

———. *The Private World of Leonard Bernstein*. London: Weidenfeld and Nicolson, 1968.

Guthrie, Tyrone. *A Life in the Theatre*. New York: McGraw-Hill, 1959.

Guthrie-Treadway, Gertrude. "Fritz Reiner, Symphony Conductor, Tells of His Early Experiences in Interview." *Cincinnati Enquirer*, September 25, 1927.

Gwiasda, Karl E. "Chicago Symphony Orchestra Popular and Special Concerts, 1953–1962." Typescript. The Fritz Reiner Society, December 1981.

Haggin, B. H. *Music on Records*. New York: A. A. Knopf, 1943.

Hailey, Christopher. *Franz Schreker, 1878–1934: A Cultural Biography*. Cambridge: Cambridge University Press, 1993.

Hamilton, David. "*Le nozze di Figaro* at the Met: A Brief History." Liner notes for *Great Operas at the Met: "Le nozze di Figaro."* MET504–CD.

———. "Recordings: *Tristan und Isolde*. Richard Wagner." *Opera Quarterly* 9.3 (Spring 1993): 162–67.

Harrison, Jay S. "Return of Reiner." *Musical America* 83.10 (October 1963): 12–13.

Hart, Philip. "Chicago Symphony Orchestra, from the Archives, Volumes I and II." *ARSC Journal* 19.2–3 (February 1989): 129–35.

———. *Fritz Reiner, A Biography*. Evanston, Ill.: Northwestern University Press, 1994.

———. "Fritz Reiner, December 19, 1888–November 15, 1963." *Opera News*, December 14, 1963, 29.

———. "Fritz Reiner—The Man with the Vest-Pocket Beat." *Keynote* 12.10 (December 1988): 8–12.

———. "How Fritz Reiner Came to Chicago: New Evidence from the Reiner Collection." *The Podium: Magazine of the Fritz Reiner Society* (Fall/Winter 1988): 7–10.

———. *Orpheus in the New World: The Symphony Orchestra as an American Cultural Institution*. New York: W. W. Norton, 1973.

———. "Recent Fritz Reiner Compact Discs." *ARSC Journal* 28.2 (Fall 1997): 248–54.

———. "Reiner in Chicago." *High Fidelity* 14.4 (April 1964): 42–46, 126.

———. "Toward a Reiner Discography." *ARSC Journal* 19.1 (May 1988): 63–70.

———. "Underground Reiner" and "New Reiner CDs." *ARSC Journal* 20.2 (Fall 1989): 209–16.

Hartmann, Rudolf. *Richard Strauss: The Staging of His Operas and Ballets*. Oxford: Phaidon, 1982.

Helmbrecht, Arthur J. "Carlotta Reiner: A Loving Remembrance." *The Podium: Magazine of the Fritz Reiner Society* (Fall/Winter 1983): 28–32.

———. "Fritz Reiner: The Comprehensive Discography of His Recordings." Typescript. The Fritz Reiner Society, 1978 and 1981.

Henderson, J. Tamblyn. "The Golden Age of Recording: Harold Lawrence and Mercury Living Presence." *The Absolute Sound* 8.29 (1983): 102–8.

Henschel, Horst, and Erhard Friedrich. *Elisabeth Rethberg: Ihr Leben und Künstlertum*. Schwarzenberg: Stadtischer Geschichtsverein, 1928.

Heyman, Barbara B. *Samuel Barber: The Composer and His Music*. Oxford: Oxford University Press, 1992.

Heyworth, Peter, ed. *Conversations with Klemperer*. Rev. ed. London: Faber and Faber, 1985.

———. *Otto Klemperer: His Life and Times*. Vol. 2, *1933–1973*. Cambridge: Cambridge University Press, 1996.

Hillyer, Stephen C. "Barber as Conductor." *The Podium: Magazine of the Fritz Reiner Society* (Fall/Winter 1981): 16–17.

———. "Chicago Symphony Orchestra Subscription Concerts, 1953–1963." Typescript. The Fritz Reiner Society, December 1981.

———. "Cincinnati Symphony Orchestra Programs, 1922–31." Typescript. The Fritz Reiner Society, 1989.

———. "NU Launches Reiner Collection." *The Podium: Magazine of the Fritz Reiner Society* (Fall/Winter 1983): 6–8.

———. "Pittsburgh Symphony Concerts, 1938–1948." Typescript. The Fritz Reiner Society, 1985.

———. "The Sound and Sense of Divided Seating." *The Podium: Magazine of the Fritz Reiner Society* (Spring 1981): 22–24.

Hitchcock, H. Wiley, and Stanley Sadie, eds. *The New Grove Dictionary of American Music.* 4 vols. London: Macmillan, 1986.

Holmes, John L. *Conductors: A Record Collector's Guide, Including Compact Discs.* London: Victor Gollancz, 1988.

———. *Conductors on Record.* Westport, Conn.: Greenwood Press, 1982.

Höntsch, Winfried, and Ursula Puschel, eds. *300 Jahre Dresdner Staatstheater.* Berlin: Henschelverlag Kunst und Gesellschaft, 1967.

Horowitz, Joseph. *Understanding Toscanini.* New York: Alfred A. Knopf, 1987.

Hudson, Richard. *Stolen Time: A History of Tempo Rubato.* Oxford: Clarendon Press, 1994.

Hughes, Spike. *The Toscanini Legacy: A Critical Study of Arturo Toscanini's Performances of Beethoven, Verdi, and other Composers.* 2d enlarged ed. New York: Dover Publications, 1969.

Humphrey, Martha Burnham. *An Eye for Music.* Boston: H. M. Teich, 1949.

Hunt, John. *Hungarians in Exile: Reiner, Dorati, Szell.* Exeter: Short Run Press, 1997.

"An Interview with Clark Brody." *The Podium: Magazine of the Fritz Reiner Society* (Fall/Winter 1982): 8–18.

"An Interview with Donald Peck/I." *The Podium: Magazine of the Fritz Reiner Society* 3 (1979): 6–14.

"An Interview with Donald Peck/II." *The Podium: Magazine of the Fritz Reiner Society* (Autumn 1980): 12–27.

"An Interview with Edward Druzinsky." *The Podium: Magazine of the Fritz Reiner Society* (Fall/Winter 1983): 15–25.

"An Interview with George Gaber." *The Podium: Magazine of the Fritz Reiner Society* (Fall/Winter 1985): 7–45.

"An Interview with Gordon Peters." *The Podium: Magazine of the Fritz Reiner Society* (Fall/Winter 1984): 8–23.

"An Interview with John S. Edwards (1912–1984)." *The Podium: Magazine of the Fritz Reiner Society* (Spring/Summer 1985): 12–23.

"An Interview with Margaret Hillis—Part 1." *The Podium: Magazine of the Fritz Reiner Society* (Spring/Summer 1983): 14–23.

"An Interview with Margaret Hillis—Part 2." *The Podium: Magazine of the Fritz Reiner Society* (Fall/Winter 1983): 33–38.

"An Interview with Morton Gould." *The Podium: Magazine of the Fritz Reiner Society* (Spring/Summer 1987): 9–21.

"An Interview with Victor Aitay." *The Podium: Magazine of the Fritz Reiner Society* (Fall/Winter 1986): 7–17.

"An Interview with Walter Hendl." *The Podium: Magazine of the Fritz Reiner Society* (Spring/Summer 1984): 11–23.

"An Interview with William Schuman." *The Podium: Magazine of the Fritz Reiner Society* (Fall/Winter 1987): 9–16.

Jablonski, Edward. *Gershwin.* Garden City, N.Y.: Doubleday, 1987.

Jablonski, Edward, and Lawrence D. Stewart. *The Gershwin Years.* Garden City, N.Y.: Doubleday, 1973.

Jackson, Paul. *Saturday Afternoons at the Old Met: The Metropolitan Opera Broadcasts, 1931–1950.* London: Duckworth, 1992.

———. *Sign-off for the Old Met: The Metropolitan Opera Broadcasts, 1950–1966.* Portland, Ore.: Amadeus, 1997.

Jacobson, Robert, ed. *Magnificence on Stage at the Met: Twenty Great Opera Productions.* New York: Simon and Schuster, 1985.

———. *Notes on the Singers.* Booklet accompanying *RCA/MET: 100 Singers 100 Years.* 6 CDs (Metropolitan Opera Guild 09026-61580-2).

———, ed. *Reverberations: Interviews with the World's Leading Musicians.* New York: W. Morrow, 1974.

Janis, Byron. Liner notes for Sergey Rachmaninov, *Piano Concertos nos. 1 and 3.* Chicago Symphony Orchestra. Fritz Reiner. RCA CD 09026-18762-2.

"János Starker Speaks about His Reiner Years." *The Podium: Magazine of the Fritz Reiner Society* 1.2 (1977): 9–14, 29–33.

"János Starker Speaks about His Reiner Years/II." *The Podium: Magazine of the Fritz Reiner Society* 2.1 (1978): 12–17.

Jefferson, Alan. *The Life of Richard Strauss.* Newton Abbot, U.K.: David and Charles, 1973.

Jones, Isabel M. *Hollywood Bowl.* New York: G. Schirmer, 1936.

Jones, Robert T. Liner notes for *Excerpts from Bizet's "Carmen."* Columbia Odyssey LP Y 32102.

"Karl Böhm (1894–1981)." *The Podium: Magazine of the Fritz Reiner Society* (Fall/Winter 1982): 5–7.

Key, Pierre. *Music Yearbook, 1925–26.* New York: Pierre Key, Inc., 1925.

———. *Pierre Key's Musical Who's Who.* New York: P. Key, Inc., 1931.

Kirsten, Dorothy. *A Time to Sing.* Garden City, N.Y.: Doubleday, 1982.

Klinger, Elizabeth Sebestyén. "Memories of Fritz Reiner as a Young Man." Typescript in the possession of Eva Bartenstein.

Kolodin, Irving. "Fritz Reiner." Liner notes for Josef Haydn, *Symphonies nos. 95 and 101.* Chicago Symphony Orchestra. Fritz Reiner. RCA Victor, LSC-2742.

———. *The Metropolitan Opera, 1883–1966: A Candid History.* New York, 1986.

———. *The Musical Life.* New York: Alfred A. Knopf, 1958.

———. *The New Guide to Recorded Music.* Garden City, N.Y.: Doubleday, 1950.

———. "Opera, American Plan." *Theatre Arts Monthly* 19.6 (June 1935): 415–25.

Koopal, Grace. *Miracle of Music: The History of the Hollywood Bowl.* Los Angeles: W. Ritchie, 1972.

Kozinn, Allan. "William Mengelberg: His Art and Tragedy." *Keynote* 10: 8–17.

Kozma, Tibor. "Ave Atque Vale—Fritz Reiner." *Opera News,* April 6, 1953, 5–6; reprinted in *The Podium: Magazine of the Fritz Reiner Society* 1.1 (1978): 10–11.

Krause, Ernst. "Im Glauze der Strauss-Oper: Fritz Busch und Karl Böhm." In *Oper in Dresden: Festschrift zur Wiedereröffnung der Semperoper.* Berlin: Henschelverlag, 1985. 73–80.

Krokover, Rosalyn. "The Pittsburgh Symphony." *High Fidelity* 7.2 (February 1957): 34–37, 119–22.

Kupferberg, Herbert. "Lukas Foss: New Found Focus for the Composer/ Conductor." *Ovation* 5.3 (April 1984): 13–17.

———. *Tanglewood.* New York: McGraw-Hill, 1976.

———. *Those Fabulous Philadelphians: The Life and Times of a Great Orchestra.* New York: C. Scribner's Sons, 1969.

Lancie, John de. "Im Gesprach mit Richard Strauss." *Richard Strauss-Blatter* 11 (June 1984): 36–42.

———. "Orchestral Malaise: The Corporate Sound." *American Record Guide* 57.5 (September/October 1994): 6–8, 10–12, 14, 16.

Laux, Karl. *The Dresden Staatskapelle.* Leipzig: Veb Edition, 1964.

Lawrence, Robert. *A Rage for Opera: Its Anatomy as Drawn from Life.* New York: Dodd, Mead, 1971.

———. *The World of Opera.* New York: T. Nelson, 1956.

Lebrecht, Norman. *When the Music Stops: Managers, Maestros, and the Corporate Murder of Classical Music.* London: Simon and Schuster, 1996.

Leinsdorf, Erich. *Cadenza: A Musical Career.* Boston: Houghton Mifflin, 1976.

Leiter, Robert D. *The Musicians and Petrillo.* New York: Bookman Associates, 1953.

Levant, Oscar. *The Memoirs of an Amnesiac.* New York: G. P. Putnam's Sons, 1965.

———. *A Smattering of Ignorance.* New York: Doubleday, Doran, and Co., 1940.

Levin, Sylvan. "Reiner and Stokowski—Plus Sylvan Levin; or, Between the Devil and the Deep Blue Sea; or, When Is a Conductor Not a Conductor?" *Maestrino* 1.2 (October 1984): 7–10.

Levine, Joseph. "Behind the Downbeat." *Emerson Flute Forum* 4.3 (Autumn 1987): 1–2.

Levy, Alan. *The Bluebird of Happiness: The Memoirs of Jan Peerce.* New York: Harper and Row, 1976.

Levy, David B. "The Contrabass Recitative in Beethoven's Ninth Symphony Revisited." *Historical Performance* 5.1 (1992): 9–18.

Levy, Janet M. "Beginning-Ending Ambiguity: Consequences of Performance Choices." In *The Practice of Performance: Studies in Musical Interpretation.* Ed. John Rink. Cambridge: Cambridge University Press, 1995. 150–69.

Library of Welte-Mignon Music Records. New York: De Luxe Reproducing Roll Corp., 1927.

Linkowski, Allen. "Chicago Symphony in Concert." *American Record Guide* 59 (September/October 1996): 228–29.

A Liszt Ferenc Zenemuvészeti Foiskola oktatói: 1875–1975. Budapest, 1975.

Lukacs, John. *Budapest 1900: A Historical Portrait of a City and Its Culture.* London: Weidenfeld and Nicolson, 1988.

Luten, C. J. "Astrid Varnay." Liner notes for RCA Soria Series. MET 9.

MacDonald, Hugh. "To Repeat or Not to Repeat?" *Proceedings of the Royal Musical Association* 111 (1984–85): 122–38.

Mann, William. *Richard Strauss: A Critical Study of the Operas.* New York: Oxford University Press, 1966.

March, Ivan, Edward Greenfield, and Robert Layton. *The Penguin Guide to Compact Discs and Cassettes.* Harmondsworth: Penguin Books, 1992.

Marek, George R. *Toscanini.* London: Vision, 1976.

Marinelli, Carlo. *Opere in Disco da Monteverdi a Berg.* Florence: Discanto edizioni, 1982.

Marrissen, Michael. "Performance Practice Issues That Affect Meaning in Selected Bach Instrumental Works." Unpublished paper.

———. *The Social and Religious Designs of J. S. Bach's Brandenburg Concertos.* Princeton, N.J.: Princeton University Press, 1995.

Marsh, Robert C. *Dialogues and Discoveries: James Levine, His Life and His Music.* New York: Scribner, 1998.

———. "Fritz Reiner's Parting Shot." *The Podium: Magazine of the Fritz Reiner Society* (Fall/Winter 1984): 6–7.

———. "Kubelik and the Thomas Tradition." Liner notes for *Chicago Symphony Orchestra: The Kubelik Legacy.* Vol. 1. Mercury MG 3-4500.

———. Liner notes for Ludwig van Beethoven, *Symphony no. 9* (1994). Chicago Symphony Orchestra. Fritz Reiner. BMG Classics CD 09026 617952.

———. Liner notes for *Reiner Conducts Wagner* (1994). BMG Classics CD 0 9026 617922.

———. "A Recluse on the Road." Carnegie Hall Program (1965).

Marshall, Robert L. *The Music of Johann Sebastian Bach: The Sources, the Style, the Significance.* New York: Schirmer Books, 1989.

Matheopoulos, Helena. *Maestro: Encounters with Conductors of Today.* London: Hutchinson, 1982.

Mayer, Martin. "Dr. Reiner's Orchestra." *High Fidelity* 10.2 (February 1960): 38–41, 110–13.

———. *The Met: One Hundred Years of Grand Opera*. New York: Simon and Schuster, 1983.

McArthur, Edwin. *Flagstad: A Personal Memoir*. New York: A. A. Knopf, 1965.

McGovern, Dennis, and Deborah Grace Winer. *I Remember Too Much: Eighty-Nine Opera Stars Speak Candidly of Their Work, Their Lives, and Their Colleagues*. New York: Morrow, 1990.

McKee, David. "Recordings: Elektra (1909)." *Opera Quarterly* 15.3 (Summer 1999): 479–503.

Mercer, Ruby. *The Tenor of His Time: Edward Johnson of the Met*. Toronto: Clarke, Irwin, 1976.

Merrill, Robert, with Sandford Dody. *Once More from the Beginning*. New York: Macmillan, 1965.

Millard, Andre. *America on Record*. Cambridge: Cambridge University Press, 1995.

Mohr, Richard. Liner notes for Josef Haydn, *Symphonies nos. 95 and 101*. Chicago Symphony Orchestra. Fritz Reiner. RCA Victor, LSC-2742.

———. Liner notes for Ludwig van Beethoven, *Piano Concerto no. 4*. Chicago Symphony Orchestra. Fritz Reiner. RCA Victor, LSC-2680.

———. Liner notes for Nikolai Rimsky-Korsakov, *Scheherazade*. Chicago Symphony Orchestra. Fritz Reiner. RCA Victor LSC-2446.

Mordden, Ethan. *Broadway Babies*. New York: Oxford University Press, 1983.

———. *A Guide to Opera Recordings*. New York: Oxford University Press, 1987.

Morgan, Kenneth. "Fritz Reiner." In *American National Biography*. Ed. John A. Garraty and Mark C. Carnes. Chapel Hill: Oxford University Press, 1999. 321–23.

———. "Fritz Reiner and the Technique of Conducting." *Journal of the Conductors' Guild* 14 (1993): 91–100.

———. "Fritz Reiner as Opera Conductor in the 1930s." *Opera Quarterly* 12.3 (Spring 1996): 59–77.

———. "Fritz Reiner in Dresden." *Journal of the Conductors' Guild* 19 (1998): 86–97.

———. "Reiner in Pittsburgh: A Survey of the Great Conductor's Earlier Commercial Recordings." *International Classical Record Collector* 2.6 (1996): 24–30.

———. "Risë Stevens: The Drama Queen." *International Classical Record Collector* 4.14 (1998): 8–16.

———. "*Salome* at the Met, 1949." *International Opera Collector* 2.7 (1998): 46–50.

Muck, Peter. *Einhundert Jahre Berliner Philharmonisches Orchester*. 3 Vols. Tutzing: H. Schneider, 1982.

Mueller, John H. *The American Symphony Orchestra: A Social History of Musical Taste*. Bloomington: Indiana University Press, 1951.

Mueller, Kate Hevner. *Twenty-Seven Major Symphony Orchestras: A History and Analysis of Their Repertoires, Seasons 1842–43 through 1969–70*. Bloomington: Indiana University Press, 1973.

Myers, Kurtz. *Index to Record Reviews*. Boston: G. K. Hall, 1978.

———. *Index to Record Reviews, 1978–1983*. Boston: G. K. Hall, 1985.

———. *Index to Record Reviews, 1984–1987*. Boston: G. K. Hall, 1989.

Newbould, Brian. *Schubert and the Symphony: A New Perspective*. Surbiton: Toccata Press, 1992.

Norton, Spencer, ed. and trans. *Music in My Time: The Memoirs of Alfredo Casella*. Norman: University of Oklahoma Press, 1955.

O'Connell, Charles. *The Other Side of the Record*. New York: A. A. Knopf, 1947.

Olmstead, Andrea, ed. *The Correspondence of Roger Sessions*. Boston: Northeastern University Press, 1992.

———. *Roger Sessions and His Music*. Ann Arbor: UMI Research Press, 1985.

O'Neil, Thomas. *The Grammys: For the Record.* London: Penguin Books, 1993.

Osborne, Richard. *Herbert von Karajan: A Life in Music.* London: Chatto and Windus, 1998.

Page, Tim, and Vanessa Weeks Page. *Selected Letters of Virgil Thomson.* New York: Summit Books, 1988.

Palmer, Christopher. *The Composer in Hollywood.* London: Marion Boyars, 1990.

Palmer, Louis O. "Chicago Symphony Rapidly Becoming Virtuoso Ensemble under Fritz Reiner." *Musical America* 74.1 (January 1954): 6.

———. "Chicago Symphony Shows Gains as 63rd Season Comes to a Close." *Musical America* 74.8 (June 1954): 14.

Papp, David. "The Great Leveller—Reiner in Chicago." *Gramophone* 71.845 (October 1993): 20–21, 23.

———. "Hindsight: Fritz Reiner." *BBC Music Magazine* 7.8 (April 1999): 44.

———. "Reiner: The Great Leveller." BBC Radio 3. Six broadcasts (1993).

Peyser, Herbert F. "Reiner Leads Brilliant *Salome* Revival." *Musical America* 69.3 (February 1949): 27, 262.

Peyser, Joan. *Bernstein: A Biography.* New York: William Morrow, 1987.

Pfeffer, Arthur S. "Michael Hobson of Classic Records and the Rebirth of Quality Vinyl." *International Classical Record Collector* 1.1 (1995): 74–78.

Pfeiffer, John. "The Superiority of a Fraction." Liner notes for Richard Wagner, *Also sprach Zarathustra.* Chicago Symphony Orchestra. Fritz Reiner. RCA Victor, ARP 1-4583.

Philip, Robert. *Early Recordings and Musical Style: Changing Tastes in Instrumental Performance, 1900–1950.* Cambridge: Cambridge University Press, 1992.

———. "1900–1940." In *Performance Practice: Music after 1600.* Ed. Howard Mayer and Stanley Sadie. Basingstoke, U.K.: Macmillan, 1989. 461–82.

———. "Traditional Habits of Performance in Early Twentieth-Century Recordings of Beethoven." In *Performing Beethoven.* Ed. Robin Stowell. Cambridge: Cambridge University Press, 1994. 195–204.

Pickett, David. "A Comparative Survey of Rescorings in Beethoven's Symphonies." In *Performing Beethoven.* Ed. Robin Stowell. Cambridge: Cambridge University Press, 1994. 205–27.

"Pittsburgh's Principal Flutist Recalls Dr. Reiner." *The Podium: Magazine of the Fritz Reiner Society* (Spring/Summer 1985): 9–11.

Pollack, Howard. *Skyscraper Lullaby: The Life and Music of John Alden Carpenter.* Washington, D.C.: Smithsonian Institution Press, 1995.

Potter, Rollin R. "Fritz Reiner: Conductor, Teacher, Musical Innovator." Ph.D. dissertation, Northwestern University, 1980.

Potts, Joseph E. "The Chicago Symphony Orchestra." *The Strad* 58 (June 1962): 49–55.

Prawy, Marcel. *The Vienna Opera.* London: Weidenfeld and Nicolson, 1969.

Raven, Seymour. "Reiner Tells Views on Art of Conducting." *Chicago Sunday Tribune,* March 19, 1950.

Reich, Howard. *Van Cliburn.* Nashville: T. Nelson Publishers, 1993.

"A Reiner Centenary Scrapbook." *The Podium: Magazine of the Fritz Reiner Society* (Fall/Winter 1988): 11–42.

"A Reiner Symposium in Bloomington/I." *The Podium: Magazine of the Fritz Reiner Society* 2.2 (1978): 9–14.

"A Reiner Symposium in Bloomington/II." *The Podium: Magazine of the Fritz Reiner Society* 3 (1979): 18–25.

Reiner, Fritz. "A Conductor on Outdoor Concerts." *The Podium: Magazine of the Fritz Reiner Society* (Spring/Summer 1986): 18–19.

———. "From Cylindrical to Long Playing Records." *WABF Program Magazine* (April 1949): 9.

———. "Mahler." Liner notes for Gustav Mahler, *Symphony no. 4*. Chicago Symphony Orchestra. Fritz Reiner. BMG/RCA CD 09026 635332.

———. "The Making of a Conductor." *Musical America* 61.16 (October 1941): 29; reprinted in *The Podium: Magazine of the Fritz Reiner Society* (Fall/Winter 1987): 23.

———. "Music for the Greatest Audience." *Music News* 39.3 (March 1947): 6–7.

———. "My Favorite Opera." *Chicago Tribune*, March 31, 1957; reprinted in *The Podium: Magazine of the Fritz Reiner Society* (Spring/Summer 1984).

———. "The Secrets of the Conductor." *Etude* (July 1936): 417–18; reprinted in *The Podium: Magazine of the Fritz Reiner Society* (Fall/Winter 1986): 23–25.

———. "Symphonies as Opera Producers." *Musical Courier* (1943).

———. "The Technique of Conducting." *Etude* 69 (October 1951): 16–17; reprinted in *The Podium: Magazine of the Fritz Reiner Society* (Autumn 1980): 9–11.

———. "Your Chances with the Symphony." *Upbeat* (1938).

Reis, Claire R. *Composers, Conductors, and Critics*. New York: Oxford University Press, 1955.

Repertoar Slovenskih Gledalisc, 1867–1967. Ljubljana: Slovenski gledaliski muzej, 1967.

Respighi, Elsa. *Ottorino Respighi: His Life Story*. Trans. Gwyn Morris. London: Ricordi, 1962.

Rink, John, ed. *The Practice of Performance: Studies in Musical Interpretation*. Cambridge: Cambridge University Press, 1995.

Robinson, Paul. *Bernstein*. London: MacDonald, 1982.

———. *Solti*. London: MacDonald and Jane's, 1979.

———. *Stokowski*. London: MacDonald and Jane's, 1977.

Rodzinski, Halina. *Our Two Lives*. New York: Charles Scribner's Sons, 1976.

Rooney, Dennis D. "Fritz Reiner on CD." *Keynote* 12.11 (January 1989): 12–15.

———. "How the LP Was Born." *International Classical Record Collector* 4.14 (1998): 30–38.

———. "The Life and Death of the LP." *Keynote* 12.5 (July 1988): 8–12.

Roos, James. "Oboist Finally Records the Concerto He Inspired." *The Double Reed* 14.3 (1991): 34–35.

Rosen, Carole. *The Goossens: A Musical Century*. Boston: Northeastern University Press, 1994.

Rosen, Charles. *The Classical Style: Haydn, Mozart, Beethoven*. Rev. ed. London: Faber, 1976.

Rosenberg, Deena, and Bernard Rosenberg. *The Music Makers*. New York: Columbia University Press, 1979.

Rosenthal, Harold. *Two Centuries of Opera at Covent Garden*. London: Putnam, 1958.

Rothe, Friede F. "Fritz Reiner." *Opera News*, February 21, 1949, 6–7.

Rubinstein, Arthur. *My Many Years*. New York: Alfred A. Knopf, 1980.

Sablosky, Irving. "The Trial and Triumph of Fritz Reiner." *Chicago* 3.1 (March 1956): 35–39.

Sachs, Harvey. *Toscanini*. Philadelphia: J. B. Lippincott Company, 1978.

Saerchinger, César. "Fritz Reiner—Perpetual Prodigy." *Saturday Review*, May 31, 1952; reprinted in *The Podium: Magazine of the Fritz Reiner Society* 2.1 (1978): 8–9.

Saleski, Gdal. *Famous Musicians of a Wandering Race: Biographical Sketches of Outstanding Figures of Jewish Origin in the Musical World*. New York: Bloch Printing Publishing Co., 1927.

———. *Famous Musicians of Jewish Origin*. New York: Bloch Publishing Co., 1949.

Sammons, Robert L. "Chicago Symphony Orchestra." *Town and Country* 115.4460 (March 1961): 80–81, 146.

Sanders, Alan, ed. *Walter Legge: Words and Music*. London: Duckworth, 1998.

Sapienza, Madeline. "Fritz Reiner." In *Dictionary of American Biography: Supplement Seven, 1961–1965*. Ed. John A. Garraty. New York: Oxford University Press, 1981. 639–41.

Sargeant, Winthrop. "The Future of Opera in America." *Nation,* April 6, 1932.

―――. *Geniuses, Goddesses, and People.* New York: E. P. Dutton, 1949.

Schabas, Ezra. *Theodore Thomas: America's Conductor and Builder of Orchestras, 1835–1905.* Urbana: University of Illinois Press, 1989.

Scherer, Barrymore Laurence. "Maxims: Octogenarian Conductor Max Rudolf Shares the Lessons and Experiences That Have Guided His Long Career." *Opera News,* December 7, 1991, 18–20.

Schickel, Richard. *The World of Carnegie Hall.* New York: Messner, 1960.

Schlachtmeyer, Al. "An Interview with Carlotta Reiner: Sunshine and Twilight in Weston." *The Podium: Magazine of the Fritz Reiner Society* 2.1 (1978): 5–7.

Schmalz, Robert F. "Paur and the Pittsburgh: Requiem for an Orchestra." *American Music* 12 (1994): 123–47.

Schonberg, Harold C. *Facing the Music.* New York: Summit Books, 1981.

―――. *The Great Conductors.* New York: Simon and Schuster, 1967.

―――. *Horowitz: His Life and Music.* New York: Simon and Schuster, 1992.

Schreiber, Ulrich. "Diskographie der mit Fritz Reiner erhältlichen Schallplatten." *Hi Fi Stereophonie* 3 (July 1964): 360.

Schuh, Willi, ed. *Richard Strauss: Recollections and Reflections.* Trans. L. J. Lawrence. London: Boosey and Hawkes, 1953.

Schuller, Gunther. *The Compleat Conductor.* New York: Oxford University Press, 1997.

Schuman, William. "Reiner in Memoriam." *The Podium: Magazine of the Fritz Reiner Society* (Spring/Summer 1988): 35–36.

Schumann, Karl. "Fritz Reiner." *Fonoforum* 7 (September 1962): 16–18.

Secrest, Meryle. *Leonard Bernstein: A Life.* New York: Vintage Books, 1995.

Seinfelt, Frederick W. "Reiner as Conductor of Opera." *Fritz Reiner Society Newsletter* 3 (n.d.).

Seltsam, William H. *Metropolitan Opera Annals: First Supplement, 1947–1957.* New York: H. W. Wilson Company, 1957.

Seltzer, George. *Music Matters: The Performer and the American Federation of Musicians.* Metuchen, N.J.: Scarecrow Press, 1989.

Selvini, Michele. "Maestri: Reiner Renaissance." *Musica* 100 (October–November 1996): 88–95.

Semple, William T. "History of the Chicago Symphony Orchestra's Recording Career." *The Absolute Sound* 8.32 (December 1983): 131–34.

Shanet, Howard. *Philharmonic: A History of New York's Orchestra.* Garden City, N.Y.: Doubleday and Co., 1975.

Shaw, Ray. "Music and the Hand." *Musical America* (special issue) (February 10, 1943): 27, 194.

Sheblessy, Sylvia K. *One Hundred Years of the Cincinnati May Festival.* Cincinnati: n.p., 1973.

Sheean, Vincent. *First and Last Love.* New York: Random House, 1956.

Sherman, John K. *Music and Maestros: The Story of the Minneapolis Symphony Orchestra.* Minneapolis: University of Minnesota Press, 1952.

Slonimsky, Nicolas. *Baker's Biographical Dictionary of Musicians.* 8th ed. New York: Schirmer Books, 1992.

―――. *Music since 1900.* 5th ed. New York: Schirmer Books, 1994.

Smith, Cecil. "*Carmen*—New Sets, New Staging in Metropolitan Revival." *Musical America* 72.3 (February 1952): 33, 126.

―――. "*Falstaff* and *Pelléas* at Metropolitan." *Musical America* 69.4 (March 1949): 5, 8.

―――. "Strauss's *Der Rosenkavalier* Opens Metropolitan Season." *Musical America* 69.15 (December 1949): 3, 8.

―――. "Strauss's *Elektra* Revived with Varnay and Hoengen." *Musical America* 72.4 (March 1952): 7, 31.

―――. *Worlds of Music.* Philadelphia: Lippincott, 1952.

Smith, William Ander. *The Mystery of Leopold Stokowski*. Cranbury, N.J.: Fairleigh Dickinson University Press, 1990.

Spendal, Monica. "Ljubljana." In *The New Grove Dictionary of Opera*. Vol. 2. Ed. Stanley Sadie. London: Macmillan, 1992. 1296.

Staatskapelle Dresden. Ed. Eberhard Steindorf and Dieter Uhrig. Berlin: Henschelverlag Kunst und Gesellschaft, 1973.

Stanley, Louis. "The Baton." *Musical America* (February 1955): 18–19, 133–34.

Steber, Eleanor, with Marcia Sloat. *An Autobiography*. Ridgewood, N.J.: Wordsworth, 1992.

Stein, Erwin, ed. *Arnold Schoenberg Letters*. New York: St. Martin's Press, 1965.

Stephens, Norris L. "Pittsburgh Symphony Orchestra." In *Symphony Orchestras of the United States: Selected Profiles*. Ed. Robert R. Craven. Westport, Conn.: Greenwood Press, 1986. 351–55.

Stephenson, Kurt. *Hundert Jahre Philharmonische Gesellschaft in Hamburg*. Hamburg: Broschek and Co., 1928.

Stern, Isaac, with Chaim Potok. *My First Seventy-Nine Years*. New York: Knopf, 1999.

Steude, Wolfram, Ortrun Landmann, and Dieter Härtwig. "Dresden." In *The New Grove Dictionary of Music and Musicians*. Vol. 5. Ed. Stanley Sadie. London: Macmillan, 1980. 612–27.

Stevens, Halsey. *The Life and Music of Béla Bartók*. Rev. ed. New York: Oxford University Press, 1964.

Stoddard, Hope. "Fritz Reiner . . . 'The Quality of Leadership.'" *International Musician* 54.5 (November 1955): 10–14.

———. *Symphony Conductors of the USA*. New York: Thomas Y. Crowell Co., 1957.

Stravinsky, Igor. *An Autobiography*. New York: Simon and Schuster, 1936.

———. *Themes and Conclusions*. London: Faber, 1972.

Stravinsky, Vera, and Robert Craft. *Stravinsky in Pictures and Documents*. London: Hutchinson, 1979.

Stuart, Philip. *The London Philharmonic Discography*. Westport, Conn.: Greenwood Press, 1997.

Suchoff, Benjamin, ed. *Béla Bartók Essays*. London: Faber, 1976.

Sutton, Wadham. "A Martinet of the Rostrum." BBC Music Weekly Broadcast, Radio 3 (December 12, 1988).

Svejda, Jim. *The Record Shelf Guide to the Classical Repertoire*. 3d ed. Rocklin, Calif.: Prima Publishers, 1992.

Swain, Jonathan. "Reputations: Fritz Reiner." *Gramophone* 76.11 (November 1998): 42–43.

Szigeti, Joseph. "Making Music with Bartók." *The Long Player* 2.10 (October 1953): 10–12.

———. *With Strings Attached: Reminiscences and Reflections*. 2d ed. New York: Alfred A. Knopf, 1967.

Talbott, Earl G. "Fritz Reiner—One of the World's Great Conductors." *New York Herald Tribune*, November 16, 1963.

Taruskin, Richard. "The Golden Age of Kitsch." *New Republic*, March 21, 1994, 28–38.

———. *Text and Act: Essays on Music and Performance*. Oxford: Oxford University Press, 1995.

Temple Savage, Richard. *A Voice from the Pit: Reminiscences of an Orchestral Musician*. Newton Abbot, U.K.: David and Charles, 1988.

Thomas, David. "A Conversation with Lukas Foss." *Journal of the Conductors' Guild* 18.1 (Winter/Spring 1997): 2–13.

Thomas, Louis R. "A History of the Cincinnati Symphony Orchestra to 1931." Ph.D. dissertation, University of Cincinnati, 1972.

Thompson, Oscar, ed. *The International Cyclopedia of Music and Musicians*. 10th ed. New York: Dodd, Mead, 1975.

Thomson, Virgil. *The Art of Judging Music*. New York: A. A. Knopf, 1948.

———. *The Musical Scene*. New York: A. A. Knopf, 1945.

———. *A Virgil Thomson Reader by Virgil Thomson*. Boston: Houghton Mifflin Co., 1981.

Tintori, Giamperi. *Cronologia opere-balletti-concerti: La Scala 1778–1977*. Gorle: Grafica Gutenberg editrice, 1979.

Totels, Robert E. "Reiner at the Met, Part I." *The Podium: Magazine of the Fritz Reiner Society* 1 (1976): 5–9.

———. "Reiner at the Met, Part II." *The Podium: Magazine of the Fritz Reiner Society* 2 (1977): 21–28.

Trezise, Simon. *Debussy: La Mer*. Cambridge: Cambridge University Press, 1994.

Turnbull, Robert. *The Opera Gazetteer*. London: Trefoil, 1988.

Uske, Bernhard. "Präzision und Dramatik des dirigenten Fritz Reiner: Ein musikalischer Draufganger." *FonoForum* (June 1989): 28–31, 34.

Valin, Jonathan. *The RCA Bible: A Compendium of Opinion on RCA Living Stereo Records*. Cincinnati: Music Lovers Press, 1993.

Vásárhelyi, Julius. *Ungarn ein Land der Musik: Ungarischer Kuenstleralmanach*. Budapest: Koeniglich Ungarische Universitaets-druckerei, 1930.

Vázsonyi, Balint. *Ernö Dohnányi*. Budapest: Zenemukiadó, 1971.

Viles, Eliza Ann. "Mary Louise Curtis Bok Zimbalist: Founder of the Curtis Institute of Music and Patron of American Arts." Ph.D. dissertation, Bryn Mawr College, 1983.

Vogt, Howard. *Flagstad: Singer of the Century*. London: Secker and Warburg, 1987.

Wachman, P. M. "The Guest Conductor." *Musical Digest*, August 12, 1924, 5.

Weingartner, Felix. *On the Performance of Beethoven's Symphonies*. Trans. Jessie Crosland. London: Breitkopf and Härtel, 1908.

Wendt, Lloyd. *Chicago Tribune: The Rise of a Great American Newspaper*. Chicago: Rand McNally and Co., 1979.

Whiteside, Shaun, and Michael Tanner, eds., *Wilhelm Furtwängler: Notebooks, 1924–1954*. London: Quartet Books, 1989.

Willier, Stephen A. "Fritz Reiner." In *International Dictionary of Opera*. Vol. 2. Ed. C. Steven LaRue. Detroit: St. James Press, 1993. 1093–94.

Willis, Thomas. Liner notes for *Chicago Symphony Orchestra: From the Archives, Vol. 3*. CSO 873.

———. "Reiner Library a Gift to N.U." *Chicago Tribune*, December 28, 1969; reprinted in *The Podium: Magazine of the Fritz Reiner Society* (Spring/Summer 1983): 26.

———. "Reiner on TV." *Fritz Reiner Society Newsletter* 10 (n.d.).

Wright, Brian. "Great Conductors: Fritz Reiner." *Classic CD* 10 (February 1991): 60–61.

Wright, Donald, ed. *Cardus on Music: A Centenary Collection*. London: Hamish Hamilton, 1988.

Young, Edward D. "Interview with Lukas Foss." *Koussevitzky Recordings Society Newsletter* 4.1 (1994): 4–11.

Zaslaw, Neal. *Mozart's Symphonies: Context, Performance Practice, Reception*. Oxford: Oxford University Press, 1989.

Index

Monte Carlo Opera, 57
Monteux, Pierre, 15, 67, 104, 145, 211, 226
Moore, Douglas, 121
Mordden, Ethan, 184
More, Louis, 62
Mörike, Eduard, 32
Moscana, Nicola, 133
Mottl, Felix, 69
Mozart, Wolfgang Amadeus, 2, 24–26, 35, 38, 39, 50, 73, 78, 115; interpretation of, 211, 214–17, 220–25; operas performed at the Metropolitan Opera, 132–34; 155, 158, 161, 169; operas performed in Philadelphia, 88–91; operas performed in San Francisco, 96; recordings of, 179, 181, 185–86, 189–90, 196–98, 204–5, 229, 273, 275–77
Mraczek, Joseph, 37, 40, 48, 49
Muck, Karl, 33, 209
Munch, Charles, 124, 155, 161, 191–92, 214
Munsel, Patrice, 188
Music Guild Productions, 103
Musicians' Symphony Orchestra, 86
Mussolini, Benito, 15
Mussorgsky, Modest, 85, 88, 122, 212–13; recordings of, 180, 182, 193, 198, 229, 273, 276–77

National Concerts and Artists Corporation, 16
National Symphony Orchestra, Washington, D.C., 124
NBC Symphony Orchestra, 11, 15, 122, 144; recordings of, 178, 187, 189–90, 192, 204–5, 217, 230, 276
Nestroy, Johann Nepomuk, 31
New Jersey Symphony Orchestra, 154
New London Consort, 217
Newman, Alfred, 57
Newman, Ernest, 97
New York, 2, 3, 8, 43–44, 62, 78, 82
New York Concert Choir, 155
New York Philharmonic-Symphony Orchestra, 15–17, 164, 167, 173; recordings of, 177–78, 184, 187, 204–5, 221, 229–30, 276; Reiner as guest conductor of, 46, 53, 58–59, 65, 80, 102, 105, 119, 122–23, 144–45, 161–62
New York Symphony Orchestra, 62
Nietzsche, Friedrich, 20

Nikisch, Artur, 29, 40, 69, 71, 209
Nilsson, Sven, 134, 136, 276
Northwestern University Choir, 155
Novotna, Jarmila, 134, 137

Oenslager, Donald, 78, 87, 90, 139
Offenbach, Jacques, 32, 34
Ohio Mechanics Institute, Cincinnati, 45
Oldberg, Eric, 148, 164–66
Onofrei, Dimitry, 85
Orchestra Hall, Chicago, 153, 160, 191–92
Orchestral Association, Chicago, 123, 148; and Reiner, 162, 164, 168, 170–71, 202
Orff, Carl, 161, 196
Ormandy, Eugene, 16, 57, 105, 161; conducting gestures, 70, 153; guest conductor in Chicago, 155; recordings of, 203, 208; rivalry with Reiner, 144
Osten, Eva von der, 36

Paley, William, 178
Palma, Mallorca, 43
Paray, Paul, 155, 191
Paris, 32, 54
Pattiera, Tino, 37
Pauly, Rose, 96
Paur, Emil, 106
Pechner, Gerhard, 135
Peck, Donald, 152
Peerce, Jan, 123, 188–89, 277
Pelletier, Wilfred, 129
Pembaur, Karl, 33
Pergolesi, Giovanni Battista, 78
Persichetti, Vincent, 79
Peters, Gordon, 152
Peters, Roberta, 137
Petina, Irra, 85, 137
Petrillo, James C., 170, 178–79, 184, 202
Pfeiffer, John, 193
Pfitzner, Hans, 36
Philadelphia Civic Opera Company, 84, 87
Philadelphia Grand Opera, 65, 78, 84–86, 176
Philadelphia Opera Company, 94
Philadelphia Orchestra, 2, 10, 15–16, 20–21, 85; and the Curtis Institute, 77, 82; and Fantasia, 103; and opera, 87–89, 93; recordings of, 176, 180, 185, 212–13, 218, 226, 276; Reiner as guest conductor of, 46, 50, 58–59, 62, 65–67, 100–101, 105, 124, 144–45, 161, 164, 173
Philharmonia Orchestra, 162

KENNETH MORGAN is a professor of history at Brunel University in Uxbridge, England. He is the editor of *An American Quaker in the British Isles: The Travel Journals of Jabez Maud Fisher, 1775–1779;* the coeditor (with Jonathan Barry) of *Reformation and Revival in Eighteenth-Century Bristol;* and the author of *Bristol and the Atlantic Trade in the Eighteenth Century; Slavery and Servitude in Colonial North America; The Birth of Industrial Britain: Economic Change, 1750–1850;* and *The Birth of Industrial Britain: Social Change, 1750–1850,* as well as many articles on historical topics. He plays bassoon and has been a regular contributor to *International Classical Record Collector.*

Music in American Life

Doowop: The Chicago Scene   *Robert Pruter*
Blue Rhythms: Six Lives in Rhythm and Blues   *Chip Deffaa*
Shoshone Ghost Dance Religion: Poetry Songs and Great Basin Context
   Judith Vander
Go Cat Go! Rockabilly Music and Its Makers   *Craig Morrison*
'Twas Only an Irishman's Dream: The Image of Ireland and the Irish in American
   Popular Song Lyrics, 1800–1920   *William H. A. Williams*
Democracy at the Opera: Music, Theater, and Culture in New York City, 1815–60
   Karen Ahlquist
Fred Waring and the Pennsylvanians   *Virginia Waring*
Woody, Cisco, and Me: Seamen Three in the Merchant Marine   *Jim Longhi*
Behind the Burnt Cork Mask: Early Blackface Minstrelsy and Antebellum American
   Popular Culture   *William J. Mahar*
Going to Cincinnati: A History of the Blues in the Queen City   *Steven C. Tracy*
Pistol Packin' Mama: Aunt Molly Jackson and the Politics of Folksong   *Shelly Romalis*
Sixties Rock: Garage, Psychedelic, and Other Satisfactions   *Michael Hicks*
The Late Great Johnny Ace and the Transition from R&B to Rock 'n' Roll
   James M. Salem
Tito Puente and the Making of Latin Music   *Steven Loza*
Juilliard: A History   *Andrea Olmstead*
Understanding Charles Seeger, Pioneer in American Musicology   *Edited by*
   Bell Yung and Helen Rees
Mountains of Music: West Virginia Traditional Music from Goldenseal   *Edited by*
   John Lilly
Alice Tully: An Intimate Portrait   *Albert Fuller*
A Blues Life   *Henry Townsend, as told to Bill Greensmith*
Long Steel Rail: The Railroad in American Folksong (2d ed.)   *Norm Cohen*
The Golden Age of Gospel   *Text by Horace Clarence Boyer; photography by*
   Lloyd Yearwood
Aaron Copland: The Life and Work of an Uncommon Man   *Howard Pollack*
Louis Moreau Gottschalk   *S. Frederick Starr*
Race, Rock, and Elvis   *Michael T. Bertrand*
Theremin: Ether Music and Espionage   *Albert Glinsky*
Poetry and Violence: The Ballad Tradition of Mexico's Costa Chica
   John H. McDowell
The Bill Monroe Reader   *Edited by Tom Ewing*
Music in Lubavitcher Life   *Ellen Koskoff*
Zarzuela: Spanish Operetta, American Stage   *Janet L. Sturman*
Bluegrass Odyssey: A Documentary in Pictures and Words, 1966–86
   Carl Fleischhauer and Neil V. Rosenberg
That Old-Time Rock & Roll: A Chronicle of an Era, 1954–63   *Richard Aquila*
Labor's Troubadour   *Joe Glazer*
American Opera   *Elise K. Kirk*
Don't Get above Your Raisin': Country Music and the Southern Working Class
   Bill C. Malone
John Alden Carpenter: A Chicago Composer   *Howard Pollack*
Heartbeat of the People: Music and Dance of the Northern Pow-wow
   Tara Browner
My Lord, What a Morning: An Autobiography   *Marian Anderson*
Marian Anderson: A Singer's Journey   *Allan Keiler*

The University of Illinois Press
is a founding member of the
Association of American University Presses.

Composed in 9.5/13 Sabon
with Sabon display
by Type One, LLC
for the University of Illinois Press
Designed by Paula Newcomb
Manufactured by Thomson-Shore, Inc.

University of Illinois Press
1325 South Oak Street
Champaign, IL 61820-6903
www.press.uillinois.edu